THE ALASKA PANHANDLE

A COMPLETE GUIDE

1ST EDITION

THE ALASKA PANHANDLE

Carol Fowler

The Countryman Press
Woodstock, Vermont

To Ken

We welcome your comments and suggestions. Please contact Great Destinations Guide Editor, The Countryman Press, P.O. Box 748, Woodstock, VT 05091, or e-mail countrymanpress@wwnorton.com.

ISBN   978-1-58157-095-3

Cover photo by the author

Interior photographs by the author unless otherwise specified
Maps by Mapping Specialists, © The Countryman Press
Book design by Bodenweber Design
Composition by PerfecType, Nashville, TN

Published by The Countryman Press, P.O. Box 748, Woodstock, VT 05091

Distributed by W. W. Norton & Company, Inc., 500 Fifth Avenue, New York, NY 10110

Printed in the United States of America

10 9 8 7 6 5 4 3 2 1

GREAT DESTINATIONS TRAVEL GUIDEBOOK SERIES

Recommended by *National Geographic Traveler* and *Travel + Leisure* magazines

A crisp and critical approach, for travelers who want to live like locals.
—*USA Today*

Great Destinations™ guidebooks are known for their comprehensive, critical coverage of regions of extraordinary cultural interest and natural beauty. Each title in this series is continuously updated with each printing to ensure accurate and timely information. All the books contain more than one hundred photographs and maps.

Current titles available:

The Adirondack Book

The Alaska Panhandle

Atlanta

Austin, San Antonio
 & the Texas Hill Country

The Berkshire Book

Big Sur, Monterey Bay
 & Gold Coast Wine Country

Cape Canaveral, Cocoa Beach
 & Florida's Space Coast

The Charleston, Savannah
 & Coastal Islands Book

The Chesapeake Bay Book

The Coast of Maine Book

Colorado's Classic Mountain Towns

Costa Rica: Great Destinations
 Central America

Dominican Republic

The Finger Lakes Book

The Four Corners Region

Galveston, South Padre Island
 & the Texas Gulf Coast

Guatemala: Great Destinations
 Central America

The Hamptons Book

Hawaii's Big Island: Great Destinations
 Hawaii

Honolulu & Oahu: Great Destinations
 Hawaii

The Jersey Shore: Atlantic City to Cape May:
 Great Destinations

Kauai: Great Destinations Hawaii

Lake Tahoe & Reno

Las Vegas

Los Cabos & Baja California Sur:
 Great Destinations Mexico

Maui: Great Destinations Hawaii

Memphis and the Delta Blues Trail

Michigan's Upper Peninsula

Montreal & Quebec City:
 Great Destinations Canada

The Nantucket Book

The Napa & Sonoma Book

North Carolina's Outer Banks
 & the Crystal Coast

Nova Scotia & Prince Edward Island

Oaxaca: Great Destinations Mexico

Palm Beach, Fort Lauderdale, Miami
 & the Florida Keys

Palm Springs & Desert Resorts

Philadelphia, Brandywine Valley
 & Bucks County

Phoenix, Scottsdale, Sedona
 & Central Arizona

Playa del Carmen, Tulum & the Riviera Maya:
 Great Destinations Mexico

Salt Lake City, Park City, Provo
 & Utah's High Country Resorts

San Diego & Tijuana

San Juan, Vieques & Culebra:
 Great Destinations Puerto Rico

San Miguel de Allende & Guanajuato:
 Great Destinations Mexico

The Santa Fe & Taos Book

The Sarasota, Sanibel Island & Naples Book

The Seattle & Vancouver Book

The Shenandoah Valley Book

Touring East Coast Wine Country

Tucson

Virginia Beach, Richmond
 & Tidewater Virginia

Washington, D.C., and Northern Virginia

Yellowstone & Grand Teton National Parks
 & Jackson Hole

Yosemite & the Southern Sierra Nevada

The authors in this series are professional travel writers who have lived for many years in the regions they describe. Honest and painstakingly critical, full of information only a local can provide, Great Destinations guidebooks give you all the practical knowledge you need to enjoy the best of each region.

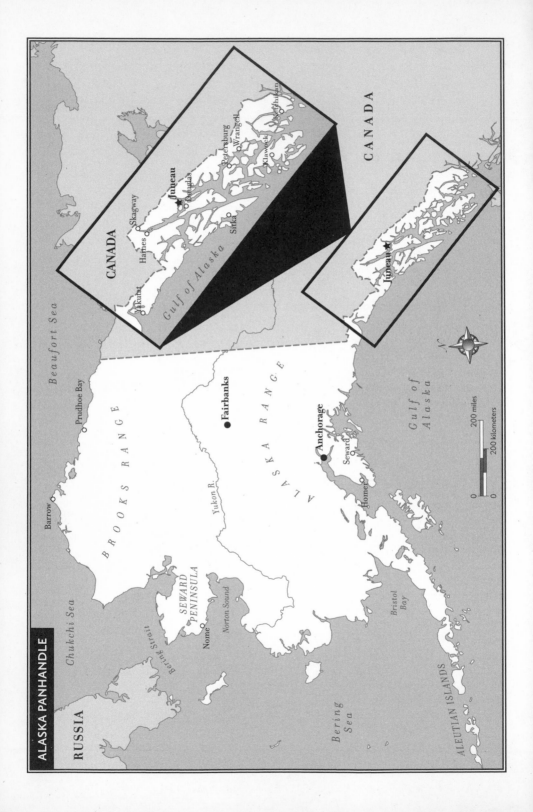

Contents

1
History
Beringia Migrants to Cruise Ship Tourists
27

2
Transportation
Getting Here, Getting Around
45

3
Lodging
Your Room in the Far North
59

4
Culture
What to Do in Town
101

5
Alaska Native People
Meeting Raven and Eagle
137

Acknowledgments

Many people eased my time in Alaska, and pointed to things I may not have discovered. My thanks go to Jennifer A. Thompson, who suggested initial contacts, and Tara Stevens, who refined itineraries and tracked down endless information. In Juneau, Sharon Gaiptman's enthusiasm and knowledge of Alaska and the Yukon set me on various enriching paths and adventures. Later on, Elizabeth Arnett helped me to tie up details. Lori Stepansky and Buckwheat Donahue served as tireless ambassadors and interpreters of Haines and Skagway, respectively.

In Ketchikan, my thanks go to Patti Mackey and Dragon London, for their time and patience with my endless queries long after I had left; and to Chuck Baird, for enlightening me about the past.

Alaska Natives provided endless kindness in their villages, particularly Lindarae Shearer, in Metlakatla, and Johan Dybdahl, in Hoonah. Many unnamed Alaskans—whose hearts are as big as their state—sought me out to share information, insights, and sometimes meals, over many years of travel.

My thanks to editors Kim Grant for her direction and later to Bill Bowers for his careful reading of the manuscript.

My appreciation goes to my children, who respected the time I needed to finish this project. And to my husband, Ken—who traveled hundreds of miles in the Alaska Panhandle on bush planes, small fishing boats, or lumbering ferries, and later fact-checked and read the manuscript with care—my gratitude and love.

Introduction

"The great fresh unblighted, unredeemed wilderness . . ."

—*John Muir on Alaska*

Haines, at the northern end of the Alaska Panhandle, lies 14 miles from Skagway along the Lynn Canal, a 90-minute ferry trip. By highway, it's a 364-mile drive that takes the better part of a day. The route runs north to Haines Junction in the Yukon, crosses over to Whitehorse, and backtracks south to Skagway. Haines and Skagway are two of only three Alaska Panhandle towns to be connected to anywhere else in North America by road. This quirk of geography explains a lot about the Alaska Panhandle terrain, its scale, and the lifestyle of its people. They get around either by sea or by air. The waterways are their marine highway, and the little floatplanes that buzz everywhere incessantly are their taxis. Cruise ships and ferries of the Alaska Marine Highway System bus numbers of people from port to port. Roads may extend out of the towns' boundaries, but they run a few miles and then dead-end in the forest.

The Alaska Panhandle stretches almost 500 miles, from the southern tip of Prince of Wales Island to Yakutat. At most, it's 100 miles wide from the British Columbia border to

Hubbard Glacier's tidewater face is 6 miles long.

the Pacific Ocean, including the islands of the Alexander Archipelago that run almost its entire length. Sandwiched into these relatively small borders are 15,000 miles of coastline, along bays, inlets, fjords, and approximately 1,100 islands. Glaciers sculpted this landmass into a vast lacy landscape, a paradise with glaciers, rainforests, abundant wildlife, and, always, the snow-covered mountains forming a backdrop, and the sea framing the foreground.

Besides scenic gifts, the Panhandle offers a rich Alaska Native culture and interesting history. Tlingit people of the Northwest Coast Indians make up most of the Native population. Some Haida and Tsimshian people live in the southern part of the Panhandle, but most of the totem poles, lodges, and Native villages you'll encounter are Tlingit.

The Alaska Panhandle, also known as Southeast Alaska and the Inside Passage, attracts more than 1 million visitors, largely by cruise ship and mostly between May and September. Glacier Bay crowns the northern Panhandle and is reason enough to come. Do it sooner rather than later, before global warming melts the glaciers. Dozens of them spill out of the Coast Mountains icefields and into the sea. In 1750, they filled what is now Glacier Bay, but have since retreated back into the mountains, creating a 65-mile fjord. Cruise ships, excursion boats, and kayakers pay homage to Lamplugh, Reid, Johns Hopkins, and Margerie glaciers. These mighty rivers of ice stretch back and back, streaked blue and white streams between mountains, in a scale beyond imagining. Smaller boats list slightly, as visitors cluster to one side or the other to view these remnants of the last Ice Age. And then, sometimes, a calving glacier shatters the silence, and awestruck visitors gasp.

This, then, is Alaska. In its immensity, and its beauty.

The Way This Book Works

Because most travelers come by cruise ship, this book is organized around the major ports of call, which are clustered into three regions of the Panhandle: Northern, Central, and Southern. It will give you an idea which towns you might visit back to back, if you are on a cruise ship or an independent traveler. Since Alaska towns are not connected by road, you are not likely to stay in one, then go to dinner in another, as you might in most other ?destinations.

The Northern Panhandle is listed first. Except for Juneau—which tops the list, since it is the state capital, and is also the most visited city in Southeast Alaska—towns are listed in alphabetical order. Chapters cover lodging, dining, recreation, culture, Native villages, and shopping, and are arranged in this geographical order. In the information boxes, Web sites are listed without the "www" part of the address. A chapter on Alaska history introduces the Panhandle, and a chapter of useful telephone numbers and Web sites, including contact information for each region's tourism bureaus, concludes the book.

My hope is that all this will make your stay more comfortable and your visit more interesting. The majesty of Alaska speaks for itself. This guide will help you uncover the details.

Prices

Fishing Lodge Price Codes
Moderate: Up to $800 per day
Expensive: $800–$1,100
Very expensive: More than $1,100

Lodging Price Codes
Inexpensive: Less than $100
Moderate: $100–$175
Expensive: $176–$250
Very expensive: More than $250

Dining Price Codes
Inexpensive: Entrées $15 or less
Moderate: $15–$25
Expensive: Most entrées more than $25

PANHANDLE TOWNS

Alaska Panhandle towns share similar histories and, in general, the same landscape of mountains meeting the sea. Most of them started as Native village sites, and, after white settlement, went through economic boom-and-bust cycles, from fur trading, to mining, to timber, and even canneries. Today, it is mainly tourism that fuels the economy of Southeast Alaska.

Even with shared histories, these towns have distinct personalities, much like the siblings of a large family. Perhaps because no roads lead from one town to the other, Wrangell can't blend into Petersburg in the way Los Angeles joins Pasadena. Perhaps because of the isolation, Panhandle towns tend to remain singular communities.

NORTHERN PANHANDLE

Juneau: The queen of the Panhandle has the air of things happening, with people scurrying between the State Capitol and the Federal Building, and meeting in the bar of the Baranof Hotel. Visitors, though, are likely to ride high above town on the Mount Robert's Tramway, shove open the doors of the Red Dog Saloon, or visit Mendenhall Glacier, Alaska's "drive-in glacier." Sometimes called the country's most beautiful state capital, Juneau is backed by mountains, and stretches out along Gastineau Channel.

Juneau's clock on South Franklin Street is an iconic landmark.

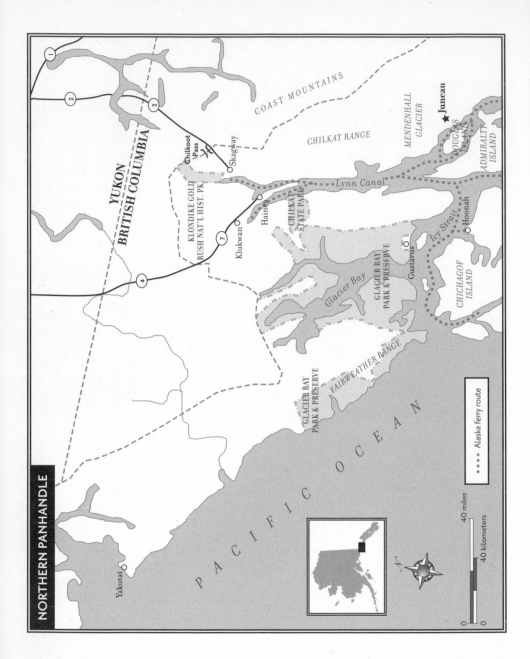

Four distinct communities make up Juneau. The historic downtown has the state capitol, the excellent Alaska State Museum, and good shopping. Visitors spend most of their time here. Lemon Creek is a largely a commercial area, and the home of Alaskan Brewing Company. Beyond that, is the airport and the Mendenhall Loop area, the newer residential district and glacier site. Across Gastineau Channel, Douglas Island attracts a sizeable number of residents and has the Panhandle's only ski resort.

The marble columns of the Alaska State Capitol in Juneau come from Prince of Wales Island.

Gustavus: This town sits at the entrance to Glacier Bay. Anyone who wants to do more than a quick in and out on a cruise ship must come through Gustavus. Most residents are small business entrepreneurs, who run inns, charter fishing services, art galleries, or cafés.

Unlike most places in the Alaska Panhandle, Gustavus has vast flat areas, the result of glacial silt. And it's growing each year because of the effect of the retreating glaciers, which cause the land to rebound and rise. Some buildings sit out on large open plots that were once homestead farms. Others are at the end of driveways, hidden in spruce trees.

It's not easy to get here, unless it's early June through August, when Alaska Airlines runs daily jet service. The Alaska ferry does not stop here. Many visitors arrive in small bush planes.

Haines: *The New York Times* has called Haines "the real *Northern Exposure*." Whether it is or not is a bit moot, though it takes grit and a certain quirky eccentricity to survive a winter here, as it does anywhere in Alaska.

Haines is another town favored with jaw-dropping beauty. Mountains surround it, and the Lynn Canal flows at its feet. It has a small downtown area at one end of town, and at the other, Fort Seward, a former U.S. Army Post, where graceful former residences now house artists' studios, a small hotel, and bed-and-breakfast inns. Bird lovers converge here each fall for the Bald Eagle Festival, and adventurers come in the spring for heli-skiing.

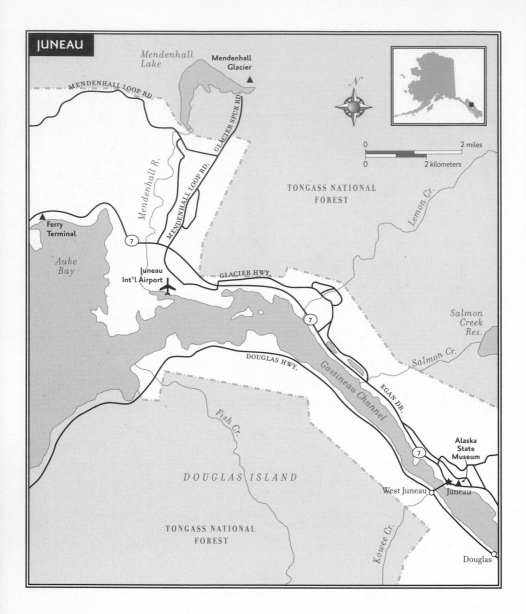

JUNEAU

Mendenhall
Lake

Mendenhall
Glacier ▲

MENDENHALL LOOP RD.

GLACIER SPUR RD.

Mendenhall R.

MENDENHALL LOOP RD.

TONGASS NATIONAL
FOREST

Lemon Cr.

Ferry ▲
Terminal

⑦

Auke
Bay

Juneau
Int'l Airport ✈

GLACIER HWY.

⑦

Salmon
Creek
Res.

Salmon Cr.

DOUGLAS HWY.

Gastineau Channel

EGAN DR.

Fish Cr.

Alaska
State
Museum

⑦

DOUGLAS ISLAND

West Juneau ○ ▲▲ Juneau

TONGASS NATIONAL
FOREST

Kowee Cr.

Douglas

N

0   2 miles

0   2 kilometers

Skagway: The Klondike Gold Rush created Skagway almost overnight, especially after the White Pass & Yukon Route railway established its base here. Today the railway exists as a tourist excursion, as far as the pass, and Skagway ranks third, in Alaska's most visited cruise ports.

The historic district at the center of town, part of Klondike Gold Rush National Historical Park, is beautifully preserved. The town must be applauded for its architectural integrity—more so than any other Panhandle community. One of the Gold Rush buildings, the Red Onion saloon, rates as an Alaska tourist icon. Walk along Skagway's board side-walks, and it's easy to imagine the town filled with scruffy miners, entrepreneurs, and opportunists, like "Soapy" Smith, a notorious swindler in Alaska's early days.

Yakutat: Once a Tlingit community, Yakutat is now a fishing town where people converge for recreational fishing on Yakutat and Disenchantment bays, and the Situk River. Nearby Hubbard Glacier, the largest tidewater glacier in North America, also draws visitors, including many on large cruise ships, though they do not visit the town. Within the past few years Yakutat has also become a magnet for surfers for the long, shore break on its ocean beaches. The town has a few stores and a Visitor Center for Wrangell–St. Elias National Park & Preserve, but except for fishing, it does

Killer whales often appear on Tlingit totem poles, including this one shown in detail.

The Chilkat Mountains dwarf buildings in Letnikov Cove in Haines.

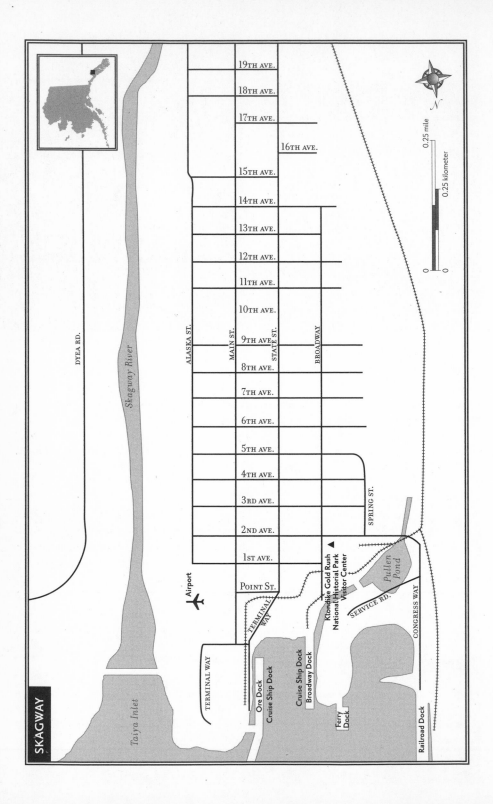

SKAGWAY

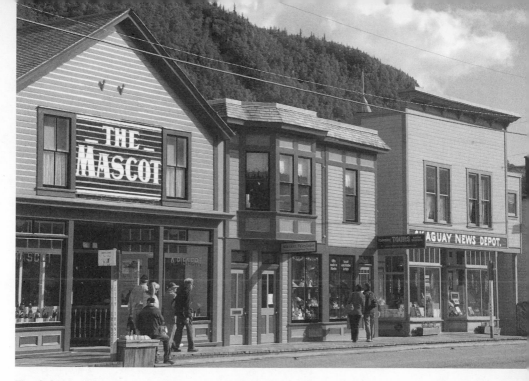

The 1898 Mascot Saloon was one of many in Skagway during the Klondike gold rush.

little to attract tourists. Town buildings are scattered in the wooded terrain, and on clear days, a gorgeous view of Mount St. Elias unfolds across the bay.

Yakutat sits at the narrow junction of the Alaska Panhandle with the main body of the state. It lies beyond the Inside Passage, with its myriad islands, and so its terrain is as a result flatter, and the mountains, though still spectacular, more distant.

CENTRAL PANHANDLE

Petersburg: This town wears its Norwegian roots with pride. The Sons of Norway Hall is the most prominent building in town, and the replica of a Viking ship, the most conspicuous artifact. Popular entertainment features the Leikarring dancers, in their charming blue embroidered costumes. Colorful rosemaling painting decorates every downtown store—even the Harbor Bar.

Peter Buschmann, a fisherman, founded the town and attracted other Norwegian immigrants. They established fisheries, and Petersburg today continues to be a fishing town, with commercial fishing boats, three canneries, and a huge charter fishing fleet. Small boats line up gunwale-to-gunwale at the docks. Excursion boats for LeConte Glacier, the southernmost tidewater glacier, also depart from Petersburg.

Sitka: This is a town with a past, and one which still bears an air of importance. Once a Tlingit site called *Shee-At'iká*, it became the capital of Russian America, and the site of the transfer of Alaska to the United States, in 1867. Sitka National Historical Park commemorates the battle between the Russians and the Tlingit, and has a splendid, adjacent totem pole park. The Russian legacy still exists, in buildings such as St. Michael's Cathedral and the Bishop's House and in place names. Sitka also has the world-class Alaska Raptor

Mount St. Elias is visible on a clear day across Yakutat Bay.

Center where injured eagles are rehabilitated and returned to the wild.

Sitka sits on the western side of Baranof Island on the Pacific Ocean, the only Panhandle town to do so. Still, it sits on a deep bay of Sitka Sound studded with islands, so the harbor is calm and protected. Its location makes it more isolated than many other Inside Passage towns.

Wrangell: Children of Wrangell come out to greet cruise ship or ferry passengers, and to sell them garnets, collected from a ledge near town, with all of the proceeds going to youth programs. People selling local handicrafts may also be seen here.

Wrangell also has Chief Shakes Tribal House, a Tlingit tribal house, and an excellent museum in the Nolan Center. It's a jumping-off place for excursions to the Stikine River and the Anan Wildlife Observatory. And of course, charter-fishing boats line the harbor. Wrangell is a little smaller than most of the Panhandle towns and hasn't used its past to create its present image, as much as some other places have. John Muir spent several weeks here on his first trip to Alaska to study glaciers. On this excursion, he got caught in a fierce rainstorm one night on the hill behind town. He built a roaring bonfire atop Mt. Dewey to keep himself warm, and caused consternation among the local Tlingits when they saw the clouds above reflecting its fiery light.

SOUTHERN PANHANDLE
Ketchikan: The gateway to the Panhandle for cruise ship passengers coming from the south, Ketchikan calls itself "Alaska's First City." Like Juneau, it is long and narrow; locals

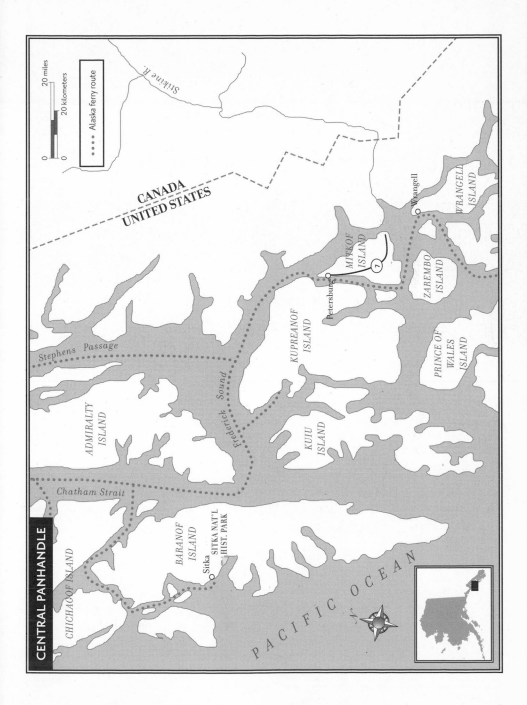

CENTRAL PANHANDLE

CANADA
UNITED STATES

20 miles
20 kilometers

Alaska ferry route

Stikine R.

Wrangell

WRANGELL ISLAND

MITKOF ISLAND

ZAREMBO ISLAND

Petersburg

KUPREANOF ISLAND

PRINCE OF WALES ISLAND

Stephens Passage

Frederick Sound

ADMIRALTY ISLAND

KUIU ISLAND

Chatham Strait

BARANOF ISLAND

SITKA NAT'L HIST. PARK

Sitka

CHICHAGOF ISLAND

PACIFIC OCEAN

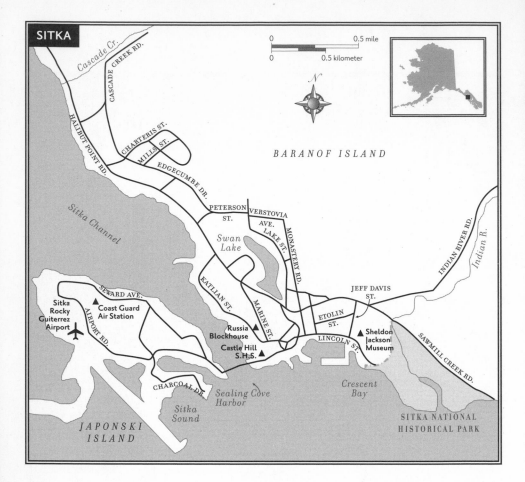

like to say it's "8 miles long and three blocks wide." Staircases connect many streets on the mountainside town. Every visitor treks up Creek Street, the former red-light district, now home to galleries and cafés. Two important Tlingit villages, Saxman and Totem Bight, each have impressive collections of totem poles, and a heritage center has significant, historic totem poles on display.

Huge cruise ships and small fishing boats crowd Ketchikan's waterfront, which is also enlivened by a series of shops and mini-malls that run the gamut, from expensive jewelry shops and serious art galleries, to souvenir shops. Ketchikan is the departure point for sightseeing flights or cruises to appropriately named Misty Fjords National Monument—a good place to spot wildlife, and find waterfalls gushing down cliffs that disappear up into wisps of cloud.

Ketchikan earned a good bit of national attention in 2007 for its bid to build the "Bridge to Nowhere." The bridge, in fact, was meant to connect the airport on Gravina Island over Tongass Narrows to town on Revillagigedo Island. After disputes over funding, the project

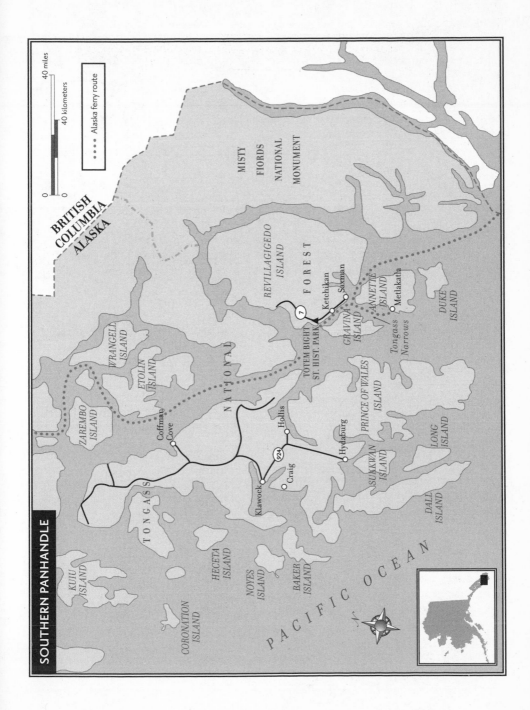

SOUTHERN PANHANDLE

40 miles

40 kilometers

····· Alaska ferry route

BRITISH
COLUMBIA

ALASKA

MISTY

FIORDS

NATIONAL

MONUMENT

REVILLAGIGEDO
ISLAND

F O R E S T

Ketchikan Saxman

7

ANNETTE
ISLAND   Metlakatla

GRAVINA
ISLAND

DUKE
ISLAND

TOTEM BIGHT
ST. HIST. PARK

Tongass
Narrows

WRANGELL
ISLAND

ETOLIN
ISLAND

PRINCE OF WALES
ISLAND

LONG
ISLAND

N A T I O N A L

Hollis

ZAREMBO
ISLAND

Coffman
Cove

924

Hydaburg

SUKKWAN
ISLAND

DALL
ISLAND

T O N G A S S

Craig

Klawock

KUIU
ISLAND

HECETA
ISLAND

CORONATION
ISLAND

NOYES
ISLAND

BAKER
ISLAND

P A C I F I C   O C E A N

N

Creek Street, once Ketchikan's red-light district, attracts visitors for its galleries and shops.

A Ketchikan artist created fanciful toppings for Thomas Basin pilings.

was cancelled, so expect to continue taking the ferry between the airport and Tongass Avenue.

Prince of Wales Island: POW stretches 140 miles by 45 miles, the third-largest island in the United States. Unlike other parts of the Panhandle, the island has more than 2,000 miles of paved and graded roads; more than the rest of the entire Alaska Panhandle. Most people come here to fish at resorts, some of them accessible by float plane or boat only. It also has excellent totem pole parks in Klawock and Hydaburg. Clear-cutting of timber has denuded some of the hills, but the island still has extensive forested areas.

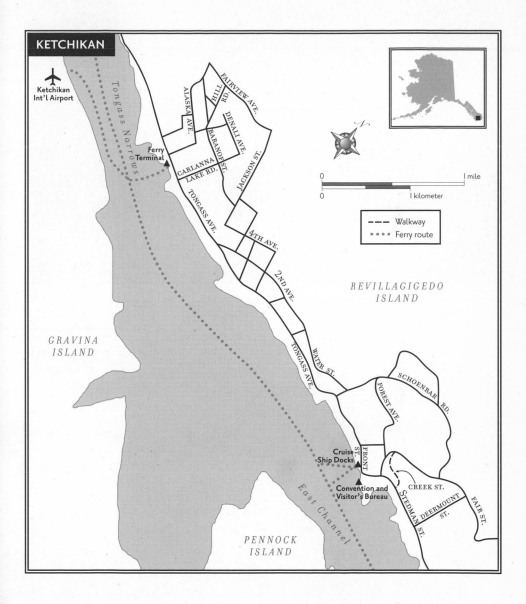

KETCHIKAN

Ketchikan
Int'l Airport

Tongass Narrows

Ferry
Terminal

ALASKA AVE.
HILL
FAIRVIEW AVE.
RD.
DENALI AVE.
BARANOF ST.
CARLANNA
LAKE RD.
JACKSON ST.

TONGASS AVE.
4TH AVE.
2ND AVE.

TONGASS AVE.
WATER ST.

GRAVINA
ISLAND

REVILLAGIGEDO
ISLAND

0   I mile
0   I kilometer

- - - Walkway
• • • • Ferry route

SCHOENBAR RD.
FOREST AVE.
FRONT ST.
Cruise
Ship Docks
Convention and
Visitor's Bureau
CREEK ST.
STEDMAN ST.
DEERMOUNT ST.
FAIR ST.

East Channel

PENNOCK
ISLAND

HISTORY

Beringia Migrants to Cruise Ship Tourists

In the beginning of time, land had to be made before mankind could be created. This duty fell to Raven.
—Tlingit creation legend

NATURAL HISTORY

The vast peninsula of Alaska tops the North American continent rather like an inverted pot. The pot body is the state's primary landmass. The Panhandle, the subject of this book, stretches downward and southward, clinging to the edge of British Columbia and the Yukon Territory, while the Aleutian Islands stretch out in the opposite direction, toward Russia and Japan, rather like steam escaping from the pot.

Pushed by tectonic plate action, the North American continent migrated here from the south, when the primordial landmass began to break up. The part drifting northward compressed somewhat, forming Alaska's mountain ranges, which include the highest peaks in North America. The continents are still drifting; but on geologic, not human, time.

Alaska's oldest rocks formed hundreds of millions of years ago, and thousands of miles away. The most dramatic evidence of this migration is Yellow Rock near Metlakatla on Annette Island. The sandstone rock, looking like a fragment of New Mexico, formed considerably south of here. The state's geology is complicated, and often rocks close to each other had vastly different origins in time and place.

The subduction zone between the North American and the Pacific tectonic plates has formed the Aleutian Islands. Where tectonic plates collide, one rolls under the other, forcing or scraping some material to the surface, and forming land. Occasionally, hot magma is forced through along this zone. Where the magma escapes to the surface, it becomes a volcano. Such volcanic regions at the edge of a plate are called volcanic arcs. The Aleutian Islands form the northern part of the largest volcanic arc on earth, the Pacific Ring of Fire. It spans North and South America, as well as Asia's Pacific coast. Volcanoes in the Aleutian Islands and Alaska Peninsula spew ash frequently, sometimes interrupting airplane service to Anchorage and Juneau. The state has 40 active volcanoes, and their presence also means seismic activity, including earthquakes and the possible threat of tsunamis.

Relief maps show alternate bands of mountains and plains dividing Alaska. The western and southernmost of these mountains are the Coast Mountains. They run up the west coast of the Lower 48, through Canada and the Alaska Panhandle. The international boundary between the United States and Canada runs along the crest of the Coast Mountains. They drop steeply into the sea, giving the Panhandle its spectacular landscape.

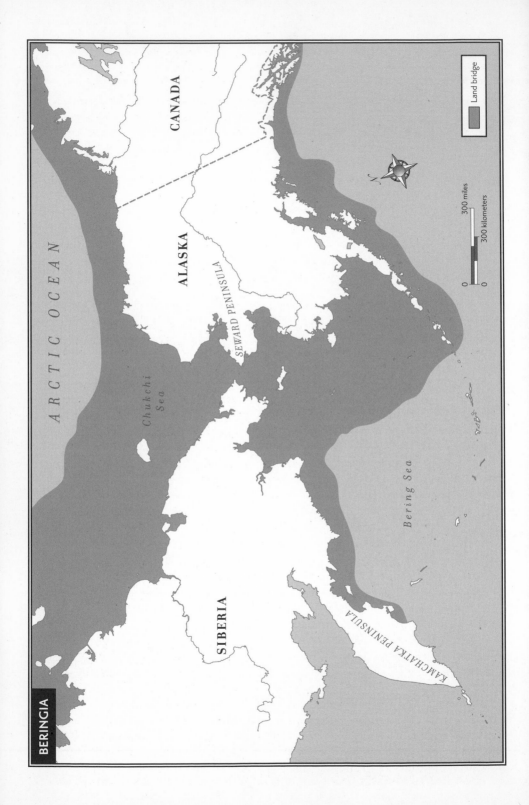

The Panhandle stretches almost 500 miles, from the southern tip of Prince of Wales Island to Yakutat, though it is at most 100 miles wide, and the mainland portion generally runs only about 30 miles from the coast to the Canadian border. Islands, about 1,100 of them, make up most of the Panhandle, like an enormous loosely arranged jigsaw puzzle. John Muir called the arrangement "land and water embroidery." Deep channels, sounds, and fjords separate the islands from each other and the mainland. They are the tips of the submerged part of the Coast Mountains. In 1867, Americans of the U.S. Coast and Geodetic Survey named the islands the Alexander Archipelago, for Tsar Alexander II of Russia.

Where the Panhandle joins the state's main landmass, the Coast Mountains curve sharply to the west, and near Anchorage are known as the Chugach Range. Then they arc south onto the Kenai Peninsula and emerge briefly again on Kodiak Island. It's as if the narrowing of the earth's sphere has bent the mountains from a north–south to an east–west axis, and then bent them back south again.

Two additional east–west ranges divide Alaska; the Alaska Range, which arcs around the southern basin and contains Mount McKinley; and the Brooks Range, which is north of the Arctic Circle. Alaska's major rivers, including the Yukon, run between these mountain ranges.

North of the Coast Mountains in the area north of Anchorage lies a basin that includes the Matanuska–Susitna Valley, a rich agriculture area with a moderate climate. Beyond the Alaska Range, are the central uplands and plains. North of the Brooks Range, the tundra-covered Arctic Plains spread over about one-third of the state's area.

Yellow Hill in Metlakatla shows evidence of continental drift.

Ice Ages

Alaska's northern latitudes made it subject to the great ice sheets that covered this part of Earth during the past 800 million years. During four periods, these ice sheets grew, and then retreated. Today's retreating glaciers are remnants of the Wisconsin glacial period, the final period of the last Ice Age that took place about 20,000 years ago.

During these glacial periods, vast amounts of seawater were locked into ice sheets and snowfields. The resulting dropping sea level created a land bridge between Siberia and Alaska, which scientists call Beringia, named for Vitus Bering, the 18th-century Danish-born mariner who explored this region on behalf of Russia.

At its greatest extent, Beringia may have been about 1,000 miles wide. Pollen recovered from cores drilled deep into the earth in islands of the Bering Sea and the Yukon have confirmed the presence of this land bridge between about 14,000 and 30,000 thousand years ago. It was probably not continuous, and it probably existed at other periods in the even more distant past. Some Bering Sea islands today are remnants of that land bridge.

Even during these Ice Ages, the northern parts of Alaska and the Beringia land bridge remained free of ice. Not enough rain or snow fell to create the ice sheets and glaciers. It was a vast, cold steppe, covered with grasslands. Thick ice sheets did cover most of present-day Southern Alaska, including the Panhandle, most of Canada, and the northern part of the United States.

Most experts agree that the North American continent was first populated when people from Asia crossed this land bridge, and probably even stayed there for a while. They began to migrate and to settle North and eventually South America. As the glacial period came to an end, the oceans rose and the land bridge was once again closed so that they were isolated from their ancestral lands in Asia. However, since Alaska and Siberia are extremely close at the Diomede Islands, certainly the migrations continued. Little Diomede Island, off the Seward Peninsula, lies about 2½ miles from Russia's Big Diomede Island.

Anthropologists and paleontologists have pushed the date back in time over the past decade or two. They used to believed that the migration occurred 10,000–12,000 years ago. Recently, however, evidence of a human settlement in Patagonia has been dated to 14,000 years ago by radiocarbon techniques.

Not everyone migrated through Alaska. Some people stayed, and in time their cultures differentiated.

People, of course, were not the only living things to have migrated over the land bridge. Alaskan and the Yukon fossils offer evidence of many animals, which are believed to have migrated from the Eurasian landmass to North America during the Pleistocene age, and earlier. These might include mammoths, bison, caribou, horses, musk oxen, wolves, and brown bear. Mammoths, especially, thrived on the cold Beringia grasslands.

The Ice Ages left one other indelible change to the landscape: The great glaciers scoured out river valleys, pushing ahead dirt and rocks, like giant bulldozers. When the glaciers began to retreat, they left behind dirt rubble, which are called moraines, and widened the V-shaped depressions into U-shaped valleys. These are all over Southeastern Alaska, evidence of this glacial action.

John Muir initially noticed U-shaped valleys in Yosemite, and theorized that glaciers had formed these valleys, yet not all experts agreed with his theories. When he went to Alaska in 1879, he found the glaciated landscape in the making. He writes, in ecstatic terms, not only of confirming his theories, but also of the scale and beauty of Southeast Alaska. He walked across the vast glaciers in Glacier Bay, up the Stikine River, and near

Salmonberry blooms in any vacant patch of dirt in May and bears yellow, orange, and red berries in late summer.

Juneau, sometimes pulling a sled behind him and spending the night in a skin sleeping bag. The U-shaped valleys are apparent anywhere along the Inside Passage, and up its channels. Some of them open directly to the sea and bays, others are hanging valleys, ending perpendicular to the side of a larger valley. Glaciers still fill some of them.

Flora and Fauna

People often marvel at cabbages the size of wine barrels and fireweed that turns roadsides crimson, with flower spikes up to 7- feet high during the summer. Alaska's growing season may be short in terms of days, but long daylight hours stimulate plants to grow and grow, and grow.

The region in general is classified as a temperate rainforest. Coniferous trees dominate the flora. Sitka spruce (the state tree), Alaska yellow cedar, and western redcedar are the more commonly found trees in the Panhandle. Totem pole carvers favor the latter, for its malleable and durable wood. The deciduous, somewhat brushy-looking, tree found growing everywhere along roadsides and in vacant lots is alder. People use it to smoke salmon and other foods.

These trees grow everywhere along the coast, covering mountains with a dense forest canopy up to about 2,500 feet, the tree line at this latitude. The conifers take hold, on islands so tiny that the trees are taller even than the islands are wide. They create a damp, dark cover for the underbrush that sports a thick tangle of berries. Late summer brings an abundance of huckleberries, thimbleberry, and salmonberry to the forest, and likely to the table as well, in many restaurants and bed-and-breakfast inns. In addition to berries, a nasty, nettlelike plant called devil's club grows on the forest floor. Alaska Natives used it widely for medicinal purposes. You can buy devil's club creams and lip balm, especially in Sitka. Skunk cabbage often joins devil's club, as one of the largest plants on the forest floor or in the muskeg. Its leaves can grow to be 2- to 3-feet long, looking like something from the tropics.

In flat, open areas, muskeg covers the ground. The swampy, marshy area is spongy underfoot, and results from the decay of plant matter in wet soil. It's the reason board-walks cover so many hiking areas, and it's why Alaskans so often wear the tall rubber boots, which they're likely to call "Petersburg sneakers" (or substitute whatever town you're in, for Petersburg). An array of wildflowers can grow on the muskeg, providing blooms all summer long.

The warm Japan Current keeps the Alaska Panhandle mild, which supports the rainfor-est environment. However, at elevations above about 2,500 feet, trees play out and are replaced by Alpine tundra. Tundra consists of short, stunted plants, which sometimes bloom in dazzling colors and can survive extreme cold. Arctic tundra grows on permafrost at northern latitudes, and Alpine tundra at high elevations anywhere. Eventually the tun-dra dwindles to lichens, and finally bare ground.

Permafrost covers most of the main body of Alaska, but not the Panhandle. Much of the Alaskan permafrost lies in patches, which presents a challenge to any sort of development. The Alaska oil pipeline, for example, is built on permafrost. The brackets supporting the raised pipeline extend deep into the ground, and had to be built of a special non-heat-conducting material so that the ground around the support would not melt and undermine the pipeline. Roads and railbeds in Alaska often buckle under unexpected

The Japan Current supports the rainforest, shown here at Auke Bay near Juneau.

Georg Steller, who came with explorer Vitus Bering in 1741, gave his name to Steller sea lions and other wildlife.

melting of permafrost. Global climate warming threatens to melt permafrost, which could have far-reaching consequences in places such as Fairbanks.

Taiga is a term used to describe an area of stunted trees, sometimes between the coniferous forests and the tundra, though it's only found north of the Panhandle.

The growing season in Alaska may be short, but it's explosive. A succession of wildflowers brings brightness to open areas throughout the summer season. Early on, skunk cabbage sends up its sexual blossom, which disintegrates with the vaguely stinky odor for which it is named. In late May, dandelions grow to flamboyant size and dot the roadsides with yellow, quite overpowering the smaller buttercups. Then the little blue blossoms of forget-me-nots, the state flower, carpet the ground with the color of the sky. Lupine, sometimes stunted, sometimes huge, emerges in early June.

Primroses, Indian paintbrush, and wild iris also brighten the muskeg and roadsides in June and July. In boggy areas, Labrador or Hudson Bay tea grows with a small white flower. Alaska Natives harvest and dry its leaves for a tea, which they believe has healing properties. The most common plant anywhere in Alaska, is fireweed. The plant easily grows to 5 or more feet, and blooms with magenta blossoms from late June until frost. Photographers love to put it in the foreground of Alaska photos.

Animal life, in addition to the gorgeous scenery, draws many visitors to Alaska. The cool oceans abound with plankton and other marine invertebrate life, which provide rich feeding ground for whales. Orcas (killer whales) and humpback whales are abundant in Panhandle waters in the summer. An occasional minke whale may also be spotted. Whale-watching excursions (See Chapter 7, *Recreation*) are a popular visitor activity.

Salmon lure fishing enthusiasts who come to Panhandle fishing resorts for a few days or a week. They spend their days on a small boat, in quest of the five varieties of salmon or halibut, and then return home. Salmon are born in fresh water along Alaska streams, or in salmon hatcheries. After about two years, the young salmon, or smolts, swim out to sea, where they stay for one or more years. Then they return to the streams where they were born, in one of nature's miracles. Sometimes they beat themselves bloody, trying to swim up waterfalls to their birth spot. Summer is prime time to see the spawning salmon, and visitors line stream bridges in Ketchikan, Petersburg, Juneau, and elsewhere, to see this phenomenon. Some people describe the salmon spawn as being so thick, "you could walk on their backs across the stream."

Harbor seal and Steller sea lion colonies populate shoreline rocks on islands and coves, and are easily seen from small cruise ships and kayaks. Sea otters are also numerous, and you'll often see them around harbors, on their backs, cracking open shells on their bellies. It's easy to project human playfulness onto these little creatures.

Bears, perhaps more than any other animal, motivate wildlife excursions and are sought for photographs. The Panhandle has black bears, the most abundant variety, and Alaska brown, or grizzly bears. A few islands, such as Annette near Ketchikan, do not have brown bears. Bears are most likely to be spotted foraging along streams or along the shore of inlets. If you're on a cruise ship, scan the beaches. You'll sometimes see them on open sandy areas, for example, in Glacier Bay. Streams with spawning salmon get the highest density of bears.

The U.S. Forest Service has created three bear-viewing sites in the Alaska Panhandle: Anan Wildlife Observatory near Wrangell for black bears; Pack Creek Brown Bear Viewing Area on Admiralty Island for brown bears; and Fish Creek Wildlife Observation Site for both brown and black bears near Ketchikan. (See Chapter 7, *Recreation*.)

Even before the Tlingit people established their culture, other people lived in the Alaska Panhandle and carved petroglyphs, like this killer whale at Wrangell.

Moose will also cause eyes to turn and cars and tour buses to stop along Alaska roads. I've seen them in the parking lot of the Captain's Choice Motel in Haines, though never in the forest. Moose may migrate to higher elevations in the summer, so they are less likely to be seen during the tourism season. Beware of moose just as much as you would bears. They are dangerous, especially a mother with a baby. Red foxes, wolves, and Arctic ground squirrels are other furry things to look for in the Panhandle.

Don't forget to look up. The white spots on cliffs and mountains are mountain goats. Dall sheep cling to the lower reaches and can sometimes be spotted on roadsides. Caribou and musk ox tend to be creatures of the far north, so you won't see them in the Panhandle.

Almost anytime you look into the tallest trees along the fjords, inlets, and coves of the Inside Passage, you're likely to see a large, dark bird with a white head—a little like a golf ball atop a dark sack. It's a bald eagle, no doubt looking for dinner in the form of fish. They're another species that can quicken the heartbeat of anyone who never expected to see this creature, except on the U.S. seal.

Unusual birds that can be spotted along the shore in colonies, especially around South Marble Island in Glacier Bay, are puffins with their colorful bills. Arctic terns, glaucous-winged gulls, and herring gulls are common in bays. Murres, murrelets, and loons can also be observed. Colonies of Arctic and Caspian terns and kittiwakes soar around cliffs near the faces of glaciers. Early summer and fall are wonderful seasons for migratory birds. Rafts of thousands of surf scoters darken big patches of water in those seasons. Other types of ducks to be seen in the area are mergansers and, very exciting for birders, harlequin ducks.

St. Lazaria Island near Sitka ranks as one of Alaska's prime birding areas. More than 500,000 birds nest on the 65-acre island. Burrowing birds such as storm petrels, rhinoceros auklets, and ancient murrelets are the most abundant species. Albatross and shearwaters also feed in waters off the island. Several companies in Sitka provide excursions to observe the birds from the sea.

Ravens populate the Panhandle towns with their boisterous presence and raucous calls. They don't inspire the excitement of a bald eagle, but Alaska Natives traditionally held them in high regard. The Tlingits held Raven responsible for bringing the land into being, and placed these birds at the center of their creation myth.

Climate and Weather

The Alaska Panhandle has a northern maritime climate, kept relatively mild by the Japan Current. Southwest winds blow over the warm waters of the current, keeping winter temperatures mild and summer temperatures cool.

Most of the Panhandle averages high temperatures in the mid-60s during the summer and the high 20s or low 30s in winter. In the interior, at Whitehorse for example, temperatures are more extreme, averaging about minus 7-degree lows in January, and 70-degree highs in summer.

Those kind winds also bring rain in summer, and snow in winter. Early summer has the least rainfall, while this increases into the fall, which is also the rainiest season. Early summer has cooler temperatures, but in general, is a good time to travel. Skies are often overcast or partly overcast, and rain is often misty rather than a downpour. Ketchikan takes the prize for heaviest rainfall, with annual precipitation measured at 160 inches. Rather than trying to ignore it, the Visitor's Bureau posts a rain gauge, called the "Liquid Sunshine Gauge," on its building. It shows the record year to be 1949, with a whopping 192 inches.

Just bring a water-repellent jacket, but don't forget the sunscreen and sunglasses, either. When the sun bounces off Margerie Glacier, it can be blinding.

Social History

Pre-History
The first migrants to Alaska arrived over the Beringia land bridge. The first human implements found in Alaska date to about 11,000 years ago, but scientists believe that people lived here before then.

Over time, as people settled in isolated regions of Alaska, they became more diverse, ethnically, culturally, and even physically. Today, anthropologists distinguish 11 distinct cultures with 20 different languages among Alaska Natives. Most people cluster the native people into seven to nine groups: Inupiat, Yup'ik, and Yupik Eskimos who generally live in the Arctic and through the Aleutian Islands; the Athabascans, the largest group, who live in interior Alaska and have more land base than any other native people; Aleut and Alutiiq, who live along the Gulf of Alaska; and Haida, Tsimshian, and Tlingit, the northernmost of the Northwest Coast people, who live in the Panhandle. Tlingit people are by far the largest group. (See Chapter 5, *Native Culture*.) The Alaska State Museum in Juneau has excellent exhibits focused on these cultures, and community museums throughout the Panhandle often have excellent Tlingit and Haida exhibits. (See Chapter 4, *Culture*.)

Over thousands of years, these people developed complex systems of subsistence living under harsh conditions, as well as religious beliefs and artistic iconography and expression. Then, beginning in the 18th century, Europeans began to nudge steadily at the coast of Alaska. First, Peter the Great sent Vitus Bering to explore the area off Russia's Far East. In 1728, Bering made two attempts, spotting St. Lawrence Island, and sailing through the strait that bears his name. He led a second 1741 expedition, and this time he landed near present-day Yakutat, though he died on the return trip. But naturalist Georg Steller was along on this second voyage, observing and collecting specimens, and eventually giving his name to several Alaskan animals. And, most important, expedition members brought fine otter pelts back to Russia, which awakened that country's interest in America. Bering's account was the first written record of outside contact with Alaska Natives.

Explorers
Next came the Spaniards, starting in the 1770s and continuing through the succeeding two decades, with their explorations the source of the many Spanish names in the Panhandle: Bucareli Bay on Prince of Wales, Malaspina Glacier near Yakutat, and Revillagigedo Island at Ketchikan. Captain Cook came in 1778, searching for the Northwest Passage. He named Mount Fairweather and Prince William Sound on the journey. Cook Inlet, near Anchorage, was later named for him, and famously Turnagain Arm, which reflected his disappointment at the inlet's dead end, inspiring him to declare it, "River Turnagain." George Vancouver, who had sailed with Cook, came back in 1793 and 1794 to chart the coast for England. He named Prince of Wales Island after the son of George III. He scattered other English names about: Lynn Canal, Douglas Island, Stephens Passage, and Admiralty Island.

The French came, too, with the La Pérouse expedition of 1786 that visited Lituya Bay, between Glacier and Yakutat bays.

Russian America

Meanwhile, the Russians hadn't been idle. Beginning about the middle of the 1700s, free-lance fur traders began island hopping through the Aleutians, harvesting sea otter, fox, and seal furs. They disrupted the Aleut's subsistence lifestyle and brought their own diseases, decimating the native population. Finally, six companies of fur traders staked out various areas, from the Aleutians through Prince William Sound.

By the 1780s, the first Russian settlement was established on Kodiak Island, and the fur trade continued to grow. By 1791, Alexander Baranov had arrived to run the operation, and by 1799 it had the exclusive trading monopoly, becoming the Russian-American Company. Baranov became known as the "Lord of Alaska" for his part in putting the colony on firm footing and expanding its sphere of influence. The headquarters moved from Kodiak to Sitka—or "Shee-At'iká" as the Tlingit called it, a site he deemed more hospitable. A fort was established. Tensions erupted with the Tlingit, who burned the fort and killed or ran off the Russians and their Aleut laborers. Eventually, the Russians returned, and in 1804, prevailed at present-day Sitka, which they called New Archangel. It became the capital of Russian America.

They established the Russian Orthodox Church, converting many of the Aleuts and Tlingits, and building St. Mark's Cathedral and a Bishop's Palace. The Orthodox religion is the most tangible remaining evidence of the Russian presence in North America. In general, Alaska furs were sold in China in exchange for tea, porcelains, and other Chinese goods, which were then traded elsewhere. The Russians did not operate in a cocoon. Americans and the English were also trading in furs along the Pacific Coast, and both were conscious of Russians flexing their muscles in America, not only with regard to claiming land, but controlling trade between the Tlingit and others. Eventually, the Russians signed an agreement with Americans that recognized the border of Russian America at 54.4 degrees north and also recognized trading and navigation rights. A similar agreement was signed with Great Britain. This also was an attempt to settle the complicated border between Canada and Russian America, a dispute that was not settled until early in the 20th century.

By then, Baranov had died at sea on his return to Russia after long service as head of the Russian-American Company. By about the mid-1800s, furs were beginning to dwindle, simply due to having been overharvested. The difficulty of maintaining these far-flung outposts also surfaced, for the Russians, British, and the Americans. The Civil War distracted the United States from further activity in the far north, until 1865. Eventually, Secretary of State William Seward promoted the sale of Russian America to the United States for $7.2 million, or as it is often defined, two cents an acre. He argued that it would extend America's sphere of influence in North America, strengthen ties with Russia, and make Japan and China more accessible for trade. The Senate ratified it, and the formal transfer took place on October, 18, 1867, now called Alaska Day. While Russian and American officials looked on, the Russian double-eagle imperial flag was lowered, and the Stars and Stripes raised. The ceremony took place at the governor's house on "Castle Hill" in Sitka.

America Strikes Gold

The Americans called the new possession Alaska, for the Aleut word meaning "Great Land," a fitting word. Some people and some press accounts ridiculed the sale, calling it "Seward's Folly," or "Seward's Icebox," but he proved correct in extending the boundaries of the country in North America. Seward visited Alaska in 1869, after he had left office.

A miner/guide stands at the entrance to a tunnel at the AJ Mine on the Gastineau Mill-mine tour. The board to his left has a brass disk with a number, which the miner moved to the top row when he went into the mine, and put back at the bottom when he came out.

Alaska became a U.S. Department, administered by the Army, followed by the Treasury Department, and the Navy. In 1884, Congress named the territory the Alaska District, with a little more authority designated for local officials through the Organic Act of 1884. One early challenge was that much of its interior was unknown, so the Army organized expeditions to chart the rivers and the areas between them, particularly between the Copper and Yukon rivers.

Prospectors, many of them veterans of gold camps in California, saw opportunity in the new territory. They made their way through Wrangell up the Stikine River to the Cassiar Gold Fields of Canada, in the 1870s. After those fields played out, in 1880, Joe Juneau and Richard Harris, with three Tlingits as guides, explored an area on the mainland where a stream tumbled into Gastineau Channel. Moving up the stream, they began to find gold embedded in quartz. It was part of the rich deposits in the Silver Bow Basin, and the beginning of Juneau, named for the prospector who died poor. Numerous claims and counterclaims came into play about the establishment of the mining district. Eventually the A J Mine operated above Juneau, and the Treadwell Mine was established across the channel on Douglas Island. Juneau mining thrived well into the 20th century, and even today, gold is still mined at Berners Bay, about 45 miles from Juneau.

Finding gold in Canada accessed through the Panhandle wasn't unique to Wrangell. Later, the same thing happened at the top of the Lynn Canal, at Dyea and Skagway for the gold more than 500 miles upstream on the Yukon River in Canada. It was the Klondike Gold Rush of 1898, maybe the continent's most momentous quest for riches. Starting in 1897, miners went through Dyea, already established as a trading post, and which subsequently became trailhead for the Chilkoot Trail. Dyea's lengthy tidal flats made it an unsuitable port. Then in 1898, the White Pass & Yukon Route was built a few miles east. It doomed Dyea, and Skagway was born an instant boomtown. Haines also served as a point of entry to the Klondike Gold Fields for those who went up the Chilkat River. Some miners made their way inland through Edmonton and others journeyed up through the Bering Sea to the mouth of the Yukon River and then took steamers upstream hundreds of miles across Alaska.

Alaska had gold finds, on the Kenai and at Nome, but none matched the frenzy of the Klondike.

Alaska drew more than prospectors. John Muir, sometimes in the company of Presbyterian missionary Samuel Hall Young, made three trips to Alaska near the end of the 1800s. The Presbyterians established missions in many of the small Panhandle towns. To this day, the Presbyterian Church plays important roles in places such as Wrangell, Haines, and Skagway. These are often among the oldest churches in these towns.

The interior of Alaska remained much more of a frontier than the Panhandle, largely because of the latter region's access to the seacoast, kinder climate, and the history of set-tlements, starting with Tlingit villages, Russian America forts, and American towns. Until the extensive growth of Anchorage in the 1940s and 1950s, the Panhandle remained Alaska's most heavily settled region.

After hordes of people flooded to Alaska during the gold rushes of the late 1800s, the government began to be aware of the need to preserve the region. Preservationists and conservationists such as Gifford Pinchot, a chief of the Bureau of Forestry, and John Muir urged the government to set aside lands. Theodore Roosevelt signed a series of executive orders creating the Tongass National Forest, which today extends over 17 million acres, almost the entire Alaska Panhandle. It is the nation's largest national forest. He also cre-ated the Chugach National Forest in South Central Alaska, which now measures 5½ million acres. Today the federal government oversees 200 million acres of Alaska public lands, which include 15 national parks, 16 wildlife refuges, and the nation's two largest national forests.

Gold and other minerals continued to be mined in the early 1900s, if at a slower pace than the Klondike. The seas were also being mined. Settlers and investors realized the value of fish, particularly canned salmon, and so many canneries were established throughout the Panhandle. Some of them were on the site of Tlingit villages, where natives had come to fish for centuries. Alaska Natives went to work in those canneries. Many of them have since closed, while others have now become fishing resorts or tourist facilities.

Territorial Days

In the early 1900s, Alaskans wanted more authority over their affairs. Finally, in 1912, Congress passed the second Organic Act, and Alaska became a U.S. Territory with an elected legislature and appointed governor. With territorial status, came the desire for a flag. The American Legion organized a contest open to students in grades 7 through 12, who were to submit a design for a flag on an ordinary sheet of paper or cardboard, with their name, age, and address on the back. Benny Benson, a 13-year-old student at the Jesse Lee Home, a mission school in Seward, won the contest. His winning design featured the Big Dipper and the North Star against a blue background.

He wrote his reasons for the design alongside the entry: "The blue field is for the Alaska sky and the forget-me-not, an Alaskan flower. The North Star is for the future state of

Alaska, the most northerly in the union. The Dipper is for the Great Bear—symbolizing strength."

The first half of the 1900s was a time of trying to build infrastructure in the main part of Alaska, with railroads and highways connecting Fairbanks, Anchorage, and the ports of Valdez, Seward, and Whittier. The Panhandle's mountainous terrain pretty much prevented any roads, so access remained largely by steamer.

Highway access got a boost at the beginning of World War II. The military immediately sensed the importance of Alaska as a strategic location for air and ground bases. It started with ferrying supplies and airplanes to the Soviet Union, who was our ally, and after the war using those bases as a deterrent to possible Russian attack during the Cold War. The problem was that there was no way to get supplies to the interior of Alaska. So a plan was hatched to build an Alaska–Canada military highway from Montana or South Dakota, up through Canada, to enter Alaska in the Yukon Valley, not far from the Klondike gold fields. A series of forts existed in Alberta, British Columbia, and the Yukon. The Army used a road scraper to clear a path between them, and as the roadbed was being level, the trucks followed. Walter R. Borneman describes this odd primitive convoy in *Alaska: Saga of a Bold Land*.

Alaska saw other action in World War II. The Japanese occupied two Aleutian Islands, Attu and Kiska, the only places in the continental United States to be occupied. It took fierce fighting to overcome the Japanese. The government sent Japanese Americans, along with some Germans and Italians, to internment camps in the West. Aleuts who lived near any military bases in the Aleutians were also sent to camps.

Military presence during World War II and the Cold War has left Alaska with a legacy of

Benny Benson, an Alaska schoolboy, designed the Alaska state flag as the territorial flag.

several fine airport runways, however. The jet service possible at places such as Gustavus and Yakutat is because of the runways built originally for the military.

In general, with the settling of Alaska by more and more people from the Lower 48, discrimination against Alaska Natives increased. Some of their fishing and hunting grounds were disturbed. They could not live in certain areas or participate in certain businesses. NO NATIVES ALLOWED signs were common in shops and movie theaters.

The Alaska Native Brotherhood and Sisterhood chapters, and some whites spearheaded a civil-rights movement. Hearings were held in the Territorial Senate in 1945. One of the white speakers said: "Who are these people, barely out of savagery, who want to associate with us whites, with 5,000 years of recorded civilization behind us?"

The last person to testify was Elizabeth Peratrovich of the Alaska Native Sisterhood, who responded: "I would not have expected that I, who am barely out of savagery, would have to remind the gentlemen with 5,000 years of recorded history behind them, of our Bill of Rights." The gallery audience and some of the Senators burst into applause, and an Anti-discrimination Act was passed. Elizabeth Peratrovich Day is celebrated on February 16.

The Forty-Ninth State

When the war was over, Alaskans intensified their efforts to become a state, though opinion was not unanimous within the state or outside. Opponents in Congress pointed to Alaska's separation from the U.S. mainland, its small population, and its unresolved Alaska Native claims. Interestingly, the strongest opposition came from Washington State leaders. Seattle, especially, has always had a strong connection to Alaska, serving as a supply base from the earliest days. To some extent, the connection is still strong. Many Alaskans are educated in Washington State, or they live and work there for periods during their lives. Goods from Seattle make the trip north to serve restaurants and shops in Alaska.

Nonetheless, a referendum for statehood passed by 58 percent and Territorial Governor Ernest Gruening and other advocates lobbied Congress and the National Governors Conference, which supported Alaska statehood. Finally, in 1956 Alaska voters approved a new constitution. The House and Senate accepted it and President Dwight Eisenhower signed the Alaska Statehood Act in July 1958. Alaska became the 49th state on January 3, 1959. The U.S. flag with 49 stars was raised in a ceremony on July 4, 1959 at a spot in front of today's Juneau-Douglas City Museum, where a 49-star flag still flies. Juneau remained the capital and William Egan became its first governor. The 50th anniversary of statehood will be celebrated throughout 2009.

Boroughs rather than counties are the governance divisions of the state, as defined in the state constitution. Five Panhandle communities, including Juneau, Haines, Sitka, and Yakutat, have consolidated borough and city governments.

Only a few years after statehood, the region's seismic under-footing reared up. On March 27, 1964 (which also happened to be Good Friday) an earthquake struck South Central Alaska with a 9.2 Richter scale intensity, among the most powerful ever recorded. It killed 131 people, most of them from the resulting tsunami, which destroyed the ports of Valdez, Seward, and Cordova on Prince William Sound. To this day, you can see cabins buried in the mud along Turnagain Arm just outside of Anchorage.

Alaska Natives had long petitioned Washington for some kind of reparation after the settlement of their lands by white U.S. citizens. Finally in 1971 Congress passed the Alaska Native Claims Settlement Act (ANCSA). The law authorized Alaska Natives to select 44 million acres of land and $962,000,000 as part of their aboriginal claim to land in the state. Some of the settlement was in the form of mineral or timber rights, while other was as land or outright cash. The state was divided into 12 geographic regions, and a corporation with Alaska Native shareholders was set up in each. Sealaska, based in Juneau, is the largest corporation and the largest landholder in Southeast Alaska. In addition, village corporations were set up within the large regions. Only the Tsimshians at Metlakatla decided not to participate; they voted to remain a reservation.

The settlement was complicated, and has generated problems as well as successes. In some cases, a village corporation may have rights to land surface, but a regional corporation has rights to the subsurface, which can lead to controversy. Some Native groups have clear-cut timber, especially on Prince of Wales Island and in the Southern Panhandle. The cutting has been criticized, but the money was often needed for other investment.

In addition to cutting and selling timber, Native corporations have diversified interests in environmental consulting, manufacturing, construction, and information technology. These companies may be outside of Alaska. Some Native corporations have invested in and operate tourism facilities, such as Icy Strait Point at Hoonah, Goldbelt at Juneau, and Cape Fox at Ketchikan.

Black Gold

In addition to ANCSA, the discovery of North Slope oil has brought huge changes to Alaska over the past 40 years. The first discovery came on the Kenai Peninsula in the 1950s, where some operations continue today. But nothing compared with the 1968 discovery of oil deposits on the North Slope, bordering the Beaufort Sea, which transformed Alaska. Oil had to be transported across the state, from the Arctic North to accessible ports in Southeast Alaska almost 800 miles away, over three mountain ranges, across permafrost, active fault lines, and across migratory paths of moose and caribou herds.

By 1977, engineers and construction workers completed the pipeline, raised above the ground to allow animals to pass underneath and resting on non-heat-conducting pilings, so the permafrost does not melt from the temperature of the oil. The oil, in turn, has to be warmed, so it will continue to flow in the often sub-zero temperatures.

Alaska's economy boomed when oil started to flow. Voters passed a state constitutional amendment setting up the Alaska Permanent Fund, run as an investment corporation, with 25 percent of revenues from oil, gas, and other minerals. Each year, Alaska residents who have lived in the state for at least one year receive a dividend from the Permanent Fund. Payment averages $600 to $1,500 per year. They pay no state income taxes, nor state sales taxes, the latter a boon to travelers. However, some cities levy a sales tax. In addition to the dividend in 2008, which was $1,200, the state paid every man, woman, and child a $1,200 "resource rebate" to offset high energy costs. Of course, the oil causes disasters as well as bringing benefits. The *Exxon Valdez* spilled 10.8 million gallons of oil into Prince William Sound in 1989, and the environment still has not fully recovered.

One of the oil boom spin-offs has been the explosive growth of Anchorage. Most of the oil companies are headquartered here, and the population has jumped by 50 percent per decade according to the U.S. Census figures. Today, Anchorage's population stands at 280,000, almost half of Alaska's 670,000 people.

This growth has brought pressure to move the state capital from Juneau to Anchorage, an especially active debate in the 1970s. Various plans have been discussed, including building a capital at communities between Anchorage and Fairbanks, but the costs of developing a new site have been more than voters wanted to pay. So, for now, the capital remains in Juneau.

Now and the Future

Oil and energy issues continue to dominate state politics and discourse. For much of 2008, the Alaska State Legislature met in special session to discuss raising tax rates on oil companies. In another session, the Legislature approved awarding a Canadian company the right to build a natural gas pipeline from the North Slope to Alberta. North Slope oil has been diminishing each year, so the state is looking for something to replace this source of revenue. The promise of more oil paired with countrywide rising oil prices has encouraged some federal officials to support allowing oil to be drilled in the Arctic National Wildlife Refuge.

Attention turned to Alaska leaders when the Republican Party presidential nominee John McCain chose Governor Sarah Palin to run as his vice president.

There is yet another growth spurt that has affected Alaska, especially the Panhandle. It's the boom in tourism, particularly from cruise passengers. At Juneau, Ketchikan, and Skagway, from mid-May through September, as many as four mega-ships tower over any of the buildings in town, while the number of passengers has grown 400 percent since the 1990s. Almost one million passengers poured off ships in Juneau in 2007, the last year for which figures were known. By contrast, only about 235,000 came in 1990.

Of course, local residents welcome the money spent by those visitors, though they may also resent the disruption to their way of life. And the visitors? Beyond the smoked salmon or silver jewelry they take home, they leave with memories of Alaska's awesome scenery, and a concern for what happens in this state to the Far North. Alaska itself has become more knowable.

Transportation

Getting Here, Getting Around

On a map, the Alaska Panhandle looks like a loosely constructed jigsaw puzzle—almost 500 miles of convoluted coast and about 1,100 islands separated by narrow channels and cut by fjords from Yakutat to Ketchikan. No blue highways or even dotted-line dirt roads join the towns. The only way to get from place to place is by airplane or boat. Fortunately, the state has good systems for both.

GETTING HERE

Airlines are the primary way independent travelers get to Alaska. Many other people come on cruise ships, with departures from Seattle, Vancouver, or San Francisco, and then fly home. Or, a cruise may be in the opposite direction, starting in Anchorage (Whittier) or Juneau, and ending in the three departure cities. Most cruises are one-way, though a few are round-trip. (See *Cruise* section.)

Other people arrive by the Alaska Marine Highway System, (see *By Ferry* section) or by driving the Alaska Highway.

By Air

NORTHERN PANHANDLE

Juneau and Ketchikan International Airports have the facilities of most major city airports. A surprising number of tiny Panhandle towns have jet-worthy runways built by the military during World War II or the Cold War. Alaska Airlines serves these communities. Tiny airports are another matter. There may be only one airstrip. Occasionally pilots have to buzz the runway to frighten away bears or moose. Allow plenty of time before a flight. Returning anglers usually have extra luggage to check, with ice chests full of frozen fish. National Transportation Safety Board (NTSB) personnel may close security checkpoints until just before flight departure. Be ready when they are.

Juneau International Airport: 907-789-7821; Juneau.org/airport/. 1873 Shell Simmons Drive, 7½ miles from downtown Juneau. Parking, cell phone lot; gift shop, restaurant, free wireless Internet.

Gustavus Airport: 907-697-2251; 1 Airport Way.

Haines Airport: 907-766-2340; Haines Highway, 3 miles west of downtown Haines.

An Alaska Airlines plane resplendent with a king salmon awaits passengers in Juneau.

Hoonah Airport: 907-945-3426; 1 mile southwest of Hoonah.

Skagway Airport: 907-983-2323; 10-minute walk to historic center and ferry dock.

Yakutat Airport: 907-784-3293; 3 miles southeast of town center.

CENTRAL PANHANDLE
Sitka Rocky Gutierrez Airport: 907-966-2960; 605 Airport Drive, on Japonski Island about 1½ miles from town, gift shop, restaurant, wireless Internet hotspot.

Petersburg: James P. Johnson Airport: 907-772-4624; 1450 Haugen Drive, about 1 mile from downtown. **Also a Seaplane Facility**, same number.

Wrangell: 907-874-3107; Airport Loop Road, 1 mile northeast of downtown.

SOUTHERN PANHANDLE
Ketchikan International Airport: 907-225-6800; borough.ketchikan.ak.us/airport/airport.htm. Located on Gravina Island, a five-minute ferry ride ($5) to Tongass Avenue, about 2½ miles from downtown. Wireless Internet hotspot.

Klawock, Prince of Wales Island: 907-755-2229. Off Big Salt Road. Because of the many bears in the area, walking to town is discouraged. Phone for a taxi in advance. The terminal has no pay phone, and many cell services don't work.

Metlakatla: A jet-worthy runway is no longer in use. Float planes serve Metlakatla and arrive at a dock near town.

Airlines

Alaska Airlines and Horizon Air, its feeder airline (1-800-252-7522; alaskaair.com) are the backbone for travel from the Lower 48, Hawaii, and international destinations, and within Alaska. Even smaller towns, such as Yakutat and Gustavus, have Alaska Airlines jet service. Ketchikan and Juneau receive several flights daily to and from Seattle, which has connections throughout the country. The airplane serving some Panhandle towns has a giant salmon painted on the side of the aircraft.

Alaska Airlines code-shares flights with Delta, Northwest, and American Airlines. Flights from the Lower 48 may start on other airlines, but they connect with an Alaska Airlines flight, usually in Seattle.

By Ferry

Alaska Marine Highway Service (1-800-642-0066; dot.state.ak.us/amhs/), the state ferry system, offers the possibility to cruise to Alaska without cruise ship froufrou, if that doesn't appeal to you. These are stately vessels with navy-blue hulls and sparkling white upper decks that look dignified compared to most of the all-white cruise ships. (Holland America Line also paints its vessels in this traditional way, so they can be confused with the ferries from a distance.)

Once a week, from spring to fall, a ferry leaves Bellingham, Washington, near Seattle, and travels up the Strait of Georgia between Vancouver Island and the British Columbia mainland, the Queen Charlotte Strait and Dixon Gateway, arriving in Ketchikan 37 hours later. Another way to come is to drive highways Canada 97 and 16 to Prince Rupert on the British Columbia coast, and get the Alaska ferry there. You can board as a pedestrian only or with your car, on any of the runs. The Prince Rupert ferry runs four times a week, and takes six hours to get to Ketchikan.

A cabin deck is available on several ferries. It's essential to book in advance both for cars and overnight berths. Those wanting to save money spread out sleeping bags in the solarium or forward passenger lounge and sleep there. The policy is lights out after a ferry leaves port, so if you want to read after dark, which comes early from late fall to early spring, bring a reading light. Some ferries have a reading room, where lights are kept on.

Ferry service is subject to change from year to year. During 2008, Alaska ferries seemed to have a good on-time record, but the schedule is erratic. You may have to board or disembark in the middle of the night.

Here are some tips:

1. Check in at the ticket office before your first trip. After that, on subsequent trips, if you are a walk-on passenger, you can simply get your ticket pulled when you board, although occasionally people get sent back to the ticket window. Automobile passengers must check in at the window. You will be assigned a lane for your car.
2. Food is available on all ferries, except for the very short Ketchikan–Metlakatla run.
3. Wireless Internet is available most of the time.
4. Cell phones generally do not work outside of towns.
5. If you need a taxi, call it in advance from the ferry, before you disembark. I've waited up to an hour in the winter in Juneau when several people wanted taxis to downtown.
6. The ferry may dock miles from the centers of towns. Check in advance.

7. Movies are often shown, and some ferries have bars.
8. Fares vary with the length of the trip, and start at $31 for pedestrians for the shortest segments; or $41 for vehicles.

GETTING AROUND

By Air

Scheduled Commuter Airlines

Most of these airlines fly three- to eight-passenger prop planes. De Havillands and Cessnas are airborne workhorses in Alaska, and may be wheeled, amphibious, or float aircraft. Amphibious aircraft have small wheels mounted inside two large floats, so they are capable of landing on a runway or on water. Some planes are equipped with skis for landing on snow or glaciers. Flights rarely last longer than an hour, and most are 30 to 45 minutes. Float planes land on a pond beside the tarmac at Juneau airport. Some float planes leave from downtown. In general, small airplanes are not handicapped accessible because of the difficulty in entering the cramped cabins. Short segments cost about $40–$100.

L.A.B. Flying Service suspended operations in 2008, and Skagway Air Service the year before.

JUNEAU

Alaska Seaplane Service: 907-789-3331; flyalaskaseaplanes.com. Service to small outlying areas; flightseeing over Juneau Icefield and Glacier Bay.

Wings of Alaska: 907-789-0790; wingsofalaska.com. Juneau, Gustavus, Skagway, Haines and Hoonah.

KETCHIKAN

Pacific Airways: 907-225-3500 or 1-877-360-3500; flypacificairways.com. Scheduled flights to Metlakatla, and Klawock, Hollis, and Thorne Bay on Price of Wales Island, plus charters and flightseeing.

Promech Air: 907-225-3845 or 1-800-860-3845; promechair.com. The largest float plane company in Southeast Alaska has scheduled flights to Metlakatla, Klawock, and Hollis, as well as charters and flightseeing, from the company's dock on Tongass Avenue.

Taquan Air: 907-225-8800 or 1-800-770-8800; taquanair.com. Serves 18 communities, more than any other carrier out of Ketchikan, on Annette, Prince of Wales, and Revillagigedo islands, and the Alaska mainland. The company also offers flightseeing and charter flights.

Air Taxis and Charter Services

These cost considerably more, but they leave on your schedule. Air taxis ferry people to remote fishing lodges or Forest Service cabins. Sometimes they are used for a day of fishing, or transporting people to a remote kayaking spot. Flightseeing companies and glacier excursions are listed in Chapter 7, Recreation. Cost for an air taxi, assessed for the aircraft, starts at $200.

NORTHERN PANHANDLE

JUNEAU

Air Excursions: 907-789-5591; airexcursions.com. Offices in Juneau and Gustavus; serves largely Northern Panhandle and Ketchikan.

Fjord Flying: 907-697-2377. Based in Gustavus, serves Juneau, Haines, Skagway, Hoonah, and flightseeing.

Tal-Air: 907-789-6968. Service out of Juneau.

Ward Air: 907-789-9150; wardair.com. Wheeled, amphibious, and float planes to all parts of Southeast Alaska and Western Canada.

YAKUTAT

Alsek Air Service: 907-784-3231; alsekair.com. Wheeled and ski-fitted aircraft; flightseeing.

Yakutat Coastal Airlines: 907-784-3831; flyyca.com. Wheel, tundra tire, float, or ski-outfitted aircraft; Northern Panhandle and Gulf of Alaska.

CENTRAL PANHANDLE

SITKA

Harris Aircraft Services: 907-966-3050; harrisaircraft.com. Float plane charters and flightseeing.

PETERSBURG

Kupreanof Flying Service: 907-772-3396; kupreanof.com. Float plane tours and charters.

A float plane awaits passengers at a dock near downtown Juneau.

The Rhapsody of the Seas *towers over the Ketchikan waterfront.*

Nordic Air: 907-772-3535. Amphibious aircraft.

Pacific Wing: 907-772-4258; pacificwing.com. Amphibious airplanes operate out of airport or Petersburg float plane dock.

WRANGELL
Sunrise Aviation: 1-800-874-2311; sunriseflights.com. Flightseeing and charters.

SOUTHERN PANHANDLE

KETCHIKAN
Ketchikan scheduled commuter services also offer air charters.

Carlin Air: 907-225-3036 or 1-888-594-3036; carlinair.com. Charters and flightseeing in a float plane.

Island Wings Air Service: 907-225-2444 or 1-888-854-2444; islandwings.com. Float plane sightseeing and charters.

By Ferry

Alaska Marine Highway Service: (See *Getting Here* section.) The Alaska ferry has daily service during summer to the major communities on the Inside Passage, and service about once weekly to smaller or distant places, such as Yakutat.

Interisland Ferry: 907-826-4848 or 1-866-308-4848; interislandferry.com. The ferry provides daily service between Ketchikan and Hollis, Prince of Wales Island, year-round. A northern route offers service about three times weekly between Coffman Cove, Prince of

Wales Island, and Wrangell and Petersburg from about May 1 to mid-September. The ferry usually runs around the weekend, though it's subject to change.

Haines–Skagway Fast Ferry: 907-766-2100 or 1-888-766-2103; chilkatcruises.com; 142 Beach Road, Haines. Catamarans connect Haines and Skagway in about 35 minutes as often as seven times daily on weekdays, and about twice daily on weekends during the summer. Docking is at small boat harbors near the center of each town. Packages are offered including a trip on the White Pass and Yukon Route. Walk-on passengers only; bicycles permitted. Fare: $31.

Ground Transportation

Rental Cars

Because the Alaska Panhandle has so few roads, the national rental car agencies are not widely represented, with the exception of Juneau. Avis has a fairly large presence and each town does have at least one local car rental agency often with rental RVs. Several agencies rent only during summer.

Vehicles may not be in good repair, and you'll sometimes get advice, such as, "The car has a lot of dings. Just ignore them."

A rental car opens up exploring a few miles outside of most towns. The 364-mile Golden Circle drive between Skagway and Haines with a long detour through the Yukon is scenically stunning and popular. You can also put a car on the Alaska ferry to get from town to town. It's sometimes necessary to get a car in one place and drop if off in another. Drop fees tend to be expensive, starting at $75 for just a short distance. Car rental rates start at about $75 per day.

Most rental companies will not allow driving standard cars on gravel roads. Most of them have four-wheel-drive vehicles for rougher terrain.

NORTHERN PANHANDLE

JUNEAU

Avis: 907-789-9450; avis.com

Budget: 907-790-1086; budget.com

Hertz: 907-789-9494; hertz.com

National-Alamo: 907-789-9814; nationalcar.com

Rent-A-Wreck: 907-789-4111; rentawreck.com/Juneau.htm

GUSTAVUS
BW Enterprises Rent-a-Car: 907-697-2403

HAINES
Alaska Eagle Tours: 907-766-2891; alaskaeagletours.com
Avis: 907-766-2733; Halsingland Hotel in Fort Seward. May through mid-September.

SKAGWAY
Avis: 907-983-2247; avis.com; Spring Street and Fourth Avenue. May through mid-September.

Sourdough Car Rentals and Tours: 907-983-2523; Broadway and Sixth Avenue. Bicycles available as well.

CENTRAL PANHANDLE
PETERSBURG
Avis: 907-772-4716; avis.com. Tides Inn and Scandia House.

SITKA
Avis: 907-966-2404; avis.com. 605 Airport Road.

Northstar Rent-a-Car: 907-966-2552 or 1-800-722-6927; northstarrentacar.com; 600 C Airport Road.

WRANGELL
Practical Rent-A-Car: 907-874-3975. Airport Way.

SOUTHERN PANHANDLE
KETCHIKAN
Alaska Car Rental: 907-225-5000 or 1-800-662-0007; akcarrental.com. 2828 Tongass Avenue, and 1000 Airport Way.

Budget Rent-a-Car: 907-225-6004; budget.com. 4950 N. Tongass Avenue and 1000 Airport Way.

METLAKATLA
Metlakatla Car Rentals: 907-886-4133; laughingberry.com. 505 Milne Street.

PRINCE OF WALES ISLAND
The island has more than 2,000 miles of paved, gravel, and logging roads, more than the rest of the Alaska Panhandle. It's ideal territory for driving.

Prince of Wales Jeep Rentals: 907-401-0997. Craig.

Wesley Rentals: 907-617-8837; wesleyrentals.com; Klawock. Cars, jeeps, trucks.

Wilderness Car Rental: 907-826-5200 or 1-800-949-2205; wildernesscarrental.com. 128 J.T. Brown Street, Craig. Cars may be picked up or dropped off at ferry in Hollis or Coffman Cove.

Taxicab Companies
Taxis are sometimes scarce at the airport or the Alaska ferry terminal. Call to arrange your taxicab as the ferry is docking, and make advance appointments for other important trips. Cabs do not ordinarily line up at hotels, but usually respond quickly when the front desk calls. Sometimes taxicab drivers will help arrange your next ride, especially if it is a very early or late run to the airport or ferry.

Juneau cab drivers tend to be like city drivers anywhere. In the smaller towns, cabbies will tell you a great deal about the place, offer tips for lodging or restaurants, and share local gossip. Often they run tours as well as taxi service.

JUNEAU
Alaska Taxi and Tours: 907-780-6400

Capital/Evergreen Cab: 907-586-2772 or 907-586-2121

Glacier Taxi and Tours: 907-796-2300

Juneau Taxi and Tours: 907-586-1111

GUSTAVUS
TLC Taxi: 907-697-2239

HAINES
Haines Taxi and Tours: 907-766-3138

SKAGWAY
At press time for this book, Skagway had no taxicab service.

CENTRAL PANHANDLE
PETERSBURG
Cab-a-Van: 907-772-2222

SITKA
Hank's Tours and Taxi: 907-747-8888; hankstours.com

More Taxi and Tours: 907-738-3210; moorebusi.com

Sitka Cab: 907-747-5001

WRANGELL
Northern Lights Taxi: 907-874-4646

Star Cab: 907-874-3622

SOUTHERN PANHANDLE
KETCHIKAN
Alaska Cab: 907-225-2133

Yellow Taxi: 907-225-5555

PRINCE OF WALES ISLAND
Shoo teen Taxi: 907-965-4949. Taxi, ferry shuttle, and sightseeing.

Arrive Local Style, by Water
Tongass Water Taxi (907-225-8294) makes the trip from Ketchikan Airport to anywhere along the waterfront more appropriate and fun. And it costs less than a regular taxi or shuttle. Look for the operator, often owner Rich Schuerger, with the sign in baggage claim at the airport. The night I rode, the next trip was to transport a cat from Ketchikan to the residential area on Gravina Island across Tongass Narrows. A classic Ketchikan moment.

The Skagway Street Car Tour has been taking visitors around town since 1923.

Limousine and Classic Car Services: Rates for limousine services start at about $80 per hour.

NORTHERN PANHANDLE

JUNEAU
Juneau Limousine Services: 907-463-5466; juneaulimousine.com

SKAGWAY
Skagway Classic Cars: 907-983-2886; skagwayclassiccars.com

SOUTHERN PANHANDLE

KETCHIKAN
Classic Tours: 907-225-3091; classictours.com. Tool around town and to totem parks in a 1955 Chevy.

Shuttle Services for Airport and Ferry

Most of these services are to-and-from the airport or ferry docks, but a few offer services elsewhere. Some of the shuttles are also tour companies. In addition, many lodgings offer shuttle services, often complimentary, from the airport or ferry dock.

NORTHERN PANHANDLE

JUNEAU
Several hotels offer van services to the airport.

SKAGWAY

Dyea Dave Shuttles and Tours: 907-209-5031; dyeadavetours.com. Shuttles to Chilkoot trailhead.

CENTRAL PANHANDLE

SITKA

Sitka Tours: 907-747-8443; sitkatours.com. Look for the big blue bus at the airport or ferry dock. No need to call. Runs May through September.

SOUTHERN PANHANDLE

Ketchikan Transporter: 907-225-9800; ketchikantransporter.com. Service to and from the airport to local hotels.

Public Transportation

Juneau, Ketchikan, and Sitka have year-round public bus transportation. Fares run $1–$2.

Juneau: Capital Transit (907-789-6901) has a printed bus schedule that is widely available in lodgings and at the tourist office. The bus works well between downtown and the Mendenhall Loop area, including visits to the glacier, and Auke Bay.

Sitka: Community Ride (907-747-7103) runs Monday through Friday and has three lines: The Red Line connects the Alaska Ferry terminal with the downtown area; the Blue Line runs from downtown out Sawmill Creek Road to Whale Park; the Green Line has a downtown loop and crosses to Japonski Island. When cruise ships are in town, a **Visitor Transit** (907-747-7290) bus runs from downtown to the Sitka National Historical Park and Alaska Raptor Center.

Ketchikan: Bus transportation is easy. It's call **The Bus** (907-225-8726) and it runs hourly: Green Line in town, Blue Line north of town, and Red Line south of town. Visitors use it to get to the totem parks, Saxman south of town, and Totem Bight to the north.

Town Tours

Tours of Inside Passage ports of call and surrounding areas are among the most popular shore excursions for cruise ship passengers. A few are in horse-drawn or old-fashioned vehicles, adding to the atmosphere. You'll generally find them lined up at the cruise ship dock, and often you can simply board. Reservations can be made in advance on the cruise ship or on the company Web sites. The companies operate seasonally, about mid-May through mid-September.

NORTHERN PANHANDLE

JUNEAU

Juneau Trolley Car Company: 907-586-7433; juneautrolley.com. The narrated tour makes 13 stops, with the option to get off and reboard. Trolleys run every 30 minutes.

SKAGWAY

North Country Pedicab: No more than two people in the bicycle-powered cab. Cabs line up near the cruise ship docks or cruise Broadway.

Skagway Street Car Tour: 907-983-2908; skagwaystreetcar.com. President Harding climbed aboard one of the yellow streetcars in 1923, and the company has offered tours ever since. Currently in use is a 1927 streetcar with costumed guides.

KETCHIKAN

Horse Drawn Trolley Tours: 907-225-3672; horsetrolleytours.com. A husky sled dog sits placidly next to the driver as you plod through Ketchikan on 45-minute living history and cultural tours.

CRUISING ALASKA

Most people visit the Alaska Panhandle by cruise ship—more than 900,000 in the 2008 May through September season. The big ships, carrying up to 2,600 passengers, bring most of them. Holland America Line and Princess Cruises have seven ships each on Alaska itineraries, and Royal Caribbean International and Celebrity, owned by the same company, have six jointly. Norwegian Cruise Line has three, and Carnival, one.

Crystal Cruises and Regent Seven Seas contribute midsize ships to the Alaska-bound fleets. Cruise West has the most small-ship sailings; others in the 200 or fewer passenger range are Silversea, Lindblad, and the yacht-size American Safari Cruises. The paddle wheeler, *Empress of the North,* a distinctive ship in 2008, will not be in Alaska waters in 2009.

A horse-drawn tour is a popular way to see Ketchikan.

People often show brand loyalty to a cruise line. Others may be puzzled by the many choices. The advice of a travel agent specializing in cruises can be of invaluable help. Cruise lines have brand identity that shapes the ship's personality. In general, Carnival is regarded as the party line; Holland America is more traditional; and Princess, the former Love Boat line, has huge ships with an abundance of private balconies. Crystal is for foodies, and Norwegian has free-style dining. Royal Caribbean offers onboard sports activities. But labels run to clichés, so check with a travel agent and consider carefully.

Look hard at the ports of call and shore excursions. If possible, do a pre- or post-cruise land trip offered by the cruise line, or arrange this on your own. Alaska is a vast state, and though the Inside Passage is a part of it with jaw-dropping beauty, you only have an inkling of its possibilities. According to industry statistics, about 25 percent of the people who take an Alaska cruise return as independent travelers within five years. So think of your Alaska cruise as an introduction to see what you'd like to visit on a return trip.

All cruise ships have on-board naturalists who can help passengers spot wildlife and offer background information about glaciers and rainforests. Shore excursions extend the chances of seeing wildlife and getting closer to glaciers. Some people are interested in more serious adventure, such as a zipline ride or a glacier trek. Go prepared, so you will know what shore excursion to book from the array offered, or what you might choose to do on your own. Many passengers also book shore excursions in advance.

If you are on a large cruise ship, you will probably see whales and bald eagles from the ship. You are not as likely to see bears or moose. Even on shore, they can be difficult to spot. A smaller ship, which can get closer to shore and navigate narrower channels, ups the chances considerably. Some lines, such as Cruise West and Lindblad, emphasize the natural-history aspect of the cruises.

Two general itineraries, Inside Passage and Gulf of Alaska, are usually offered by most lines, although all of them traverse the Inside Passage. Most cruises are seven days, either northbound, usually from Vancouver or Seattle, terminating in Juneau or Anchorage; or southbound, which is simply the reverse. Juneau, Ketchikan, and Skagway are the main ports of call, and Sitka gets several ships per week. Whittier or Seward is the port for Anchorage, and the end or starting point for a Gulf of Alaska cruise.

The small lines tend to have more 10- or 14-day choices, and may stop at small communities, including Alaska Native villages, on the Inside Passage—Metlakatla, Petersburg, Kake, Hoonah, or the whimsically named Meyers Chuck. Small ships can also navigate Misty Fjords National Monument, and manage Wrangell Narrows.

Here are cruise lines offering Alaska itineraries. Some lines, though not all, discourage phone calls. Contact links are on the Web sites.

American Safari Cruises: 1-888-862-8881; amsafari.com
Carnival Cruise Line: 1-800-227-6482; carnival.com
Celebrity Cruises: 1-800-437-3111; celebritycruises.com
Cruise West: 1-888-851-8133; cruisewest.com
Crystal Cruises: 1-888-722-0021; crystalcruises.com
Holland America Line: 1-877-932-4259; hollandamerica.com
Norwegian Cruise Line: 1-866-234-7350; ncl.com
Princess Cruises: 1-800-PRINCESS; princess.com
Regent Seven Seas Cruises: 1-877-505-5370; rssc.com
Royal Caribbean International: 1-866-562-7625; royalcaribbean.com
Silversea Cruises: 1-800-722-9955; silversea.com

Ports-of-Call Highlights

The following activities highlight visits to the main Panhandle ports of call. Glacier Bay and Hubbard Glacier certainly are the climax to a cruise for many people, but they are not ports of call.

JUNEAU

Activity: Alaska State Museum
Adventure: Mendenhall Glacier walk
Lunch: Tracy's King Crab Shack
Souvenir: Glacier Smoothie Soap
Keepsake: Baleen basket from Raven's Song

SKAGWAY

Activity: Train excursion on White Pass & Yukon Route
Adventure: Day-hike on Chilkoot Trail
Lunch: Sweet Tooth Café for cheeseburgers
Souvenir: Train Shoppe cap
Keepsake: Gold-nugget necklace from Taiya River Jewelry

HAINES

Activity: Carving workshop at Alaska Indian Arts
Adventure: Raft trip on Chilkat River
Lunch: Halibut and chips at Bamboo Room
Souvenir: Local writer Heather Lende's *If You Lived Here, I'd Know Your Name*
Keepsake: Glass sculpture by Greg Horner from Alaska Indian Arts

PETERSBURG

Activity: Leikarring Dancers at Sons of Norway Hall
Adventure: Fish with Magicman or Petersburg Creek charters
Lunch: Tina's Kitchen halibut-cheek taco
Souvenir: Rosemaling kit from Cubby Hole
Keepsake: Norwegian sweater from Lee's Clothing

SITKA

Activity: Sitka National Historical Park/Alaska Raptor Center
Adventure: Diving with Island Fever
Lunch: Reindeer sausage from Lincoln Street stand
Souvenir: Matryoshka nesting dolls
Keepsake: Sitka rose beaded earrings by Cathleen Pook

KETCHIKAN

Activity: Saxman and Totem Bight totem parks
Adventure: Alaska Canopy Adventures rainforest zipline
Lunch: Steamers seafood chowder
Souvenir: Ray Troll T-shirt
Keepsake: Tlingit carving from a Mission Street gallery

3

Lodging

Your Room in the Far North

The earliest Alaska travelers either camped out in a tent, even during winter, or accepted hospitality from the missions. A tradition of roadhouses sprung up early on. These crude shelters dotted remote areas, but certainly were welcome to those out in the cold or the rain, offering travelers a bed and meals. The term holds in a few Panhandle places, but it's more for nostalgia's sake than anything else.

Tourists began to come to Alaska not long after the U.S. purchase in 1867. John Muir writes about a steamer at Glacier Bay in 1890. Just like today's cruise passengers, these people usually spent the night on board the ships, but they also began to spend time in the larger towns, especially Juneau, and so small hotels soon made an appearance.

HOTELS AND MOTELS

A few older hotels exist in Juneau, Ketchikan, and Sitka, but most Panhandle lodgings are motels dating from the last few decades, when the boom in Alaska travel began with the advent of cruise ships, the ferry, and motor travel on the Alaska Highway. The Panhandle has many comfortable, but few luxury, properties. Overall, the number of rooms—or beds, as it's measured in the industry—is small compared to the number of visitors, since most people are aboard cruise ships. Spending the night on shore will bring you closer to Alaska, its wilderness, and its towns and people.

Motel décor seems consistent from Ketchikan to Yakutat. Most rooms have pale walls, golden or pale wood trim, a cheerful flowered or printed comforter or bedspread, and enough drawer or desk space to stow belongings and hold a television set. Wireless Internet, though not always free, is often available, and most lobbies have a computer with Internet access for guests. King-size beds are not yet as common as they are in the Lower 48. Bathrooms run to plain-label standards, with tub-shower, toilet, and a single or double sink with a Formica or perhaps granite counter, and separate from the tub-toilet chamber. It's not the lap of luxury, but it works.

BED-AND-BREAKFAST INNS

Many Panhandle towns have several B&Bs, which usually have more character than motels. They are often in historic houses, or have unusual architecture. Some owners rent out two or three bedrooms in their homes, but others are stand-alone inns. They may be modest by Lower 48 standards, and they may have kitchenettes. In some cases, breakfast ingredients will be provided, but you make your own. Units like this are sometimes let on a vacation rental basis.

B&Bs also encourage lingering over the final cup of coffee at breakfast, trading stories with other travelers, or getting tips on local attractions from the owners. You come away knowing a little bit more about Alaska.

In general, Panhandle B&Bs are not given to teddy bears, tea cozies, or multiple pillows on the bed. Maybe it's the long, cold winters or the isolation, but rooms tend to be clean, light, and given to pale colors, and lots of expansive windows looking out to extraordinary views.

Be prepared to remove your shoes when you enter a B&B, a practice most Alaskans observe at home. You may find a shoe rack just inside the front door. It's usually fine to wear slippers or flip-flops inside the house, however.

An easy way to find B&Bs is through a listing service. These cover the Alaska Panhandle.

Alaska Travelers Accommodations: (907-247-7117 or 1-800-928-3308; alaska travelers.com; 4672 S. Tongass Highway, Ketchikan, AK 99901.) Dozens of listings in Ketchikan and other parts of the Panhandle. A few are in Ketchikan's historic district, but most of them are several miles from town.

Bed & Breakfast Association of Alaska—Inside Passage Chapter: (accommodations -alaska.com.) This lists several B&Bs in Ketchikan and throughout the Panhandle. They range from one to four bedrooms.

You'll climb the stairs into the four poster at Grandma's Feather Bed Inn.

FISHING LODGES

Fishing lodges are an Alaska institution. The staff will take care of everything—all fishing gear, charter boats, guides, even appropriate clothing, including waders, bibbers (overalls with a bib in front), jackets, and boots are part of the package. After you land the big one, lodge employees will clean, vacuum pack, and flash-freeze it. For the trip home, it's stored in a duct-taped ice chest, which can be checked in like luggage. Some fishing resorts will ship your fish.

Overnight accommodations may range from bare-bones to luxurious; meals range from basic catch-of-the-day to gourmet fare prepared by imported chefs. Fishing lodge visitors may never see a totem pole, visit a museum, or shop for wood carvings. That's not what they came for. Many people return year after year to such lodges.

The price scale for fishing lodges soars compared to regular lodgings. This is because so many services are included, including cost of the float plane or airport van to and from the lodge.

Expect to pay about $1,000 per person, per day, at most lodges. Some offer flexible packages with options for room and meals only, an unguided fishing expedition with use of a boat, or guided fishing.

Most Alaska fishing lodges do not currently provide handicapped access.

Fishing Lodge Price Codes

Moderate: Up to $800 per day

Expensive: $800–$1,100

Very expensive: More than $1,100

FOREST SERVICE CABINS

Imagine yourself in a dense conifer forest on the shores of a lake, miles from any road, town, or any other house. To keep you company, black bears, and maybe brown, forage around a stream that feeds into the lake. During the day, bald eagles sit at attention in the trees and ravens soar overhead. At night, wolves howl and other creatures scurry about.

Some days and nights it's likely to rain, but moss on the roof mutes the sound. Come dinnertime, you're likely to take the rod to the stream and perhaps catch some Dolly Varden. Afterward, you might sit out late and enjoy the long northern twilight.

This is a forest service cabin, which some travelers consider the only way to truly experience Alaska. More than 150 of them are scattered in Tongass National Forest on remote lakes, rivers, streams, and saltwater beaches. Most are accessible by float plane or boat only. They are in all parts of the Panhandle, with access from Ketchikan, Prince of Wales Island, Wrangell, Petersburg, Sitka, Admiralty Island, Hoonah, Juneau, and Yakutat.

Their architecture varies from A-frames to boxy pitched-roof, log cabins, and pan adobe. Some of them have wheelchair accessibility. Usually sleeping four to six or more people, they are bare-bones inside; plumbing consists of an outhouse and a pump. Water may be from a lake or stream, and must be treated. A broom, ax, table, benches, cooking counter, and sometimes a skiff are provided. You bring your own camping equipment, including a stove, sleeping bags, lanterns, and all food, pots, pans, plates, and utensils. Cabin etiquette means taking out what you bring in, so include garbage bags, a fire extinguisher, and fire starter.

Bears inhabit much of the Tongass National Forest, so you must be alert and careful to keep food concealed or in bear containers. Many people carry pepper spray.

Air services provide transportation to the cabins, which you will have to arrange; equipment can be rented from Panhandle outfitters. The cabins get booked very early. Rental fees range $25–$45 per day.

For more information: 907-225-3101; fs.fed.us/r10/tongass/

To reserve: 1-877-444-6777; reserveusa.com

RV PARKS

Taking an RV to Alaska or renting one appeals to many travelers. In certain parts of Alaska, competition to find hookup spaces is keen. The RV traveler's grapevine is rife with rumors about where you may or may not park, including Wal-Mart or Fred Meyer parking lots. Full hookups cost about $20 or more per night. Partial hookups and dry camp sites are less. Haines and Skagway are popular RV sites, since both towns connect to highways, unusual in Alaska. But many travelers put their RVs on the Alaska ferry and go from town to town.

VACATION RENTALS

Almost all towns have apartments, condos, or houses that may be rented for a week or more. A good source of information is the tourist bureau or chamber of commerce (See Chapter 9, Information). Many motels and B&Bs will rent out on a long-term basis. Many people find listings at vrbo.com, the largest Internet listing of rentals by owner.

Alaska Juneau Suites: 907-789-3772; alaska-juneau.com

Welcome Home Vacation: 1-800-750-4712; sitkavacation.com

Alaska Travelers Accommodations: 1-800-928-3308; alaskatravelers.com

Lodging Notes

Lodging anywhere in Alaska during summer is tight. Be sure to reserve early. Rates vary widely between summer and winter. Expect summer rates to be somewhat higher than they would be for similar accommodations and amenities in the Lower 48.

Hotels, motels, or B&Bs rarely require minimum stays. Fishing lodges usually must be booked for at least a three-night stay.

Price Codes

Inexpensive: Less than $100
Moderate: $100–$175
Expensive: $176–$250
Very expensive: More than $250

The rates shown are for summer season since that is when most people visit the Panhandle. Many hotel rates are as much as half-price during the winter. Some Panhandle towns have a local tax, but Alaska does not have a state sales tax.

Handicapped Accessibility

The public areas of most hotels are compliant with the Americans with Disability Act (ADA). Many hotels and motels, especially if they are new or have been renovated, have at least one room with wheelchair and bathroom accessibility. In general, B&Bs and fishing lodges are not handicapped accessible. Anything requiring small airplane or float plane transportation is generally not accessible.

Season

Some Panhandle accommodations are open mid-May through mid-September only. This is generally true of fishing lodges or inns and B&Bs in smaller places. Town lodgings tend to be open year-round. Policies may change from year to year, so check before you count on a room.

Smoking

Some Panhandle lodgings are fully nonsmoking and others have both smoking and non-smoking rooms. Be sure to request your choice. Most bed-and-breakfast inns are non-smoking. Petersburg has a law prohibiting smoking in hotel beds. Most Panhandle towns, including Juneau, Sitka, and Ketchikan, now ban smoking in public places and the work-place. Some make exceptions for bars. In Skagway, almost all restaurants and hotels are nonsmoking, though the town does not have an ordinance. The same situation exists in Wrangell. State law prohibits smoking on all public transportation facilities, and in government and educational buildings.

Gay Travelers

Alaska is not generally high on the radar as a gay or lesbian destination. However, Alaskans, though generally conservative politically, have a live-and-let-live attitude, so gays and lesbians can be comfortable here. **Out in Alaska** (1-877-374-9958; outinalaska .com) organizes cruises and adventure trips for gay and lesbian travelers throughout the state.

Spas

The Alaska Panhandle lacks spas, as compared to other resort areas. Cruise ship passengers return to onboard spas after a day of shore excursions and shopping. Other people seem to come largely to fish, hike, or enjoy the vast outdoors. Ketchikan and Juneau have a few day spas. Visit spaindex.com/day/usa/alaska.html for list of day spas.

NORTHERN PANHANDLE

JUNEAU

Juneau, the largest Panhandle town and the Alaska state capital, has the largest and the most lodgings. Juneau has several bed-and-breakfast inns, which are listed in a separate sections. In most other cases, B&Bs are listed with other lodgings in a town.

Hotels and Motels

Best Western Country Lane Inn

Owner-Managers: Mel and Sharon Perkins
907-789-5005 or 1-888-781-5005
countrylaneinn.com
info@countrylane.com
9300 Glacier Hwy., Juneau, AK 99801
In the Mendenhall area, close to Juneau
International Airport
Price: Moderate
Credit Cards: Yes
Handicapped Access: Two rooms
Special Features: Cheerful motel with extra
amenities.

The Country Lane Inn is close to the Juneau
Airport and Nugget Mall, though its setting
seems quiet and woodsy. While the two-story
room arrangement with external corridors is
much like motels anywhere, other things ele-
vate this inn from the ordinary. Pretty bedspreads with a tiny floral print cover beds.
The dark wood furniture is buffed and polished, and the rooms offer high-speed
Internet access and a coffeemaker.

Breakfast, included in the room rate,
features an elaborate continental buffet
with a microwave for the oatmeal, and
toasters for bagels and English muffins.
With the hard-cooked eggs, you could con-
struct a hearty breakfast for the Alaska
morning. It's served in the lofty two-story
lobby, where floor-to-ceiling windows
flood the spot with light. Guests gather here
and trade travel tales.

A free shuttle service ferries guests to
and from downtown during the day, and
transportation to the airport or the ferry is
also complimentary. People working here
were particularly helpful, being careful to
write down directions or shuttle times.

The Driftwood Lodge

Owner: Rick Kasnick
907-586-2280 or 1-800-544-2239
driftwoodalaska.com
driftwood@gci.net

435 Willoughby Ave., Juneau, AK 99801
Near corner of W. Third St
Price: Inexpensive to Moderate
Credit Cards: Yes
Handicapped Access: One room
Special Features: Kitchenettes in most
units.

Families gravitate to this hotel since some
of the 63 units have two bedrooms and
most of them have kitchenettes. Though the
building looks like a three-story motel on
the outside, the units are more like apartments than motel rooms. The location is
convenient to the waterfront, historic
buildings, and downtown shops.

State representatives and senators often
stay here during January through May,
when the legislature is in session. It's near
the state office building and the Alaska
State Museum.

The Kasnick family has owned the hotel
for more than 20 years. They will arrange
tours of the area, rent bicycles, and offer
airport and ferry shuttle service.

Extended Stay Deluxe Juneau

907-790-6435; 1-888-559-9846
extendedstayhotels.com
JSS@extendedstay.com
1800 Shell Simmons Dr., Juneau, AK 99801
On the entrance to Juneau International
Airport
Price: Moderate
Credit Cards: Yes
Handicapped Access: Two king, three
queen
Special Features: Suites with full kitchen;
indoor swimming pool.

The Extended Stay Deluxe has a complimentary airport shuttle, but there's no need
to use it. Simply roll your bag out of the
baggage claim, along the airport entrance
road for a short distance, and you've arrived
at the lobby of this suite-style hotel.
Chances are logs will be flickering in the
gas fireplace to welcome you.

Part of the Extended Stay series, the hotel offers units that come with a full kitchen and sleeping and sitting area large enough for small business meetings, or simply room to stretch out. In spite of having a full-size refrigerator and two-burner stove, you won't have to cook. Complimentary continental breakfast is offered every morning.

An indoor swimming pool with a spa, and a fitness room with a television in front of the treadmills add to the amenities.

Extended Stays tend to cater to the business traveler and have something of the predictable chain look, though there are homey touches here: A barbecue is outside for those who do want to cook; flowers brighten a lobby table, and green shutters are on the windows.

Goldbelt Hotel

907-586-6900 or 1-888-478-6909
goldbelttours.com
mail.gbh@goldbelt.com
51 Egan Dr., Juneau, AK 99801
On the downtown waterfront, at the corner of Willoughby Ave.
Price: Expensive
Credit Cards: Yes
Handicapped Access: Two rooms
Special Features: Extraordinary Native Alaska art collection in lobby.

Even if you don't spend a night at the Goldbelt Hotel, do visit its lobby. The Chilkat blanket, masks, and decorated canoe paddles are simply stunning. A Native corporation made up of Tlingit and Haida shareholders owns the hotel. The parent company owns other hotels and runs tours to Glacier Bay and elsewhere. They will even book an entire Alaska vacation.

Rooms in the 105-unit hotel overlook the waterfront or the mountains. They have two double beds or a king-size bed, and the amenities of any city or business hotel: free wireless Internet, meeting rooms, voice-mail, and room service. Airport shuttle is also complimentary, a significant service since Juneau International Airport is about a $25 cab ride from downtown. The lobby staff is attentive.

Stylish Zen Restaurant, which rates favorable review from Juneau locals, is off the lobby. It serves Asian fusion cuisine. (See Chapter 6, *Restaurants and Food Purveyors*.)

Historic Silverbow Inn

Owner-Managers: Jill Ramiel and Ken Alper
907-586-4146 or 1-800-586-4146
silverbowinn.com
info@silverbowinn.com
120 Second St., Juneau, AK 99801
In the center of downtown
Price: Inexpensive to Expensive
Credit Cards: Yes
Handicapped Access: No
Special Features: Small, European-style inn in 1914 building.

There are just six rooms at the Historic Silverbow Inn, and each of them is distinctive. Interesting bed covers, unique chairs, and quirky art on the walls bring character to each. Some of the rooms are small, but they all have a private bath, and many pleasing amenities. Sheets are silky 400-count, little treats may appear in the rooms, and coffee and tea are always hot.

There are other unexpected things: free wireless Internet, free local calls, and CD players.

Breakfast is in a homey dining room downstairs, and is provided by Silverbow Bakery, known all over Juneau for its terrific breads and bagels. The sideboard always holds something interesting: perhaps a frittata and some lovely coffeecake, and later in the day, irresistible cookies. The inn is popular with locals. On Monday, Tuesday, and Wednesday evenings, independent and classic movies are shown in the restaurant. And it's free, including the popcorn.

Prospector Hotel
907-586-3737 or 1-800-331-2711, except Alaska
prospectorhotel.com
prospect@ptialaska.net
375 Whittier St., Juneau, AK 99801
Whittier St. and Egan Dr.
Price: Moderate to Expensive
Credit Cards: Yes
Handicapped Access: Two rooms
Special Features: Waterfront location, nicely appointed rooms.

The entrance to this 63-room hotel seems a bit hidden off a parking lot, but once inside, the welcome is warm. Even the woman vacuuming the floor smiles and nods. Rooms seem more spacious than usual and are furnished with some flair, with dark cherry wood, draperies, and buttery walls. Bedspreads are cheerful with crewel embroidery. Adding to convenience are a refrigerator and microwave, and a bright packet of locally roasted Heritage coffee. T.K. Maguire's restaurant is in the hotel, which is pet-friendly.

Many of the rooms overlook Gastineau Channel and Douglas Island, with the mountains beyond. The oversize desks with ergonomic chairs, and free wireless Internet, add up to comfort and convenience for the business traveler. Although the hotel is firmly modern, the image of a grizzled prospector prominently decorates the façade. The entrance is just below it.

Travelodge Hotel Juneau
907-789-9700
travelodge.com
gmtravelodge@gci.net
9200 Glacier Hwy., Juneau, AK 99801
Glacier Hwy. and Egan Dr.
Price: Moderate
Credit Cards: Yes
Handicapped Access: Three rooms
Special Features: Very close to airport; fully nonsmoking.

Many Juneau hotels cluster near the airport in the Mendenhall Loop area, about 8 miles from downtown. This 86-room hotel, pretty much a typical Travelodge, is one of them. It's also within walking distance of Nugget Mall and has a Mexican restaurant, Mi Casa, on the premises. Complimentary shuttle to the ferry and airport operate around the clock, and a scheduled shuttle connects guests to downtown during the day.

It may be snowing outside, but it's steamy as a jungle in the indoor pool area. Water temperature soared to 87 degrees on one winter day. A whirlpool and fitness room complete the workout amenities.

Rooms are pleasant, with double, queen, or king bed arrangements, bright bedspreads, and dark motel-style furniture. Free wireless Internet, room safes, complimentary "bear bites" breakfast, and room service add to convenience and comfort. The lobby has welcoming apples and coffee, but otherwise could be a motel anywhere, with one exception—the big bearskin on the wall.

Westmark Baranof Hotel
907-586-2660
westmarkhotels.com/juneau.php
127 N. Franklin St., Juneau, AK 99801
On North Franklin St. near Front St.
Price: Moderate to Expensive
Credit Cards: Yes
Handicapped Access: No, but will add accessories in room to accommodate
Special Features: Juneau's most "big-city" hotel; popular with state legislators; nonsmoking rooms.

You can identify the state legislators and staffers in the Baranof Hotel's lobby. They're wearing dark dress shirts and neckties under their Gore-Tex jackets, and possibly even a suit. The tourist crowd, who are likely starting or ending a cruise, wears Gore-Tex, too—but they're likely to have a plaid flannel or turtleneck shirt on underneath.

The nine-story, 196-room hotel is a downtown landmark and is within walking distance of the State Capitol, cruise ship docks, and cultural and historical sites. Listed on the National Register of Historic Places, the hotel was built of concrete in 1939, and the Art Deco elegance of those years still shows. A spectacular flower arrangement, often of exotic Hawaiian blooms, graces the lobby.

The rooms are comfortable, and those on the top floors have stunning mountain or channel views, and are also quieter. Updated within the last few years, they are furnished with understated dark wood furniture, cheery floral bedspreads, and pale walls.

Rooms have Internet access for a fee, and cable television. This is Juneau's only big-city hotel, with two restaurants, a lively bar, meeting rooms, and hair salon. Tour services are available in the lobby.

Bed-and-Breakfast Inns

Alaska's Capital Inn Bed and Breakfast

Owner-Managers: Linda Wendeborn and Mark Thorson
907-586-6507 or 1-888-588-6507
alaskacapitalinn.com
innkeeper@alaskacapitalinn.com
113 W. Fifth St., Juneau, AK 99801
Uphill from downtown, close to the State Capitol
Price: Expensive
Credit Cards: Yes
Handicapped Access: One room
Special Features: Restored 1906 mansion furnished with antiques and respect for its heritage.

Even the wallpaper gives reason enough to stay at the Capital Inn. Owner Linda Wendeborn sought out companies that

An antique organ feels at home in the parlor at Alaska's Capital Inn Bed & Breakfast.

hand-screen sumptuous, richly patterned wallpaper reminiscent of the Arts-and-Crafts style of the early 20th century. It sets the tone for every loving detail—even the notepads have William Morris prints—that bring elegance and grace to the 1906 mansion.

The house had fallen on hard times and into the hands of multiple owners, when Wendeborn and her husband Mark Thorson bought it in 1985. They gutted, refitted, decorated, and furnished it in a style true to its architecture and heritage. They honored its first owners, the John Olds family, by naming the bedrooms after the children. Lila's Room is the original master bedroom outfitted with a king-size bed, sofa bed in a sitting area, and fireplace. John's room has a massive, oak, king poster bed that you'll climb three stairs to reach. Clawfoot tubs, stained-glass windows, and hand-sewn quilts evoke its past, when Juneau's wealthiest and most notable citizens lived on this hill beside the State Capitol.

The large dining room still serves that purpose. Guests gather at 8 AM for a full gourmet breakfast, which may be crab eggs Benedict—a great favorite—or lemon soufflé hotcakes. Should you have to leave early, Linda will send you off with bagels and smoked salmon. At almost any time of day, something delicious to eat is set out—fruit and cheese with wine in the late afternoon, coffee early in the day, or tea and cookies later.

Wireless Internet throughout the house and a computer in the living room with Internet connections offer modern convenience. All rooms have television and telephones, and the back deck has a hot tub.

Best Western Grandma's Feather Bed Inn
907-789-5566
grandmasfeatherbed.com
2358 Mendenhall Loop Rd., Juneau, AK 99801
Price: Moderate to Expensive

Credit Cards: Yes
Handicapped Access: No
Special Features: Country elegant décor; slightly eccentric room arrangements in Victorian house; nonsmoking facility.

Our room was called the Martha Stewart Suite, since she once stayed in it, and its décor certainly lives up to the standards of America's domestic doyenne. The creamy wallpaper had tiny floral patterns that varied from the bedroom to the bathroom, but harmonized well with each other. A folding screen set off the tub, with a larger version of similar flowers. The huge whirlpool bath sat in a raised area like a throne. The four-poster, which indeed was a featherbed, also was raised and took a double stepstool to reach. Eyelet trim embellished the dust ruffle, sheets, and pillowcases.

Formerly a restaurant, the inn has a slightly eccentric look, with asymmetrical rooms and interesting nooks and crannies on different floor levels resulting from the rooms being carved out of a larger space. It has a lot of character and is well-maintained.

At breakfast, don't be tempted to overdo the buffet with cereals, yogurt, fruit, and muffins. There's also a plate to be delivered, which may have sourdough or blueberry pancakes, or scrambled eggs, bacon, and biscuits. With just 14 suites, this is the smallest Best Western property in the country. A complimentary shuttle service provides transportation to the airport and ferry terminal, and to downtown Juneau during the day.

Pearson's Pond Luxury Inn and Adventure Spa
Owners: Diane and Steve Pearson
907-789-3772
pearsonspond.com
book@pearsonspond.com
4541 Sawa Circle, Juneau, AK 99801
Off Mendenhall Loop

Price: Very expensive
Credit Cards: Yes
Handicapped Access: No
Special Features: Gorgeous gardens surround this luxury inn beside a pond; full
breakfast; reserve months or a year in
advance; fully nonsmoking.

Imagine walking into a beautiful two-story
atrium, bedraggled at the end of a long
travel day and being handed a glass of
wine—exactly the varietal you prefer—or a
cup of hot tea. Elegant snacks, and home-
baked hot bread, follow. At your suite, a fire
flickers on the hearth and soft music plays.
Ever-active hosts, Diane and Steve Pearson
satisfy needs before you're aware that they
even exist.

The suites all feature a kitchenette with
a refrigerator and microwave, and barbecues are nearby on decks, so you can handily prepare dinner. A hot breakfast dish is
served each morning, and guests can help
themselves to cereals, yogurt, juice, and
other snacks from a refrigerator stuffed to
the edge of each shelf. The Pearson's efforts
have earned several awards, including
fourth place in the World's Most Romantic
Hotel Destination by MSN and both Fodor's
and Frommer's Best Inn of Alaska ratings.
This is Alaska's only AAA four-diamond
property.

Suites have four-poster queen beds,
with pillow-top mattresses, comforters,
and pillows—down or synthetic, as you
wish. In one premium suite, tapestry and
silk in muted magenta, umber, and gold
fabrics elegantly draped the canopied bed.
Although the property has just five rooms,
it has all the amenities of a full-scale
resort. The pond on the grounds has
kayaks, a paddleboat, and rowboat for
guest's use. Bicycles are available, especially handy for nearby Mendenhall Glacier
and Auke Bay. Diane will book any kind of
Juneau-area adventure trip, from fishing to
kayaking and glacier adventures. (She is

also is a wedding planner and performs
ceremonies on the grounds or even glaciers. See the Destination Wedding section
of this chapter.)

Steve is an avid hiker, who knows trails
on Juneau's peaks, so he has suggestions for
walkers. At the end of a long hiking day,
guests soak in a hot tub set within the lovely
gardens, or book a massage with one of the
therapists who comes into the spa room. Or
they may choose to simply sit on the deck
built onto the terminal moraine of
Mendenhall Glacier and contemplate the
glacier itself, visible about 2 miles away.

A rental car is recommended for stays at
the inn, set in the Mendenhall Loop residential area.

Hostels
Juneau International Hostel: (907-586-
9559; juneauhostel.net; 614 Harris Street,
Juneau AK 99801.) Open year round, the
hostel has dormitory separate arrangements for men and women. A common
room with a fireplace, kitchen, laundry is
available, as are bike racks. It's located
in a former historic home and is near
downtown and about six blocks from the
waterfront.

RV Parks
Auke Bay RV Park: (907-789-9467; 11930
Glacier Highway, Juneau. AK 99801.) The
full service park is 1½ miles from the
Alaska Ferry terminal. Trails and opportu-
nities for paddling are nearby.

Spruce Meadow RV Park: (907-789-1990;
JuneauRV.com; 10200 Mendenhall Loop
Rd., Juneau, AK 99801.) This full-service
park with all hookups has private spaces
amid alder, spruce, or meadow areas.
Wildlife, including black bear, deer, and
porcupines roam the area. Located at the
edge of a residential area, it's near
Mendenhall Glacier and Auke Bay Boat
Harbor and ferry terminal. Bus connections

link the park to historic and downtown Juneau. Reservations recommended. Rates: $30 per night.

GUSTAVUS (GLACIER BAY)

Gustavus marks the entrance to Glacier Bay, though the national park visitor center is about 8 miles north at Bartlett Cove. Most people who come here spend at least one day taking the Glacier Bay cruise, which the inns will arrange. Icy Strait fishing packages are also popular. Gustavus inns are open only in late spring through summer. They offer American plan with all meals; some are known for their cuisine. Reservations are essential for a room or for dining.

Alaskan Angler's Inn

Manager: Steve Brown
907-697-2343 or 1-866-510-2800
alaskasportfish.net
anglersinn@infowest.com
31 State Dock Rd., Gustavus, AK 999826;
1173 S. 250 W., Suite 107G, St. George, UT 84770
Next to Bear Track Store
Price: Moderate to Expensive
Credit Cards: Yes
Handicapped Access: No
Special Features: Convenient location near dock, store, and a golf course.

The buildings are the color of a barn and hold rooms with two queen beds each, kitchenette, full bathroom, satellite TV, and Internet connection. Most people come for five-night fishing packages, which cover guided fishing provided by Deep Blue Charters, license, guides, and bait and tackle.

Meals are provided in the package, or you can cook them yourself, either in the room kitchenette or in a kitchen in the lodge common room. The beamed room has a pool table, and is a gathering place at the end of the day.

The inn is beside the Bear Track Mercantile and Deli, and the Mount Fairweather Golf Course, where there usually is enough light to golf after a fishing day. The dock is just down the road, making this a convenient location.

Bear Track Inn

Owner-Manager: Janie Sheahan
907-697-3017 or 1-888-697-2284
beartrackinn.com
beartrac@aol.com
255 Rink Creek Rd., P.O. Box 255, Gustavus, AK 99826
Price: Very expensive
Credit Cards: Yes
Handicapped Access: One room fully accessible; one room partial
Special Features: Spectacular log building, gourmet dining.

The great room of this spruce-log lodge soars 30 feet to the peaked ceiling, reminiscent of national park lodge architecture. An open fireplace dominates the center of the room, and soft lighting emanates from moose antler chandeliers. It's a wonderful place to curl up with a book or to trade fish stories.

The 14 rooms have two queen beds, down comforters, high thread-count sheets, log beams, private baths, and bath sheets. Second floor rooms have spectacular views over meadows, forest, and toward Icy Strait.

Dining may feature a whole Dungeness crab sitting on the plate, salmon in parchment, Alaska spotted prawns, or game, including musk oxen or caribou. Service is family style. A hearty breakfast starts the day, and lunch is sent along with whatever activities you may choose.

The inn arranges fishing or à la carte excursions, including Glacier Bay cruises, kayaking, and trips to Skagway for the White Pass & Yukon Route train. The inn is located outside of town behind the airport.

Glacier Bay Lodge is tucked into the trees above the dock at Bartlett Cove.

Glacier Bay Lodge

Aramark Hotel
907-264-4600 or 1-866-761-6634
visitglacierbay.com
At Bartlett Cove and entrance to Glacier Bay
Price: Moderate
Credit Cards: Yes
Handicapped Access: Four rooms
Special Features: Only lodging in Glacier Bay National Park.

Tucked into the Sitka spruce forest at water's edge, this rustic-style lodge looks appealing, with its peaked gables and wide front porch. It is a convenient base for exploring Glacier Bay, hiking at the edge of the park, kayaking, or whale-watching.

The building houses the National Park Visitor Center, so you can easily visit exhibits and attend its interpretive programs. Logs are always burning in the massive stone fireplace, which draws in guests, who sit writing postcards or reading. Beyond, in the open dining room, the spectacular Tlingit mural of Raven and Eagle guards over the whole scene.

Rooms have two beds covered with plaid spreads, private baths, and knotty-pine walls. Windows look out toward the water or into the forest. The lodge books any activities for the park, including Glacier Bay cruises or whale watching. One of the unique trips is a whale-watching trip to Point Adolphus at the dinner hour. The long Alaska twilight allows sightseeing far into the evening.

Gustavus Inn

Owner-Managers: JoAnn and David Lesh
907-697-2254 or 1-800-649-5220
gustavusinn.com
dave@gustavusinn.com
P.O. Box 60, Gustavus, AK 99826
Gustavus Road, just west of the crossroads

Price: Moderate to expensive
Credit Cards: Yes
Handicapped Access: One room, plus four
at ground level
Special Features: Graceful old farm house,
top-notch cuisine, May through Sept. season.

Since 1965, the Lesh family has been providing hospitality in this graceful farm
homestead and sharing their table in its
original dining room. It's the classic
Gustavus experience.

JoAnn and David Lesh now manage and
run the inn, including cooking your dinner
and making arrangements for activities.
His parents started the inn, and their children are now helping.

Everything adds up to comfort and
warmth. The hall bench is filled with rubber boots, the better to slog through the
marshy meadow in the rain. Bicycles are
lined up outside under a shelter, to ride
along Gustavus's flat roads. A map to local
trails is in the room, along with a wildlife
guide to the area. A library has wildlife
guides and Alaska books. Wireless Internet
is available throughout the inn, and a computer terminal is provided for guests.

Like the rest of the inn, the bedrooms
are decorated with a kind of unfussy country style. Craftsman oak furniture, a striped
quilt cover, muted wallpaper prints, and a
quilt wall hanging added to the cozy, but not
overwhelming detail. All the rooms but two
have a private bath, and reading lights are
provided beside the bed.

The inn books many activities: Fishing
at Icy Strait, Glacier Bay cruise, hiking and
kayaking excursions. Some guests come
just for the Lesh's cuisine, which is excellent. As much as possible, things come
from the garden and from local fishermen.
(See Chapter 6, *Restaurants and Food
Purveyors.*) At the end of the day, people
gather around the tiny bar to trade stories
and enjoy salmon spread with a glass of
wine or Alaska beer. It's a place to wind

down from Alaska's awesome size and
scenery.

HAINES
Haines is one of the few Alaska Panhandle
cities connected by road to somewhere else,
so some of the lodgings offer SUV or van
rental. Most of them have airport or ferry
dock pickups.

Alaska Guardhouse
Owners: Phyllis Sage and Joanne Waterman
907-766-2484 or 1-866-290-7445
alaskaguardhouse.com
info@alaskaguardhouse.com
P.O. Box 853, Haines, AK 99827
On the Fort Steward grounds
Price: Inexpensive
Credit Cards: Yes.
Special Features: Former Fort Seward jail,
one kitchen unit, whirlpool bath, gay-
travel.com approved.

During its days as a fort building, this
cheerful tanzanite-colored cottage housed
the jail and offices. Today the three "cells"
look pretty cheerful with pale walls, and
deep lavender, gray, and pink comforters
and pillows. One of the rooms is quite
small, but large common rooms expand the
possibilities. A six-person whirlpool bath
is on the glassed-in area overlooking the
mountains. You are challenged to find the
"Santa Claus" in the range across Lynn
Canal.

A fireplace draws in people in the sitting
room, and an enclosed porch divides a
quiet area for reading. The porch swing is a
favorite place to while away the afternoon.
Continental breakfast is provided each
morning.

Beach Roadhouse
Owner-Manager: Phil Busby
907-766-3060 or 1-866-736-3060
beachroadhouse.com
frontdesk@beachroadhouse.com

1 Mile Beach Rd., P.O. Box 1293, Haines, AK 99827
At the Battery Point Trailhead
Price: Inexpensive to Moderate
Credit Cards: Yes
Handicapped Access: Two units
Special Features: Cabins and small lodge, SUVs for rent, open Feb.–Dec.

Set about a mile from town, the simply furnished rooms and cabins allow you to stay in the forest with the conveniences of home and town. Each of the six units has a fully equipped kitchenette or full kitchen. Some units have heated tile floors, a welcome comfort on cool or cold Alaska mornings. The cabins have a loft sleeping area that works well for families and for those interested in fishing.

The resort offers SUVs for rent, and a day trip up the pass. There are also a kayak and a canoe available to guests. Inside, the units have motel-style décor, with pale walls, honey-colored wood furniture, and floral bedspreads.

Captain's Choice Motel

Owner-Manager: Ed Lapeyri
907-766-3111 or 1-800-478-2345
capchoice.com
capchoice@usa.net
108 Second Ave., P.O. Box 392, Haines, AK 99827
Corner Second Ave. and Dalton St.
Price: Inexpensive to Moderate
Credit Cards: Yes
Handicapped Access: No
Special Features: Nautical touches to room, free wireless Internet.

The Captain's Choice looks pretty much like a motel on any interstate in the Lower 48, which makes it an exception in Haines. Most lodgings here are distinctive or quirky. But the Captain's Choice knotty-pine walls and rope trim, as well as the view out to the largest fjord in North America,

pretty much bring Alaska into the scene. You might even glimpse a moose in the parking lot, something you'll never find in Kansas.

The 39-room Captain's Choice offers van service and car rental, and it has a Laundromat. The breakfast room, where a complimentary continental breakfast is served, is a good place to trade Alaska stories with other travelers over bagels, toast, or cereal. People behind the desk seem particularly friendly and helpful and know all there is to know about this part of Alaska.

The lobby is a bustling place. Sit there for awhile, and eventually all 2,400 residents of Haines will come through.

Eagles Nest Motel

Owners: Shane and Janis Horton
907-766-2891 or 1-800-354-6009
alaskaeagletours.com
eaglesnest@aptalaska.net
1 Mile Haines Hwy., P.O. Box 250, Haines, AK 99827
Price: Inexpensive
Credit Cards: Yes
Handicapped Access: Several rooms accessible
Special Features: Car rentals, and wildlife viewing or fishing arranged.

Rooms and suites in the 13-unit motel are outfitted with queen beds, phones, and cable television. The suites feature a bedroom, large living room, and kitchenette. Continental breakfast is included with the room rate, and a courtesy van ferries people to the airport or to town. Guests may rent front-wheel drive cars for day trips or overnights on the Golden Circle.

During winter the owners put snow tires on the cars. The owners run fishing and wildlife excursions in a pontoon boat on Chilkoot Lake.

Fort William H. Seward Bed and Breakfast Inn

Owners: Norm and Suzanne Smith
907-766-2856 or 1-800-615-6676
fortsewardalaska.com
fortseward@yahoo.com
House No. 1, Fort Seward Dr., P.O. 5,
Haines, AK 99827
One of the large white houses on the top end of parade ground
Price: Inexpensive to Moderate
Credit Cards: Yes
Handicapped Access: No
Special features: Elegant house on National Register of Historic Places; open May–Sept.

A row of elegant Jeffersonian houses lines the parade ground at Fort Seward. They belonged to the post officers, and now the one belonging to the post surgeon is Haines's oldest bed-and-breakfast inn. Owners Norm and Suzanne Smith run the inn and live on the top floor.

The freshness of paint and décor makes this a particularly welcoming inn. Deep, plush towels are folded on cheery floral spreads on queen beds. Lace curtains, lavender walls, white woodwork, and high ceilings all reflect the period refinement of the house. Three rooms have Belgian tile fireplaces, and Persian carpets line the halls and stairs. Others with two queen beds and a kitchenette are suitable for families. The view from some rooms overlooks the parade ground and on to the Lynn Canal and mountains.

A full breakfast, including the inn's famous whole-wheat sourdough pancakes, fuels guests for the day. The owners estimate they have flipped 250,000 of the famous cakes. It'll be more, by the time you read this.

Fort Seward Lodge and Restaurant

General Manager: Scott Sundberg
Operations Manager: Nicholas Trimble
907-766-2009 or 1-877-617-3418

One of the old Fort William H. Seward officer's houses is now a Haines bed-and-breakfast inn.

ftsewardlodge.com
fortseward@gmail.com
39 Mud Bay Rd., P.O. Box 307, Haines, AK
99827
In Fort Seward near Haines Highway
Price: Inexpensive to Moderate
Credit Cards: Yes
Handicapped Access: Yes, with some help
Special Features: Formerly the Fort's Post
Exchange; restaurant and bar and gathering
place; open February through the American
Bald Eagle Festival in November.

The double bed in a room near the front of
the building, one of 10 units, is set one step
up from the rest of the room. The lodge
wing follows the sloped level of the fort.
Each of the rooms is different and a little
eccentric, since they are carved out of the
former fort buildings from 1904. There are
nooks and crannies, and plenty of odd corners that make the rooms more interesting.

They all have one or two double beds,
wainscoting, and pale walls in simple but
serviceable décor. They also look out to
Portage Cove or to the mountains. The
room at the front of the building has a
kitchenette, complete with Heritage Coffee.
Two of the rooms have a shared bath, and
come at a considerably lower rate.

The building, constructed in the early
1900s, was once the Post Exchange.
Soldiers and their families came to attend
movies and to bowl, and get ice cream. Its
bar and restaurant are still one of the town's
gathering places.

Hotel Hälsingland

Owner-Manager: Jeff Butcher
907-766-2000 or 1-800-542-6363;
hotelhalsingland.com
Reservations@HotelHalsingland.com
P.O. Box 1649, Haines, AK 99827
13 Fort Seward Drive, on the parade
ground, Haines
Price: Inexpensive to Moderate

Credit Cards: Yes
Handicapped Access: One room fully
accessible
Special Features: Historic fort hotel;
Haines's largest lodging; some original
fireplaces; open year-round except for a
few weeks in winter; free wireless Internet
in the lobby.

There are Alaska hotels far more luxurious
than this one, but there are few more fitting
for its location. Housed in the former commanding and bachelor officers' quarters of
Fort Seward, the Victorian board building
sits proudly at the head of the parade
grounds. It's named for the homeland of
the original owner.

Without being overly fussy, the lobby
area and 50 rooms express the fairly pared-
down Victorian décor of turn-of-the-20th-
century Alaska. Some of the rooms have
original Belgian tile fireplaces and claw-
foot tubs. Pale walls, dark wood furniture,
and earth-toned floral printed bed spreads
set the tone. Room size and nature vary
widely, and some of them are a bit eccentric
in shape, since they are in a building converted from other purposes. And be aware,
many of the rooms have chipped paint,
peeling wallpaper, and need renovation.
Beds, however, are up to date and comfortable.

Some guests share a bath with other
rooms, which drops their rates to less than
$100. Some windows look out to the spec-
tacular mountains surrounding Haines, or
over the parade grounds. The comfy chairs
and free wireless Internet in the lobby
invite whiling away the afternoon. Among
the hotel's claims to fame was that Eleanor
Dusenbury composed the song celebrating
the Alaska flag here.

Summer Inn Bed and Breakfast

Owner-Manager: Lori Webster
907-766-2970

summerinnbnb.com
innkeeper@summerinnbnb.com
117 Second Ave., P.O. Box 1198, Haines, AK
99827
Between Dalton and Union streets
Price: Inexpensive
Credit Cards: Yes
Handicapped Access: No
Special Features: Historical inn with legendary tie to Soapy Smith gang; full breakfast with room; open year-round.

This tidy, cheerful five-bedroom inn is a home away from home in Haines. Five bedrooms have comforters on the beds topped by a handmade quilt in soft pastel colors. Pale walls and white curtains at the window add to the light look. Beds may be twins or doubles.

All rooms have private baths, and one of them has a circa-1912 bathtub that belonged to Tim Vogel, who built this house. It is believed that Vogel belonged to the Soapy Smith gang that terrorized Skagway, just up the Lynn Canal, during the Yukon Gold Rush.

RV Parks

Haines Hitch-up RV Park: (907-766-2882; higtchuprv.com; 851 Main Street.) The large park has 92 full hookups, cable television, a gift shop, and a Laundromat.

Oceanside RV Park: (907-766-2437; oceansiderv.com; 14 Front Street.) The ocean-front park has 23 hookups, restrooms, showers, a laundry, and cable television, as well as wireless Internet access. It's open year-round, and the owners have gold-mine tours June through August.

Salmon Run Campground and Cabins: (907-766-3240; salmonrunadventures .com; 6.5 Mile Lutak Road.) About two miles from the ferry terminal, the site has 30 spaces in a forest setting along Lutak Inlet. Restrooms, showers, picnic tables, and tent-camping sites available.

Skagway

Skagway is another seasonal destination. It's population drops wildly in winter, and so do available inn rooms.

The Historic Skagway Inn

Owner-Managers: Karl and Rosemary Klupar
907-983-2289 or 1-888-752-4929
skagwayinn.com
reservations@skagwayinn.com
Seventh and Broadway, Skagway, AK 99840
Price: Moderate
Credit Cards: Yes
Handicapped Access: No
Special Features: Historic inn, complimentary van to airport, ferry dock, train station; open year-round.

The Skagway Inn, an attractive white house on Broadway at Paradise Alley, has been welcoming guests since 1897, though they came for more than a good night's sleep in the old days. It was a brothel during the Gold Rush, and to this day the 10 rooms are named for women who worked here. After the heady days of the Klondike, it became a family residence, a boarding house, and finally a hotel.

Rooms are individually furnished, with white or delicately flowered bed linens, brass beds, and antique chests. Sheer curtains cover the windows, and are pretty, but screen out little light during the summer. Bed sizes vary: Some rooms have queens, others double, or twin beds. Some rooms share a bath, or have a half-bath with a shower down the hall, so be sure you have the arrangement you would like.

An elaborate full breakfast is served. The owners have planted a lovely garden, and periodically have culinary demonstrations that use vegetables and herbs grown right here. Olivia's Restaurant on the premises (temporarily closed) will reopen in 2009.

Mile Zero Bed & Breakfast

Owner-Manager: Tara Mallory
907-983-3045
mile-zero.com
milezero@starband.net
901 Main St., Skagway, AK 99840
At the corner of Ninth Ave.
Price: Inexpensive to Moderate
Credit Cards: Yes
Handicapped Access: One room
Special Features: Attractive cozy inn, in a residential neighborhood; new building looks like an older home, nonsmoking.

Skagway is at Mile Zero for the Chilkoot Trail, the White Pass & Yukon Route railroad, and the Klondike Highway. Bed-and-breakfast owner Tara Mallory sees the seven-room inn as Mile Zero for one's adventures in Alaska. The comfortable inn has two wings that jut out from the corner entrance of etched glass double doors. Rooms, named for Yukon places, have both private entrances and access through the common room at the apex of the two wings.

Built to be an inn in 1995, Mile Zero has updated bathrooms, double-insulated walls, and handicapped access, yet it has a cozy, old-fashioned look. A porch surrounds the building and flowers grow in the front yard. A feminine touch guided room décor, done as though for a private home, with a vine wreath and birdhouses. A big recliner and an armoire add to comfort, and the wildlife prints remind you that you're in Alaska.

Breakfast is expanded continental, with yogurt, granola, oatmeal, banana bread, bagels, English muffins, and cereals. Guests linger, and trade stories and advice with the owner.

Westmark Inn Skagway

General Manager: Jim Sager
907-983-6000 or 1-800-544-0970
westmarkhotels.com/skagway.php
P.O. Box 515, Skagway, 99840
Third Ave. and Spring St.
Price: Moderate

Mile Zero sits at that point on Main Street, the extension of South Klondike Highway in Skagway.

Credit Cards: Yes
Handicapped Access: Two rooms
Special Features: Convenient location; free ferry and airport pickup; mid-May–mid-Sept.

This hotel has 151 rooms, an enormous hostelry compared to Skagway's other inns. Owned by Holland America, it caters to cruise ship passengers staying before or after the land portion of cruise tours. The building, about a block off Broadway, Skagway's main street, has a board exterior painted a startling ochre. Rooms are spread into two buildings, the original with the Chilkoot Dining Room and another wing across the street, which looks like a two-story motel. Rooms are comfortable, and cover the basics. The bar and informal restaurant, Bonanza Bar, are on Broadway.

An outdoor garden in a courtyard with a fountain is a quiet spot of retreat from otherwise busy Skagway, and is one of the hotel's biggest assets.

Sgt. Preston's Lodge

Owner-Managers: Chris and Teri Valentine
907-983-2521 or 1-866-983-2521
http://sgtprestons.eskagway.com
sgt-prestons@usa.net
370 Sixth Ave. P.O. Box 538, Skagway, AK 99840
Sixth Ave. and Broadway
Price: Inexpensive to Moderate
Credit Cards: Yes
Handicapped Access: One room
Special Features: Variety of rooms, gas barbecue, complimentary airport and ferry shuttle.

The cluster of buildings that make up Sgt. Preston's Lodge look as if they might be the Northwest Mounted Police barracks. In fact, they were a U.S. Army barracks, though Skagway once had a Mounties headquarters and the Yukon border is just a few miles up the road.

The 40 rooms have various configura-

tions with double or queen beds. All of them have a private bath, though the bath may have a shower stall. Others are more spacious, with two queen beds and a full bath. All rooms have cable television and telephone with free local calls. Microwaves and refrigerators available on request, and coffee, tea, and hot chocolate available in the lobby.

The White House Bed and Breakfast

Owner-Managers: John and Jan Tronrud
907-983-9000
atthewhitehouse.com
whitehse@aptalaska.net
475 Eighth Ave., P.O. Box 41, Skagway, AK 99840
Eighth Ave. and Main St.
Price: Moderate
Credit Cards: Yes
Handicapped Access: One room
Special Features: Historic white house, quiet location.

A beautiful original wooden staircase and family antiques grace the foyer of this 1902 house, which is part of the Skagway Historic District. An extended continental breakfast is served on the buffet in the dining room that looks as if it belongs to someone's grandmother. Hot tea and filled cookie jar are available any time. Those who depart early can arrange a breakfast-to-go delivered the night before.

The 10 rooms have colorful hand-sewn quilts on the beds, private baths, a refrigerator, cable television, and ceiling fans. Some rooms have armoires. A general feeling of comfort and refinement characterizes the inn.

Hostels

Skagway Home Hostel & Gardens: (907-983-2131; skagwayhostel.com; 456 Third Avenue near Main Street.) A garden surrounds the restored historic home of this family-run hostel. A mixed dorm, gender-specific dorm, and family room make up the arrangements. A kitchen is available or you can take dinner with the family. It's popular with a range of travelers—backpackers, families, and seniors.

RV Parks

Pullen Creek RV Park: (907-983-2768 or 1-800-936-3731; pullencreekrv.com; end of Second Avenue at waterfront.) Full hookups and tent sites, some with a harbor view. Convenient location close to historic district and ferry terminal.

Skagway Mountain View RV Park: (907-983-3333 or 1-800-323-5757; bestof alaskatravel.com; Twelfth Avenue and Broadway.) Complete electrical and water hookups, an RV wash, as well as a Laundromat and fully accessible showers, and restroom facilities are in the spacious park. Dry sites and tent area also available. Staff is on hand to help with reservations.

YAKUTAT

Yakutat's lodgings are scattered fairly widely in the tiny community. Most of them serve as fishing lodges, and are open seasonally.

Blue Heron Bed and Breakfast Inn

Owner-Managers: Fran and John Latham
907-784-3287
johnlatham.com
bluhern@yahoo.com
218 Bayview Dr., Yakutat, AK 99689
Located on the waterfront about one quarter mile from boat dock
Price: Moderate to Expensive
Credit Cards: No; personal checks or cash, only
Handicapped Access: No
Special Features: Beautiful setting in graceful lodge-home, wonderful duck decoys; open year-round.

Fran and John Latham welcome guests to this four-room lodge, which is also their home, as if they are personally greeting friends. It's a graceful Alaska home with a panoramic view over an inlet from Yakutat Bay, and in the distance, Mount St. Elias. The rooms are tastefully decorated with bird prints and rich blue-gray tones. Elegant duck decoys and bird carvings stand on tables and shelves throughout the home. A mounted salmon hovers over the fireplace, where logs are usually flickering.

John Latham is a famed Alaska hunting and fishing guide, and he's likely to be taking guests out during the day. The facility operates on a fishing lodge basis for those guests, with complete fishing-room packages. Many guests have been coming here for 20 years or more. It also operates as a bed-and-breakfast inn. The Lathams also offer a nearby vacation rental.

At breakfast, served on a tablecloth with cloth napkins, you may find mangoes, delivered by air from Seattle, with blackberries and sourdough waffles and endless cups of coffee. The Lathams are exceedingly helpful and will book excursions, such as a boat trip to Hubbard Glacier. Should you take a hike, Fran will send you along with pepper spray in case you meet a bear.

Glacier Bear Lodge

Owner-Manager: Sharesse Edwards
907-784-3202
glacierbearlodge.com
info@glacierbearlodge.com
Glacier Bear Ave., off Yakutat Rd., P.O. Box, 303, Yakutat, AK 99689
About halfway between the airport and town
Price: Moderate
Credit Cards: Yes
Handicapped Access: Wheelchair ramp, will accommodate
Special Features: Open Apr.–Oct. for steelhead through coho salmon season.

A glacier bear is indeed a separate variety, a black bear that carries a gene that gives it a blue-black coat, a coloring that makes them hard to spot on glaciers. The people at Glacier Bear Lodge couldn't say if one had ever crossed the grounds. The fishing lodge, wonderfully located on the Situk River with steelheads and spawning salmon right outside the door, stays open April through October to take advantage of the long fishing season. The lodge's 31 rooms each have two double beds and one roll-away, to accommodate large family or fishing groups. Free wireless Internet is available, as well as complimentary airport pick-up and drop-off. The main building with the restaurant and very lively bar is a soaring two-story structure with tall windows. Motel-style wings house lodge rooms.

Fishing packages are extremely flexible, with some as short as two days, or the lodge may be booked for room and breakfast only.

Yakutat Lodge

Managers: Dan and Hope Anderson
907-784-3232 or 1-800-925-8828 (YAKUTAT)

yakutatlodge.com
yakutatlodge@starband.net
P.O. Box 287, 111 Airport Rd., Yakutat, AK 99689
Beside Yakutat Airport
Price: Moderate
Credit Cards: Yes
Handicapped Access: Several rooms
Special Features: Close to airport, rustic lodgings.

You can't miss this cluster of buildings just outside tiny Yakutat Airport terminal. The rustic lodge has 16 rooms, which accommodate four people, with private bath in two buildings, and four cabins with a bathhouse. You'll need a sleeping bag for the cabins.

The largest of the buildings houses a cozy lobby, restaurant, bar, and gift shop. Moose antlers serve as handles for the big double door opening to this area. Huge rockers surround an iron stove in the sitting area that has a chess game set up and ready to start. The shop has nice, quality logo-wear. Everywhere, photos show the

Moose antlers serve as the door handle at Yakutat Lodge.

trophy fish to be captured in Yakutat Bay or the Situk River.

Fishing packages are flexible, with choices for fully guided trips, or unguided, and fishing on fresh or salt water. The restaurant serves three meals daily. (See Chapter 6, *Restaurants and Food Purveyors.*)

Yukon Territory

WHITEHORSE

Whitehorse is a territorial capital and the largest city in the Yukon, so it has several large hotels.

Edgewater Hotel

867-667-2572 or 1-877-484-3334
edgewaterhotelwhitehorse.com
edgewater@northwestel.net
101 Main St., Whitehorse, Yukon Y1A 2A7, Canada
Corner Main and First Avenue
Price: Moderate to Expensive
Credit Cards: Yes
Handicapped Access: One room
Special Features: Prime location at town center.

The lobby at the 30-room Edgewater Hotel can be hard to cross. People jam the area, which is surprisingly small for a hotel with two restaurants, a bar, and a busy meeting room. They may be members of the Territorial government, or tourists. The hotel is directly across the street from the White Pass & Yukon Route station, something of a magnet for tourist activities.

Rooms are nicely furnished with one or two extra-long double beds and all of the amenities of a well-planned hotel aimed at business travelers: spacious desks with a comfortable work chair, high-speed Internet connection, flat-screen television, ironing board, and coffeemaker. Cheerful flowered spreads cover the beds, and a flower arrangement brightens the cabinet-counter against creamy walls. There's even air-condition-ing for the Yukon's sometimes hot, summer days. This isn't the Alaska Panhandle with its cooling, temperate, rainforest climate.

Be aware that main floor rooms at the front of the building open directly to the sidewalk, so you will have to keep the drapes closed, unless you don't mind passersby spying from the outside.

Best Western Gold Rush Inn

867-668-4500 or 1-800-780-7234
goldrushinn.com
411 Main St., Whitehorse, Yukon Y1A 2B6
At the corner of Fourth Avenue
Price: Moderate
Credit Cards: Yes
Handicapped Access: Two rooms
Special Features: Gold Rush décor and artifacts in public areas; modern guest rooms.

This hotel covers a long city block, with 106 rooms and suites. The public rooms celebrate the 1898 Gold Rush with lavish use of artifacts, including globe lighting fixtures, spindle banisters, and stuffed animals. But, once upstairs, the artifacts are left behind and the rooms are modern and suitable for the business traveler.

A comfortable desk chair, high-speed and wireless Internet connections will please those who have to check e-mail. Each room has a microwave and fridge. Stylish bowl washbasins and spas in suites add to comfort. Some rooms are air-conditioned. Dry cleaning service, a coin-operated laundry, and beauty salon are available. A full-service restaurant serves breakfast, lunch, and dinner, and a lounge is on the premises.

Hostels

Beez Kneez Bakpakers: (867-456-2333; bzkneez.com; 408 Hoge Street.) Bright yellow, the color of a bee's belly, accents this cheerful and popular hostel near downtown. Dorms and private rooms, a fully equipped kitchen, showers, and laundry facilities. A free bicycle, barbecue, and free wireless Internet connections.

Hide on Jeckell Hostel: (867-633-4933; hide-on-jeckell.com; 410 Jeckell Street.) A book exchange, free bicycles, and Internet connections add to the appeal of this hostel. Lockers are available in dorms, and a lounge area with fireplace and equipped kitchen add to convenience.

RV Parks

RV parks probably cover more acreage than any other developed land along the Alaska Highway. They are essential to the many people who bring their accommodations with them on what has been dubbed "The Last Great Road Trip."

HAINES JUNCTION

Kluane RV Kampground: (1-866-634-6789; kluanerv.ca; 1016 Alaska Highway.) This large park has 60 pull-through sites with all hookups, including wireless Internet and cable television, and 40 wooded campsites. Gorgeous views of Kluane Mountains from grounds; hot showers and Laundromat, and gas and diesel fuel available.

Fas Gas RV Park: (867-634-2505; beside Fas Gas service station.) Twenty-three pull-through sites have all connections but sewer, and hot showers. Hiking trails nearby.

WHITEHORSE

Hi Country RV Park: (867-667-7445; hicountryrvyukon.com; 91374 Alaska Highway.) The popular park has 130 pull-through and back-in sites with full hookups. Coin-operated Laundromat, convenience store, free cable television and coin-operated wireless Internet. A meeting cabin with wood stove accommodates up to 50 for meetings or barbecues. Wheelchair access to all buildings.

Pioneer RV Park: (867-668-5944 or 1-866-626-7383; pioneer-rv-park.com; 91091 Alaska Highway.) Fifty pull-through sites and 100 back-in slots are nicely situated in forested area. Full and partial hookups are available, along with wireless Internet, coin-operated Internet kiosk, Laundromat, showers, meeting room, and store.

CENTRAL PANHANDLE

PETERSBURG

Petersburg has two main inns, as well as several B&Bs.

Herons Rest Bed and Breakfast

Owner-Managers: Deidre and Ronn Buschmann
907-772-3373 or 1-888-450-3373
petersburg.org/businesses/bnb/html
buschmann@gci.net
613 Rambler St.; P.O. Box 1367, Petersburg, AK 99833
Off S. Nordic Dr.
Price: Inexpensive to Moderate
Credit Cards: Yes
Handicapped Access: Two rooms
Special Features: Secluded 13-acre setting; free bikes; wireless Internet; beautifully designed; open year-round.

This new inn is beautifully designed, with a soaring ceiling and Palladian windows that look out to the surrounding 13 acres, where you might spot deer or in the nearby trees, perching herons, which gave the inn its name. Bikes provided by the inn make it easy to get to town, and the owners will do airport and ferry pick-ups.

Deidre and Ronn Buschmann designed and built the inn beside their residence, though it's a separate building with a private entrance. Pale woods, including a yellow cedar banister, finish off the rooms. Light floods into the downstairs common room with a kitchenette including refrigerator and microwave. Deidre cooks a full breakfast every morning. Two downstairs rooms share a bathroom and are ideal for families; the upstairs suite has its own sitting area.

The owners don't promote the connection, but Ronn Buschmann is the great-grandson of Petersburg founder Peter Buschmann. Ronn has updated the family history in *Petersburg Pioneers*, a book available at the Clausen Memorial Museum.

Scandia House
Managers: Don and Charlene Anderson
907-772-4281 or 1-800-722-5006
scandiahousehotel.com
info@scandiahousehotel.com
110 Nordic Dr., P.O. Box 689, Petersburg, AK 99833
Nordic Drive near the beginning of Sing Lee Alley
Price: Moderate
Credit Cards: Yes
Handicapped Access: One room
Special Features: Attractive hotel at the edge of downtown; free wireless Internet; some nonsmoking rooms.

This Scandinavian-style hotel fits right into Petersburg's Nordic ambience. A rosemaling band decorates the pale walls of each room, outfitted with oak furniture in simple lines that reinforces the contemporary Norwegian spirit. The rosemaling tones appeared in floral bedspreads, carpeting, and chairs.

The 33 guest rooms have unique configurations to meet the needs of various travelers. You'll find double, queen, and king beds; some units also have a kitchenette. A wall-mounted lamp aids bedtime reading. Some rooms look out to mountains and others to the waterfront and Nordic Drive, busy during the day, but quiet at night.

Scandia House is Petersburg's oldest and newest hotel. Originally built in 1905, it burned and was rebuilt, opening again in 2005. Its newness shows in the bathrooms and unscuffed surfaces.

Car and boat rentals can be arranged through the hotel, and it has the adjacent Java Hüs coffee shop on one side and a hair salon on the premises. Tina's Kitchen, one of Petersburg's most popular eating places, is just next door. A courtesy van usually sits in the *porte-cochère* ready for service for the airport and ferry. A complimentary continental breakfast has house-made muffins, juice, and coffee.

Tides Inn
Owner: Gloria Ohmer Koenigs
General Manager—Kelsey Martinsen
907-772-4288 or 1-800-665-8433
tidesinnalaska.com
tidesinn@Alaska.com
305 First St.; P.O. Box 1048, Petersburg, AK 99833
Corner of First and Dolphin St.
Price: Inexpensive
Credit Cards: Yes
Handicapped Access: One room
Special Features: Spectacular views from some rooms; free wireless Internet; some nonsmoking rooms.

The 45 rooms here are clean, spacious, and bright with patterned bedspreads, and plenty of lamps. But this isn't the reason to stay at the Tides Inn. It's for the panoramic view of Petersburg Harbor, Wrangell Narrows, and Kupreanof Island. The rooms without views have the same conveniences, which include a fairly large refrigerator and a microwave, but may face the opposite wing, and are dark. Rooms are in two parallel buildings with indoor halls and a sheltered walk between them. The wing closest to the lobby is oldest; the newer one, slightly downhill, has the best views on its waterfront side. Although clean and bright, some bathrooms show signs of wear. There is no elevator for second-floor rooms.

Though she isn't often around these days, owner Gloria Ohmer Koenigs is something of a local Petersburg legend. She came here as a pioneer during territorial days in 1947, stayed, and eventually started this hotel. She used to bake Norwegian cakes for breakfast. Nowadays, the continental breakfast consists of juice, coffee or tea, and muffins, and they still taste homemade. The motel is within walking distance of the harbor and scenic Petersburg sites, and offers complimentary van service to the airport or ferry.

Waterfront Bed and Breakfast
Owner-Managers: Sammy Parker and LeeRoy Newton
907-772-9300 or 1-866-772-9301
waterfrontbedandbreakfast.com
waterfrontbb@gci.net
1004 S. Nordic Dr., P.O. Box 1613, Petersburg, AK 99833
Near the Alaska ferry dock
Price: Inexpensive to Moderate
Credit Cards: Yes
Handicapped Access: Five rooms
Special Features: Set right over waterfront beside ferry terminal; hot tub; open all year; nonsmoking.

White woodwork and cheerful printed comforters on each bed add character to rooms at this B&B next to the Alaska ferry terminal. A piano in the sitting room and family photos on the wall add to the homey atmosphere. A kitchen is the gathering spot for breakfast, which Sammy Parker cooks each morning.

Guests may also use the kitchen facilities. The deck overlooking the ferry dock and Wrangell Narrows is another gathering spot for guests.

LeeRoy Newton occasionally initiates a wildlife show. He bangs on an outdoor table, whistles, and scans the skies. Then he begins to cut up salmon carcasses with a cleaver. "Watch for the white head," he says. First one, and then another, and another bald eagle begin to head in this direction, sometimes from Kupreanof

Island across the Narrows. They soar in, seem to brake in mid-air, and then, talons extended, pounce on the salmon he has thrown on the shore. Sometimes they impale a piece mid-swoop, and wheel back over the narrows. Only the youngest birds settle on the beach to eat the treat.

Fishing Lodges

Green Rocks Wilderness Lodge
Owner-Manager: Tim Harper
907-772-5050 summer; 702-301-9657 rest of year
greenrockslodge.com
info@greenrockslodge.com
P.O. Box 29, Petersburg, AK 99833
Price: Moderate
Credit Cards: Yes
Handicapped Access: No
Special Features: Cabins near waterfront; Dungeness crab, in addition to fish.
Often single groups rent this small fishing resort with accommodations for just 12 people in two large cabins. Located on the eastern edge of Kupreanof Island, the lodge offers guided fishing for all five salmon species, halibut, and Dungeness crab. In spring and fall, bear hunting is available. Lodge employees clean, vacuum pack, and flash-freeze fish for their guests.

Breakfast and dinner are served in a central lodge, where people also socialize and take showers. Lunches are packed for the 18-foot Lund boats, or served in the lodge. Cabins have bunk beds, all bedding, and heaters. Transportation is provided from Petersburg to the lodge, which is inaccessible by road.

Hostel
Alaska Island Hostel: (907-772-3632; alaskaislandhostel.com; 805 Gjoa St., P.O. Box 892, Petersburg, AK 99833.) Reservations are required for this dorm-style lodging, with a kitchen, wireless Internet, Alaska books and videos, and

lockers. It's about eight blocks to downtown and the harbor.

RV Parks

Ohmer Creek National Forest Campground: (907-228-6220; Mitkof Highway.) The campground with 10 sites is 22 miles south of town on a gravel road for the last 5 miles. Fishing in the creek and an interpretive nature trail are activities at the isolated spot.

Twin Creek RV Park: (907-772-3244; twincreekrv.com; 741 Mitkof Highway) The park is 7½ miles outside of town with full and partial hookups, and tent sites. Self-service snacks and drinks, fishing tackle, and rental videos available. Trails lead to the beach on Wrangell Narrows or forested areas.

SITKA

Sitka is larger than most of the other Panhandle cities, with 9,000 people, and its hotels seem to have a little more city veneer than most Panhandle hostelries, as well. The desk clerk may ask if you need the wireless Internet code, and the key is a magnetic card instead of a metal one.

The town has three large hotels and several bed-and-breakfast inns. Almost every property takes advantage of the stunning setting with views over Sitka Sound, Japonski Island, and Mount Edgecombe. During the fishing season, people stay in town hotels and go out with charters, especially at Salmon Derby time in early June. Music lovers come for the Sitka Music Festival the same month.

Sitka has a nonsmoking ordinance, so hotel public areas and restaurants are nonsmoking.

Sitka Hotel

Owner-Manager: Cynde Stangl
907-747-3288
sitkahotel.com
stay@sitkahotel.com
118 Lincoln St., Sitka, AK 99835
Near the foot of Lincoln Street at Totem Square
Price: Inexpensive to Moderate
Credit Cards: Yes
Handicapped Access: One room
Special Features: Cheerful, old-fashioned-looking lobby, excellent location.

This 60-room inn is Sitka's oldest hotel, though it's décor would suggest an even older date than 1939. Bright wallpaper, lace curtains, white wood-spindle decorations, and an unusual clef couch bring to mind Victorian times. Outside, however, especially the Totem Square façade, has a boxy front with a sidewalk overhang suggesting the Old West.

The hotel has two wings, and most guests are happy to pay the premium for the more updated rooms in the newer section, toward the back. Wireless Internet access, free local calls, and ironing boards are some of the conveniences.

Coin-operated laundry, free parking, and a convenient location are other plusses. Victoria's Restaurant and Pour House are off the lobby in the older part of the hotel.

Totem Square Inn

Owner-Manager: David Malone
907-747-3693 or 1-866-300-1353
totemsquare.com
201 Katlian St., Sitka, AK 99835
South side of Totem Square at waterfront
Price: Moderate
Credit Cards: Yes
Handicapped Access: Two rooms
Special Features: Free expanded continental breakfast, waterfront location.

As soon as you check-in, the desk clerk hands each guest a bottle of Sheet'ka Heen bottled water, and explains breakfast hours and wireless Internet codes. Questions seem to be anticipated. Owned and operated by the Alaska Native-owned Shee

The Totem Square Inn, at left, sits at Sitka's waterfront.

Atikä, Inc., this 67-room hotel is designed for comfort and convenience. Spacious rooms feature bedside lamps and ample bathroom counter space A *porte-cochère* protects you from rain when checking in or out. Free wireless Internet, two lobby computer stations, flat-screen television, and complimentary airport shuttle add to convenience.

Rooms facing Totem Square overlook the Pioneer Home, totem pole, foot of Lincoln Street, and O'Connell Bridge. Other rooms face directly over the harbor or the mountains. Room décor runs to subtle tones, with textured, tan wallpaper and bedspreads with muted red and earth tones, in an abstract botanical print.

Breakfast starts at 6:30 AM—late, by Sitka standards—and has wide choices, with oatmeal, cold cereals, juices, and yogurt, in addition to English muffins, bread, and breakfast pastries.

The staff will make restaurant reserva-

tions or check the Alaska ferry schedule. Some Alaska hotels will happily supply the phone numbers; here, they make the call.

Westmark Sitka

General Manager: Ron Hauck
907-747-6241 or 1-800-544-0970
westmarkhotels.com
330 Seward St., Sitka, AK 99835
Between Seward and Lincoln sts.
Price: Moderate
Credit Cards: Yes
Handicapped Access: Four rooms
Special Features: Large restaurant and bar off hotel lobby; fireplace and seating area; nonsmoking.

Owned by Holland America Lines, this 101-room hotel seems like a crossroads. The lobby bustles with people checking in or leaving for tours, or waiting to meet business associates. The lobby seating area is a good place to linger, especially on a cool night when a fire burns on the hearth. A large restaurant and lounge are just off the lobby.

Rooms overlook busy Lincoln Street or toward the mountains. Configuration varies with two double beds, a queen or two queens, and even twin beds. Free high-speed Internet access and coffeemakers are available in all rooms.

The hotel is large and sits at a prominent corner of town, but can go unnoticed. Colorful retail shops sit at ground level on Lincoln Street, where the hotel sets up the Chowder Hut, a kind of sidewalk café–beer garden during the day, in summer. An entrance is on Lake Street and the main entrance on Seward Street, though it's hardly imposing. The hotel and restaurant are open year-round.

Fishing Lodges

Baranof Wilderness Lodge
Owner-Manager: Mike Trotter
1-800-613-6551
flyfishalaska.com
mtrotter@flyfishalaska.com
P.O. Box 2187, Sitka, AK 99835
Price: Moderate to Expensive
Credit Cards: Yes
Special Features: Season May–Oct.; secluded bay 20 miles from Sitka.

A float plane transports guests the 20 miles to the lodge on Warm Springs Bay on the east side of Baranof Island. Cabins have pine paneling, wood-burning stoves, and private bathrooms with showers. A genera-tor powered by a turbine at nearby Sadie Creek supplies lodge electricity. Fishing options vary, from salmon and halibut in salt water to trout fishing in streams and lakes. Guides take out guests in skiffs or 24-foot cabin cruisers. The lodge also has some wilderness campsites. Barbless tackle and catch-and-release practices support sustainable fishing for freshwater species. One box of saltwater fish are cleaned, vac-uum packed, and frozen for guests to take home.

Seminars in fly fishing and photography are held periodically throughout the summer.

Dove Island Lodge
Owners: Duane and Tracie Lambeth
Manager: Nicole Bilinski
907-747-5660 or 1-888-318-3474
aksitkasportfishing.com
gofish@doveislandlodge.com
P.O. Box 1512, Sitka, AK 99835
Island in Sitka Sound
Price: Moderate to Expensive
Credit Cards: Yes
Special Features: Ultraluxe fishing resort; flexible fishing packages; free wireless Internet.

Were Hollywood to film an Alaska fishing lodge, they might choose Dove Island. Located on a private island, the luxury property has soaring windows overlooking Sitka Sound, river-rock fireplaces, yellow cedar walls, antler chandeliers, thick sapling beds, and log furniture. The main lodge has five two-bedroom suites, and there are also two cabins. Guests may have twin or king-size beds.

Two chefs create gourmet meals that culminate each day in a five-course dinner. The most famed is the Alaska Night menu that features local ingredients in each of the courses.

Fishing is in the ocean waters, or guests are transported by the resort float plane to fresh water streams or lakes. King and sil-ver salmon and halibut are targeted for ocean fishing. The lodge is accessible by a short boat ride from Sitka. There also are bed-and-breakfast options, and day trips to Sitka or the surrounding areas.

Hostels
Sitka International Youth Hostel: (907-747-8661.) The hostel is currently closed, and a new one is under construction.

RV Parks

Sitka Sportsman's Association RV Park:
(907-747-6033; 5211 Halibut Point Road.)
Space for 16 RVs with electrical and water
hookups, showers and restrooms, is provided in this park that is open year-round.
An indoor shooting range, and an outdoor
trap and skeet range will appeal to hunters
and marksmen.

WRANGELL

Alaskan Sourdough Lodge

Owner-Manager: Bruce E. Harding
907-874-3613 or 1-800-874-3613
akgetaway.com
info@akgetaway.com
1104 Peninsula Rd., P.O. Box 1062,
Wrangell, AK 99929
On the harbor, south of town center
Price: Inexpensive to Moderate
Credit Cards: Yes
Handicapped Access: Street-level access
Special Features: Cedar-pole construction,
breakfast included.

Potted plants and flowers brighten the
porch at this rustic 16-room lodge, overlooking Wrangell Harbor. Built by former
Wrangell mayor Bruce Harding, it has red
cedar-pole construction that adds to the
rustic, rough-hewn look. Most rooms are
small, but they have private baths, telephone, and high-speed Internet connection. One large family room will sleep six
people. The resort makes complimentary
shuttle pick-ups from the airport or the
ferry.

The lodge also packages the room and
meals with Stikine River jet-boat excursions, kayaking, rafting, golf at Wrangell's
Muskeg Meadows, or fishing.

Grand View Bed and Breakfast

Owner-Managers: John and Judy Baker
907-874-3225
grandviewbndb.com
2 Mile Zimovia Hwy., Wrangell, AK 99929
Two miles south of town
Price: Inexpensive to Moderate
Credit Cards: No; personal checks and cash,
only
Handicapped Access: No
Special Features: Hillside location overlooking Zimovia Straits.

A complimentary robe adds to the comfort
of this three-room, bed-and-breakfast inn.
Each room has a private entrance and bath,
queen bed, and use of a common area with
living room, kitchen, and dining room.

The owners, 50-year Alaska residents,
are known for their helpfulness in suggesting and arranging bookings for activities, as
well as cooking custom breakfasts. They
also offer courtesy transportation to and
from the airport or ferry terminal. The B&B
is south of town, about halfway to
Shoemaker Bay, with access to good hiking
and biking trails. Perched on a hillside, it
offers sweeping views of Zimovia Straits.

Rooney's Roost Bed & Breakfast

Owner-Managers: Gordon and Rebecca
Rooney
907-874-2026
rooneysroost.com
reservations@rooneysroost.com
206 McKinnon St., P.O. Box 552, Wrangell,
AK 99929
Downtown
Price: Inexpensive to Moderate
Credit Cards: Yes
Handicapped Access: No
Special Features: Graceful old house with
window boxes; antique-furnished rooms.

Staying at Rooney's Roost, now in the second generation of the Rooney family, is like
stepping back into early 20th-century
Alaska. Each of the six rooms in the two-
story house expresses a unique theme.
Cheerful, patterned fabrics brighten the
four-poster bed of the Provence Room. Sun
does indeed flood into the Sunshine Room,
which sits under the sloping roof on the

second floor, which has dormer windows. Some rooms have a harbor view.

Three rooms have a shared bath; private baths have a claw-foot soaking tub or shower. A full gourmet breakfast may feature Alaska berries or seafood, and is served in the dining room. Transportation to and from the ferry terminal and airport is available.

Stikine Inn
Owners: Bill and Cheryl Goodale
Manager: Jake Harris
907-874-3388 or 1-888-874-3388
stikineinn.com
info@stikineinnak.com
107 Front St., P.O. Box 662, Wrangell, AK 99929
On the Zimovia Straits waterfront
Price: Moderate
Credit Cards: Yes
Handicapped Access: One room
Special Features: Mountain or water views, one block from ferry terminal; nonsmoking.

Bill and Cheryl Goodale have gradually remodeled the 35-room Stikine Inn since they took over in 2006. A wine bar-lounge has been completed downstairs. Several rooms already are completed, in soft, neutral tans, browns, and greens.

The prime rooms are on the third floor and overlook the busy Wrangell Harbor and Zimovia Strait. It's fun to watch the fishing activity in the morning. Gill netters cozy up to a packing boat to drop their catch. The packer boat takes the catch to the cold-storage facilities. You will have to carry your bags up to the third floor to reach these rooms. The staircase was somewhat steep during my visit, though plans are underway to change and lengthen it.

There's nothing pretentious about this inn, but it is utterly comfortable and convenient. Everything in town is within walking distance. The Stikine Inn Restaurant on the premises serves breakfast, lunch, and dinner (See Chapter 6, *Restaurants and Food Purveyors*) and Alaska Waters off the lobby can book any sort of Stikine River or LeConte Glacier trip (See Chapter 7, *Recreation*).

Zimovia Bed & Breakfast
Owner-Managers: Barb and Mike Rugo
907-874-2626 or 1-866-946-6842
zimoviabnb.com
zimoviabnb@rgbwebs.com
319 Weber St., P.O. Box 1424, Wrangell, AK 99929
Near Reid St.
Price: Inexpensive
Credit Cards: Yes
Handicapped Access: No
Special Features: Garden setting near the center of town.

Although it's not far from the center of town, this brown-shingled house has an unusually quiet garden setting. Hand-crafted touches, such as fish-themed mosaic tiles in the bathrooms, and inlaid garnets in the floor, add to the character of the two-bedroom inn. Each room has a kitchenette, private entrance, and one even has a sauna.

Homemade breads are served for the continental breakfast, and van transport is offered to the ferry dock or airport, as well a town tour. The owners welcome children and pets. Satellite television and free wireless Internet allow guests to stay connected.

Fishing Lodges
Rain Haven
Owner-Manager: Marie Oboczky
907-874-2549
rainwalkerexpeditions.com
marieo@aptalaska.net
P.O. Box 2074, Wrangell, AK 99929
Wrangell Harbor or remote location
Price: Moderate.
Credit Cards: Yes

Special Features: Houseboat accommodation.

This may be among the most unique, and yet most appropriate Panhandle lodging. It's a houseboat that may be used right in Wrangell Harbor, or towed to more remote locations, giving access to wilderness trails and opportunities for kayaking or canoeing, or viewing the brown bears at Anan Creek.

Associated with Rainwalker Expeditions, which rents kayaks, canoes, and bikes, as well as planning custom expeditions, the houseboat boasts featherbeds, a library, and an enclosed solarium. A fully equipped galley and hot showers only add to the comfort. The houseboat sleeps five people on bunk beds.

Hostel

Wrangell Hostel: (907-874-3534; presby @aptalaska.net; 220 Church Street.). Alaska's oldest protestant church, the Wrangell First Presbyterian Church, houses the Wrangell Hostel, open June through August. Air mattresses are provided for sleeping, and kitchen facilities and showers are available. A private room and a family room are also available. There is no lock-out. You'll be keeping good company. John Muir stayed at the Wrangell Presbyterian Mission on his first trip to Alaska.

RV Parks

Alaska Waters RV Park: (907-874-2378 or 1-800-347-4462; alaskawaters.com; 241 Berger Street.) The Native-owned corporation also offers Stikine River wilderness tours, three-night safaris, and Petersburg–Le Conte Glacier day trips. The RV park is in a quiet wooded area on the south side of the harbor. The wooded site is level, and has a "hot spot" for free wireless Internet and full hookups. Complimentary shuttle to town.

Shoemaker Bay RV Park: (907-874-2444; parksrec@aptalaska.net; Shoemaker Bay

Recreation Area.) Located 5 miles south of town, the 16-unit, city-run site is open all year. All sites have picnic tables, electricity, and fireplaces, but no running water. A dump station, restrooms, and water spigot are located in an adjacent harbor parking area. Availability is on a first-come, first-served basis. No reservations.

SOUTHERN PANHANDLE

KETCHIKAN

Ketchikan is long and narrow, so hotels are widely scattered from one end of town to the other. The largest hotel is near the ferry dock, about 2 miles from downtown. A few cluster in the center, but others are at the far edges of town. Many of them have complimentary shuttle service, necessary for guest convenience.

Bed-and-breakfast inns and vacation rentals are even more widely scattered on Revillagigedo Island, though a few are in town. If you're going to stay in Ketchikan for even a few days, a rental car is recommended, and for several days it opens the possibility for more activities.

Some Ketchikan properties are entirely nonsmoking; others have smoking rooms.

Best Western Landing Hotel

General Manager: Linda Peters
907-225-5166 or 1-800-428-8304
landinghotel.com
info@landinghotel.com
3434 Tongass Ave., Ketchikan, AK 99901
Along waterfront across from ferry terminal and about 2 miles from downtown
Price: Expensive
Credit Cards: Yes
Handicapped Access: Several rooms, fully equipped
Special Features: Excellent location for ferry passengers; one building is nonsmoking.

Ketchikan's largest hotel stretches over two buildings across from the Alaska ferry dock. The 107 rooms range over various configurations, with queen rooms with one or two beds, king beds, and suites with separate sitting room. The North Court building is nonsmoking.

Creamy walls, warm-toned cherry wood, and bright floral bedspreads bring cheer to the rooms. Some of them have fireplaces and balconies overlooking Tongass Narrows.

Large desks with ergonomic chairs, high-speed Internet access, and meeting rooms meet business travelers' needs. A lobby gift shop adds to the citified facilities. The library with a fireplace is a good place to curl up on one of Ketchikan's rainy afternoons. The on-site laundry facilities are also welcome.

A complimentary shuttle whisks guests to downtown or the airport ferry, from early in the day through the evening. The Landing Restaurant and Jeremiah's Pub are on the property.

The Gilmore Hotel

Owner-Manager: Suzi Kimberley
907-225-9423 or 1-800-275-9423
gilmorehotel.com
info@gilmorehotel.com
326 Front St., Ketchikan, AK 99901
Across from the waterfront near Pioneer Alley
Price: Inexpensive
Credit Cards: Yes
Handicapped Access: No
Special Features: Historic boutique hotel.

Try to shut out the sight of multistory cruise ships, crowded sidewalks, and glutted streets, and this hotel will give you some idea of what a quieter Ketchikan looked like. It was built in 1927, and is on the National Register of Historic Places.

The boutique hotel has 38 rooms, many of which overlook Tongass Narrows. Warm earth tones dominate the décor of rooms, which tend to be compact. Queen beds with high-thread count, Egyptian-cotton sheets,

free wireless Internet access and local telephone calls, and flat-screen television are other amenities. Complimentary breakfast and van shuttle service are included.

Should you catch any fish in Ketchikan, you can store them in a hotel freezer until you're ready to go home. Even Ketchikan visitors who do not stay here are likely to find their way to the Gilmore Hotel for Annabelle's Keg and Chowder House, a popular restaurant.

The New York Hotel and the Inn at Creek Street

Owner-Manager: Renee McLaughlin
907-225-0246 or 1-866-225-0246
thenewyorkhotel.com
newyorkhotel@att.net
207 Stedman St., Ketchikan, AK 99901
Across from Thomas Basin harbor at Stedman and Creek streets
Price: Moderate
Credit Cards: Yes
Handicapped Access: No
Special Features: Rooms furnished with antiques; fully nonsmoking.

You'll look out to the small boat basin and the activity on Ketchikan's main street through lace curtains in this small, charming hotel. The 10-room inn has been taking in guests on this spot since 1924, though the business has existed since the early 1900s.

The niche on the second floor where the guest computer is housed was the former check-in window for the rooms. Oak antique dressers and armoires furnish the rooms and beds may have tufted comforters. Bathrooms look crisply redone and the amenities on the shelf—including cotton balls and Q-tips—are more than hotels in this price range usually offer. The reading lamps are also a welcome modern addition to the rooms.

The lobby was once an ice-cream parlor. The adjacent Ketchikan Coffee Company still serves refreshments, but now it's likely a latte and muffin, or soup. Vintage photos hang in the lobby, showing the hotel and family who owned it in the 1920s and 1930s.

The Inn at Creek Street, in a separate building, is the suite section of the hotel.

The street-side rooms are scenic, but traffic starts rolling early on this spot at the bridge at Creek Street.

Narrows Inn

Owner-Manager: Donna LaForce
907-247-2600 or 1-888-686-2600
narrowsinn.com
reservations@narrowsinn.com
4871 N. Tongass Ave., P.O. Box 8296, Ketchikan, AK 99901
Northwest of town, right on the water
Price: Moderate
Credit Cards: Yes
Handicapped Access: Two rooms
Special Features: Waterfront setting; complimentary breakfast.

Ask for a balcony room, for there is always something going on along Tongass Narrows. Float planes zip past like high-powered mosquitoes, the Alaska ferry slips toward its dock, and across the channel on Gravina Island, Alaska Airline jets land and take off. In quieter moments, herons and eagles may glide over the water, or orca or humpback whales may cavort in the narrows.

The 44-room gray-board inn at a small boat harbor looks at one with this place. Rooms have one or two double beds, with blond wood headboards and colorful spreads. The inn provides a complimentary shuttle to the airport ferry, or you can take a water taxi from the airport directly to the hotel landing. Shuttle service also connects the inn to the Alaska ferry, and to downtown Ketchikan.

The hotel will arrange fishing and flightseeing excursions, and provides a freezer for your catch. The Narrows Inn Restaurant, which is completely nonsmoking, is a homey place specializing in steaks and seafood. Inn guests have a complimentary continental breakfast here.

WestCoast Cape Fox Lodge

907-225-8001 or 1-800-325-4000;
westcoasthotels.com
capefoxsales@westcoasthotels.com
800 Venetia Way, Ketchikan, AK 99901
At the top of the funicular in the center of town
Price: Moderate
Credit Cards: Yes
Handicapped Access: Four rooms
Special Features: Funicular access to lobby; stunning Native artworks; totem poles on circular drive.

Even if you don't stay here, take the funicular up to the lobby to view the artworks. A cluster of totem poles out front and stunning lobby art greet visitors to this handsome hotel built and owned by the Cape Fox Native Corporation. Famed carver Nathan Jackson created the carved mural on the stair landing.

The hotel perches on a hillside above tall conifer trees with a view over the Ketchikan harbor. Almost every room has a view, and it's tempting to run to the window each time the buzz of a seaplane taking off from the harbor interrupts the quiet. Spacious rooms are done in warm-toned plaids and wood accents. Amenities include wireless Internet connection, dataport, Nintendo, and pay-per-view movies. A river-rock fireplace dominates the lobby, surrounded with comfy chairs that invite reading or snoozing.

The Heen Kahidi Restaurant serves breakfast, lunch, and dinner and also has a river-rock fireplace. This is one of Alaska's most beautiful hotels.

Bed-and-Breakfast Inns

KETCHIKAN

Ketchikan has more than a dozen B&Bs, which stretch out on the waterfront either north or south of town and to other parts of Revillagigedo Island. Almost every Ketchikan accommodation has a gorgeous view over the Tongass Narrows. An easy way to find them is with the following listings.

Ketchikan Reservation Service Bed & Breakfast Lodging: (907-247-5337 or 1-800-987-5337; ketchikan-lodging.com; 412-D Loop Rd., Ketchikan, AK 99901.) The service lists vacation rentals and bed-and-breakfast inns on all parts of Revillagigedo Island.

Captain's Quarters

Owner-Manager: Toni Bass
907-225-4912
ptialaska.net/~captbnb/
captbnb@ptialaska.net
325 Lund St., Ketchikan, AK 99901
Off Water St. near downtown
Price: Moderate
Credit Cards: Yes
Handicapped Access: No
Special Features: View and nautical décor, no pets or children.

This hillside home could indeed belong to a ship captain since it offers a sweeping view of town and the Ketchikan waterfront. Nautical touches appear throughout the three-unit inn, though in general, the rooms have a tidy, light look, with golden oak trim, pale walls, and pastel spreads. Rooms have queen beds, private bath, and cable television. One large room has a full kitchen.

A continental breakfast is served in a common room in this nonsmoking facility.

Eagle Heights Bed & Breakfast

Owner-Manager: Cherry Ferry
907-225-1760 or 1-800-928-3308 (booking agent)
eagleheightsbb.com
eagleheights@kupnet.net
1626 Water St., P.O. Box 9597, Ketchikan, AK 99901
Northwest of downtown
Price: Moderate
Credit Cards: Through booking agency
Handicapped Access: No
Special Features: Eagle viewing, spacious rooms, gold rush artifacts.

This hillside three-unit B&B is named for the concentration of eagles that gather nearby, in June and July. Built into the hillside, the building looks something like an eagle's aerie. Rooms are spacious, with soaring ceilings, lots of windows, and beams. Some rooms have lovely honeyed wood or cedar trim, and other special touches, such as a down couch. A downstairs room has a kitchenette, and an additional bed.

The inn even has its own museum. The Yukon Room, the common room where guests gather, contains artifacts from the Yukon Gold Rush, where the ancestors of the current owners staked claims at Dawson City and Ruby, Alaska.

Fishing Lodges

Ketchikan enjoys the moniker "Salmon Capital of the World," so several fishing lodges make their home here. Some of them are even accessible by road, though others need a float plane or boat connection to the airport.

Salmon Falls Resort

Owner-Managers: Paul Cyr and Chris Garman
907-225-2752 or 1-800-247-9059
salmonfallsresort.com
information@salmonfallsresort.com
P.O. Box 5700, 16707 N. Tongass Hwy., Ketchikan, AK 99901
About 20 miles northwest of Ketchikan on

North Tongass Hwy.
Price: Moderate to Expensive
Credit Cards: Yes
Handicapped Access: One room
Special Features: Architecturally spectacular log building; full-scale resort and fishing lodge.

Cabin cruisers, large jet boats, and skiffs line up at the Salmon Falls Resort dock. They indicate the variety of activities and fishing packages available at the fishing lodge and full-scale resort. The four-passenger cabin cruisers are for guided fishing, the jet boats for wildlife and historic-site excursions, and the skiffs for fishing on your own.

A fleet of vans and a bus are there for guests who would rather go into Ketchikan for a day of shopping. Salmon Falls is accessible by paved road, though once you turn in at the salmon-shaped mailbox and go down the steep drive you are as isolated as anywhere. (And the road stops just 2 miles farther on, at Settler's Cove.) The property sits on a steep hill overlooking Clover Pass and Betton Island and beside Second Creek, which drops into the channel in a roaring waterfall beside the dining room. Eagles spend a lot time around the creek mouth, and occasionally black bears stroll on the gravel beach. Come late summer, spawning salmon fill the creek mouth.

All salmon species lurk in these waters, as well as cod, sea bass, halibut, and red snapper. "The captain knows where the fish can be found, and some of our guests know where they want to fish," said co-owner and manager Paul Cyr. After you pull up to the dock with your catch, the staff takes over, cleaning, dressing, and packing the fish in containers for the trip home.

The bar-dining room area is a soaring log room, with a 270-degree view over the Clover Pass and an array of islands (See Chapter 6, *Restaurants and Food Purveyors*). Lodge rooms also have log walls, and Mission furniture. Otherwise, the arrangement is similar to hotel rooms.

Salmon Falls Resort is a spectacular log structure outside of Ketchikan.

Fishing boats await anglers at Salmon Falls Resort.

Packages are flexible. You can arrange for guided fishing, fishing on your own, or simply no fishing at all.

Silverking Lodge
Managing Partners: Kirk and Pam Thomas
Radiophone. To contact, call: The Cedars,
907-225-1900
silverkingalaska.com
info@silverkingalaska.com
P.O. Box 8331, Ketchikan, AK 99901
20 miles from Ketchikan
Price: Inexpensive to Moderate
Credit Cards: Yes
Handicapped Access: No
Special Features: Unguided fishing, rustic cabins

At the end of the day, it's pleasant to sit around the picnic table on the deck and trade fish stories at Silverking Lodge. Guests also gather in a spacious common area over board games or to watch satellite television. Knotty pine finishes off the walls in rooms with two twin beds, and private bath with a shower.

During May and June the lodge is available for family reunions or corporate retreats.

The lodge provides 14-foot, two-person outboard open boats for unguided fishing. Penn 209 levelwind reels are used with 6-foot, 6-inch combination rods. Rain gear is provided, as well as professional processing of fish. Transportation to Ketchikan Airport, about 20 miles away, is by float plane or boat.

Hostels

Eagleview Hostel: (907-225-5461; eagle-viewhostel.com; 2303 Fifth Avenue.) The hostel is open April through October. Sheets and pillowcases are provided for beds; sleeping bags are prohibited. Shelf space is provided for guests' food. Free coffee and tea.

Ketchikan Youth Hostel: (907-225-3319; ktnyh@eagle.ptialaska.net; 400 Main Street.) Open June through August, the hostel is affiliated with Hostelling International. Dormitory beds for nineteen. Lock-out during the day. No credit cards.

RV Parks

Clover Pass Resort and RV Park: (907-247-2234 or 1-800-410-2234; cloverpass resort.com; P.O. Box 7322, Ketchikan, AK 99901.) A 35-space RV park, with full hookups, coin-operated laundry, and showers. Guided and self-guided fishing available with skiff rentals from the resort, or mooring space for your own boat. The facility also has a 36-room motel. Located 15 miles north of Ketchikan on Clover Pass waterway.

METLAKATLA
In spite of its isolation, Metlakatla has overnight lodging.

Metlakatla Inn and Restaurant
Owners: Edith and Dale Olin
907-886-3456
metlakatlainn.com
Third and Lower Milton Street, Metlakatla, AK 99926
Price: Inexpensive
Credit Cards: Yes
Handicapped Access: No
Special Features: Attractive, cozy, board building with paned windows.

Two distinctive totem poles support the roof at the entrance to this cozy-looking inn, the only full-service hotel in Metlakatla. Curtains hang on paned windows in the lobby, and Tsimshian artwork and paintings are displayed in public areas.

Each room has a private bath with granite and marble counters, and most rooms have flat-screen televisions. DVD movies are available at the hotel as well as cable television and wireless Internet. Rooms have a microwave and fridge, and the hotel restaurant also serves meals.

Like other Alaska inns in isolated places, the inn has rental cars. They will also provide van service from the ferry or float plane docks.

PRINCE OF WALES ISLAND
Few lodgings on Prince of Wales Island (POW) are open year-round, unless otherwise indicated. Fishing, fishing, and more fishing are the reason most people come, though most of the fishing lodges will also arrange nonangling activities.

Fishing Resorts

Fireweed Lodge
Owner-Manager: Bob Anderson
907-755-2930; Oct.–March, 206-910-7702
fireweedlodge.com
fireweedlo@aol.com
P.O. Box 166, Klawock, AK 99925
Hollis Highway, at Jody's Seafoods
Price: Moderate to Expensive
Credit Cards: Yes
Handicapped Access: Some ramps on ground floor
Special Features: Homey atmosphere, lovely setting.

The lobby at Fireweed Lodge looks like someone's living room, with comfortable leather couches, wide-screen television, a big rock fireplace, and dogs stretched out on the floor. Soaring two-story windows look out at the Klawock River widening to an estuary. The clue that the room might be a lodge comes with the piles of logo-wear shirts on tables, and the taxidermied salmon, bear, king crab, and deer on the wall. The lobby is a good place to spot bear on the beach across the water, and river otters on the dock.

Bob Anderson has owned the lodge since 1990 and gradually added rooms, including the most recent, six suites in a small complex of buildings in addition to 12 rooms. Many units look out to the same waterfront view as the lobby, and are pro-

Fireweed Lodge on Prince of Wales Island has the comforts of home and world-class fishing.

vided with television and telephones. Anderson has also added a basketball and horseshoe courts, hot-tub room, fitness and sauna and recreation room, and a card and conference room.

Guided fishing in the resort's 10 boats offers numerous opportunities in both fresh and salt water, in a season that extends from April for steelhead to early summer for king salmon, coho, and rock-fish, to October. Halibut are caught at any time of the year.

Reservations will be taken for nonfish-ing guests if rooms are available. The resort serves three meals (See Chapter 6, *Restaurants and Food Purveyors*) and guests dine well.

Fishing Bear B and B
Owner-Manager: Rob Shaw
907-329-2924 May–Sept.
fishingbearbandb.com
fishingbear lodge@q.com
P.O. Box 18123, Coffman Cove, AK 99818

Price: Moderate
Credit Cards: Yes
Handicapped Access: Grab bars and seat in shower
Special Features: Remote location, spacious units.

Most people want to put a toe in the wilder-ness, but not really be in the wilderness, says Rob Shaw, the owner of Fishing Bear B and B. You're certainly at the edge of the wilderness in tiny Coffman Cove, but you enjoy comforts at the homey, tiny fishing lodge. One of the three units has three bed-rooms, sleeping six to eight, and is fur-nished in L.L. Bean style, with plaid blankets and flannel sheets. Shaw rents skiffs, or he will arrange for a local charter for guided fishing.

Most people who come here do their own cooking in a well-equipped kitchen. But you must pick up your groceries in Thorne Bay, where most guests arrive by float plane from Ketchikan. Coffman Cove has no grocery store or restaurant. The tiny bait shop sells a few canned things. Shaw will also arrange for his neighbor to cook your dinner, from a menu featuring shrimp and chicken baskets, onions rings, and French fries.

In the evening, it's pleasant to sit on the deck in the long twilight. Except for the occasional crunch of tires on the gravel road, it's utterly silent. You'll be able to hear your own breathing.

Coffman Cove is a good location for access to different fishing grounds, and for the Interisland Ferry Northern Route, which connects to Wrangell and Petersburg on weekends, May through September. It takes about an hour to drive from Klawock to Coffman Cove.

Shelter Cove

Managers: Traci McIntire and David Creighton
907-826-2939 or 1-888-826-3474 (FISH)
sheltercovelodge.com
shelterc@aptalaska.net
703 Hamilton Drive, P.O. Box 798, Craig, AK 99921
One half mile from Craig
Price: Moderate to Expensive
Credit Cards: Yes
Handicapped Access: One room
Special Features: Waterfront setting on Bucareli Bay; open year-round.

Fishing packages dominate the June through August season, though the waterfront lodge is open year-round. A fleet of seven boats serves the ten-room lodge; most people choose a four-day package, with three full days of fishing, and meals included. Guides, gear, and proper clothing are supplied for all fishing boats. The location gives access to hundreds of miles of water on the western side of POW for world-class fishing. Nearby streams give anglers the chance for freshwater fish as well. After the catch is landed, the staff,

which is almost at the ratio of one-to-one, cleans the fish, cuts it to order, and vacuum packs and flash-freezes it for shipping home.

Rooms are comfortable, with two beds, television, and Internet connections. Massive stone fireplaces attract guests in the lodge common room and lounge. After the fishing season has ended, the lodge functions as a regular hotel.

Waterfall Resort

General Manager: Steve Cockrell
907-225-9461 or 1-800-544-5125
waterfallresort.com
wfreservations@kpunet.net
Resort: Prince of Wales Island; sales office: 320 Dock St., #222, Ketchikan, AK 99901
Accessible by float plane
Price: Very expensive
Credit Cards: Yes
Handicapped Access: No
Special Features: Former cannery; large, luxury fishing resort.

Once Southeast Alaska's largest salmon-processing plant, Waterfall Resort today boasts luxury amenities for 92 guests, and state-of-the-art fishing boats and equipment. The building's exterior still bears the spare look of a cannery, but the lodge rooms and cabins are spacious and comfortable, the cocktails are cold, and the food, gourmet. This is the swankiest fishing lodge on Prince of Wales.

Staff members greet guests the moment they arrive. At a one-to-one ratio, guests' needs are quickly met; everyone is assigned a guide. Fishing is done from 25-foot Almar cruisers, with heated cabins, air-suspension seats, and advanced marine electronics. At trip's end, the fish are cleaned, frozen, and packed in wet-lock fish boxes for travel. An Alaska Airlines representative at the resort serves as departure check-in agent.

Located on the west side of Prince of Wales Island, Waterfall Resort attracts

Weddings

Destination weddings in tropical places have gained a great following over the past decade or two. But Alaska weddings, even a wedding on a glacier, are also growing in popularity, especially among those who love adventure and the out-of-doors. Another option is a rainforest wedding

Diane Pearson, a certified wedding planner and owner of **Pearson's Pond Luxury Inn and Spa** (907-789-3772; juneau-guide.com) in Juneau, will plan a wedding, from a simple ceremony in the inn garden to a full-blown event. She specializes in glacier weddings, arranging for the bride, groom, and wedding party to be whisked to a spot on Mendenhall Glacier in a helicopter. She's thoroughly familiar with the glacier and knows how to choose the most spectacular and private spots.

Like wedding planners everywhere, Pearson takes care of every detail, from transportation to customized ceremony, flowers, witnesses, photographer, cake, champagne, and honeymoon plans. Or she arranges for couples making a single-day stop on a cruise ship to be married in a splendid Juneau setting.

anglers for its legendary fishing grounds teeming with salmon, halibut, red snapper, and lingcod. The resort sponsors the King of Kings Salmon Tournament during the season. Catching record-setting salmon here happens with some frequency.

Hotels

Ruth Ann's Hotel
Owner-Manager: Ruth Ann Parsons
907-826-3378
ruthanns@aptalaska.net
300 Front St., Craig, AK 99921
Price: Inexpensive
Credit Cards: Yes
Handicapped Access: No; two ground-level rooms available
Special Features: Individual character to rooms, some kitchenettes.

You'll check into the hotel on one side of the street, in the building with flower boxes and porches that houses Ruth Ann's Restaurant. The hotel is across the way, and up the hill a bit, and is a more bare-bones building. The complex has been here since 1976 and is something of an institution in Craig. Everyone who comes to Prince of Wales Island eventually passes through here.

Inside, the rooms have individual furnishings. Quilts on the brass beds, and other touches look as if they'd be at home in the frilly restaurant across the way. All rooms have private baths, and four of them have kitchenettes as well. A few have private balconies with waterfront views. People arranging fishing charters often stay at the 17-room hotel. It's open year-round, except January.

4

CULTURE

What to Do in Town

Cultural activities—at least the kinds of things usually done inside—capture less visitor attention than Alaska's great outdoors. But often museums or performances bring richer meaning to outside activities.

Visual arts dominate the cultural scene of the Alaska Panhandle, with the powerful, rhythmic totem images of Tlingit, Haida, and Tsimshian people. Those groups are part of Northwest Coast people, stretching from British Columbia through the Panhandle. Every public space in the Alaska Panhandle, it seems, is graced with a totem pole, carved wall panel, or a spectacular mask. Galleries carry prints and silver jewelry in those designs, and imitations fill gift shops; even the Alaska Airlines beverage napkin has a Raven-and-Eagle design. Museums often interpret these symbols as well and have some good examples of totem poles. (See Chapter 5, *Alaska Native People,* for totem parks.)

Plays and concerts are performed in most towns, but these generally take place during the winter and are aimed at locals. The hometown folks often perform in these things as well; they're fun, and they offer insight into the bootstrap lifestyle. Alaska Native dance (See Chapter 5) and some ethnic dances are aimed at visitors.

Historic sites and excellent historical museums cover Alaska's precontact period and its days as Russian America, and look at the impact of fishing, mining, and lumbering economies on the life of the people and the place. If you can take your eyes off the gorgeous scenery, or time away from fishing, hiking, or other outdoor activity, here are some alternatives.

ARTS CENTERS AND MUSEUMS

|JUNEAU
As might be expected, the state capital is also Alaska's cultural capital.

Juneau Arts & Culture Center
907-586-2787 (ARTS)
jahc.org
350 Whittier St., Juneau, AK 99801
Open: Gallery, Mon.–Fri., and Sat. afternoons; performing space for events
Admission: None for gallery

The former Juneau Armory has been reborn as an arts-and-culture center, run by the Juneau Arts and Humanities Council. The spacious gallery meanders in small rooms outside the large open room that was once a gym and is now a performance and event space.

The gallery exhibition program changes monthly and focuses on artists from Juneau and other parts of Alaska. Openings are held in the early evening, on the first Friday of the month, a program embraced by several Juneau art galleries. Watch for the special logo flags to see who's open.

Exhibits at the Juneau Arts & Culture Center may be photographs and paintings of Alaska's remote and beautiful places, such as Mihael Blikshteyn's photographs of coastal scenes, and Alexis Rippe's abstract, vivid, oil paintings.

Be sure to look into the large room used for events and performances. The Northwest Coast wall paintings have a poignant origin. The building was used as a morgue after an Alaska Airlines crash in the early 1970s. Afterward, Ivan James painted the designs as a memorial to the people who perished.

Haines
Alaska Indian Arts
907-766-2160
alaskaindianarts.com
Building No. 13, Fort Seward Drive, P.O. Box 271, Haines, AK 99827
Open: Mon.–Fri.
Admission: Free
Gift shop

The revival of an art form that was almost lost has taken place over the last 50 years, in one of the Fort Seward's spacious white buildings, the former fort hospital. Here, master

Carvers at Alaska Indian Arts in Haines created these masks.

Tlingit carvers train other apprentice carvers in the art of making knives, bentwood boxes, halibut hooks, and totem poles. Started more than 50 years ago by Carl Heinmiller, to revive traditional carving skills among Tlingit youths, Alaska Indian Arts today is led by his son, Lee Heinmiller. Commissioned totem poles made here are found around the world. During summer 2008, carvers were at work on a 35-foot totem pole that barely fit into the workroom.

Carvers are almost always at work at the facility. Some of the Tlingit imagery is translated to prints, which are sold at the center. Proceeds from them help support the program. Elegant silver bracelets by Greg Horner, who has a studio in the building, are also available.

Some of the artists combine carved cedar with glass or create glass sculpture in Tlingit figures. A totem pole created in Haines, with elements of glass, was erected at Pilchuck Glass School near Seattle. Among its images is one of Pilchuck star artist, Dale Chihuly.

Art Galleries

Art galleries fill more storefronts in Juneau, Ketchikan, and Sitka than any other type of shop or service. Most of their artworks are done in the curved, interlinking forms of the Tlingit, Haida, and Tsimshian people. But not all are created by Alaska Natives. Many artists have embraced the style. Watch for the "Alaska Native" tag with an open hand and name identity tag.

Galleries have artworks by other Alaska Natives: whalebone, baleen baskets, masks, and ivory carvings by Yup'ik and Inupiat Eskimos, tiny, printed baskets from Aleuts, and additional carvings from Athabascan groups.

The distinction between art gallery and gift shop often traces a narrow line. Art galleries, listed in this chapter, focus on one-of-a-kind work by artists and artisans. They are usually carvings, prints, paintings, handcrafted jewelry, beading, and weavings. Gift shops may have unique items, but they fall into the realm of functional or decorative objects, such as tote bags, coffee mugs, or notecards. (See *Shopping* chapter.)

The quality of the artwork varies greatly, but much of it is excellent. The price surges from one extreme to the other. In general, things seen in the cities near the cruise ship docks are the most expensive. Those in Native villages or smaller places, less so. Remember, too, that shops at art centers and museums (covered in other sections in this chapter) offer high-quality artworks.

Juneau galleries tend to be open year-round; galleries in other towns are often closed in winter, though hours are unpredictable.

NORTHERN PANHANDLE

JUNEAU

Juneau galleries and shops stretch from the cruise ship docks up South Franklin and its cross streets, to the clock corner in historic downtown. Northwest Coast and Eskimo art is the strong suit, though you'll find oil paintings and contemporary sculpture.

A well-worn path leads from the dock to these galleries, which are jammed when four ships are in town. If you're spending the night in Juneau, better to wait until late in the day when the crowds have returned to dinner and dancing.

The quality of the Alaska Native art rates high in Juneau galleries, perhaps exceeding Anchorage and often matching Vancouver, which has spectacular galleries. In Vancouver, where indigenous people are called First Nation, works come largely from Kwakiutl and Haida groups. In Alaska, works come largely from Tlingit people, though Haida and Tsimshian are certainly represented. The iconography is similar, though the use of color varies.

Gallery of the North: (907-586-9700; alaskangallery.com; 147 S. Franklin Street.) The gallery seems to focus on wall-hung works more than other Franklin Street galleries, though it also has carvings and carpets featuring Northwest Coast designs. One unusual item was a canoe paddle shaped like a halibut. The gallery also has watercolors and prints by Barbara Lavallee, a popular artist who works in the same cheerful folk art style as Rie Muñoz.

Juneau Artists Gallery: (907-586-9891; juneauartistsgallery.com; 175 S. Franklin Street, Suite 111 inside the Senate Mall.) This cooperative gallery features work by about 30 Juneau artists. The array ranges from Ukrainian pysanky eggs—and they range from quail to ostrich eggs—to prints, art glass framed mirrors, watercolors, photography, ceramics, and jewelry. Prices range widely, too—from less than $20 to several hundred dollars. Gallery artists serve as salespeople, so someone will always be on hand to chat about the work or about Juneau.

Raven's Journey Gallery: (907-463-4686; ravensjourneygallery.com; 435 S. Franklin Street.) If you've come on a cruise ship, this bright yellow building across the street from the dock is likely the first place you will see. The selection inside is museum quality, and the gallery will educate you about Northwest Coast and Arctic art, with pieces that cut a wide swath across these cultures. Walrus ivory carving, totem poles and masks, totemic jewelry, baleen baskets, and marine-mammal bone figures are here. The works set a high standard for Alaska Native art.

Johnny Ellis, who grew up in Juneau, owns the gallery with his wife Kathy. As a boy he was fascinated with Alaska Native art and objects in the Territorial Museum. After stints in the Navy and construction work, he started to make fossil ivory jewelry. In 1991, he opened the gallery, which still features his bracelets and pendant earrings embellished with abalone shell.

Alaska Ivory

Panhandle galleries and museum shops have many ivory objects. Only Alaska Natives can hunt for walrus and seals and carve the tusks. An array of complicated federal and state laws regulates harvesting of ivory from dead animals or fossilized ivory on beaches. Most ivory carvings and jewelry come from fossilized ivory collected by Alaska Natives in the Arctic. Non-natives may use it for artworks.

Rie Muñoz

Once you've seen a Rie Muñoz watercolor or print, you'll forever recognize her images. They might show parka and mukluk-clad children, playing games or picking berries in a snowy coastal landscape. Each shape is rendered in simple form, in clear color patches, with pleasing rounded lines. Humor often enters the scene, such as children playing hopscotch on ice floes, or hints of surrealism reminiscent of Chagall in works inspired by folklore and legends. She describes the work as "expressionism." By any name, it will make you smile.

A spectacular totem pole by Tsimshian carver Heber Reece dominates a corner at Raven's Journey Gallery in Juneau.

A stained glass panel based on a Rie Muñoz image hangs in her Juneau gallery.

Children playing games are not always her subjects; sometimes she shows people at work, crabbing or fishing. But the style is consistent, and carries across the artworks. You will find her paintings and prints throughout Alaska and the Lower 48, though her own **Rie Muñoz Gallery** (907-789-7449; riemunoz.com; 2101 N. Jordan Avenue) in Juneau's Mendenhall Loop neighborhood and **Decker Gallery** (907-463-5536; 233 S. Franklin Street) have the widest selection in Juneau. Now well into her 80s, she produces thirty-eighty watercolors per year, and selects six to twelve of those for limited-edition prints.

She adopted Alaska in 1951 because she loved it, and has lived in the state ever since, currently residing in Juneau. She has lived in many remote coastal communities, including King Island, a 13-hour umiak ride from Nome. She taught Eskimo children on King Island, the beginning of her inspiration.

Most things at the Raven's Journey come from others. They are beautifully displayed, with full documentation of the artwork and the artist. A sign reads: ARTWORK HONORING ALASKA'S FIRST PEOPLE.

GUSTAVUS

Fireweed Gallery: (907-697-3005; fireweed@gustavus.ak.us; Gustavus and Wilson roads.) You may find Jim Healey with white paint on his hands from priming his salmon wall plaques, which also hang on the gallery walls. An eclectic assortment by Alaska artists ranges from exquisite small masks to bold woodblock prints, beaded serving spoons, and silver jewelry. And, should you need something sweet, Jim or anyone else there will scoop up some homemade ice cream.

HAINES

Haines has attracted a number of artists from the Lower 48 who, along with the native Tlingit carvers, have created an arts colony.

Catotti and Goldberg Art Studio: (907-766-2707; artstudioalaska.com; 6.5 Mile Mud Bay Road.) offers paintings, silkscreen prints, and giclée prints of the paintings. Several artists live along Mud Bay Road. Open by appointment.

Chilkat Valley Arts: (907-766-3230; www.chilkatvalleyarts.com; 209 Willard Street.) Debi Knight Kennedy is among Haines artists showing at this gallery, antique shop, and bead-supply store (See Chapter 8, *Shopping*).

Artist Jim Healey often works at his Fireweed Gallery in Gustavus.

Extreme Dreams Fine Arts and Crafts: (907-766-2097; extremedreams.com; 6.5 Mile Mud Bay Road.) It's worth the trip to see the tall timber building here, erected by the artists, John and Sharon Svenson. It houses the gallery showing paintings, fused and slumped glass objects, art glass beads, and prints. Open by appointment.

Sculpture by Judd: (Fifth Avenue and Union.) You can't miss the sculptures by the artist who goes by the name Judd. A large eagle stands out front at Captain's Choice Motel, and another is at the Trading Post Shop. The artist also has an outdoor garden at his studio, along with a small shop.

Sea Wolf Gallery: (907-766-2558; tresham.com; Fort Seward Parade Grounds.) Tresham Gregg, whose parents were among the Fort Seward founders, shows dreamlike images of animals, birds, and human forms, in the graceful curves inspired by Tlingit design. Carved masks, silver jewelry, prints, shamanistic charms, and wall plaques are among artworks. Gift items include inexpensive birch brooches. His studio is nearby, so you may catch him here. He also has work at **Whale Rider Gallery** (907-255-2540; 16 Portage Street in Fort Seward), which features handmade jackets by Annette Smith, and at **Uniquely Alaskan Arts** (907-766-3525, 201 Willard Street). This gallery covers a wide range of things, including "goddess" T-shirts, clothing, and spirit figure dolls.

SKAGWAY

Lynch and Kennedy: (907-983-3034; lynch-kennedy.com; 350 Broadway.) An eclectic assortment ranges from very large totemic rugs to gold-nugget jewelry. Sculpture leans to wildlife art genre; prints by Aleut artists.

Skagway Artworks: (907-983-3443; skagwayartworks.com; 555 Broadway.) Work by 12 Skagway artists jams this gallery, where owner Tina Cyr greets browsers as if they've come to her home. She does watercolors and beaded jewelry and her husband Ralf Gorichanaz carves fossil ivory in sinuous shapes, and casts some of the work in silver.

CENTRAL PANHANDLE

PETERSBURG

Petersburg has several attractive shops, but not true galleries. However, it does have public artworks throughout town. The Petersburg Arts Council has published a pamphlet for a self-guided walking tour of public art, available at the Visitor Information Center, First and Fram streets.

SITKA

Some of Sitka's most interesting artwork is found in the shops at the Sitka National Historical Park (See Chapter 7, *Recreation*), the Sheldon Jackson Museum and Cultural Center (See *History and Culture Museums and Parks* section), and the Made in Sitka Gift Shop in the community house where Naa Kahídi dancers perform (See *Alaska Native People* chapter).

Artist Cove Gallery: (907-747-6990; artistcovegallery.com; 241 Lincoln Street.) Weavings, carvings, and jewelry come from Inupiat and Northwest Coast artists, and oil paintings and prints, from Sitka-area artists. Works range from elaborate sculptures and bentwood boxes to charming pendants of spruce-root baskets filled with "berries."

Cathleen Cass Pook's fine beadwork may be found at several Sitka galleries, including Devilfish and Sitka Rose, and shops at the Sheldon Jackson Museum and the Southeast Alaska Indian Cultural Center.

Devilfish Gallery: (907-747-5656; nicholasgalanin.com; 315 Lincoln Street.) The gallery shows the work of Tlingit artists Nicholas Galanin and Tommy Joseph, as well as others. Much of it is contemporary, including Galanin's carved masks made from hundreds of sheets of stacked paper. Some of Joseph's carved pieces have been cast into bronze.

Fishermen's Eye Gallery: (907-747-5502; fishermenseye.com; 239 Lincoln Street.) Sitka artists created most of the paintings, photographs, and sculpture in this gallery, a long-time fixture in town.

Sitka Rose: (907-747-3030 or 1-888-236-1536; sitkarosegallery.com; 419 Lincoln Street.) The gallery is worth a visit just to get inside the 1895 Hanlon-Osbakken house, which is on the National Register of Historic Places. Willis Osbakken, one of the artists, was born in the house. His beautiful carved alder bowls are among other Alaska Native art, paintings, and sculpture of exception quality.

SOUTHERN PANHANDLE

KETCHIKAN

Mission Street has several interesting art galleries among Ketchikan's many shops. Don't forget **Saxman Totem Village** (see *Alaska Native People* chapter) for hand-carved work from native craftsmen.

Alaska Eagle Arts Gallery: (907-225-8365; alaskaeaglearts.com; 5 Creek Street.) The gallery showcases Marvin Oliver, whose modern interpretation of Northwest Coast design appears in glass, carvings, sculpture, and prints, as well as in Pendleton blankets, denim jackets, and notecards.

Arctic Spirit Gallery: (907-225-6626; arcticgallery.com; 310 Mission Street.) Artworks here tend to be big and bold, and they're shown to maximum effect, hanging from the wall or standing widely spaced on the floor. Carvings and masks are from the Alaska North, as well as Northwest Coast totems and other artworks.

Crazy Wolf Studio: (907-225-9653; crazywolfstudio.com; 607 Mission Street.) Masks, canoe paddles, drums, plaques, and prints cover the walls of this store. Baleen and spruce baskets, silver bracelets, and dance rattles fill cases. Seek out the work of owner Ken Decker, a Tsimshian, who works in almost all genres. He designed the raven-eagle "love birds" on the Alaska Airlines napkin.

Ketchikan's Carver at the Creek: (907-225-3018; normanjackson.com; 28 Creek Street.) Tlingit artist Norman Jackson is often at work carving in the gallery devoted to his work. He displays silver bracelets, bentwood boxes, and silkscreen prints. The work is a little more elemental and powerful than some Tlingit images.

Mainstay Gallery: (907-225-2211; ketchikanarts.org; 716 Totem Way.) This is Ketchikan's community art gallery, where local work is showcased. Often by emerging artists, it may be outside of the mainstream or quirky—such as decorated vending machines, or wearable art.

METLAKATLA

Metlakatla Artists Village: (907-886-7491; metlakatla.com; 34 Western Avenue.) Studio-galleries are in the building next to the Long House. Generally open on summer after-noons when dance performances are held, the studios are gallery-work spaces. Lindarae Shearer shows beaded necklaces and earrings, as well as plaited and twined red and yellow cedar baskets.

DANCE AND MUSICAL THEATER

NORTHERN PANHANDLE

HAINES

Chilkat Dancers Storytelling Theater: (907-766-2540; tresham.com/show; Totem Village Tribal House, Fort Seward Parade Grounds.) Actors and dancers bring Tlingit legends to life with carved masks, elaborate costumes, and dialogue in this dance-theater production. Haines artist-performer Tresham Gregg has created and directs the performances. Late afternoon and early evening performances in summer. $12.

Troll's Drollery

Ray Troll's Soho Coho (907-225-5954; trollart.com; 5 Creek Street) doesn't quite fit one-of-a-kind criteria for art galleries in this section, since his artwork is largely screened onto T-shirts, or appears on coffee mugs, cards, or Raven's Brew coffee packages. But his humor certainly is one-of-a-kind, and he translates it with such skill that he's certainly an artist.

His images run to visual and verbal puns about the Alaska experience, and almost always use fish, usually salmon, as the central subject. The salmon are anatomically correct. You can even tell whether it's a sockeye or a humpy. He renders them in a cartoon-like, vaguely rock-poster style. He "frames" the central motif on the wearer's chest with a title above it or even surrounding the image. *Spawn Till You Die* may be his most famous. A skull hovers above "crossbones," which are actually sockeye salmon. *Archfishop* has a fish wearing a mitre and robes and holding a scepter, in a church setting that includes stained glass. Another spoofs Grateful Dead shirts. It's tie-dyed and bears a skull, a frequent motif, and the title, "The Baitful Dead."

Troll shows his considerable skill as a wildlife artist in some images of a kingfisher and other birds, and another of the forest. The Academy of Natural Sciences awarded him a Gold Medal for Distinction in Natural History Art in 2007, along with John McPhee and Ansel Adams. At times, the images have a surreal beauty, such as a trilobite floating in a starry sky. If you want to buy Troll T-shirts, you pretty much have to do it in Ketchikan, or order them from the Ray Troll Web site. The cards and coffee packages appear elsewhere, but Soho Coho, which Troll owns with his wife, is the best place to find the full array. The gallery features work by a few other artists, including some attractive trivets crafted from salvaged metal.

He's also a musician and composer, and the lead guitarist and vocalist for a garage band, the Ratfish Wranglers. He's probably Ketchikan's most famous citizen.

Two of Ray Troll's best-known designs

HOONAH
Native Heritage Center Theater: (See Chapter 5, *Alaska Native People.*)

SKAGWAY
The Days of '98 Show: (907-983-2545; thedaysof98show.com; 6th and Broadway in the F.O.E. Hall.) When you hear the rinky-dink tunes coming out of the flag-bedecked F.O.E. Hall, it's not an imaginary figment of the past. Since 1925, the people of Skagway have put on "The Days of '98 Show" for visitors. Dubbed the longest-running show in the north, it celebrates the last days of Soapy Smith, with a cast of gamblers, thieves, and dance hall girls. The show started with local people acting and dancing the parts, but professional actors now fill the roles.

It traces some of the mayhem caused by the character who tried to pass himself off as a model citizen, including leading the July 4th parade just four days before Frank Reid shot him down. Music, dance, lots of flash and brass. $20.

SITKA
Naa Kahídi Dancers: (See Chapter 5, *Alaska Native People.*)

New Archangel Dancers: (907-747-5516; newarchangeldancers.com; Harrigan Centennial Hall, Harbor Drive.) These energetic dancers perform three or four times daily during the summer. Couples perform the spirited dances of Russia, Belarus, Moldavia, and Ukraine. The Cossacks kick in deep knee bends, and leap into splits. Look hard; only women perform in the 40-member troupe. Not one of them is Russian; not one is a professional. But they look convincing. Fee is $8, cash only.

Don't miss the New Archangel Dancers in Sitka.

HISTORY AND CULTURE
MUSEUMS AND PARKS

The splendid Alaska State Museum in Juneau interprets the state's human history perhaps better than anything else in the state. Museums in smaller communities are important, too, because they define the history and culture of those places. When you get home, sometimes the photos of the crowded harbors of Sitka, Petersburg, and Wrangell begin to all look alike. The vintage photos and objects in a museum document their distinctiveness and help set it in your mind.

Even the façade of the Alaska State Museum in Juneau suggests Northwest Coast integrated designs.

In Alaska it's difficult to separate museums of history and culture from the art museums, because Alaska Native people express their culture through art. Totem poles in museums illustrate the lives and stories of the people who made them. When they stand alone as an aesthetic object, they're likely to be in an art museum, covered in the section above.

These museums cover the story of Alaska people, from the Native groups, through explorers, Russians, the English, and finally Americans.

NORTHERN PANHANDLE
JUNEAU
Alaska State Museum
907-465-2901
museums.state.ak.us
395 Whittier St., Juneau, AK 99801
Open: Daily, mid-May–late Sept.; Tues.–Sat., late Sept.–mid-May
Admission: Adults, $5 summer, $3 winter; age 18 and under, free
Gift shop

Even the architecture of the Alaska State Museum fits its contents: A subtle relief in Northwest Coast designs covers its outer wall. Just inside on the first level, signage, objects, and an excellent relief map give an orientation to the state. The museum covers both the cultural and historical background of the state's people and the events that directed their lives.

The first level focuses on Native Alaskans and has sections devoted to each group: Aleuts, Athabaskans, Eskimos, and Northwest Coast Indians. Especially stunning are the dazzling Thunderbird screen from Yakutat, and the Wolf House posts from Sitka. Photographs complement objects to give a context to the originals.

The adaptations of Aleut, Yupik, and Inupiat Arctic dwellers amaze visitors from kinder climates. They used animal gut for clothing and boots. Some of the objects, such as the Aleut baskets and slender, beaded Athabascan moccasins are exceedingly refined.

The second floor covers the Russian period and the history of American development, including the U.S. purchase and development of its natural resources—fishing, timber, mining, and oil. Perhaps the most interesting aspect is what's in between the floors. To get from the first to the second, you ascend a ramp that spirals around a tree outfitted with a display of a huge bald-eagle nest, large enough to be the size of a settler's cabin.

Every inch of the museum is used to portray Alaska's past, and its rich cultural heritage. Among the more memorable things are the ivory gavel that opened the first Alaska Territorial Legislature, a Fresnel lens, and a huge samovar from the Russian era.

The excellent gift shop reflects the museum mission, with a wide assortments of books and DVDs, beautiful masks, jewelry, and wall plaques made by Alaska Natives, Russian nesting dolls, and inexpensive Athabascan birchbark baskets. There is also a branch store downtown.

Juneau–Douglas City Museum
907-586-3572
juneau.org/parksrec/museum
Fourth and Main streets, Juneau, AK 99801
Open: Daily in summer; Tues.–Sat. Oct. 1–April 30
Admission: Summer, $4; free in winter
Gift shop

The huge relief map just inside the entrance to the Juneau–Douglas City Museum attracts visitors before they even move on to the other exhibits. It reinforces Juneau's dramatic topography, of a city clinging to mountains that plunge into a narrow sea channel.

A timeline and objects in one wing of the museum relate to the Tlingit people who lived along Gastineau Channel before contact. A 9-foot basket fish trap, discovered a few miles away on Montana Creek, is truly impressive, both for its size and age. Dated to 500–700 years old by radiocarbon dating techniques, it survived the centuries since it was preserved in mud. The museum also has an excellent video and numerous objects and vintage photographs that tell about Juneau's origins as a gold-mining site, and the role that gold played in the town's development in the heyday of the Treadwell and A J Mines.

Before you leave, look up. The large painting depicts what appears to be Venice, though instead of gondolas, Northwest Coast canoes glide over the canal.

The U.S. flag was first raised in Alaska on the museum lawn, on July 4, 1959. A totem pole on the lawn near Calhoun Street is a prime example of contemporary themes on traditional totem poles. While it looks like any other, with an eagle and raven and human faces, its title, *Harnessing the Atom,* shows the contemporary role that totem poles might serve. The eagle represents the United States, a Russian priest stands for Russia, and the human figure on top of the sun represents the harnessing of energy. Carver Amos Wallace of Ketchikan added the raven, as the Tlingit creator of all things, supporting the other figures.

A brochure for a self-guided walking tour to historic downtown Juneau is available at the museum.

HAINES

Sheldon Museum & Cultural Center
907-766-2366
sheldonmuseum.org
11 Main St., P.O. Box 269, Haines, AK 99827
Open: Daily, Mon.–Fri. and Sat.–Sun. afternoons, summer; Mon.–Fri. afternoons, winter
Admission: $3 adults; under age 12, free
Gift shop

The Sheldon Museum rates attention for its splendid artifacts and it's chronicle of Haines history. The building, which was built as the museum in the 1970s, sits on the grounds of the former Presbyterian Mission, which dates to the town's origins. The local Chilkat Tlingit chief invited delegates of the Presbyterian Church to discuss a mission in 1879. A church official sent Rev. S. Hall Young, who brought his friend John Muir. With the Chilkats, they picked the current town site on Portage Cove, opposite the Tlingit village near their meeting point.

The museum has numerous artifacts that relate to the neighboring Chilkat people, including a splendid blanket and a wonderful small Friendship totem pole. It was originally carved for Stephen Sheldon and his wife, Haines residents in the first half of the 20th century who contributed much to the town. A large version of the pole stands at the Haines library. Many of the artifacts in the museum come from Sheldon's collection.

Dozens of vintage photos also tell the story of the town, from the early mission days through the building of Fort Seward, and its later conversion to housing and an arts center after World War II. Many of them are taken in winter, when deep snow covers everything.

Hammer Museum
907-766-2374
hammermuseum.org
108 Main St., P.O. Box 702, Haines, AK 99827
Open: Mon.–Fri., May–Sept.
Admission: $3 adults, free under age 12

Did you know there are hammers for clapping, canceling checks, stunning cattle, and smashing sugar cubes? Dave Pahl's Hammer Museum also has autopsy, double-claw, and Roman battle hammers. The little house holds about 1,400 hammers, grouped by function on the walls and in cabinets. You can't miss it. There's a huge hammer out front.

Pahl, who came to Alaska with his wife to pursue a self-sufficient lifestyle, needed tools to survive. This led to the start of the hammer collection. On trips to the Lower 48, he encountered more and the collection grew. The manikins in the museum come from the Smithsonian Museum. After he bought the cottage for his museum, he dug a basement by hand. Under the foundations he unearthed a Tlingit ceremonial stone hammer. It was an omen, and underscored the rightness of his decision.

SKAGWAY

Visitors walking into Skagway from the docks stumble into Klondike Gold Rush National Historical Park. The whole center of town is a U.S. Historic District.

Klondike Gold Rush National Historical Park
907-983-2921
nps.gov/klgo
P.O. Box 517, Skagway, AK 99840
Visitor Center, Broadway at Second Avenue
Open: Visitor Center open daily in summer
Admission: No park fees; fees for camping and hiking the Chilkoot Trail
Gift shop

This may be the most widely far-flung park in the U.S. system. Part of it is along Pioneer Square in Seattle, Washington, where the Klondike Gold Rush started for many people. The next segment is in Skagway, launching point to the Klondike gold fields. It continues at Dyea, 9 miles northwest of town, where the Chilkoot Trail begins. Dyea (see *Historic Buildings and Sites* section) was once as large as Skagway, but it was abandoned when the White Pass & Yukon Route Railroad began operation in 1900.

The park follows the Chilkoot Trail across the border, and combines with Canadian sites at Bennett Lake and finally Dawson City, 550 miles north of the lake, to become the Klondike Gold Rush International Historical Park.

A park visitor center and museum (see below) is in the historic district, where the Park Service has restored several buildings. A map is available at park headquarters. Rangers lead walks through town.

In the Skagway segment of the park, the National Park Service owns 15 buildings along Broadway. Each of them has been painted its original color. Some of them house shops, and are designated by a plaque on the building, such as the **Lynch and Kennedy Dry Goods Store** at Broadway between Third and Fourth avenues. The **Arctic Brotherhood Hall,** Broadway between Second and Third, is covered with 8,933 driftwood sticks, and is believed to be the most photographed building in Alaska.

Some buildings are restored to their original functions. Several figures lean on the massive wood bar at the **Mascot Saloon**, at Third Avenue and Broadway, just as they did in 1898. This may be the only barroom in the National Park Service. The **Moore Cabin and Homestead,** built by Skagway's founder William Moore and his son, J. Bernard, shows what Alaska pioneer homes looked like. Some pieces are original, and others are true to the period, including a jammed-full roll-top desk and walls covered inch-to-inch with flower prints and some family portraits.

Klondike Gold Rush Museum
907-983-9223
nps.gov/klgo/
Corner Second Ave. and Broadway
Open: Daily, year-round
Admission: Free

The museum, adjacent to the National Park Visitor Center (open mid-May through late September) focuses on the great stampede of 1897–'98 that brought Skagway and neighboring Dyea into being. It was the start of the 503-mile journey to the Yukon gold fields. Most impressive is the miner surrounded by the year's worth of supplies, a one-ton load required by the Canadian government to cross the border. Miners worked with a partner, trudging back and forth over the Chilkoot Pass, carrying 150 pounds at a time. Sometime Tlingits were used as porters. Vintage photos show the real loads and people.

View the film *Days of Adventure, Dreams of Gold*, and then sign up for the ranger-led walk of Skagway, including several buildings owned by the National Park Service (see *Historic Buildings and Sites* section).

Skagway Museum and Archives
907-983-2420
Seventh Ave. and Spring St. P.O. Box 521, Skagway, AK 99840
Open: Daily during summer; hours vary in winter
Admission: $2; $1 students; free age 12 and under
Gift shop

One of the most extraordinary objects in the Alaska Panhandle is in this museum. It's a quilt made of the neck skins of scores of Alaska ducks. The beautiful iridescent teal, tan, and white feathers are woven into rich textures. A photograph of it graces *Quilts of Alaska*, a book published on the Alaska Quilt Survey.

The museum focuses on Skagway history and exhibits are well organized. Most of the things come from Skagway Gold Rush families, and exhibits look to its mining past, and to survival in this cold climate. Sleds, snowshoes, lanterns, and a model of a mine are among exhibits. A collection of furniture is embellished with twigs, just like the Alaska Brotherhood Hall on Broadway. It's a style called Victorian Rustic, and the furniture and building come from the same period. Another section features changing exhibits by local artists.

The museum was gutted and renovated in 2001. A designer from the Alaska State Museum did the plans for the new space, and the professionalism shows. The museum shares a granite, gabled building with Skagway City Hall. It sits apart from downtown, so much grander than the clapboard buildings. It was built as McCabe College in 1899 in the flush of the Gold Rush. It became a federal courthouse, and now houses the City Hall and Skagway Museum.

WHITEHORSE, YUKON
Two Yukon museums complement the story learned in Alaska towns.

Yukon Beringia Interpretive Centre
867-667-8855
beringia.com
Mile 914 Alaska Hwy., Whitehorse, Yukon, Canada Y1A 2C6
Open: Daily, mid-May–late Sept.; Sun. afternoons rest of year
Admission: $6 Canadian
Gift Shop: Books

We all learned as children that Asian people migrated over a land bridge into what is now North America, 10,000 years ago or more. The Yukon Beringia Interpretive Centre gives real substance to the notion, with films, exhibits, signage, and artworks.

Maps show the land bridge, perhaps 1,000 miles wide, that formed when the sea level dropped during the Ice Ages, an event that scientists now believe happened more than once. Glaciers never formed here because the area was too dry. It was a vast grassland that supported woolly mammoths, Jefferson's ground sloths, scimitar cats, and people, who

The Yukon Beringia Interpretive Centre in Whitehorse, Yukon, brings to life the Ice Age land bridge between Siberia and North America.

became Alaska Natives and First Nation people in Canada. Examples of all of these animals are here. A diorama shows a winter camp. with a skin tent amidst the snow and wolves.

Fossils from the Yukon and on some of the Bering Sea Islands give evidence of plants and animals in eons past. Docents at the center are eager to help interpret the exhibits.

MacBride Museum
867-667-2709
macbridemuseum.com
1124 First Ave., at the corner of Wood St. Whitehorse, Yukon Y1A 1A4, Canada
Open: Daily, summer; Tues.–Sat. afternoons, winter
Admission: $7; $6 students; $3.50 age 6–12
Gift shop

This museum is much larger than it looks. It's a series of buildings around a courtyard, with both indoor and outdoor exhibits. The tiny log building, a former telegraph office, is but one part of the museum. The collections cover the natural and human history of the Yukon.

A pair of stuffed moose, wood bison, grizzly and polar bears, mountain goats, caribou, and cougar fill the Mammal Hall. Another building has historic photographs and First Nation objects, including an exquisite pair of beaded mukluks, and objects and photographs relating to the Klondike Gold Rush and building the White Pass & Yukon Route. Another large hall traces Yukon's modern history with a series of full-size rooms and street scenes. A pioneer cabin that belonged to Sam McGee, made immortal by Robert Service, is in the courtyard.

CENTRAL PANHANDLE

PETERSBURG
Clausen Memorial Museum
907-772-3598
clausenmuseum.org
203 Fram St. P.O. Box 708, Petersburg, AK 99833
Open: Mon.–Sat. during summer; 10–2 Tues.–Sat. Sept.–Dec.; Call rest of year
Admission: $3; free under age 12
Gift shop

A Petersburg bride once wore the silk *Hardanger* embroidered wedding dress that, along with some cheerful children's embroidered clothing, is one of the few objects in this museum made for sheer beauty and elegance. Most displays celebrate fishing, fox farming, and cannery labor that have gone on in Petersburg since Peter Buschmann came to town in 1896 and saw the potential for commercial fishing. Not only did the waters teem with fish, the ice of nearby LeConte Glacier could cool it down and transport it. Of course, the Alaska Natives had set traps on Sandy Beach 2,000 years previously.

A back room has photographs of trophy halibut hanging beside dwarfed people, traps for king, Tanner, and Dungeness crab, and a Fresnel lens. The front room has domestic objects

If you have time, watch the movie, *Petersburg: The Town that Fish Built*. It's available to purchase in the gift shop, along with a good selection of books on local history, as well as Hardanger embroidery and rosemaling Christmas ornaments.

SITKA
Isabel Miller Museum
907-747-6455
sitkahistory.org
Harrigan Centennial Hall, 330 Harbor Dr., Sitka, AK 99835
Open: Daily, early May–late Sept.; Tues.–Sat. rest of year
Admission: $1; $4 with a Theobroma chocolate bar included

A scale model of Sitka from 1867, the year it was transferred from Russia to America, highlights the museum, with well-considered objects representing each of Sitka's eras: Tlingit spruce-root baskets and dance rattles; a Victorian parlor with a pump organ and proper lace curtains; a photograph of William H. Seward signing the transfer document on March 30, 1867; and objects and photographs relating to the military presence in Alaska.

The Sitka Historical Society runs the museum, and this represents their collection. The museum store has books, cards, and prints related to the museum collections. Handmade objects are hand-carved Russian *matryoshka* dolls, Tlingit carvings, painted mugs, and trivets.

Sitka National Historical Park and Southeast Alaska Indian Cultural Center
907-747-0110
nps.gov/sitk
103 Monastery St., Sitka, AK 99835
Visitor Center at the end of Lincoln Street
Open: Year-round
Admission: $4 during summer only
Gift Shop: Excellent books, high-quality items from the Indian Cultural Center

Alaska's oldest federally designated park marks the site of an 1804 battle between the Kiksadi Tlingit and the Russians. The Tlingit repulsed the Russians for about a week, but eventually ran out of flint and gunpowder. The Russians quickly established a settlement, call New Archangel. By 1808, it became the Russian America capital, the colony's political, cultural, and religious center.

The Visitor Center for the park also houses the Southeast Alaska Indian Cultural Center. Most locals know it simply as the Totem Park, for the extensive collection of totem poles in a wooded area on the site. (See *Alaska Native People* chapter.) It's a lovely place to stroll or picnic, and probably looks much as it did in 1804. Two loop trails take visitors to the site of the Tlingit Fort and, on the opposite side of the Indian River, to the Memorial to the Russian Midshipmen.

The park also includes the Russian Bishop's House (501 Lincoln Street). The most impressive relic of the Russian America period, it was a center of learning and culture. Many of the objects and furniture used by Bishop Innocent in the 1840s are still here.

Sheldon Jackson Museum
907-747-8981
museums.state.ak.us
104 College Dr., Sitka, AK 99835
Near Lincoln St.
Open: Daily, mid-May–mid-Sept.; Tues.–Sat. rest of year
Admission: $4 summer, $3 winter; free for 18 and under
Gift shop

You can't miss this octagonal building on the campus of the now-closed Sheldon Jackson College. It was built in 1895 to house the extraordinary collection amassed by the Rev. Dr. Sheldon Jackson, a Presbyterian missionary who collected the items in his travels between 1898 and 1900. He was the first General Agent of Education for Alaska.

It would be easy to spend a day among the hundreds of objects from all of Alaska's Native cultures. The largest part of the collection comes from Inupiat and Yupik Eskimo people from the north. A hunter with a skin anorak in a *baidarka*, a kayak-like boat, sits atop display cases, a startling display. Baskets, skin pouches, bentwood containers, masks, dance bibs, and button blankets fill cases. A set of carved figures engaged in the Eskimo blanket-toss game and the Aleut baskets with tiny colorful details, like printed calico, will charm the visitor.

Drawers below the cases may be opened with yet more things, such as labrettes, fish hooks, and toys, lined up neatly and labeled. Native artists sometimes demonstrate their skills in the museum.

WRANGELL

Petroglyph Beach State Historic Park: About 1 mile north of the ferry dock on Evergreen Avenue, this site has excellent interpretive panels and replicas of the petroglyphs, available for rubbing on a series of stairs and landings down to the beach site. The petroglyphs are on the beach, and finding the real thing can be difficult. When you reach the bottom, turn to the right. Most of them are on rocks just at the high tide mark, and face perpendicular to the water. The spiral is among the most famous, but there is also a killer whale, and a human face. Visitors should only do rubbings on the replicas, since continued touching can cause wear to the real artifacts.

Wrangell Museum
907-874-3699
wrangell.com/visitors/attractions/history/museum/
296 Campbell Dr., Wrangell, AK 99835
Open: Mon.–Sat. May–Sept.; Tues.–Sat. afternoons, Oct.–Apr.
Admission: $5; $3 seniors
Gift shop

This excellent museum is housed in the James & Elsie Nolan Center, an impressive facility for a town of 2,300 people. The lobby area has massive totem house posts dating to the late 1700s, which are believed to be the oldest in existence today.

Exhibits are arranged thematically and trace Wrangell's development with interpretive signs, vintage photographs, and objects. An especially impressive basket collection features functional and fanciful spruce and cedar-root baskets, including one with a human face woven into the fabric. The Russian and British fort sections are covered with signage and uniforms, and the town's role as a supply center in the Alaska gold rushes is given space.

Lumbering, fishing, and photos of the last great potlatch are here. If you're confused about the five varieties of salmon, a display board with models might set you straight. The museum shop is fairly large, and offers many Alaska food items, as well as books, mugs, Simply Sterling petroglyph jewelry, and necklaces made out of miniature baskets.

SOUTHERN PANHANDLE

KETCHIKAN
Dolly's House Museum
907-225-6329
24 Creek St.
Open: Daily, May–Sept.
Admission: $5

Dolly Arthur, one of Ketchikan's ladies of the night, certainly loved bright wallpaper with flowers. Blue-green wallpaper with dazzling flowers lines the tiny dining room; her bedroom is hot pink with more blossoms the size of dinner plates. She even decorated her shower curtain with flowers made out of French silk condoms. Dolly, who ran this brothel on her own from sometime in the 1920s until prostitution was outlawed in Alaska in the 1950s, lived in this house until shortly before her death at 87 in 1975. It's Ketchikan's most expensive museum, keeping up with Dolly's entrepreneurial ways.

Tongass Historical Museum

907-225-5600

city.ketchikan.ak.us

629 Dock St.

Open: Daily, May–Sept.; Wed.–Fri. and Sun. afternoons and Sat. Oct.–Apr.

Admission: $2 May–Sept.

This small museum, housed in the same building with the Ketchikan Library, offers some real gems. One is the Harry Truman totem pole, with an unmistakable carving of the president atop Churchill and Stalin. Another very elegant piece is the beadwork bag in a case called "First People." Other sections cover Ketchikan's lumbering days, fishing, air service, and fires.

Roll a Log

The **Great Alaskan Lumberjack Show** (907-225-9050; lumberjackshows.com) falls outside of most categories in this book, but it's probably as close to historical insights as anything, though it's pure, corny entertainment. It's something to trade stories about later, at the dinner table.

Logging also was once a mainstay of the Ketchikan—and Southeast Alaska—economy, though it no longer is. Two loggers, representing former Ketchikan and Yukon camps, compete in sawing, pole climbing, and finally log rolling. The audience gets in the act by cheering for one or the other. It takes place several times daily, May through September, at Salmon Landing at the cruise ship dock. You'll hear the crowd before you see it.

Competing lumberjacks roll a log in Ketchikan's rollicking show.

A carving of the former president takes top place on the Truman Totem Pole at the Tongass Historical Museum in Ketchikan.

Photos of old Ketchikan, including some evocative images of Creek Street, make the museum worth a stop. One of them showing the street in fog at night appears in copies around town. Another of the famous Dolly Arthur, remembered in a museum of her own (Dolly's House Museum), shows her to be a statuesque beauty.

Historic Buildings and Sites

NORTHERN PANHANDLE

|JUNEAU
Alaska State Capitol Building
907-465-2479
Fourth Street between Main and Seward streets, Juneau
Open: Mon.–Fri., and Sat. afternoons
Admission: Free
Tours: Every half hour during the summer

You never know who might greet you in the Alaska Capitol corridors. On a winter afternoon, the friendly chair of the state Resources Committee took us to his office and let us witness his signing documents. (With all of that oil and gas, this is an important committee.) In the other wing, the State Senate President greeted us as if we were old friends. We didn't get to meet the governor, but the impressive double doors to her offices looked welcoming. During the summer months, you will get an official tour of the capitol, which may be more informative, but perhaps not as much fun.

In one of the rooms, there's a photo of the late Senator Bettye Fahrenkamp, who presided over committee hearings in this room. Her favorite pair of earrings is displayed along with it: Fashioned in gold, one is the word "In"; the other is "Out."

The legislature chamber is nothing grandiose. The ceilings are fairly low and the desks modest. It looks more like a county courtroom with comfortable seating.

The appearance of the whole capitol building belies its function. Although it sits on a rise above downtown and Gastineau Channel, the boxy structure looks much more like an office building than the seat of state government. Built in 1931, it originally served as the Federal and Territorial Building. When Alaska became the 49th state, in 1959, it was given to the state.

State Senate and Legislature offices are on the second floor. The governor's and lieutenant governor's quarters are on the third floor.

Tours may be reserved in the summer, and a self-guided tour sheet is given to visitors the rest of the year. Don't leave before you pay homage to Elizabeth Wanamaker Peratrovich, the Alaska Native from Petersburg who so eloquently pleaded the rights of natives in front of the Territorial Legislature, which led to the Alaska Anti-Discrimination Act of 1945 (See Chapter 1, *History*).

St. Nicholas Russian Orthodox Church
907-523-0986
stnicholasjuneau.org
326 Fifth St.
Open: Daily, May–Sept.; for services only, rest of year
Admission: $2
Gift shop

The octagonal building was built in Siberia, disassembled, and rebuilt in Juneau by Tlingit and Serbian people. It is the oldest continuously functioning Orthodox church in Alaska.

No Russians lived in Juneau at the time it was built, in 1894, many years after Alaska was already a U.S. Territory. Area Tlingits, who had converted to the Orthodox religion, requested the church. The Eastern Orthodox Christian priests allowed the Tlingits to conduct services in their own language, unlike Christian missionaries from the States. It led to the Tlingits embracing Eastern Orthodoxy.

The blue-and-white building, looking exotic among nearby state buildings, is designated a National Historic Place.

SKAGWAY

Some people consider all of Skagway a museum, and indeed the center of town is a designated historic district filled with Klondike Gold Rush buildings preserved by the National Park Service (see *History and Culture Museums and Parks* section).

DYEA

Located 9 miles northwest of Skagway on Dyea Road
Open: Year-round, unless snow closes the road

A single standing façade in the forest and a random scattering of boards are all that remains. Dyea, part of Klondike Gold Rush National Historical Park, erupted briefly in 1897–'98 when it became the departure point for the Yukon gold fields. Wharves extended into Taiya Inlet; 48 hotels and 47 restaurants served the transient population waiting to get on the Chilkoot Trail. Then, overnight, action shifted to Skagway. Prospectors dismantled

This supported façade is the only standing relic of Dyea, briefly the booming trailhead for the Chilkoot Trail.

buildings and transported boards to Bennett Lake and even Dawson City. Dyea vanished. Today, trees still trace the outline of town streets, but grass and underbrush have erased the rest.

CENTRAL PANHANDLE

SITKA
St. Michael the Archangel Russian Orthodox Cathedral
Middle of Lincoln St. at Cathedral Way; P.O. Box 697, Sitka, AK 99835
Open: Daily, except during services

The Mother of God icon in the Sitka Orthodox Cathedral is said to produce miracles. Even skeptics may believe in its powers. In 1966 the cathedral caught fire from another building on Lincoln Street, and a human chain of about 100 church members worked feverishly to save the icons and altar treasures. One man stacked benches and climbed up to get the chandelier that hangs from the domed ceiling. He lifted it off its chain and carried it to safety; it weighs 300 pounds.

This cross-shaped church is a replica of the original. Some icons have been covered with silver with a replica of the original painting embossed on top.

The cathedral's onion dome dominates Sitka from its prominent position in the center of Lincoln St. It's not just a reminder of Sitka's Russian past; it remains the bishop's seat of the Russian Orthodox Church for Alaska. The bench in the center of the room is the "seat." Services are still held here, occasionally in Russian, and some may even be in Tlingit.

Baranof Castle Hill State Historic Site: The small park on a hill near the downtown waterfront marks the site of a Tlingit fort and later the spot where Alexander Baranof had his home. Baranof's home was hardly a castle, but after he left, Russian governors built a more elaborate house, which earned it the "Castle Hill" nickname. The Russians transferred Alaska to the United States here on October 18, 1867, and the governor's house later burned. The view over downtown Sitka and the waterfront is great.

Old Sitka State Historic Site: Located 7 miles from downtown just beyond the Alaska ferry terminal, the site marks the first Russian settlement on Baranof Island, and has been designated a National Historical Landmark. Interpretive signs offer information about the short-lived settlement. The area beside Starrigavan Bay is enjoyed more for its recreational use with trails (the 1½-mile Forest and Muskeg Trail is barrier-free) and a public boat ramp.

HISTORICAL WALKING TOURS

Historic Downtown Juneau

The Juneau–Douglas City Museum has an excellent brochure for a self-guided walking tour to the historic parts of downtown. Also look for the three-sided, blue historic signposts scattered throughout downtown.

A good place to start is with the **Governor's Mansion** (916 Calhoun Avenue), a New England saltbox crossed with a Southern mansion. Built in 1912, it stands prominently on one of Juneau's ascending streets, so most other sites are downhill and toward the waterfront from here. Note the totem pole beside the house, which is not open to the public. From here, you can jog up some of Juneau's street-connecting stairways to the town's own "Nob Hill," and see the **Hammond-Wickersham House,** an Alaska State Historic site, through it is closed for renovation at this writing. Downhill on Gold Street is octagonal **St. Nicholas Russian Orthodox Church**, the oldest unaltered church in Southeast Alaska.

Several buildings are on Main and Fourth streets: the **State Capitol, Juneau–Douglas City Museum**, and **State Office Building.** The latter is built into Juneau's hilly terrain; its main lobby is on the eighth floor. The observation deck on this floor affords a great view of Juneau. Note the totem pole, which came from the Haida village of Sukkwan in the Southern Panhandle.

Nearby Village Street reminds visitors of the past with a **wall mural and Raven and Eagle totem poles** on the Tlingit-Haida Regional Housing Authority. They commemorate the Aak'w Indian Village that stood at this site.

The rest of the buildings cluster in the commercial area of downtown along Franklin and Front streets. Front Street was Juneau's shoreline, until tailings from the AJ and other mines extended the waterfront about two blocks. The **Valentine Building** (119 Seward Street) represents Alaska's frontier architecture. It housed stores in 1913 when it was built, and it still houses stores and a coffee shop. The **Alaskan Bar and Hotel** (167 S. Franklin) still takes in guests, and its bar still attracts a lively crowd. It's listed on the National Register of Historic Places. Across the street, the **Alaska Steam Laundry** (174 S. Franklin) is now the Emporium Mall, with more shops. Walk into the mall and toward the back you'll find vintage photographs along the hall.

If you're thirsty after all this walking, drop by the **Imperial Bar** (241 Front Street), once the Louvre Saloon, built in 1891 for thirsty miners. This may be Alaska's oldest saloon and in 1914 was one of 30 watering holes. Most tourists head for the **Red Dog** (278 S. Franklin), with its T-shirts and stuffed bears, but the Imperial is more authentic.

HAINES

Fort William H. Seward, National Historic Landmark

Pick up the informative walking tour brochure at the **Haines Visitors Bureau** (122 Second Avenue). One side recounts the fort's unusual history; the other gives the numbered points of interest for the tour. Shots were never fired at this fort, nor did it play a direct part in any war.

The fort stands apart from the town, and brings an iconic look to Haines. Large, white, board buildings surround expansive open parade grounds, on a slight rise behind Portage Cove. The buildings stand in a precise formation, like soldiers on review. The U.S. government put the fort here in 1904 because of a continuing border dispute with the Canadian government. Two infantry companies were posted here. A good bit of energy went to dealing with winter snow, though Alaska soldiers did train at the fort in World Wars I and II.

Just after World War II, the government sold the fort, which was purchased by five World War II veterans, none of whom had ever been to Alaska. They bought 85 buildings and 400 acres and set about establishing a planned community, certainly an audacious military conversion.

Their legacy is **American Indian Arts**, originally the fort hospital (No. 6) , and the **Chilkat Tribal House** and **Dancers Storytelling Theater,** added later to the 6-acre parade grounds. Descendants of the veterans run both of them. Officers lived in the large houses on the southern and western edges of the parade grounds. The commanding officer's digs are now the **Hotel Halsingland** (Nos. 10, 11, and 12). It was here that Elinor Dusenbury composed "Alaska's Flag."

The Post Exchange (No. 16) has become the **Fort Seward Lodge. Fireweed Restaurant,** and **Dejon Delights** foods are the former commissary. The smaller houses (near Alaska Indian Arts (No. 2) belong to noncommissioned officers.

Skagway

The federal government has designated Skagway as part of a registered National Historic District. It is Southeast Alaska's most architecturally consistent town, though not all of the buildings are historic. The excellent **"Skagway Walking Tour"** map identifies the old and the new. It's done beautifully, with each building on Broadway given an architectural drawing from an overhead vantage and, beside it, the building's date of construction and provenance.

The reverse side of the map details the history of each building, including those that are still private residences. Pick up the map at the Visitor Center at the **Alaska Native Brotherhood Hall** (Broadway between Second and Third avenues), the building covered with driftwood sticks.

Another way to see historic Skagway is to take a walk with a park ranger from the **Klondike Gold Rush National Historical Park Visitor Center** in the old White Pass & Yukon Route railroad depot. The tracks once marched up the center of the street, which is the reason it's so wide. Now they bypass it, just to the south of Spring Street.

Formerly Gold Rush-era McCabe College, the Skagway Museum is one of the town's rare stone buildings.

KETCHIKAN

Start your walking tour at the **Ketchikan Visitors Bureau,** 131 Front Street, and pick up the Ketchikan Walking Tour Map. It divides the long, thin town into a downtown and oldest section, and West End or "New Town." It identifies many historic buildings and sites, and totem poles. Head up Mission Street under the **Ketchikan Arch,** originally erected in the 1920s to welcome steamship passengers. Looking up the street, big white **St. John's Episcopal Church,** built in 1902 with cedar from a Saxman mill, was originally on pilings at the waterfront. Fill moved the shore out by two long blocks. Whale Park has the **Chief Kyan and Chief Johnson totem poles,** replicas carved by Israel Shotridge about 1990.

The route climbs the hill to take in the hatchery and **Totem Heritage Center** and then drops back to the waterfront on Deermount Avenue. Detour out **Thomas Street,** a wood-plank road that was the Ketchikan dock in the 1890s. Then as now, it's home to boating businesses and bars. Back on **Stedman Street,** a historical kiosk tells about Asian people who lived and ran small businesses on this street. And then the walk passes **Creek Street,** which snares most visitors.

Continuing toward the tunnel, the hillside area, known as Nob Hill, held some of Ketchikan's grandest houses. Note the stairway needed to negotiate steep **Edmonds Street.** The **West End** tour covers several cannery sites, which earned Ketchikan its **Salmon Capital of the World** title.

MOVIE THEATERS

You won't need to forgo the latest movie releases on the big screen. Most major Panhandle towns have movie theaters, including some multiplex palaces. Smaller places may use school facilities or other public rooms to show movies. Tickets prices are about the same as the Lower 48, $9–$10 for adults, and about $6 for seniors and children.

NORTHERN PANHANDLE

JUNEAU

Juneau's large multiplex is in the Mendenhall Loop area, and three smaller movie theaters are downtown. One shows recent runs on two screens and the others offer foreign films or alternative cinema.

20th Century Theatre: (907-586-4055 or 907-463-3549 for show times; grossalaska.com; 222 Front Street.) Two screens offer recent films.

Glacier Cinemas: (907-789-9191 or 907-463-3549 for show times; 9091 Cinema Drive.) The five-screen multiplex in the Mendenhall Loop area shows current releases.

Gold Town Nickelodeon: (907-586-2875; 171 Shattuck Way or 174 S. Franklin.) Films run Thur.–Sun. in the late afternoon and evening. An annual theater pass is available, and dinner packages with a menu themed to the movie are available. The cinema specializes in foreign films.

Silver Bow Inn and Back Room Restaurant: (907-586-4146 or 1-800-586-4146; silverbow.com/cinema.htm; 120 Second Street.) An alternative movie space in the Back Room Restaurant, associated with the Silver Bow Bakery and Inn, shows new and classic films on an 11-foot screen. You can dine or have a drink with the movie, which is free on Mon.–Wed.

HAINES

Haines doesn't have a movie theater, but videos and DVDs may be rented at **Haines Quick Shop**, (907-766-2330; Mile Zero Haines Highway.)

SKAGWAY

The town at the top of the Lynn Canal does not have a movie theater. You'll have to go to Whitehorse in Yukon Territory, about a two-hour drive.

CENTRAL PANHANDLE

PETERSBURG

Northern Lights Theater: (907-772-7469; 500 N. First Street.) The Syd Wright Auditorium at Petersburg Middle School auditorium becomes a movie theater on weekends when recent films are shown. The theater is a joint partnership with the schools and is aimed at family entertainment. All movies are PG-13 or G.

SITKA

Coliseum Theatre: (907-747-0646; Lincoln Street downtown and 1321 Sawmill Road.) The Coliseum shows current releases.

WRANGELL:

The last picture show to run in Wrangell was *Jaws*, in 1975. But recent movies are frequently screened weekends at the Nolan Center, 296 Campbell Drive. Ask at your hotel.

SOUTHERN PANHANDLE

KETCHIKAN

Coliseum Twin Theatre: (907-225-2294; 405 Mission Street.) Four screens are available, though not all may be used. The Coliseum has shown movies since the mid-1900s.

Music

NORTHERN PANHANDLE

Juneau Jazz & Classics: (907-463-3378; jazzandclassics.org.) Charlie Musselwhite, Hot Tuna, Lannie Garrett, Butch Thompson Trio, and the Apollo Trio have highlighted the classical, jazz, and blues festival. Performances take place in a variety of venues, including the University of Alaska Southeast campus, an office building, Chapel at the Lake, and boats. Seating is true festival style with first come, first served. Some events are free. The festival takes place annually in May.

SITKA

Home Skillet Festival: (907-747-5656; homeskilletrecords.com.) The independent record label produces a three-day festival in mid-July featuring artists such as Sonny Smith, Tom Brousseau, and Macklemore.

Sitka Summer Music Festival: (907-747-6774; sitkamusicfestival.org; Harrigan Centennial Hall, Harbor Drive.) During June, classical musicians converge on Sitka for chamber music concerts, which started in 1972. Free noontime brown-bag concerts are held at Sitka churches; other social events may precede or follow the concerts.

NIGHTLIFE

The Alaska Panhandle is not big on nightlife for visitors. They're either back on the cruise ships or they've gone to bed early in anticipation of going fishing the next day. The liveliest places are bars where locals hang out. Often live music or karaoke keeps things hopping. High on the agenda in Juneau and Skagway are the tourist saloons, listed separately.

NORTHERN PANHANDLE

JUNEAU

During summer, tourists dominate the downtown bar scene. During winter and spring, it's likely to be state legislators and lobbyists. There's always a sprinkling of local folks and it's not hard to meet them. Juneau bars are nonsmoking; most others allow smoking.

Hangar on the Wharf (See the *Restaurants and Food Purveyors* chapter) and **Red Dog Saloon** (see *Tourist Saloons* sidebar) are extremely popular.

Alaskan Bar and Grill: (907-586-1000; thealaskanhotel.com; 167 S. Franklin Street.) Most bars in downtown Juneau have a history, and this one has even made it to the National Register of Historic Places. Behind etched glass doors, the large, high-ceilinged space with a balcony often has live music. Several beers are on tap, but I've encountered a night when they were out of Alaskan amber. It even has a ghost.

Bubble Room Lounge: (907-586-2660; westmarkhotels.com; 127 N. Franklin Street.) If you're going to find anyone with a tie in a Juneau bar, this is it. And the person is likely to have come from an appointment with the governor. Located in the Westmark Baranof Hotel, it's a good place for a quiet drink, but you're not as likely to meet locals.

Doc Waters: (907-586-3627; 2 Marine Way.) This may be a pub, restaurant, or sports bar, depending on the time of day or where you sit. On warm nights the deck is great; early in the evening it tends to be filled with the dinner crowd. The bar is big, but the big-screen television may dominate things. Occasionally, live music fills up the bar and the deck.

Historic Imperial Saloon: (907-586-1960; 241 Front Street.) Once called the Louvre, this was Juneau's oldest bar. Klondike Kate danced here in 1896. Someone is usually knocking balls around at the pool table, and there are vintage photos to look at in the dim light. DJs do hip-hop on Friday and Saturday. The doors roll up on warm days.

Viking Lounge: (907-586-2159; 315 Front St.) This was built as a billiard parlor in 1915, and people still come here to play pool. Alaska Native artworks hang on the wall among the beer signs; karaoke and dancing some nights.

HAINES

Fog Cutter Bar: (907-766-2555; 188 Main Street.) Sooner or later, everyone who lives in Haines stops by here and talks with each other and with strangers. Pool tables and a big-screen television fill the gaps in conversations.

Harbor Bar: (See Chapter 6, *Restaurants and Food Purveyors.*)

Pioneer Bar: (907-766-2800; Second Avenue near Main Street.). The graffiti on the ceiling and bumper stickers behind the bar are good conversation starters. Locals are friendly, and the pub grub from the adjacent Bamboo Room restaurant is pretty decent. Nonsmoking.

Tourist Saloons

Two of the most visited places in the big cruise ports are saloons; relics, in spirit at least, of Alaska's mining eras. Like similar bonanza watering holes in Colorado or California, they try to re-create a racy, cut-loose character. But for blatant tourist commercialism, nothing beats the Alaska saloons—Red Dog in Juneau, or the Red Onion in Skagway.

Everyone walking through the doors knows it, yet everyone from the Lower 48 has to stop at these places, if only to tell their friends they've been there. They combine entertainment with souvenir shopping and dining. The food certainly isn't the best in Alaska, but it's filling. (Brewpubs and micro-breweries are listed in the Restaurants and Food Purveyors section.)

So important was the saloon in frontier Alaska, that the National Park Service has also re-created one in Klondike Gold Rush National Historical Park. Walk into The Mascot in Skagway, and you'll expect to order a beer.

JUNEAU
Red Dog Saloon

907-463-3658
reddogsaloon.com
278 S. Franklin St., Juneau, AK 99801
Open: Daily, May–Sept.
Price: Inexpensive to Moderate
Credit Cards: Yes
Cuisine: Alaska pub fare
Serving: L, D
Handicapped Access: Yes
Special Features: Huge shop; huge crowds; huge servings.

The Red Dog Saloon gets more than a half million visitors in just four months—the summer cruise season. Most restaurants or shops would envy that record. The current saloon, which matches any-one's idea of a Victorian drinking establishment, is actually a re-creation. The original Red Dog, located farther up Franklin Street, was a more conventional-looking bar.

Unless you approach the Red Dog directly from the corner of South Franklin, at its swinging door, you might confuse it for a shop. Windows on either side of the building are filled with sweatshirts, caps, logo glasses, and suspenders. This is as much retail outlet as drinking-and-eating place.

But this hasn't diminished the crowd in the bar. People jam the space, with wooden chairs back-to-back on the sawdust-covered floor. The walls are equally crowded, with stuffed animal heads, sleds, wagon wheels, a naked lady painting, vintage photos, and notes people leave for each other . A special place of honor goes to Wyatt Earp's gun. A country singer is usually belting out songs. The sign in his tip jar reads: RETIREMENT FUND.

SKAGWAY
Red Onion Saloon

907-983-2222
redonion1898.com
Second Avenue and Broadway, Skagway, AK 99840
Open: Daily, May–Sept.

Price: Inexpensive to Moderate
Credit Cards: Yes
Cuisine: Bar food, chili, and pizza
Serving: L,D
Handicapped Access: Yes
Special Features: 1898 saloon; *de rigueur* tourist stop; nonsmoking.

Everyone walking along Broadway's wooden sidewalks from the cruise ship docks makes a stop here. The folks here even offer a tour of the brothel upstairs ($5–"the same it cost in the old days"), with the usual stories about Lydia the ghost, and the habits of the house. Women in flounced red-and-black dresses, lots of curls, and sometimes sporting beauty spots serve as guides.

The Red Onion was built in 1897, flourished in 1898, and by 1899, had ended its life as a brothel-bar. The women had moved on to Dawson City. The building housed a series of other businesses, much tamer than its saloon and brothel origins. On the whole, the Red Onion is tamer than Juneau's Red Dog. It has the look of a classic, gold-country saloon, with a dark wood bar, tables and chairs, and vintage photos. Sometimes the upstairs girls come down to entertain.

Several choices from Alaskan Brewing Company are kept on tap, including the popular amber ale and IPA.

And a lot of people eat here, as well. The menu runs to bar food with nachos, barbecued chicken wings, and chili. Sandwiches are standard choices with clever names: Strumpet Roast Beef, Turkey Trollop, and Harlot Ham. Many people order pizza, and here the names get personal: Madame Jan, Bombay Peggy, Big Dessie, and Lady Lavoie. Most people don't come for the food, but most order it and leave satisfied.

The Red Onion in Skagway offers more than beer and pizza.

SKAGWAY
See Saloons sidebar.

CENTRAL PANHANDLE

PETERSBURG

Even bars in Petersburg are pretty. The entrance to Harbor Bar is painted in cheerful red rosemaling. The real nightlife is at the Sons of Norway Hall, but you'll have to be invited.

Harbor Bar: (907-772-4526; 310 Main Street.) Fishermen at this popular place will often strike up a conversation with visitors. Pool tables and a big-screen TV add to the entertainment.

SITKA

Pioneer Bar: (907-747-3456; 212 Katlian Street.) The bar sits directly across the street from commercial docks, so it's popular with fishermen. They must feel at home, since every inch of the wall is covered with photographs that relate to fishing, boats, and the sea. Sandwiches and snacks are served.

Victoria's Pour House: (907-747-3288; 118 Lincoln Street.) The bar of Hotel Sitka has big windows at the front, buttery walls, and a tidy bar fitting Hemingway's standards for a "clean, well-lighted place." The mix is about half locals, half visitors. A bar menu with hamburgers and fish and chips is available. It's smoke free.

WRANGELL

On a summer holiday weekend, Wrangell shops, cafes, and restaurants were buttoned up. But the saloons in town were open and jumping.

Marine Bar: (907-874-3005; 274 Shakes Street.) This is one of those hybrids you'll sometimes find in Alaska. It's a bar, a pizza parlor, Laundromat, and public shower house. It also rents rooms.

Totem Bar: (907-874-3533; 116 Front Street.) Pool, darts, dancing, and dancing girls (the Totem Bar cancan troupe) keep patrons entertained at this popular bar. Appetizers and a grill menu are available. A sign posted outside reads: SMOKERS STAND UP AND BE COUNTED. You know where they stand on that issue.

KETCHIKAN

Most Ketchikan nightlife for visitors centers around the Cape Fox Hotel, and Annabelle's Keg and Chowder House. (See *Restaurants and Food Purveyors* chapter.) Locals gravitate to the bars near the docks after the cruise ships leave.

Fat Stan's: (907-247-9463; 5 Salmon Landing.) In the evening, this tiny bar in the Wines International shop attracts people who work in the tourist shops. It's a good place to try an Oregon pinot noir or reserve Chianti. The barkeep with also make a terrific mojito with fresh mint leaves. If you're hungry, there's only potato chips, but if Alaska Fish House is open, you can have food delivered to Fat Stan's.

Potlatch: (907-225-4855; 126 Thomas Street.) Sitting right over Thomas Basin, the Potlatch often has live music, which draws the local crowd, including a band named

Potlatch that is popular in Southeast Alaska. Pool tables and friendly locals, including fishermen from the basin, are always on hand.

THEATER

Many community theater companies help entertain Panhandle people over the long, dark winter.

|JUNEAU

Perseverance Theatre
907-364-2421; tickets 907-463-TIXS
perseverancetheatre.org
914 Third St., Douglas, AK 99824
Performances: Wed.–Sat. evenings, Oct.–May
Admission: $17–$27

This is Southeast Alaska's only professional theater company, and its reputation reaches far beyond Alaska. Since its founding in 1979, it has premiered 50 plays, including in the 2007–2008 season the world premiere of *Yeast Nation*, the newest musical by the authors of *Urinetown*. Pulitzer Prize-winning *How I Learned to Drive* also premiered there.

The resident professional company is obviously not afraid to experiment. Some productions combine the classics with Alaska Native traditions. *Moby Dick* was based on Melville and Inupiat Eskimo whaling traditions. A production of *Macbeth* was set within the context of the Tlingit culture and performed by an Alaska Native cast. The production toured the state, and later was presented at the Smithsonian's National Museum of the American Indian.

The main stage has a season of five plays; experimental works are presented on a second stage. The 140-seat theater has a square configuration. People sit on steeply raked seats, never very far from the actors. Perseverance Theatre is the resident theater at the University of Alaska Southeast, located in Juneau, which offers theater minors to students.

Theatre in the Rough
907-364-3858
Old Elks Club, 109 S. Franklin, Juneau
Performances: Thur.–Sat. during productions
Admission: $16–$18

This company exhibits the frontier "can-do" spirit that one expects to find in Alaska. A fire destroyed all of its lighting equipment, sets, and costumes when it was burned out of its former home at the Holy Trinity Church in 2006.

Plans went ahead for a 2007–2008 season. A performing space was procured at the Old Elks Club, once the Alaska Territorial Hall, and a limited season was planned. Instead of choosing a simple script, artistic director Aaron Elmore chose *The Three Musketeers*, based on the story by Alexandre Dumas. He had to write the script; sew dozens of elaborate costumes; choreograph sword fights; and play a leading role. He also had to create a theater out of a bare room. The audience sat on bleachers lined up along two sides of the hall. The action took place in the center on the floor between the bleachers, and actors exited at either end.

The Alaska Governor's Mansion in Juneau looks like an antebellum home.

The company brought it off, giving substance to some of the mythic stories that swirl around Alaska and Alaskans.

KETCHIKAN
First City Players
907-225-4792
ketchikanarts.org

During July the group offers *The Fish Pirate's Daughter,* an original melodrama in Ted Ferry Civic Center on Saturday evenings. About ten additional shows are offered, including a musical, children's theater performance, and collaborative dance festival.

5

ALASKA NATIVE PEOPLE

Meeting Raven and Eagle

Tlingit introductions take time. A Tlingit youth, sitting next to me on a flight from Juneau to Yakutat, started with his name, followed by his moiety, which is Eagle, and then his clan, which is the same as his mother's in this matrilineal society. Without taking a breath, he repeated the same information for his father, and then his grandparents. Only then, Tlingits believe, will you know who they are.

Even in newspaper stories, Tlingits are identified by moiety, which is either Raven or Eagle, sometimes known as Wolf or Eagle/Wolf. Even today, some Tlingits observe the old practice of marrying someone in their opposite moiety. In addition, they belong to a clan, which usually consists of several families. Among the common clans are Brown Bear, Killer Whale, and Coho Salmon.

Tlingit people, along with some Haida and Tsimshian people in the southern Panhandle, make up most of the Alaska Natives in the Ketchikan-to-Yakutat region. They are part of the Northwest Coast people who inhabit the Pacific Coast from southern British Columbia through the Alaska Panhandle.

Even in precontact days, these people migrated and intermarried with other groups. After widespread settling by Caucasians began in the early 1900s, they dispersed to towns, often built around salmon canneries, and in cities in Alaska or the Lower 48, especially the Seattle area.

Like Native Hawaiians and American Indians in the Lower 48, generations of Alaska Natives were discouraged from learning their language or observing cultural practices, especially holding potlatches. Since the 1930s, when there was something of a revival of totem pole carving, this attitude has been reversed. Even though most Alaska Natives are integrated into mainstream culture, many of them belong to dance groups, young people learn the language, families hold potlatches in honor of those who have died, and men carve totem poles and silver bracelets, while women create beaded jewelry and ornaments, and button blankets.

You'll soon become aware of Alaska Native culture through its strong visual language. A design by a Tsimshian artist appears on Alaska Airlines beverage napkins; logos for numerous businesses are stylized raven, bear, eagle, beaver, frog or other animal figures; souvenir shops and galleries offer miniature totem poles, bentwood boxes, and carved silver bracelets in the distinctive interwoven designs. Some of this is mass produced, but a strong native artisan tradition survives.

The Alaska State Museum in Juneau (See Chapter 4, *Culture*) interprets the Alaska Native cultures and is an excellent place to start. Then it's time to move on by attending a cultural program in a longhouse, visiting a village, and "reading" the carvings on a totem pole. All of this is within easy reach of the cruise passenger, the sportsman who comes to fish, or the casual Alaska visitor.

Tlingit Language

Nonnative people pronounce the word Tlingit like KLINK-it, though the correct first syllable sound is something between a "t" and "k" made by expelling breath from the sides and back of the mouth. Listen to the native speakers. It's easier to hear than to describe. Sometimes identified as a guttural language, Tlingit has many sounds that come from the back of the mouth or by placing the tongue against the roof of the mouth.

The complex language has 24 sounds not found in English, which are hard for English-speaking people to articulate. The Tlingit "l" is silent. Scholars have come up with a way to write these sounds using letters from the Roman alphabet. Sometimes letters are underlined, which indicates the sounds made at the back of the mouth. The apostrophe indicates a pause when the air is cut off, like a glottal stop. "W" is sometimes added to syllables, and indicates that the lips are rounded at the same time that the "K" or "X" sound is being made. In some cases, a period separates syllables. Like Chinese, Tlingit syllables range in tone, which changes the meaning of a word. A high tone is marked with an acute accent.

Villages

Some villages, such as Hoonah, have elaborate visitors centers, cultural performances, and recreation programs. They welcome many visitors daily during the summer season. Others, such as Hydaburg on Prince of Whales Island, have no organized programs, but they may have splendid totem pole parks. Some villages are best visited on a tour, which may be part of cruise shore excursions, or easily booked online or at the destination; others may be explored on your own.

Alaska Native villages are regular towns, usually organized with a tribal or legislative council and a mayor. The native population is usually about 75–80 percent, and supports a rich cultural life. Until the mid-20th century, many villages were larger, especially if the town had a salmon cannery where many people worked. Most of these facilities have closed, though now many towns have cold-packing plants for fish. Unemployment in the most isolated villages is high, and many people practice some level of subsistence living with fishing and hunting.

When visiting a village, observe certain courtesies. Don't barge into anything that isn't obviously open to visitors; don't photograph performances unless you're invited to do so; don't photograph people without permission. When you drive into an Alaska Native village without obvious visitor or cultural centers, stop at the village hall or tribal office, or even a store, to ask about the location of totem poles or other places of interest.

In almost all cases, you will be treated with courtesy, and people will be eager for you to see their best totem poles or a newly carved canoe. For the most part Alaska Natives are eager to share their culture and artistic endeavors, though in rare instances you may be discouraged from poking about the village. Respect this wish.

As in other parts of the book, the villages are arranged roughly from north to south. Those listed are among the most accessible. Two other villages, Angoon and Kake, are stops on the Alaska Ferry (See Chapter 2, *Transportation*), but are somewhat more remote. Angoon is known for its pretty harbor, and Kake, aside from its Tlingit associations, is known for its oysters.

The cost of organized tours ranges from about $50 to $100, depending on the extent of the activity.

NORTHERN PANHANDLE

NEAR JUNEAU

Hoonah: (visithoonah.com). Located on Chicagof Island about 25 miles south of Glacier Bay and 40 miles from Juneau, Hoonah consists of two parts: A developed tourist site at Icy Strait Point, and the nearby Tlingit village and harbor. The tourist site is in a converted salmon cannery where almost daily from May through September, a large cruise ship is docked and visitors come ashore to ride the world's longest zipline, go whale watching, fishing, or bike riding (See Chapter 7, *Recreation*). A cultural theater presentation is also offered. Independent travelers may book any of the recreational facilities and village tours, but only if space is available.

Hoonah is also the country's largest Tlingit community, with 900 residents. On a village tour booked through Icy Strait Point, our guide traced Huna Tlingit history—the last Ice Age drove the group out of its ancestral home in Glacier Bay—and told us about the devastating 1944 fire that burned the town to the ground. With verve and humor, she showed us the nuts-and-bolts character of the present-day town. She described its lifestyle as "high sub-sistence," meaning fishing and hunting are more than sport. She pointed out the Ace Hardware ("one-stop shopping"), cold-storage facility, Presbyterian Church, the Alaska Native Brotherhood and Sisterhood halls, and Halibut Pizza, "the heart of town."

She took us to the schoolyard, where she had just graduated from the 130-student K–12 school, to see the totem poles. She showed us how to "read" them from the bottom up. She explained that students carved the canoes, stored under a shed, and use them to fish for halibut in the traditional way. "In this community we believe, 'It takes a village to raise a child,'" she said.

Hoonah is reached by the Alaska Ferry or by air on a 20-minute flight from Juneau, on Wings of Alaska or Air Excursions. (See Chapter 2, *Transportation*). **Icy Strait Lodge** (907-945-3636) has 23 rooms with private bath, a restaurant, and bar.

NEAR HAINES

Klukwan: Klukwan is about 21 miles north of Haines, along the Haines Highway. The Tlingit once controlled this key position on the Chilkat River. Anyone traveling up the river or the footpath had to pass Klukwan, and pay a toll. The trail was known as the "grease trail" because the Tlingits traded eulachon fish oil and coastal goods with interior native groups. During the Klondike Gold Rush it was the Dalton Trail, and was an alterna-tive to the Chilkoot Trail.

Today, without a guided tour, you won't see much of Klukwan except for the long row of houses along the river. During summer 2008, construction was starting on the Klukwan Cultural Heritage Center near the village entrance, so that may change. A large sign shows a drawing of the building. **Keet Gooshi Tours** (907-766-2168; keetgooshi.com), organizes tours from Haines or from Skagway, with connections on the Fast Ferry.

A massive totem pole stands in the schoolyard at Hoonah. It's paired with another on the opposite side of the canoe shed.

Village elders have allowed visits to tribal houses for these tours. One, the Killer Whale House, has a rare screen and artworks. "This is our history book," said my guide. "When you see this, you know where you come from, and who you are." You will also visit the Alaska Native Sisterhood hall and see smokehouses where salmon has long been prepared along the river. The Tlingit also still render oil from eulachon.

Getting to Klukwan from Haines, you'll pass through the Alaska Chilkat Bald Eagle Preserve, which attracts thousands of the birds in late fall and winter, though in summer, just a few birds are around. Float trips along the river are popular. (See Chapter 7, *Recreation.*)

Klushu: (Milepost 108 on the Haines Highway, Yukon Territory.) This tiny, seasonal fish camp, about 100 miles north of Haines, provides fine photo ops, with its log buildings, a food cache, and picturesque setting. It doesn't have a Web site or even a highway sign, nor promote itself in any way, but a tiny museum, craft shop, café with tea and bannock bread, and a storyteller, encourage a visit. It's on the banks of the Klushu River, and you'll see fish traps and be able to read panels describing First Nation (the Canadian name for native groups) village life and techniques for salmon fishing. Late summer and early fall during the salmon runs are the best time to find people fishing, but the museum and shop are open at other times. The river is a lovely backdrop for a picnic.

SOUTHERN PANHANDLE

Near Ketchikan
Annette Island
Metlakatla: Just 12 miles from Ketchikan on Annette Island, Metlakatla is Alaska's only Indian Reservation and Tsimshian community. The people who founded it followed Anglican missionary William Duncan here from British Columbia, in 1887. Duncan was leaving the constraints of Canadian mission authorities. The U.S. government created the

Klushu, on the Haines Highway in Yukon Territory, is a seasonal salmon fishing village, where food is stored in a raised cache.

Annette Islands Reserve, a federal Indian reservation, granting them the right to the 86,000-acre island. The Metlakatla Indian Community decided to maintain the status and their land control rather than participate in the Alaska Native Claims Settlement Act of 1971. To this day, people in town whose ancestors came with Duncan are recognized as pioneers.

Metlakatla is larger than other Alaska Native villages, with 1,400 year-round residents, which increases to about 2,000 during the summer. It has a modern city hall, and the houses and yards are tidy and colorful, with flowers during the summer. Changes may be in the works for Metlakatla. A military task force has built a 15-mile road connecting Metlakatla to the northern part of Annette Island, where ferry connections to Ketchikan will be much faster and more frequent.

A good way to see Metlakatla is in the company of Lindarae Shearer, who runs **Laughing Berry Tours** (907-886-4133; laughingberry.com). Her grandfather was well-known photographer Benjamin A. Haldane, who documented community life in the early part of the 20th century. She drives people about the community in vans, which are also available for rent, and she runs the town's car-rental service.

She always includes a visit to Duncan Cottage Museum, where she has served as curator. She explains his missionary practices as enlightened, especially for his time. He learned the Tsimshian language and preached in it. He never discouraged the people from speaking their native language, nor from following some of their cultural practices. The church that he built, once known as the "Westminster Abbey of Alaska," burned in 1948, but has been rebuilt.

Another tour stop is Yellow Hill, certainly a strange landmark, geologically speaking.

The Duncan Cottage, now a museum, was once the home to missionary William Duncan, who brought his followers here in 1887.

Made of sandstone, it looks as if it should be part of New Mexico, and indeed it's a relic of continental drift; geologists believe it originated somewhere considerably south. If you hike to the top, you'll get a panoramic island view.

The local clinic has an outstanding art collection, and though it's not open to the public, the totem pole outside, by Wayne Hewson, is of great interest.

Cruise West ships visit about three or four times a week, when Tsimshian dances and songs are performed in full regalia in the Long House, followed by a visit to Metlakatla Artists Village, where local residents, including Lindarae, offer beading, jewelry, spruce-root baskets, and other crafts. The community's most famous product is Purple Mountain Pure bottled drinking water, which you will see all over the southern Alaska Panhandle.

Metlakatla has ferry and float plane connections to Ketchikan (See Chapter 2, *Transportation*). It's about a 10-minute flight. **Metlakatla Tours** (metlakatlatours.net) also arranges island visits. For more information about visiting and touring Metlakatla Indian Community, contact **the tourism office** (907-886-8687; metlakatla.com).

Prince of Wales Island

Hydaburg: Located on Prince of Wales Island about 42 miles south of Craig, Hydaburg was created in 1911, by the consolidation of several tiny Haida communities on the island. Though its population only numbers about 380, it is the largest Haida settlement in Alaska. Haida people normally make their home on Canada's Queen Charlotte Islands. They settled here around 1700, on land given to them by the Tlingits in recompense for the accidental killing of a Haida chief. Except for access by boat or float plane, Hydaburg was isolated until 1983 when the road was paved. It has no visitor-oriented cultural programs, but a stunning totem park beside the school (see below) and a handsome setting on Sukkwan Strait make a visit worth the effort.

Several artists and craftsmen live in the village, and people in general have a subsistence lifestyle. An AC store, Haida Market, has food and directions to the totem park. A good time to visit is during late July, when the annual Hydaburg Culture Camp takes place. For information, contact the **Hydaburg Cooperative Association** (907-285-3666).

Klawock: Although Klawock has the island's only airport, a strip shopping mall, and several fishing lodges, it is also a significant center of Tlingit culture. Its totem park, considered to hold the largest collection of authentic poles in the state, and totem restoration center (see below) attract widespread interest. The Alaska Native Brotherhood and Sisterhood sponsor an annual celebration honoring Native rights activist Elizabeth Peratrovich in February.

The town has the Gaanax Adi longhouse, and St. John's Catholic Church, which is known for its stained-glass windows of Alaska Native totemic figures.

The town is named for Kloo-wah, a Tlingit leader who used this for a summer fishing camp and then moved his clan here permanently in the mid-1800s after Caucasian settlers had arrived. Salmon has always been important to the town. Alaska's first cannery was built here in 1878, and a salmon hatchery followed. The hatchery, which supplies sockeye, coho, and steelhead to local waters, is open to visitors.

Klawock, which stretches along a river and inlet, is more accessible than some of the Native villages. It's also one of the main towns of Prince of Wales Island. The island is reached by daily Interisland Ferry (See Chapter 2, *Transportation*) from Ketchikan, 56 miles away. The Alaska Ferry and Pacific Airways also serve Prince of Wales from Ketchikan. The ferry docks at Hollis, 24 miles from Klawock.

The edge of the Hydaburg totem park overlooks a cannery, which once thrived on Prince of Wales Island.

Culture Centers and Performances

Even if you don't have the opportunity to visit an Alaska Native village, the Panhandle's major cities offer cultural programs.

Several of them present the Tlingit creation myth, which centers on the role of Raven. There are several interpretations of Raven's obtaining the Box of Daylight, which is the story of bringing the sun, moon, and stars to the people. The raucous call and sight of ravens, which seem clumsy when they are not on the wing, seems always present in the Panhandle. It's easy to understand why these creatures played such an important role in the people's myths.

Performers appear in full regalia, often a button blanket and masks, in a form that is really story theater. They chant or sing, drum, narrate the story, and dance. They often perform with their backs to the audience because the design on the back of the blanket denotes their clan. "We're not being rude," said the woman who introduced the film *Seeing Daylight*, in Juneau. "The design tells you who we are."

The following programs are aimed at visitors, and take place during the summer. There are others, sometimes in the Alaska Native Brotherhood or Sisterhood halls, or local schools. Be alert to the possibilities.

Ticket price for these programs ranges from about $10 to $30. Dancers usually pose for photographs before and after dances, but not during a performance. You may also be asked to participate, which most people do with good humor, if not with the skill of the native dancers.

NORTHERN PANHANDLE

JUNEAU

Chilkat Theater: The award-winning film *Seeing Daylight* is shown every 30 minutes, atop the Mount Roberts Tramway. The poetic documentary traces Tlingit history and expresses the idea of balance in the culture. It may be purchased at Raven Eagle Gifts (raveneaglegifts .com). The theater is in Mountain House (Shaa Hit), the complex at 1,800 feet at the top of the tram. It takes just six minutes to ride up from the Juneau waterfront below. The movie is free, but you'll have to buy a ticket to ride the tram, at about $25.

HOONAH

Native Heritage Center Theater: Live performances of dance, song, and drumming portray Huna Tlingit legends at the Icy Strait Point complex. When I visited, it featured an elder describing the performance in English and then reciting in his language. The dancer-actor who portrayed Raven was especially talented in bringing the legend of the Box of Daylight to life. This is one of the more polished versions of the Tlingit creation legend, with talented dancers/actors, impressive masks, and engaging ways to encourage

This dancer portrays Raven in Hoonah's Native Heritage Center Theater performance.

audience participation. Photos are permitted before and after the performance, but not during.

CENTRAL PANHANDLE

SITKA

Naa Kahídi Dancers: The group performs up to twice daily in the Tlingit Long House on Totem Square near the waterfront. The sight of Raven, performed by a youngster perhaps seven years old, immediately captures the hearts of those watching, and encourages them to get up at the end and try their best at stamping their feet and following his lead. The group's ages range from youngsters through tribal elders, and they have the look of dancers you might find at an Alaska Native Brotherhood hall social in almost any Panhandle town.

Southeast Alaska Indian Cultural Center: Chances are you'll find Cathleen Pook creating her exquisite beaded earrings, working with vintage beads so tiny you'd need several to fill a pinhead, or Tommy Joseph carving a totem pole. This is the place to see Alaska Natives creating the pieces you'll find in museums and galleries, or displayed in totem parks and public buildings. They work in a series of studios in the Sitka National Historical Park visitor center, or out back in a carving shed. They tell visitors about their craft and culture while they work. The park is at the end of Lincoln Street, and includes an extensive totem pole collection (see below).

The bear with many faces surrounds the low entrance to Chief Shakes Tribal House in Wrangell.

WRANGELL

Chief Shakes Tribal House: No formal programs currently take place at the house, but it's not unusual to find Tlingit residents on hand, ready to tell stories, answer questions, or tell you about their culture. Chief Shakes is the name given to a series of six Stikine Tlingit leaders who lived here during the late 1700s and 1800s. Chief Shakes IV was on hand when the Russians established a fort here, in 1833. Chief Shakes VI was the last of the succession. Constructed in 1939 as a Forest Service project, the house is a replica of a house that stood at this site. When it was completed in 1940, more than 1,500 people streamed into Wrangell to attend the last great potlatch of the Stikine Tlingit.

To get inside, you'll crouch and enter through the low door that is surrounded by a dramatic painted figure that has a human body and head of a bear. Faces peer out at the elbows, knees, palms, and ears. The painting gave the house its Tlingit name, which when translated, means "House of Many Faces." The original house doorposts

This old totem pole, dating from around 1900 or earlier, shows a simpler style and is displayed at Sitka National Historical Park.

are now in the Wrangell Museum. The Wrangell Cooperative Association cares for the current house. The grave of Chief Shakes IV is visible from the island. A totem with a weathered killer whale marks the grave.

SOUTHERN PANHANDLE

KETCHIKAN

Saxman Native Village: A short video introduces the Cape Fox Tlingit culture and Saxman history, followed by a performance of elaborately costumed dancers in the Beaver Clan House. You'll see people in tunics, button blankets, Chilkat blankets, and dramatic masks. The dancers encourage visitors to join them for the final dance. The Tlingits in the Ketchikan region came from nearby Cape Fox. The tour is booked through **Cape Fox Tours** (907-225-4846; capefoxtours.com) on cruise ships, or tickets may be bought at the shop at Saxman village. If a performance is not taking place, the house may be open. Sometimes the performers are there and will answer questions.

METLAKATLA

Performances from the Tsimshian culture take place in the Long House (32 Western Avenue) when Cruise West is docked, about two to three times a week in the summer. Non-cruise passengers may buy a ticket from the **Metlakatla Indian Community tourism director** (907-886-8687).

TOTEM POLE CENTERS AND PARKS

The Alaska Panhandle offers some of the best opportunities to see totem poles in the world. Ketchikan, which may have more poles than any other place, Sitka, Wrangell, Hydaburg, and Klawock all have clusters grouped in "parks."

Even the casual visitor is drawn to these powerful images. It's been an ongoing habit. In 1890, John Muir wrote about passengers on a steamer wanting to see the Wrangell totem poles. Tlingit, Haida, and Tsimshian people erected these poles in their villages to tell their neighbors who they were, what heroic things they had done, and what legends and myths they believed. Totem poles often commemorated an event, such as the transfer of Alaska from Russia to the United States.

Almost all of the "older" poles that you see in the Alaska Panhandle are replicas of earlier poles. After the turn of the 20th century, Alaska Natives left their tiny villages and moved to the white settlements, often to work in canneries. They left behind the totem poles in their villages, which were decaying or had fallen by the 1930s. The U.S. Forest

Celebration

Every two years, hundreds of Alaska Natives converge on Juneau for a celebration of dance, music, juried art displays, canoeing events, recipe contests, and general reaffirmation of their cultural identity. A grand entrance, with costumed dancers, launches the weekend event. A parade from Mount Roberts Tramway to Centennial Hall starts a day of dance. The next one will be held in 2010.
Sealaska Heritage Institute (sealaskaheritage.org) sponsors the event.

This detail of a pole from Old Kasaan, now at Ketchikan's Totem Heritage Center, still bears flakes of paint.

Service started a program to rescue these poles, and enlisted Alaska Native workers through the Civilian Conservation Corps (CCC). They brought the poles, sometimes only fragments, into more accessible towns, and laid them side-by-side with fresh western redcedar longs. The carvers, often descendants of the original totem carvers, then copied them using only an adze or other means available to their ancestors. These people also knew the stories behind the poles, and sometimes the particular circumstances of their being raised in the villages.

Unfortunately, the original poles were often destroyed after the new ones were made. Only a few pre-1930s totem poles exist. Now, because of normal weathering and decay, some of the 1930s poles are being replicated. Many of them are not carved fully in the round, but on the front of a hollowed-out log, supported by a metal rod. The pole also stands on a metal base that secures the pole to the ground. These will last longer, according to master carver Nathan Jackson.

These 1930s poles still stand in "parks," created at the time. You may find the parks with a few more or a few less poles than I did, in early summer 2008. From time to time, Alaska Native carvers take down poles for restoration, or even recarving, if they have deteriorated.

In addition to the 1930s totem parks, other sites are good places to find the poles, especially in the Southern Panhandle. Ketchikan has the Totem Heritage Center, with several poles rescued from nearby uninhabited Haida and Tlingit village sites. Most of these date

Nathan Jackson is today's greatest Tlingit carver.

to the late 1800s. This is an excellent place to start a visit to totem parks. Sitka National Historical Park is also a fine place for display and information about totem poles.

Totem poles mark important buildings throughout the Panhandle, including the Governor's Mansion and Mount Roberts Tramway in Juneau, the Wrangell post office, and several locations in Ketchikan. Quite often the poles are commissioned for new buildings, much in the same spirit that totems were erected to mark important events in precontact days.

The world's tallest totem pole, at 132 feet, stands at Kake on Kupreanof Island. It was created in 1970 for the Osaka World's Fair. It has a figure for every Tlingit clan on the pole. Sometimes the most touching poles are the smallest. A single pole, perhaps 6-feet tall, stands at a small lake in Yakutat. It is a memorial for a child, Nathan Harry Bremner. It honors his lineage, and his father's clan with Raven, Brown Bear, and Silver Salmon on the pole.

Totem poles are larger and more concentrated in the Southern Panhandle, probably because the redcedar grows larger and more densely there. It was the favored tree for carving.

NORTHERN PANHANDLE

HAINES

American Indian Arts: (907-766-2160; alaskaindianarts.com; Fort William H. Seward.) Master carvers peel away curls of western redcedar, making commissioned totem poles in this workshop, where for 40 years the practice of totem carving has been nurtured, and new carvers have apprenticed to the masters. In mid-2008, a 35-foot totem pole angled from one end of the carving room to the other, as carvers gradually fashioned the figures from the wood. A simple drawing was all they needed as guide. Open 9 AM–5 PM Mon.–Fri.

CENTRAL PANHANDLE

SITKA

Besides the major historical totem park, Sitka has another important pole, at Totem Square at the waterfront. It speaks to the city's Russian heritage. The Russian crest appears near the bottom, and at the top, the small figure of a man is said to be Count Alexander Baranov, the first Russian governor. He's a modest figure, and he's unclothed. Some people think it's an undignified portrayal of the governor.

Sitka National Historical Park: (907-747-8061; nps.gov/sitk; 103 Monastery Street, end of Lincoln Street.) Totem poles have been gathered here since about 1900, when Alaska Native leaders from several villages donated them to Alaska District Governor John G.

Brady. Brady sent them on tour to be exhibited at the 1904 World's Fair in Saint Louis and the following year at the Lewis and Clark Exposition. This was the first time many people in the Lower 48 had ever seen totem poles.

After the tour, he arranged for them to be displayed in Sitka. A few of them still survive, and are displayed in Totem Hall inside the park visitors center. Replicas of many of the poles given to Brady and more contemporary poles now stand outdoors in the forested area behind the visitor center, between the Indian River and Sitka Sound. The fog often curls through the Sitka spruce and hemlock trees, and around the fearsome images of Killer Whale, Wolf, Brown Bear, and Raven carved into totem poles. This was the scene of the battlefield between the Kiks.ádi Tlingit and Russian forces in 1804 and it's easy to imagine the ghost of K'alyaan, the Tlingit chief defeated in that battle, among the trees and the poles. The federal government established the park in 1910, to commemorate this battle.

There are 15 totem poles, both Haida and Tlingit, found along a 2-mile footpath in the 113-acre park. One by one, you'll come upon them, each standing in its own place, in widely spaced areas among the trees.

Among the more unusual poles is the Mosquito Legend Pole, with a wolf, salmon, and, on top, a village watchman, but no insect. It relates to the mosquito legend, however. Another raven pole stands grandly on a grassy area marking the Kiks.ádi Fort site. The older poles, including some house posts, are in general simpler than those carved later on. Even replicas were sometimes interpretations, rather than exact copies of the older poles.

Wrangell

Wrangell has two clusters of important totem poles. Kiks.ádi Totem Park is just off Lincoln Street in the center of town. The other larger park surrounds the tribal house on tranquil Chief Shakes Island.

Chief Shakes Tribal House and Totem Poles: (Across pedestrian bridge at the end of Front Street.) Chief Shakes Tribal House, or Tribal House of the Bear, is right at the edge of downtown, and beside Wrangell's busy fishing boat harbor, but there is a sense of isolation about it. First, you'll walk through town and then over a narrow pedestrian bridge to get to this weathered Tlingit tribal house on Chief Shakes Island. It's a replica of the original that stood on the island, named for a succession of Stikine Tlingit chiefs (See *Culture Centers and Performances* section).

Totem poles surround the house on this grassy oasis. It's very pleasant to sit on one of the split-log benches, and pick out the details on the poles. Most of them are story totems, including the Eagle totem at the entrance and Bear-Up-The-Mountain totem near the house. It tells the story of a flood and the two bears that led the people to safety up a mountain. Note the bear tracks on the pole, leading ever upward. One of the Chief Shakes poles ridicules the Frog clan. As late as 1980 it stirred controversy, because some Frog clan people took it as a personal insult.

The Tribal House is on the National Register of Historic Places. It may occasionally be open, and Tlingit elders may be on hand to answer questions.

Kiks.ádi Totem Park: (Corner Front and Episcopal sts.) The park was created in 1987, the culmination of a major totem restoration. Four poles, which once stood in other parts of Wrangell, were replicated and brought here. The major pole at the front honors the Kiks.ádi Tlingit clan, who settled here. The original pole, erected in 1895, has symbols representing the origin of the clan, up the Stikine River. It is believed that the people who settled Wrangell originally came from upriver, in what is now British Columbia, and worked their way to the coast.

Raven and Killer Whale poles are behind it, as well as one with an intriguing name, "One-Legged Fisherman." The base of the pole has salmon carved onto a plain surface, topped with a raven. The Killer Whale pole is a mortuary pole (See sidebar, *"Reading" Totem Poles*).

SOUTHERN PANHANDLE

KETCHIKAN

Ketchikan may be the best place in Alaska to see totem poles. It has the most concentrated collections of poles, in two parks, a center with heritage poles, and several poles by famous carvers, including Nathan Jackson, scattered about town. Examples from each of the area's cultures, Tsimshian, Haida, and Tlingit, stand side-by-side at the **Ketchikan Indian Community (KIC) building** (2960 Tongass Avenue, near the ferry terminal) and in the Southeast Alaska Discovery Center lobby (See Chapter 7, *Recreation*).

Although not officially a park, the grassy area in front of the **Cape Fox Lodge (**See Chapter 3, *Lodging*) has a totem circle of six poles, carved by Lew Wallace, a member of the Eagle clan, and of Tlingit, Haida, and Tsimshian ancestry. Two of them depict the story of Raven stealing the sun, and the moon and stars.

Totem Heritage Center: (907-225-5900; city.ketchikan.ak.us/departments/museums/totem.html; 601 Deermount Street.) A rescue operation created the Totem Heritage Center in the mid-1970s, when a group from the Alaska State Museum and the Alaska Native Brotherhood rescued the poles from abandoned Tlingit communities on Tongass and Village islands and the Haida village of Old Kasaan, on Prince of Wales. They did so with the permission of native elders. Carved in about 1850–'60, the poles were decaying, sometimes severely. Some of them had fallen over. The five displayed in the center are heraldic, memorial, and mortuary poles, and are the largest collection of historic totem poles in existence.

The center displays the poles effectively, in a darkened room, adding to their power. Unlike contemporary, bright totem poles, the paint and some of the forms have weathered away, though you can find traces of paint around the eye on the Beaver Pole from Old Kasaan. You'll find the Raven, Bear, and Eagle, and human faces and figures on the poles.

Photographs of the poles from their original settings provide context for the visitor. The interpretive material is excellent, and the guides who work at the center are eager to share information. The Tlingit mortuary pole may be the first photographed totem pole from Alaska. The center offers classes, and additional poles in even more fragile state are shown horizontally in other rooms. The center is reached on a pleasant walk through residential or wooded areas from the center of Ketchikan, and sits at the edge of City Park. Open daily, May–Sept., and Mon.–Fri., Oct.–Apr.

Saxman Native Village: (About 2½ miles south of Ketchikan, on South Tongass Highway.) A grand entrance road lined with totem poles introduces Saxman, the largest collection of poles and house posts in the world. Other poles stand at attention on a grassy area in front of a Beaver Clan House, creating a forest of images. The originals came from several abandoned Tlingit villages and cemeteries near Ketchikan, and most of them represent family lineage. Most of these poles come from the late 1930s project and get periodically repainted.

This Saxman totem pole, shown in detail, depicts a legend about a giant oyster eating a man.

Several of them have an eagle atop the pole. One of the most famous has a man, a small crouched figure, with his arm extended into the mouth of a creature that seems to be clutching an oyster shell in its teeth. It relates to the story of a man who drowned by having an oyster clamp its shell around his arm. Another has a figure of Lincoln atop the pole, and represents the Tlingit hope for peace between warring villages after Alaska became part of the United States. Among the more unusual poles are one with an opening at the bottom (once the doorway to a house), and another, a memorial to a chief who died in 1880, bearing a plaque written in English.

Nathan Jackson, probably the most famous Tlingit carver, is often at work in the carving shed on the grounds. Poles he has carved may be found all over the world, including the National Museum of the American Indian in Washington, D.C. He talks easily to visitors, about the past tradition and today's young carvers, including his son, Stephen. Other artisans may be at work, making bentwood boxes or plaques. When I visited, Leroy Hughes showed plastic bags of pigments used in the old days: black from charcoal; turquoise from copper oxide; red-orange from saliva infused with salmon roe. Yes, the carver did chew the roe, spit it out, and collect saliva, for the paint.

A visitors center and excellent gift shop complete the facility. The small village of

Saxman, where some of the artisans live, is adjacent to the totem park. The Bus, Ketchikan's public transportation, makes hourly trips to Saxman. Ketchikan tour companies (**Ketchikan Visitors Bureau,** 907-225-6166 or 1-800-770-3300) offer visits to Saxman and, below, Totem Bight State Historical Park.

Totem Bight State Historical Park: (907-247-8574; alaskastateparks.org; 10 miles north of Ketchikan on North Tongass Highway.) The magic of Totem Bight is that the poles are in a wooded area, facing out to the water, as they would have been in a village. To get there, you walk about 10 minutes through the forest, as though through a time tunnel back to the late 1800s. Now a state historical park, the site has poles from Tlingit and Haida villages and a clan house. Most of these illustrate stories, and feature animals and people atop one another, with sometimes fantastic-looking creatures between them.

Like Saxman, Totem Bight dates to the 1930s. Charles Brown designed the painting on the clan house, its entrance pole, and the welcoming pole on the point near the water. New poles replicate some of the 1930s poles, including one with a Thunderbird and whale, and another unusual pole with a land otter. Fresh paint and sharp carving are clues to the newer poles. You can enter the Wandering Raven clan house by ducking through a small opening at the base of the pole that stands against the façade. This was useful for defense. Another unusual pole is at the entrance to the site. An eagle sits atop the pole, and appears to be wearing a Chilkat blanket.

The Bus, Ketchikan's public transportation system, runs hourly to Totem Bight. A lot of people use it, especially during the cruise season. Overall, Totem Bight seems quieter than Saxman, which adds to its magic. A "bight" is an inlet from a major body of water. It's really the same as a bay, but smaller. The spot takes its name from the bight at the entrance to the totem park.

Prince of Wales Island

Two impressive totem parks and a major carving shed make Prince of Wales a rich destination for totem pole seekers.

Hydaburg Totem Park: (Beside Hydaburg School.) A contemporary pole by master carver Stanley Marsden stands at the middle of this totem park. It's dedicated to Haida elders, and was raised in 1998. Like the other large totem parks in the southern Panhandle, this one was created in 1939, based on poles brought in from other outlying Hydaburg villages. Several of them were so deteriorated, they had to be replaced in 1971. Today, many of these poles show signs of weathering and peeling paint.

Nineteen poles were standing in the summer of 2008. An unusual flesh-colored paint covers many of the faces, even those of animal figures. The shorter ones are likely mortuary columns. The Hydaburg poles may be more squat, more massive than Tlingit poles. The columns seem denser and closer together in this park, than elsewhere.

The totem carving tradition lives in Hydaburg today. School children carved a pole that stands between two houses about a block away from the park, on a parallel street one block closer to the waterfront. It can be seen above the roofs of houses from the totem park. There's also a traditional canoe under a shed at the end of this street. People in town will direct you to this pole.

Hydaburg is a 42-mile drive south of Craig.

Stanley Marsden carved this pole dedicated to Haida Elders for Hydaburg's totem park in 1998.

Klawock Totem Park and Carving Shed: One of the more interesting stops in Klawock is the carving shed. Dozens of deteriorating poles lie prone in the yard in front, awaiting their chance to be replicated. Close at hand, the figures stare, with huge eyes. Some of the paint seems relatively fresh, but the base of the poles has rotted.

Some interesting details are on these poles. One figure appears to hold a canoe paddle. Carved shells encrust other poles, and include a carved clam shell with a crab resting on it. Several of these poles have the squared, straight shaft, characteristic of Klawock. The carvers are often here, which offers an opportunity to see an ongoing project for replacing Klawock poles.

The carving shed is on the Hollis Highway on the way into town. It's across the road from the Klawock strip mall, and near the entrance to Fireweed Lodge.

The totem park crowns a rise near the school on Spring Street, closer to the center of town. On a summer morning, ravens were the only creatures in sight, to keep me company. Their constant call seemed to reiterate the importance of the raven figures on the poles.

Seven of the poles were replicated and replaced in 2005, with accompanying festive ceremonies of dancing and drumming by Tlingits in full regalia. By 2008, they had mellowed slightly, though it was easy to distinguish the newer poles with Killer Whale, Raven,

Dozens of downed totem poles await restoration or recarving at Klawock's carving shed.

The totem pole bear and blackfish, or killer whale, stands at the center of Klawock's totem park.

Eagle, Sea Monster, and Salmon carvings. The park was created between 1939 and 1940, with poles brought here from Tuxekan, the abandoned Tlingit winter village about 20 miles to the north. People moved from there to Klawock, when a cannery was established in the late 1870s.

Blackfish (Killer Whale) appears repeatedly in the poles. One of them takes center place on the park's rise, and has Blackfish poised horizontally over Brown Bear. Another pole tells the story of the first blackfish, this time placed vertically, with its prominent dorsal fin thrust out into space.

Some of the Klawock poles seem more playful than fearful. In one, land otters balance on each other's shoulders, and another has a platter of salmon at its base. Don't miss the one down the hill, with a winsome little girl at the bottom.

Several of these poles have a plain, straight-sided, central column, a relatively unusual feature that appears on Prince of Wales, the northern end of the western redcedar range. There are normally 21 poles here, making it the largest collection in Alaska (Saxman has more, if you count house poles and totem poles), though some may be down for repainting and repair. The totem park is beside the school, near the center of town.

"Reading" Totem Poles

Totem poles confounded Captain Cook when he visited Alaska in 1778, searching for a Northwest Passage. The British navigator didn't much like them, and described them as "monstrous." Generally, they were found along the shoreline of villages, facing the sea. All of the Northwest Coast people created these poles.

Totem poles were the first North American "public art": They expressed who people were, and what they believed in. They honored the dead, and they sometimes were a visual account of stories repeated endlessly, in these cultures of oral tradition.

In the past, Alaska Natives and British Columbia First Nation people made no attempt to restore the poles, as they weathered and fell. Carved out of western redcedar, the poles lasted about 80 to 100 years. The wood is durable, but the moist, temperate, rainforest climate speeds decay. Creating the poles was an ongoing thing: When someone had the resources to pay for it, and an event to commemorate, or someone to memorialize, a pole was commissioned. It was usually raised with a potlatch that featured feasting and dancing.

An excellent source of information about totem poles is in *The Wolf and the Raven: Totem Poles of Southeastern Alaska*, by Viola E. Garfield and Linn A Forrest.

Explorers and missionaries assumed that the poles had religious purposes, though that idea has been discounted. Experts define three categories for totem poles: heraldic, story, and mortuary. Heraldic poles, particularly, are akin to big billboards that might announce the status of a family or its lineage. A story pole might commemorate an event, usually with heroic dimensions, or, quite commonly, a myth or legend. Mortuary poles honored the dead, and may have a container for the ashes of the deceased.

The Tlingit moiety figures Raven and Eagle appear frequently on the poles, though almost never together, as do clan figures Brown Bear, Beaver, Halibut, "Devil Fish" or octopus, Killer Whale, Salmon, and human figures. Raven has a long, straight beak, which may project out or lie along the bird's chest, and is considered the Tlingit creation figure. Eagle has a hooked bill. Bear has a toothy grin, wide round nostrils, and ears that stand straight up. Beaver has two prominent teeth, as well as a tail with hatched marks. Halibut, Killer Whale, and the "Devil Fish" (octopus) look very much like the real thing. Killer Whale usually has a prominent, vertical dorsal fin.

One common totem pole image is Raven sitting atop a box, which relates to the story of Raven as trickster, who persuaded an elder, sometimes portrayed as his grandfather, to give him a box containing the sun and moon. Raven then released them from the box, for the people to have daylight and moonlight.

Human figures may be a chief or leader of a community. After contact, they were often public figures. Abraham Lincoln, who was president just before the United States purchased Alaska, appears at the top of some poles, as does William Seward, who presided over the sale. A Seward pole at Saxman Village ridicules him. When he came to Alaska, in 1869, about two years after the treaty, the people of Tongass Village treated him royally, sending him off with a gift of furs, a carved chest, and ornamented hat. Seward did nothing to reciprocate. A few years later, they carved the pole to commemorate the event. He sits atop a plain pole with no heraldic symbols or other carvings to denote his importance.

The practice continues. A pole at the Tongass Historical Museum in Ketchikan honors Harry Truman, who was president when Alaska became a state.

The person commissioning the pole often appears on the pole, sometimes at the bottom, contradicting the expression "low man on the totem pole." The round hat that human figures wear is based on traditional Tlingit spruce-root hat. Story totem poles are usually read from the bottom to the top.

Although many people in Tlingit society carved bowls, spoons, and canoes, those who were especially skilled were recognized as an artisan class. When a person of rank or wealth commissioned a pole, he would turn to one of these skilled carvers. Western redcedar logs are the wood of choice for a totem pole. These trees grow more abundantly and larger in the southern part of the Alaska Panhandle, and in British Columbia.

As you travel northward, western redcedar trees have smaller trunks. One theory behind the poles that have figures only at the top and bottom, with a narrow column between, is that the trees were not large enough for the massive poles with one figure set atop the other.

In addition to totem poles, Northwest Coast people carved house posts to support their large community or clan houses. It is believed that house poles preceded the totem poles, though by the late 1700s, pole carving had started. Anthropologists also believe that totem pole carving reached its peak during the late 1800s, around the time of more extensive contact. Fur traders, missionaries, and whalers who encountered Alaska Natives encouraged them to create smaller versions of the totem poles so the newcomers would have something to take home. The Alaska State Museum in Juneau has a good exhibit documenting this development.

6

Restaurants and Food Purveyors

Gifts from the Sea

Alaska's most basic food group comes from the sea. Every Panhandle menu, from Ketchikan to Yakutat, lists halibut, salmon, and king crab. Halibut may appear as fish and chips, in tacos, or on burgers. Salmon is often grilled or blackened. It's usually listed by variety: king, coho, or sockeye. King crab, or Tanner or Dungeness crab, are most often boiled in a pot and served with drawn butter. Shrimp has a season in Petersburg and Wrangell. Steak, roasts, and chicken certainly get listed, and are perhaps ordered most often by local residents.

The words "fresh" and "local" appear frequently. Almost every kitchen will stress these qualities, but the question of "fresh" is ambiguous. While it's true that you may be served fish from a local fisherman, caught that morning and sold to the restaurant at noon, what's called "fresh" may have been flash-frozen. Rules concerning the temperature and length of time fish is kept away from refrigeration are stringent. Every town in the Alaska Panhandle used to have a cannery; now cold-packing plants dot the shoreline.

Done properly, experts say, you won't be able to tell the difference between flash-frozen and fresh, which may be why some restaurants still call fish that has been frozen, "fresh."

What matters most is whether the fish is cooked properly. If anything, Alaska restaurants tend to overcook fish, so ask for it to be served "medium" or "rare," if you dislike dry edges.

Many Choices

You won't need to forgo good or exotic produce in Alaska. I had mango for breakfast in Yakutat. Baby greens are served almost everywhere. Barges, arriving weekly or more, bear crates of carrots, romaine, and peaches. Alaska gardens produce copious amounts of rhubarb, lettuce, radishes, cabbage, and strawberries. Wild blueberries and salmonberries grow in every dirt patch. The season lags behind the Lower 48, and it ends sooner, but the long daylight hours produce explosive summer growing conditions.

Ethnic restaurants are popular, and almost every menu has Asian or Mexican dishes. But halibut and salmon are likely to be the basis of a stir-fried dish; halibut tacos are Alaska "soul food."

The purse seiner fleet empties its catch at the processor's boat, at Wrangell's waterfront.

Cruise ship passengers and other tourists pack Panhandle restaurants during the summer. If you have your heart set on a certain place, make a reservation. Book the most popular restaurants before you leave home. Most Panhandle restaurants are casual. No one wears a tie, except the state legislators in Juneau.

Some Southeast Alaska restaurants close during the winter, especially in the popular cruise ship ports, except for Juneau. Those that stay open may run out of things. A little tolerance puts dining in perspective. Southeast Alaska is not a culinary destination. It's isolated and it's seasonal, which challenges keeping a lengthy menu current, and retaining a well-trained service staff.

RESTAURANT NOTES

Restaurants are listed by Panhandle region, starting in the north. Juneau, which gets the most cruise ship passengers and is the state capital, is listed first; other communities follow in alphabetical order in each section. The term "Alaska American" is a common description for cuisine style. This means that the restaurant serves the same kinds of dishes you'll find in the Lower 48, but halibut or salmon may be the main ingredient instead of chicken or beef.

Cafés open only for breakfast or lunch, or self-service eateries are listed in the Food Purveyors section.

Price and Meal Codes
The price categories are based on the cost of average dinner entrées, or a full lunch.
Inexpensive: Entrées $15 or less

Moderate: $15–$25
Expensive: Most entrées more than $25
B = Breakfast, L = Lunch, D = Dinner, Sbr = Sunday Brunch

Handicapped Accessibility

Most restaurants comply with Americans with Disabilities Act requirements. Only those without wheelchair access are noted.

Smoking Regulations

Each Panhandle city determines its own smoking policy in restaurants and bars. Juneau and Sitka have bans on smoking in public places, including restaurants. In other towns, most restaurants are nonsmoking. At press time, Ketchikan and Haines town governments were considering smoking bans, and advocates were circulating a petition in Wrangell.

NORTHERN PANHANDLE

JUNEAU

Juneau gives you more dining choices than anywhere else in the Panhandle, with a wide range of cuisines and prices. Except for the open-air stands near the cruise ship dock, most of its restaurants stay open year-round.

If you're staying downtown, it makes sense to eat at the center of town. If you're near the airport or Auke Bay, the Mendenhall neighborhood is most handy.

Chan's Thai Kitchen

907-789-9777
11806 Glacier Hwy., Juneau, AK 99801
Across the road from Auke Bay
Open: Tues.–Sat.
Price: Inexpensive
Credit Cards: Yes
Cuisine: Thai
Serving: L, D
Special Features: No reservations; no alcohol; extremely popular.

Be prepared to wait outside in the strip mall for a table at this hugely popular restaurant. The owners make few concessions to ease the wait, but the popularity of *tom yum* soup and *pad thai* keeps people lining up.

Diners crowd around tables vibrant with steaming bowls of halibut in red-curry coconut milk, or vegetables with tofu. The kitchen is expert at vegetables, which come out bright, and cooked just enough to heighten flavor, but not destroy crispness. Exotic flavors may perfume the dish, but they are the subtext to broccoli, zucchini, tomato, lotus root, and asparagus.

The University of Alaska Southeast is nearby, so a university crowd often fills the restaurant. A few Thai artworks are on the wall, and a tablecloth may cover the Formica, but there's nothing here to prettify the premises.

The restaurant is relatively close to the Mendenhall Loop area and ferry dock. If you're staying downtown you'll need a rental car or cab.

Donna's Restaurant

907-789-1470
donnasrestaurant.com
9131 Glacier Hwy., Juneau, AK 99801
Open: Daily
Price: Inexpensive
Credit Cards: Yes
Cuisine: American diner
Serving: B, L, D
Special Features: Breakfast all day, with additional lengthy menu.

Donna's is a good place to eat if you're

shopping at Nugget Mall or need something before going to the airport. It starts serving breakfast at 6 AM and continues all day, adding lunch and dinner items later. You may choose from among 16 hot sandwiches and four cold, in a nod to Juneau's mostly cool or cold weather. Hamburgers appear in 10 different variations.

Dinner is available after 3 PM and the choices include such Alaska staples as chicken-fried steak, broiled halibut, and fish and chips. A whole section of pastas and an appetizers list rounds out the ambitious menu. You'll also find some unexpected items: a gyro or Monte Cristo sandwiches, and a Greek salad.

Diner-style décor runs to laminated tabletops and booths. Locals come for breakfast.

Douglas Café
907-364-3307
916 Third Ave., Douglas, AK 99824
Across Gastineau Channel from Juneau
Open: Daily, but varies
Price: Inexpensive to Moderate
Credit Cards: Yes
Cuisine: Breakfast, burgers, eclectic
Serving: B, L, D
Special Features: Extremely popular weekend breakfast; terrific burgers.

Sunday breakfasts are so popular at Douglas Café that its famous burgers and entrées are not served that day of the week. However, that doesn't stop locals from jamming this friendly place, elbow to elbow. Pancakes run to Frisbee size, but you'll have the option to order one or two, which will be top limit for most diners. A Hawaiian-style breakfast features garlicky fried rice with eggs; or the house favorite, the Douglas Deluxe, with fried potatoes, onions and tomatoes, topped with spinach, cheddar cheese, eggs and salsa. Quite a stomach challenger.

Other people make a pilgrimage to Douglas Island for the burgers, which come with a variety of toppings, including blue cheese, jalapeños, avocado, and mushroom. Their Hawaiian burger even has ham and pineapple added to the beef patty. Dinner is equally eclectic, with dishes from Italian, French, and Cajun cuisines, as well as a simple steak.

Tables in bold primary colors—red, blue, and yellow—brighten the simple room. Hours vary, so call before you go.

The Gold Room
907-586-2660
westmarkhotels.com/Juneau-food.php
127 N. Franklin St., Juneau, AK 99801
Open: Daily
Price: Expensive
Credit Cards: Yes
Cuisine: Contemporary American, leaning toward seafood
Serving: D
Special Features: White-cloth hotel restaurant; reservations suggested.

A mirror runs the length of one wall at the Gold Room, Juneau's most refined restaurant, though it's so subtle that you finally realize the attractive person staring at you from across the room is yourself. You'll dine under chandeliers with the lights turned low, at *the* place to celebrate birthdays and anniversaries.

The waiter delivers crisp flatbread and tapenade along with the menu, which has many choices of Alaska seafood and fish, as well as chicken, duck, and steak, which may be ordered with a choice of sauces. Some items stand alone in simplicity, such as steamed king crab legs, served with drawn butter and rolls. Others are more elaborate, such as the sea scallops with orange-horseradish sauce and au gratin potatoes.

The macadamia-crusted halibut was excellent. Crab cakes leaned more on starchy fill, than crab. The house salad with raspberry vinaigrette balanced sweet and tart elements nicely.

The wine list matches the complexity on the menu, and the restaurant has special wine dinners, including some interesting choices, such as a focus on South African wines.

The adjacent Bubble Room, the hotel lounge, serves a light menu in the evening, featuring the Gold Room appetizer menu.

Grandma's Feather Bed

907-789-5567
grandmasfeatherbed.com
2358 Mendenhall Loop Rd., Juneau, AK 99801
Open: Tues.–Sat.
Price: Moderate
Credit Cards: Yes
Cuisine: American and Mexican
Serving: D
Handicapped Access: No
Special Features: Charming dining room in Victorian-style farmhouse, no reservations.

Located in the small hotel, the tiny restaurant seems to largely serve people who stay at the inn.

Its cozy décor fits the inn's Victorian architecture. Some tables have a straight-backed bench on one side, chairs on the other. Other tables sit beside the tall windows or in small corners. A shelf displays dainty china plates and cups and saucers. Tiny flower-print wallpaper, found in the inn's rooms, complete the look.

The menu is surprisingly ambitious. Fish is the menu mainstay, but diners have a choice of getting it cooked three ways— Cajun, teriyaki, or sautéed. Vegetable sides are generous, and one night at least, included corn on the cob. The menu also had a Mexican section, for those in the mood for tacos or enchiladas. It was pleasing homestyle food that may not merit a detour, but the setting is attractive.

Hangar on the Wharf

907-586-5018
hangaronthewharf.com
2 Marine Way, Suite 106, Juneau, AK 99801
Open: Daily
Price: Inexpensive to Moderate
Credit Cards: Yes
Cuisine: American pub food
Serving: L, D
Special Features: Waterfront dining; historic aviation building; reservations.

The waterfront scene here is busy, busy, busy. Float planes take off like maddened mosquitoes, or land with a whisper; small boats slip by, and enormous cruise ships loom several stories above the building. The restaurant is built right over the water, in a building that once housed Alaska Coastal Airlines. You will probably be so distracted with the marine traffic, which can be seen from most parts of the room, that you'll miss the beer tap handles hanging above the windows. The bar keeps at least 20 beers on tap at all times, and with what's available in the bottle, offers about 100 choices.

A fairly lengthy appetizer menu complements the various beers, and these dishes get shared around tables. Coconut prawns, generally more at home in Hawai'i, and shrimp with prosciutto, are favorites.

Caesar salads with a choice of several toppings seem to be delivered to all parts of the cavernous dining room. There's more, from pasta to paella, and chicken and dumplings to rib-eye steak, served up in huge portions. Almost anyone in Juneau for more than two hours finds his or her way here.

Mi Casa Restaurant

907-789-3636
9200 Glacier Hwy., Juneau, AK 99801
Open: Daily
Price: Inexpensive
Credit Cards: Yes

Cuisine: Mexican
Serving: B, L, D, SBr
Special Features: Colorful serapes and
Mexican chairs set the scene.

Mi Casa, like other Juneau Mexican restaurants, tames its seasonings for Lower 48 taste, but that doesn't get complaints from travelers or locals. The restaurant covers the gamut of Mexican combo plates, with nods to Alaska. Halibut appears in tacos, which are quite tasty, and fajitas, which went sizzling by to several tables. A beef tamale comes with a dark red sauce that has the earthiness of *mole* and was zestier than other Mexican dishes encountered in the far north. Locals flock to the Sunday brunch, where you'll find classics, such as eggs Benedict, in addition to Mexican dishes.

Salsa and chips are delivered the moment you slide into a booth or Mexican chairs. Service was attentive—almost too attentive—throughout dinner. If you pause between bites, the wait staff may snatch your plate.

Mi Casa is known for its desserts. Surely the fried ice cream is one of the more eccentric sweets around, but its combination of crunchy and creamy, warm and cold, is surprisingly good. The décor is cheerful, especially on a misty Juneau evening. Bright serapes, a glitzy sombrero, and strings of hot chili pepper lights add to the cheer.

Seong's Sushi Bar and Chinese Take-Out
907-586-4778
740 W. Ninth St., Juneau, AK 99801
Open: Mon.–Sat.
Price: Inexpensive to Moderate
Credit Cards: Yes
Cuisine: Sushi and Chinese
Serving: L, D
Special Features: Eat-in or take out; a full sushi spectrum; no reservations; no alcohol.

Need a sushi fix? This is the place locals and government workers alike head when they absolutely have to have some fresh fish with vinegar-seasoned rice, zinged up with wasabi and pickled ginger. Favorites are the Alaska roll and Seong's roll, with salmon, shrimp, avocado, and flying-fish roe. Many locals name this as the best sushi in Juneau, if not Alaska.

The tiny restaurant also has a full Chinese menu, with soups, stir-fried dishes, and noodle dishes. On cold winter days, nothing satisfies more than the chicken-broth based soups here. The restaurant lies within the shadow of Juneau's federal building.

Sweet Dream Teas
907-789-4401
sweetdreamteas.com
8585 Old Dairy Rd., Suite 102B, Juneau, AK 99801
Upstairs in K-Plaza near the airport
Open: Daily
Price: Inexpensive
Credit Cards: Yes
Cuisine: Asian tea shop
Serving: L, D
Handicapped Access: Ground-level entrance
Special Features: Anime rental plus tea shop with food.

If you want lunch, you may think you've come to the wrong place, at Sweet Dream. Shelves with Japanese anime DVDs fill the front of the shop. Keep going, and you'll come to a counter where you can place an order for *pho bo* (Vietnamese beef noodle soup) or *udon* (Japanese wheat noodle soup), or green-tea ice cream or bubble tea. The shop-café-tea bar has a multi-faceted personality. It's even an entertainment venue, with karaoke and anime screenings on weekend nights. At any time, you can check your e-mail with free wireless Internet.

The big bowls of soup will warm you up on cool Juneau days. Terrific Vietnamese salads and sandwiches are loaded with crunchy vegetables. Kids will be happy with the corn dogs and toasted-cheese pocket sandwiches.

The snack-drink known as bubble tea—various choices of iced tea with tapioca pearls or coconut jelly candies at the bottom—appeals on mild days. They even provide an extra-wide straw so you can take in the little bits of sweetness instead of having them plug up the straw.

T. K. McGuire

907-586-3711
prospectorhotel.com/restaurant.htm
375 Whittier St., Juneau, AK 99801
Open: Daily
Price: Inexpensive to Moderate
Credit Cards: Yes
Cuisine: Alaskan-American
Serving: B, L, D
Special Features: Hotel restaurant; bi-level dining room, to maximize view.

Historic mining photos and teal wainscoting carry out the old Alaska theme in this light, airy restaurant. Two levels optimize the views over Gastineau Channel and Douglas Island from all tables.

Homey entrées, including chicken-fried steak, pot roast, and salt-rubbed, slow-roasted prime rib, draw visitors and locals. The beer-battered halibut and chips is a good example of that ubiquitous dish, fluffy on the inside, delicately crisp on the outside. At lunch, sandwiches and wraps, including a delicious teriyaki wrap, join the lineup. The "T.K." stands for Terry and Kay, owners of this cheerful and welcoming hotel restaurant.

Twisted Fish Company

907-463-5033
twistedfish.hangaronthewharf.com
info@hangaronthewharf.com
550 S. Franklin St., Juneau, AK 99801
Open: Daily, May 1–Oct. 1
Price: Moderate
Credit Cards: Yes
Cuisine: Alaskan pub-style
Serving: L, D
Special Features: Fish house atmosphere, channel view; reservations recommended.

Twisted Fish Company is the younger, and more sophisticated, sister of nearby Hangar on the Wharf. It shares the waterfront building near the base of the Mount Roberts Tramway with Taku Smokeries, whose salmon products appear on the menu.

The Twisted Fish has the expected salmon, halibut, and king crab, but prepares them in unexpected ways. In addition to broiled, salmon comes baked on a cedar plank or in puff pastry. Halibut comes with wild berry salsa, either as an entrée or in a burger. Oysters, not very common in Alaska, are among appetizers. A good way to sample widely is to share the fish bites platter.

One night, salmon croquettes—three crispy cakes, with a sauce that wakes up the taste buds—sat on a bed of utterly crisp and fresh leaf lettuce. The smoked salmon Caesar pasta salad has crunchy romaine and rotini pasta, topped with a shower of shredded Parmesan. Thin-crust pizza, including trendy smoked salmon, is also popular and it's not unusual for people to order it to go.

The dining room is large and cavernous, with golden oak walls and tables, and, on one side, a window wall overlooking Gastineau Channel. Fancifully colored fish hanging from beams add splashes of color. When cruise ships are in town, passengers jam the big room, so reservations are recommended. The atmosphere is "refined fish house," though it's not too fancy: A paper napkin wraps the cutlery, and ketchup, mustard, and malt vinegar bottles stand on tables.

The wine list offers more than 40 wines by the glass, with some especially interesting red wines from smaller wineries. Three large fish restaurants are along Juneau's waterfront. The Twisted Fish seems to get the most votes from locals.

Wild Spice

907-523-0344
thewildspice.com
140 Seward St., 99801
Open: Daily
Price: Moderate to Expensive
Credit Cards: Yes
Cuisine: Asian Eclectic
Serving: L, Mon.–Fri.; D
Special Features: Mongolian barbecue.

Asian aromas waft through Wild Spice, a downtown restaurant. Photos of exotic Asian spice markets complement the aromas. It's an informal place, with laminated tabletops, booths, and lots of families on a weeknight.

At dinner, you have a choice of à la carte entrées, or a do-it-yourself entrée, called "Wild Bowl." You select the ingredients from a buffet, and a chef cooks them over a huge Mongolian barbecue grill. The restaurant gives a crib sheet, but faced with the array of vegetables, shrimp, squid, beef, and coconut milk sauce, it's much more fun to follow your impulses.

Amazingly, the guy behind the grill separates elements from the bowl, starting meat and sauces first, then adding vegetables and starch, so that everything seems to finish cooking at the same moment. The à la carte menu is truly global, with African shrimp *chermoulah*, Peruvian-crusted halibut, and elk *piccata*. If you don't want to take chances, the lengthy menu offers crab cakes and pan-seared scallops. Lunch items run more to mainstream tastes, with burgers, a salmon BLT, and chicken-salad sandwich—beware of the jalapeños—and a terrific-looking spinach salad with shrimp.

The restaurant labels its food "adventure cuisine." That, it is.

Zen Asian Fusion Restaurant

907-586-5075
zen-restaurant.net
51 Egan Dr., Juneau, AK 99801
Open: Daily
Price: Moderate to Expensive
Credit Cards: Yes
Cuisine: Asian Fusion
Serving: B, L, D
Special Features: Attractive décor; reservations recommended

This lovely dining room, accented with a long swag of burnt-orange silk and a bamboo screen, is popular with local residents as well as Alaskans who make the trip to the state capital for government business. Although it's right at the waterfront, it doesn't seem to have as many cruise passengers as other nearby places. People enter off the lobby of the Goldbelt Hotel, and it's a little hidden from the busy street.

The menu roams across many Asian cuisines: Chinese hot and sour soup joins Japanese *miso* and *udon* on the soup list; Chinese stir-fry dishes appear beside Thai curries. And for those who don't like to stray from heartland fare, steaks and a rack of lamb are offered.

Items appear in themed sections labeled "Earth"(vegetarian), "Water," (fish and seafood), and "Land" (meat and poultry.) Most people order Alaska seafood. The black cod stir-fry balances a deep brothy sauce with crisp, green pea pods, bean sprouts, mushrooms, onions, and the delicate fish. The shrimp also earns raves.

Breakfast departs from the Asian-fusion theme, with American comfort food, such as eggs, French toast, biscuits and gravy, and hash browns. Even smoked pork chop and prime rib show up at breakfast.

Zephyr Restaurant

907-780-2221
200 Seward St., Juneau, AK 99801
Open: Tues.–Sat.
Price: Moderate
Credit Cards: Yes
Cuisine: Mediterranean leaning toward Italy
Serving: D
Special Features: Stylish store-front restaurant; reservations recommended.

Sometimes the diner welcomes a break from so much Alaska salmon and halibut, delicious though they are. The Zephyr offers this opportunity, with Mediterranean dishes spanning from Italy to Turkey. Hummus, *baba ghanoush*, and olive tapenade appear on the appetizer list, followed by an assortment of salads, pastas, and entrées.

Sun-dried tomatoes work their way into several choices, including a vinaigrette and the Aegean pasta. A lengthy pasta list and several entrées bring an Italian flair to the menu. Large servings will satisfy the most ravenous appetites, and some of the salads, including one with asparagus, pancetta, and gorgonzola serve as an entrée. Polenta lasagna is both hearty and light, with pan-fried polenta substituting for the usual lasagna noodles.

Service was very friendly and prompt, almost too prompt, with our main courses arriving before we had finished the salads.

The corner store front is extremely stylish, with burnt-orange walls and tablecloths, an allegorical mural, and crystal-pendant chandeliers hanging above the room. It's the kind of place where people linger over the last glass of wine, and join in conversation with diners at the next table.

GUSTAVUS

Gustavus has few stand-alone restaurants or cafés. Most dining rooms are within full-service lodges or bed-and-breakfast inns.

Zephyr's sophisticated surroundings and Mediterranean menu bring variety to downtown Juneau.

Taste of Local Culture

Each week during the summer, Juneau families host others in their homes in a program benefiting the **Juneau Arts & Humanities Council** (907-586-2787; jahc.org). You must preregister, and indicate any dietary restrictions. Hosts pick up people at the Council's headquarters and return them after dinner, with four to six guests hosted most evenings. It's an excellent way to meet local residents, enjoy Alaska specialties from some of Juneau's best cooks, and support a good cause.

It is possible to dine at these places, but you must make an advance reservation. Most Gustavus restaurants are open only May through September.

A Bear's Nest Café
907-697-2440
gustavus.com/bearsnest/index.html
P.O. Box 216 on Wilson Rd., Gustavus, AK 99826
Open: Daily in summer
Price: Inexpensive to Moderate

Credit Cards: Yes
Cuisine: Homey, with organic produce
Serving: L, D
Handicapped Access: Ramp in rear
Special Features: Lots of character; vegan items; reservations.

Gustavus oldest restaurant looks like the Alaska of the imagination, with weathered boards and baskets hanging from the ceiling. It operates on the cooked-from-scratch, and local, philosophy. Produce and

The Village Bakery and Deli in Haines Junction, Yukon, is the scene of a weekly salmon bake in summer.

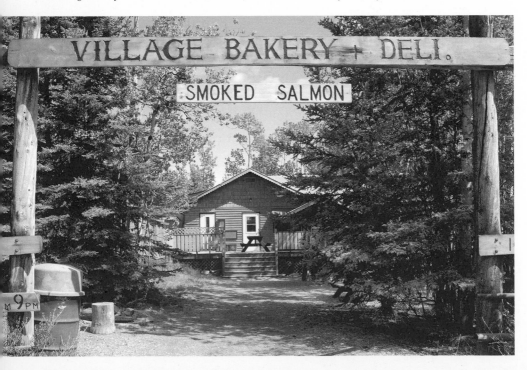

herbs come from the organic garden; the fish and crab from local fishermen. Owner-chef Lynne Morrow also offers vegetarian and vegan dishes. Soup and breads are homemade daily, and the decadent desserts will keep you at the table through another course. Strawberry-rhubarb pie, ginger-bread with lemon curd, and cream-cheese brownies are known throughout Glacier Bay. Live music on Saturday nights.

Glacier Bay Lodge

907-697-4000 or 1-888-229-8687
visitglacierbay.com/lodging-food/
index.cfm
179 Bartlett Cove Rd., Gustavus, AK 99826
At Bartlett Cove in Glacier Bay National Park
Open: Daily, late May–early Sept.
Price: Moderate to Expensive
Credit Cards: Yes
Cuisine: Alaska American
Serving: B, L, D
Special Features: Dining room and outside deck; reservations.

A spectacular Tlingit painting of Raven and Eagle highlights one end of the Fairweather dining room, named for the nearby mountain range. It also has a window wall and, in nice weather, a deck where you might spot whales.

Dungeness crab is the house specialty, though halibut and salmon will almost certainly be on the menu. Breakfast—which pretty much covers American standards—starts early, for those heading to a cruise on Glacier Bay, and dinner is served until late evening, for those enjoying outdoor activities in the long Alaska twilight. Lunch covers the burger-sandwich-salad-soup gamut. This is the only lodge-restaurant within the national park. Campers will also appreciate the small grocery store.

Smoked Salmon—Hot or Cold

The terms cold-smoked salmon or hot-smoked salmon appear frequently on menus. As you might expect, the difference relates to the smoking temperature, but there are other differences.

The following information comes from Taku Smokeries on the Juneau waterfront, where you can peer into the smoking kitchens. According to them, all smoked salmon, halibut, or cod starts the same way. The fresh fish, which usually has been flash-frozen, is brought to the smokery. It's cleaned, and cut into filets or slices. A skilled crew can do 1,000 pounds of salmon in an hour.

Then it's brined, either in liquid brine with salt and water, or dry-brined with table salt and spices. Never, ever ask anyone for his or her brine recipe—it's a serious breach of fish etiquette. Brining lasts several hours or overnight.

Hot-smoked salmon: The fish is put into the smoker and kept at 150 degrees F or higher for the smoking period. The heat is circulated with a vertical airflow. The result is cooked fish, sometimes called kippered salmon. It is what you will find in cans or jars, or in refrigerated plastic packs.

Cold-smoked salmon: The brined fish is put into a Smith smoker, and kept at a low 60–80 degrees F, with the air circulation horizontal. The result is similar to lox, and the salmon must be kept refrigerated. At Taku, sockeye is the salmon of choice for hot- or cold-smoked fish.

Dry-smoked salmon: This is a variation on cold-smoked salmon. The fish is flash-frozen after brining so it can be cut into extremely thin slices with a band saw. Smoking is overnight, and the result is salmon jerky.

Eskimo candy or salmon candy: A term used either for the smoked, rich, belly strips of salmon, or salmon smoked with a bit of brown sugar. Either way, it's smoked almost to a caramelized sweetness.

Salmon Bake

A salmon roast, or bake, bestows a kind of "really been there" mantle on the whole Alaska experience. It's a group activity, and likely to be touristy. The salmon or halibut may not be the best you'll have in Alaska, but salmon bakes are fun. You won't go away hungry, and you may meet some of the Alaska characters you'll remember best, long after the dinner blurs into a memory.

Service is usually from a buffet and includes a salad bar. Baked beans and corn or cornbread often round out the menu. And the salmon, usually king or sockeye, will be wild, line-caught fish. It may be barbecued, baked, or smoked. Beer-battered halibut is also a staple, and a meat dish or chicken is usually offered.

Salmon bakes are seasonal, usually May through September, and if outside of town, provide bus transportation from hotels or cruise ships. The cost ranges about $25–$35 for adults. Almost all salmon bakes have tiered prices, with half price or less for children, and very young children are sometimes free.

JUNEAU

Gold Creek Salmon Bake: (907-586-1424; 1601 Salmon Creek Lane.) Here, the scent of alder-smoked salmon greets visitors. The menu also includes barbecued chicken and ribs, Chilkoot baked beans, Tongass wild-rice pilaf, and salads. You'll dine under translucent domes in the rainforest, and afterward get to toast marshmallows. A lively waterfall where salmon may be spawning adds to the excitement. Visitors may also see relics of the historic Wagner Mine. Transfers from hotels or cruise ships are included.

Taku Glacier Lodge: (907-586-6275; wingsairways.com; office: 2 Marine Way.) This is the Cadillac of salmon bakes. A float plane gives you a scenic tour over Taku Glacier, fed by the Juneau icefields, before depositing you in front of the lodge. You can poke about the grounds before settling into the huge feast of salmon with baked beans, coleslaw, fruit compote, and cookies. If you can rouse yourself up from the feast afterward, you may take a guided walk. Sometimes black bears will wander onto the grounds, which inspires a lot of camera clicking. Then the float plane whisks you back to Juneau. The entire experience takes about four hours. The lodge was built in 1923, and has operated almost continuously since then. Price runs a bit over $200, but this includes the float-plane excursion.

Thane Ore House Salmon & Halibut Bake: (907-586-3442; thaneorehouse.com; 4400 Thane Road.) The salmon bake takes place in rustic buildings about 4 miles south of Juneau. It's located on the waterfront at the old Thane town site, which was near the A.J. Mine. On warm days it's pleasant to eat outside and enjoy the view over the waterfront and mountains. A heated indoor dining room is comfortable in Juneau's often misty weather. A mining museum displays artifacts.

SKAGWAY

Liarsville Gold Rush Trail Camp and Salmon Bake: (Sponsored by an RV Park, 907-983-3333.) A Klondike Gold Rush town has sprung to life outside of Skagway, complete with saloon, dance hall girls, tents, gold pans, and a stream. Lunch or dinner features salmon roasted over a wood fire, coleslaw, baked beans, potatoes, sourdough rolls, apple strudel, and lemonade. You'll eat in a cookhouse on rustic tables. A dance hall show follows, along with the chance to try panning for gold.

And how did Liarsville get its name? During the Klondike Gold Rush, journalists camped out at this spot. They filed daily dispatches about the hardships of trudging over the 33-mile Chilkoot Trail and the challenges of getting passage on the Yukon River to Dawson. The hardships were hearsay. They never left the camp to investigate their stories.

YUKON

Haines Junction

Village Bakery and Deli: (867-634-2867; corner of Kluane and Logan, across the road from Kluane National Park Visitor Centre.) Just once a week, on Friday, during the summer, the Yukon Territory bakery-deli has a salmon barbecue. People enjoy their salmon, salad, and home-baked things on the picnic tables on the deck. It's down a gravel road, about 1½ blocks from the Alaska Highway. Ask anyone in town.

Gustavus Inn at Glacier Bay

907-697-2254 or 1-800-649-5220
gustavusinn.com
1 Gustavus Rd., P.O. Box 60, Gustavus, AK 99826
Open: Daily, mid-May–mid-Sept.
Price: Moderate to Expensive
Credit Cards: Yes
Cuisine: Sophisticated home-cooking
Serving: B, L, D
Special Features: Reservations required for those not staying at the inn.

Each day, the entrée for dinner is posted in the bar by late afternoon. Will it be barbecued salmon with a luscious and faintly sweet sauce? Ginger-steamed sablefish? Guests look forward to that announcement, for some of the best cooking in the Alaska Panhandle. The menu depends on the garden and the catch of the day.

Diners sit around large tables family style, and the cooking is like the best home-cooking imaginable. Little bowls with condiments and jams sit on the table.

Eagle and Raven look out from their panel over the Fairweather dining room at Glacier Bay Lodge.

Rhubarb grows abundantly in the Gustavus Inn garden and appears frequently in the dining room.

They might hold kelp pickles, kalamata olives, or rhubarb jam. Rhubarb flourishes in the garden, and it will come to the table in jams, crumbles, and compotes. As summer progresses, the garden supplies most vegetables for the table.

Balsamic vinaigrette dresses salads, and the bread and desserts are homemade. Lemon pound cake and brandy Alexander pie are among the memorable sweets. Owner David Lesh serves as the main chef; his reputation for ginger-steamed sablefish is legendary.

Breakfast starts with homemade granola and stewed fruit, followed by sourdough pancakes, eggs, French toast, or anything else you can imagine for breakfast. Lunch usually includes an excellent soup, perhaps gingered carrot, and homemade bread, including a crusty Irish soda bread.

Homeshore Café

907-697-2822
Wilson Rd., at the Gustavus crossroads
Open: Tues.–Sat.

Price: Inexpensive
Credit Cards: Yes
Cuisine: Homey, pizza, sandwiches
Serving: L, D
Special Features: Small café beside art gallery; no reservations.

Locals gather at this cheery restaurant, with its bright lattice wallpaper, blue-and-white ceilings, and big windows. A large section of pizza and calzones leads off the menu. They might include specialty pizzas with smoked-salmon and Alfredo sauce, or a spicy Thai pizza with peanut sauce. Servings are generous.

Oven-roasted sandwiches are another hearty choice with inventive fillings: a halibut melt or "dawnita," which features smoked turkey, balsamic onions, Swiss cheese, and spinach. Creative soups and salads round out the menu. A chopped salad adds dried berries, apricots, and spiced walnuts to the usual mix of greens. Add roasted chicken, and you have a feast. Food may be ordered to go.

HAINES

Mexican food seems popular in Haines. Almost every restaurant has tacos, taco salad, burritos, or quesadillas on the menu, usually incorporating Alaska halibut, salmon, or crab in a kind of Alaska-Mex fusion. Most Haines restaurants are open year-round, unless otherwise noted, and are nonsmoking.

33 Mile Roadhouse

907-767-5510
33 Mile Haines Hwy., HC 60 Box 3300, Haines, AK 99827
Open: Daily during summer, limited days rest of year
Price: Inexpensive
Credit Cards: Yes
Cuisine: Alaskan, through and through
Serving: B, L, D
Handicapped Access: No
Special Features: Old Alaska board-and-log building; picnic tables for good weather.

If you need gas or food on the Golden Circle drive between Haines and Yukon Territory, this is the place to stop. There won't be another café or gas pump until you reach Haines Junction, about 130 miles up the road in the Yukon.

33 Mile Roadhouse sits on the Haines Highway, once an old Alaska Native trail and Gold Rush route, and now a modern, paved road. The log building, supported with massive posts and bedecked with caribou antlers, is classic Alaska architecture. The heavy log picnic tables on the deck are popular in good weather.

The snug, beamed interior and friendly waitstaff make you feel safe from the weather. The food runs to typical roadhouse fare, including the self-proclaimed "best burgers in Alaska," soups, and sandwiches. The pie is memorable.

A bear named Gus stands guard outside the Homeshore Café in Gustavus.

Built of logs, 33 Mile Roadhouse outside of Haines is a classic Alaska institution.

Bamboo Room and Pioneer Bar

907-766-2800
bamboopioneer.net
Second Avenue, near Main Street
Open: Daily, year-round
Price: Inexpensive to Moderate
Credit Cards: Yes
Cuisine: Alaska American
Serving: B, L, D
Handicapped Access: In rear
Special Features: Reservations recommended for groups; historic restaurant-bar, local institution.

The improbable name for this restaurant comes from a bamboo panel that the owner put up in the 1950s, to separate the Pioneer Bar, which starts serving at 8 AM, from the restaurant, which opens at 6 AM. Diner-style booths line one side of the restaurant, and tables line up against a banquette on the other. Red is the theme here: It's the color of the false-front building that has

stood here for more than a century, the booths and banquettes, the T-shirts worn by the wait staff, and the edge of the plastic menu holder. The ketchup bottles on Formica tables add one more red accent.

Like so many Alaska establishments, this was once a brothel and a poker parlor, and before that the Hotel de France, serving French cuisine.

Now, almost everyone comes for the halibut and chips, which are big crusty chunks with fluffy, white fish inside. Halibut also appears in sauté dishes or in the halibut taco salad.

At breakfast, expect burritos, eggs any way you can imagine, and even blintzes. But do try the fluffy homemade biscuits with whatever you order. The homemade soups can be warming in brisk Haines, especially the comforting tomato bisque. Most of the food is Alaska American, but Portobello wraps, espresso milkshakes, and chocolate spoon cake could be lifted from trendy menus in the Lower 48.

The adjacent bar is darker, and funkier, with writing on the ceiling. The full restaurant menu is served in the bar.

Chilkat Restaurant and Bakery

907-766-3653
Fifth Ave., and Dalton St., Haines, AK 99827
Open: Mon.–Sat.
Price: Inexpensive to Moderate
Credit Cards: Yes
Cuisine: Homestyle American and Thai dinners
Serving: B, L, D, Wed.—Sat., and B, L, Mon. and Tues.
Special Features: Cheerful flower baskets, lace curtains, flowered wallpaper.

It's best to get here early for breakfast, since the tables fill up quickly with regulars. The delicious doughnuts—the only place in Haines that makes them—Danish pastries, a dozen kind of muffins, bagels, coffeecake, turnovers, and croissants are all made from scratch. At lunch, the same is true for the soups, salads, and sandwiches. Unusual twists are the sweet-potato fries that may be ordered with a sandwich, and the bagel sandwiches.

Flexibility ought to please even the most finicky eaters. Breakfast covers all the basics, but includes breakfast burritos, even a low-carb version, custom-built omelets, and fresh fruit-topped oatmeal. Dinner brings another surprise: A full Thai menu, with curries, stir-fried items, and noodle and rice dishes. You may order chicken, shrimp, beef, or fish as the basis for most dishes. And, if you don't like Thai, a basic American menu, with halibut, salmon, chicken, and halibut and chips is also offered.

Lace valances, bright floral wallpaper, and an antique clock bring the look of grandmother's cheery dining room to the café. A lot of people stop by to get something out of the bakery case.

Commander's Room Restaurant and Officers' Club Lounge

907-766-2000
hotelhalsingland.com
Hotel Halsingland in Historic Fort Seward; P.O. Box 1649, Haines, AK 99827
Open: Mother's Day—mid-Sept.
Price: Moderate to Expensive
Credit Cards: Yes
Cuisine: Contemporary cuisine with focus on Alaska seafood and produce
Serving: D
Special Features: Historic hotel setting; elegant dining room; bar menu.

The chef may make a detour through the garden on the way to the kitchen, for some of the vegetables and herbs grown right on the property. During the winter, the owners travel to sample cuisine in other places, and bring these idea to Haines. Lower-48 *au courant* influences, such as duck *confit* and Asian-inspired spicy Thai noodle salad may appear alongside French Provençal or Moroccan dishes. If white king salmon is available, it may be served over a bed of vegetables or with ginger-rhubarb chutney. Kalamata olive tapenade may embellish halibut. A lamb dish and chicken usually join the list.

Halibut and chips highlights the bar menu, as well as blackened-salmon, Caesar, and duck confit salads, and the irresistible house-made flatbread with various mushroom, caramelized onion, or cheese toppings. Flatbread and salad make an appealing light dinner.

The dining room befits the dignity of the former commander's quarters when Fort Seward was a U.S. Army Post. A fireplace, white tablecloths, window tables with views, Victorian wallpaper, and oak chairs complete the scene. The restaurant is a special place for locals, and a destination

Crusted halibut over vegetables is worthy of an officer at the Commander's Room Restaurant at Hotel Halsingland.

for visitors, and the waitstaff treat diners attentively; sometimes over-attentively.

Fireweed
907-766-3838
Bldg. 37, Blacksmith Rd. Fort Seward, Haines, AK 99827
Open: May–Sept.
Price: Inexpensive to Moderate
Credit Cards: Yes
Cuisine: Organic, contemporary Alaska
Serving: L, D daily
Special Features: Reservations recommended in summer; sophisticated and simple.

A placid malamute, with one blue and one topaz eye, waited quietly at the entrance to Fireweed. He scarcely raised his head when diners stepped over him to get into the door. Inside, local families and tourists sat around big, wooden tables, taking in the yeasty aromas wafting from the kitchen.

Breads and pizzas are freshly baked here. A special house-baked sandwich, a kind of calzone, arrives steamy and fragrant with smoked turkey, eggplant Parmesan, or smoked salmon.

The list of beer from Haines Brewing Company is impressive, and may include spruce tip ale, in season. Several varieties are usually on tap. The clean, pale, bare-wood tables, chairs, and floors make an appealing backdrop to the home-cooking style of the food. Windows on one side of the room overlook the Lynn Canal, and in good weather, deck seating provides an even wider view.

Fort Seward Lodge
907-766-2009 or 1-877-617-3418
ftsewardlodge.com
39 Mud Bay Rd., Haines, AK 99827
Open: May–Oct; limited days rest of year
Price: Moderate
Credit Cards: Yes

Cuisine: Contemporary roadhouse fare
Serving: D
Handicapped Access: Three steps
Special Features: Reservations recommended in summer; historic building, lively atmosphere.

The whole Dungeness crab sitting on a plate is both spectacular and intimidating. But never fear, owner-server Kim Sundburg shows you how to extract every bit of succulent meat using a crab leg tip for an implement. It works better than a cracker. This is just one of the Alaska specialties that may be ordered at this restaurant, which gets high ratings from Haines locals. Of course there's halibut and prawns, and if the halibut didn't come in at the dock across the road, it won't be on the menu that night.

This is the sort of place where you may expect *beurre blanc* sauce with the halibut and cumin rub on the salmon. Crab cakes, raspberry chicken, Korean ribs, and a gigantic Porterhouse for two may round out the sophisticated menu. Lighter entrées include pastas or grilled seasonal vegetables.

For the nights when you're not up to a full dinner, a bar menu fills in nicely, with a Caesar salad topped with chicken, halibut, or salmon, a burger with toppings, or halibut and chips. During mild weather, you can sip your drink on the deck overlooking Lynn Canal.

If you're wondering about the swing in the center of the dining room, it dates back to the Lodge's bawdier days. Vintage photos show the room with women in dance hall attire seated on the swing.

Lighthouse Restaurant and Harbor Bar
907-766-2442
theharbor@aptalaska.net
1 Front St., Haines, AK 99827
Open: Daily year-round
Price: Inexpensive
Credit Cards: Yes
Cuisine: Down-home with sophisticated touches
Serving: B, L, D
Special Features: Impressive 1886 bar on one side, sweeping view over Lynn Canal; smoking in bar.

Bright gerbera daisies in window bays bring a cheerful down-home look to this restaurant popular with locals and visitors. The windows look out over the water and the mountains beyond and are likely to capture attention when you're not looking at the plate with hefty servings and bright colors.

Although the food has a down-home feel, with burgers, taco salad, and halibut-and-chips on the menu, there are exotic touches, such as a guava vinaigrette on mesclun greens for a salad, blackened chicken, and shrimp quesadillas. At breakfast you will find the classics, including eggs cooked familiar ways.

Servings are large and plates look colorful, with fruit garnishing a chicken pita, and a taco salad as big and bright as Mexican paper flowers. At dinner, there may be teriyaki salmon or other Asian-inspired dishes.

If you're sitting in the restaurant, do make a trip to the bar. It's a huge room, easily as large as the restaurant, and the truly massive bar, a relic of the Yukon Gold Rush, dominates the room. Lots of games keep bar patrons entertained.

Mosey's Cantina
907-766-2320
31 Tower Road. At Soapsuds Alley, Fort Seward, P.O. Box 1509, Haines, AK 99827
Open: Mon.–Sat., Mar.–Sept.
Price: Inexpensive
Credit Cards: Yes
Cuisine: Mexican
Serving: L, D
Special Features: Front-porch dining.

The signs at Mosey's Cantina in Haines match the colors on a Mexican combo plate.

You could order that New Mexican specialty called "Christmas" here, since Mosey's offers both red and green chili sauces. The owners go to New Mexico to get the proper chilies to serve in the restaurant painted bright yellow and red with a sunburst on the façade.

Look for all of the classics: tacos, enchiladas, and chiles rellenos, served with fresh house-made sauces. Locals love this restaurant, and often recommend it.

HOONAH

Hoonah restaurants listed here are located at Icy Strait Point complex, which is visited primarily by cruise ships, though the Alaska ferry stops in town and independent travelers are of course welcome. The complex is open in summer only. This once-productive cannery in a relatively remote area has been transformed into a modern facility, to entertain, inform, and feed visitors. **The Crab Station** (icystraitpoint.com; info@icystraitpoint.com) opened in 2008.

It serves only Dungeness crab, brought to the Hoonah docks fresh daily, on an all-you-can-eat basis. **The Landing Zone** is at the end of Icy Strait Point's exciting ZipRider attraction, where riders soar down the mountain for more than a mile, at speeds up to 60 miles per hour. They're in a celebratory mood by the time they get here to relax over lunch, or maybe one of the specialty drinks or beer on tap. The Alaska trinity—salmon, halibut, crab—are the specialties at Icy Strait Point restaurants, though burgers and salads are also served. All of the fish is line-caught, and delivered to the dock that you see from the restaurants. **The Cookhouse** is at the former cannery building, which now houses shops and the Icy Strait Museum. The menu is the same as the Landing Zone. Both restaurants have views over the dock and water, and both have outdoor seating. The Cookhouse facility also has an espresso and snack bar where you can get a reindeer hot dog, chips, and other lighter fare.

Skagway

Skagway restaurants are nonsmoking, unless otherwise noted; most of them open only in summer, unless otherwise noted.

Bonanza Bar & Grill
907-983-6214
westmarkhotels.com/skagway.php
330 Broadway, P.O. Box 525, Skagway, AK 99840
Open: Daily
Price: Inexpensive to Moderate
Credit Cards: Yes
Cuisine: Alaska American
Serving: L, D
Special Features: Re-created Klondike-era saloon; smoking permitted.

You'll be tempted to burst through the door, and say "Howdy, pardner," at this re-created Klondike saloon right on Skagway's Broadway. It's part of the Westmark Inn, though it's entered separately. The huge false-front building has a cavernous bar-room, lit up with Alaskan amber ale signs. It attracts a lot of tourists during the day when cruise ships are in town, but turns quiet after 5 PM.

You can enjoy a burger or ribs with a brew, or salad, including a reasonably good Caesar. Mostly, it's the kind of place to belly up to the bar and order something big and high-calorie.

Port of Call
907-983-2411
363 Second Ave., between Broadway and State St., Skagway, AK 99840
Open: Daily
Price: Inexpensive to Moderate
Credit Cards: Yes
Cuisine: Italian and Middle Eastern
Serving: L, D
Special Features: Television, Internet café; nonsmoking.

This is the kind place where you can get a quick bite to eat, or you could linger for hours, checking e-mail or watching sports on the big-screen television. A lot of people come for the pizza, which some locals rate as the best in town. There is a create-your-own option with a lengthy list of toppings to mix and match as you please. If you can't decide, there are themed pizzas—the White Pass Route and Orient Express. They come out of the oven with a crispy, blistered crust. A salad bar adds to the healthful options, a relatively rare thing in Alaska.

Some Middle Eastern items offer a refreshing change on this menu, including a Greek salad and Turkish meatloaf entrée. A wide variety of sandwiches is also on the menu.

The Skagway Fish Company
907-983-3474 (FISH)
201 Congress Way, Skagway, AK 99840
Open: Daily
Price: Inexpensive to Moderate
Credit Cards: Yes
Cuisine: Alaska American
Serving: L, D
Special Features: Waterfront restaurant with view near docks; reservations recommended for dinner.

Thick rope hangs in swags on the façade of this cheerful red building. Inside, floats and nets hang like garlands from the rafters. The décor fits the menu at this waterfront restaurant. It's a neighbor of Stowaway Café and overlooks the Small Boat Harbor.

Chowder, halibut, and salmon are specialties, and you'll find oysters, crab, clams, and almost anything else that comes out of the sea. The kitchen shows skill at frying, which is a popular preparation method. The halibut and chips have been deemed the best this side of London, and many people like the creamy chowder. Crab lovers have a choice of cakes or king crab. Daily specials are more elaborate, but for the most part preparations run to the straight-forward, which suits the plain, bare tabletops and casual atmosphere.

Those who develop a taste for Alaskan amber ale or other local beers have good selections from brews on tap. The noise level can be high, but it adds to the liveliness.

Starfire

907-983-3663
Fourth Ave. between Spring and Broadway, Skagway, AK 99840
Open: Daily
Price: Inexpensive to Moderate
Credit Cards: Yes
Cuisine: Thai, Chinese, some Southwestern
Serving: L, Mon.–Fri.; D
Special Features: Tiny, colorful, 10-table dining room.

Mustard and maroon walls bring vibrant color to this tiny restaurant and match the bright seasonings on the plates. Stir-fried dishes are a mélange of vegetables with chicken, shrimp, or beef, and sauces. Most of the menu is Thai, with curries, noodle dishes, including *pad thai*, and, of course, *tom kha* and *tom yum*, the classic Thai soups. Curries range from purple through green and red.

One menu section focuses on Chinese stir-fried dishes with great flexibility: Each one may be ordered with chicken, shrimp, or beef, and the vegetables and sauces for each vary. One night the freshness of the vegetables was greatly appealing after so many dinners of halibut and chips. Most surprising is the menu section with burritos and Frito chili pie, a dish that had its origins at the Woolworth's in Santa Fe.

Pay attention to the stars on the menu: They indicate the hotness of each dish. No star, for wimps; one star, faint heat; two stars, you'll know a chili pepper's in there; three stars, your eyes may water; four stars will start a fire.

Starfire's stir-fried veggie-rich dishes make an appealing contrast to overindulging on halibut and chips.

The dining rooms at Stowaway Café and Skagway Fish Company overlook the harbor and the waterfront promenade.

The Stowaway Café
907-983-3463
205 Congress Way, Skagway, AK 99840
Open: Daily
Price: Moderate
Credit Cards: Yes
Cuisine: Seafood with contemporary interpretation
Serving: D
Special Features: Innovative seafood preparations; harbor view; reservations highly recommended.

Passengers going to and from cruise ships will pass this café. It looks tempting to drop in, but to be assured you'll get a table, make a reservation. It's not very large; it's popular—it almost always tops the list of local recommendations—and it's only open for dinner.

Salmon and halibut star on the menu, but the preparations are innovative. Salmon may be grilled or blackened in the Cajun manner, but there also are some nods to Thai and French dishes, or Italian influences. One night, a halibut special came topped with pesto and roasted peppers. A delicious soup with spinach, mushrooms, and garlic launched dinner on another cool night. An appetizer of crab toasts is so good you'll be tempted to fill up on that.

Meat lovers may choose steak or ribs. Not only does imagination spark up the menu, the preparation lives up to the promise. Fish is moist, and salads are not overdressed.

The gray board building, on the Small Boat Harbor, has a home-built look, which adds to its charm. A mermaid mural adorns one side and, during warm weather, diners may sit on a deck overlooking the harbor.

YAKUTAT
Dining options in Yakutat are either in the lodges or the grocery store, which has a hot bar and a few tables.

Glacier Bear Lodge

907-784-3202
glacierbearlodge.com
Glacier Bear Ave., off Yakutat Rd., P.O. Box, 303, Yakutat, AK 99689
Open: Daily, Apr.–Oct.
Price: Moderate
Credit Cards: Yes
Cuisine: Alaska American
Serving: B weekends only, L, D
Special Features: Cheerful, light-filled dining room; popular with locals; nonsmoking.

Almost every night offers some special activity at Glacier Bear Lodge. On Saturday, it's boxing (televised) and prime rib, served in the bar with the big-screen television; on Thursday, it's Girl's Night Out with special drink prices. There are special wine-tasting nights, and brunches on special days during the summer.

The restaurant and large bar are in the light-filled blue building, which is relatively new, though the lodge has been in Yakutat for about 30 years. Like other lodgings in Yakutat, this one attracts fishermen.

The restaurant also has fresh, locally caught salmon and halibut on the menu in season almost every night. A big slab of sautéed salmon arrived moist in the center and delicately ivory on the outer edges. The garlic mashed potatoes didn't really need the big pool of gravy, but that may be what most diners prefer. Several entrée salads, including grilled steak, taco, and Caesar with toppings, as well as a pasta section, expand the menu.

One item on the dessert menu is called the "Widow Maker." It's a chocolate extravaganza, with multiple layers sandwiched together with rich, buttercream chocolate icing. The room's white walls, beveled-glass light fixtures, and big windows, create an airy, light-filled space, almost reminiscent of places at lower latitudes. The bearskin on the wall, however, reminds you that this is Alaska and, at the edge of Yakutat, this is pretty much deep country.

Yakutat Lodge

907-784-3232
yakutatlodge.com
P.O. Box 287, Yakutat, AK 99689
Open: Daily year-round
Price: Inexpensive to Moderate
Credit Cards: Yes
Cuisine: Alaska American
Serving: B, L, D
Special Features: Rustic, convenient to airport.

Sooner or later, everyone who comes to Yakutat pulls open the lodge's heavy wooden door by its moose-antler handles. It's right beside the airport, making it handy for meals before and after a flight, for contacting someone in town (cell phones do not work here), or for killing time.

It's large bar, which overlooks the runway, seems to be where most of the meals are served. Maybe it's because fishing movies run continuously on a big screen. The menu covers the usual salmon-to-halibut range, along with steaks and chicken. People in Yakutat will recommend it as the place to go for a halibut burger and, indeed, they make quite a feast of this basic combo of fish and bread. It's piled high with a generous filet of the fresh fish, along with enough lettuce and tomato to make a salad, as well as pickles and a slather of a mayo-like sauce. Besides the burger, the paper-lined basket overflows with french fries. For many, it's a first and a last meal in Alaska.

Yukon

Visitors to Haines and Skagway often make a side trip to Whitehorse or Haines Junction in Yukon Territory, on the Golden Circle Drive. Tiny Haines Junction has one of the best restaurants in western Canada or Alaska. Whitehorse, with a population of 27,000 (about the same size as Juneau), has several good restaurants.

Yukon Territory passed an antismoking law in 2008, so restaurants and bars are

The halibut burger at Yakutat Lodge is as good as any in Alaska.

now all smoke-free. Just remember to bring your passport.

HAINES JUNCTION
The Raven
867-634-2500
kluaneraven@yknet.ca
181 Alaska Hwy., P.O. Box 5470, Haines Junction, Yukon Y0B 1L0 Canada
At the junction with Kluane Rd.
Open: Daily, May–Sept.
Price: Expensive
Credit Cards: Yes
Cuisine: Continental
Serving: D
Handicapped Access: No
Special Features: Gourmet Continental dining; reservations required.

This restaurant gets whispered about in Juneau and Anchorage by people who are embarrassed to admit that perhaps the best restaurant in the Far North is in tiny Haines Junction, and not their relatively cosmopolitan cities. But it may be true. *Where to Eat in Canada* rated it as one of that country's best restaurants. It's simply remarkable to see this small crossroads hotel on the Alaska Highway, serving this exalted fare.

Owner Gwen Watson produces exquisite salmon, handmade pasta, elk with mushroom sauce, and a divine chocolate mousse. Of course, the menu changes frequently and depends on what's the freshest and best available, including ingredients from the inn's garden. Although ownership of The Raven changed in 2008, the restaurant maintains the high standards that earned its stellar reputation.

The dining room of the 12-room Raven Hotel, which has a spartan, gray-board look, sits on the second floor of the building and overlooks the stunning St. Elias Mountains. An outdoor deck provides seating on warm days.

The Raven is a dining destination. Plan your trip to the Yukon around the opportunity to get reservations here.

WHITEHORSE

Whitehorse and Juneau are the two largest cities in the Alaska Panhandle–Southwest Yukon area. Both of them are capitals, so restaurants get a lot of regional travelers as well as those from more distant places.

The Cellar Steakhouse and Wine Bar

867-667-2572
edgewaterhotelwhitehorse.com
101 Main St., Whitehorse, YT Y1A 2A7
Open: Tues.–Sat.
Price: Moderate to Expensive
Credit Cards: Yes
Cuisine: International and steaks
Serving: D
Handicapped Access: No
Special Features: Tapas, extensive wine list; fireplaces, reservations recommended.

Territory legislators, judges and court officials, and bank boards of executives may be seated at the group tables at this power-dining place in the Edgewater Hotel. This low-ceilinged space, with a dining room and a wine bar, each decorated with fireplaces with flickering gas logs, attracts locals who come to celebrate or hold meetings, as well as travelers wanting a good dinner.

After being seated, you'll be handed a lot of reading material—the regular menu, special menu, small plates list, and a wine list. They each offer many options, from a multicourse elaborate dinner, to a few shared tapas with a glass of wine. Cuisines of France, Italy, and Greece inspire menu dishes, along with North American steakhouse fare. The prime rib is a great favorite, according to our server. The kitchen also does interesting things with salmon and halibut when it's in season. Small plates feature crab cakes made with an abundant amount of Alaska king crab, a lamb rib chop, and a rum-marinated salmon filet. A small salad dresses these plates, making them an appealing light entrée.

Wines cover interesting international selections, including varietals from Argentina and Chile, as well as Italy and California, but not many Canadian wines.

Giorgio's Cuccina

867-668-4050
giorgioscuccina.com
202 Jarvis Ave., Whitehorse, YT
Open: Daily
Price: Moderate to Expensive
Credit Cards: Yes
Cuisine: Italian and Greek
Serving: L, D
Special Features: European atmosphere; mesquite broiler; reservations recommended for dinner.

European-Mediterranean décor sets the tone in the large room, with arches, frescoes, classical statues, and terracotta tile floor. The menu follows through with an extensive pasta section, thin-crust pizza, and even some Greek items. A mesquite grill brings a smoky taste to several varieties of fish and steak.

Mostly, though, this is a classic Italian restaurant with an especially lengthy menu. Even the choice for Caesar salad isn't limited to a single item: Diners may opt for "regular size" or "Giorgio's size," or it may be ordered with smoked salmon, garlic chicken, or Cajun chicken. The pasta list runs to more than a dozen varieties with several ingredients and sauces.

Souvlaki and moussaka are unusual finds in this North Country. But, you can order the Alaska-Yukon favorites salmon, halibut, or Alaska king-crab legs, and various steaks and chicken.

Klondike Rib and Salmon BBQ

867-667-7554
2116 Second Ave. at Steele St., Whitehorse, YT
Open: Daily, May–Sept.
Price: Inexpensive to Moderate

Credit Cards: Yes
Cuisine: Barbecued fare with Northern interpretation
Serving: L, Mon.–Sat; D, daily.
Special Features: Heated deck; house-smoked meats and salmon; no reservations.

You'll find smoky, infused meats, such as ribs and chicken, in barbecue joints anywhere. But this is definitely a restaurant of the Far North. Caribou and musk ox go into the burgers, and Arctic char is served along with halibut and salmon. Bannock, the bread of the Canadian north, comes with the halibut chowder, though you might choose focaccia instead.

The lively restaurant is housed in what looks like a tent, and indeed the building started life around 1900, as a tented bakery. Later it became a mail-and-freight business, whose legacy, "Klondike Airways," is still painted on the building's side. (Actually the company carried mail to Dawson City by snowmobiles and Caterpillars during the winter, and in sum-

mer, by steamer.) Later, it became a mortuary shop where coffins were made.

In addition to the chowder and salads, including a yummy spinach salad with red onion, dried cranberries, feta cheese, and crunchy things, the menu has wraps, burgers, sandwiches, and Alaskan halibut and chips. A seafood dip named for onetime Whitehorse resident Robert Service is popular for sharing. The house smoked salmon is delicious. Most things at lunch overflow the baskets in which they're served. The dining room fills easily, and heat lamps keep the crowd on the decks warm. Waiting diners often line up, but service is fast, so the line moves quickly.

CENTRAL PANHANDLE

PETERSBURG

Rosemaling trim and the Sons of Norway Hall bring Petersburg's Norwegian heritage to every bit of Nordic Drive. Unfortunately, there's not a single Norwegian or Scandinavian restaurant in town. The closest

Rarely is Klondike Rib and Salmon BBQ in Whitehorse without a line down the sidewalk.

you'll get to the kind of fare that the locals might serve at home is at Coastal Cold Storage (See *Food Purveyors* section) or perhaps you'll luck into a private event at the Sons of Norway Hall.

Restaurants serve a spectrum, from halibut tacos to hamburgers, stir-fries, Korean beef, and Philly cheese steaks, sometimes on a single menu. Petersburg has some good takeout choices (See *Food Purveyors section*).

Petersburg restaurants are largely non-smoking, though not the bars. Most of them stay open year-round.

Beachcomber Inn

907-772-3888
384 Mitkof Hwy, Petersburg, AK 99833
About 4 miles south of town
Open: Tues.–Sat. May–Sept.
Price: Moderate
Credit Cards: Yes
Cuisine: Alaska American

Serving: D
Special Features: Waterfront dining on porch and small dining rooms; courtesy van; reservations highly recommended.

Hope for a warm night when you're in Petersburg. At the Beachcomber Inn, people gravitate to the porch overlooking Wrangell Narrows. Sitting there, in the sunset glow of Alaska's eternal twilight, can be utterly magical. Should the evening cool, heat lamps keep the temperature comfortable. Most people have a glass of wine or a beer before getting down to serious ordering.

The building was once a cannery, though you'd never know it. Flower tubs, porch seating, intimate dining rooms, and stained-glass windows have transformed it into a graceful restaurant.

The relatively short menu reflects Petersburg's being a fishing town. Among the local catch, prized white king salmon may be on the menu. Embellished with a

Dining on the deck at Petersburg's Beachcomber Inn lingers long into the Alaska twilight.

soy glaze, the fish is still moist, the better to appreciate its delicacy. Seafood fettuccine is a feast in itself, with tender pasta and poached fish and a mound of shrimp over the top. Parsley speckles the plate edge like green polka dots.

Salads are a popular starter. Balsamic vinaigrette brings a slightly sweet note to baby greens with dill, dried cranberries, pecans, and tangy feta cheese. The Caesar has huge pieces of romaine, tempting one diner to pick up the pieces with her fingers.

This is a popular restaurant with locals, many of whom seem to order steak, perhaps a change from the fish at home. The restaurant, about 4 miles from town, offers a van service.

Joan Mei

907-772-4222
1103 S. Nordic Dr., Petersburg, AK 99833
Open: Daily, except Wed.
Price: Inexpensive to Moderate
Credit Cards: Yes
Cuisine: Chinese and some American dishes
Serving: L, Mon. and Tues., Thurs.–Sat.; Sbr; D, Mon. and Tues., Thurs.–Sun.
Handicapped Access: No
Special Features: Lengthy Chinese menu and décor; smoking allowed.

Joan Mei stands just across the road from the ferry dock. The lavender building has faded and needs a paint job, but inside the walls are bright red, and Chinese lanterns and paintings decorate the room. The owner is likely to give you a sunny greeting when you walk through the door.

The menu spans the Chinese range, with stir-fry dishes with crisp vegetables, fried and glazed appetizers, soups, and a variety of noodle dishes. Crispy egg rolls and fried rice are the kitchen's specialties. Things taste fresh, particularly vegetables in stir-fried dishes. Beyond the lengthy menu of Cantonese, Szechuan, and Mandarin

dishes, you can get standard American burgers and baskets and, most surprising of all, a short list of Mexican dishes. Anything on the menu is available for take-out, convenient for the ferry.

Rooney's Northern Lights Restaurant

907-772-2900
203 Sing Lee Alley, P.O. Box 1987, Petersburg, AK 99833
Open: Daily
Price: Inexpensive to Moderate
Credit Cards: Yes
Cuisine: American eclectic
Serving: B, L, D
Special Features: Sits right on dock overlooking harbor; dinner reservations recommended.

Rooney's menu ranges widely, offering starters, wraps, Mexican dishes, sandwiches, pastas, and entrées. Alaska fish and seafood dishes are on the front of the menu, so even before you open the folder, you know that cod, halibut, and smoked salmon are likely to be fresh and available. And, though based on Alaska fish, seafood, and beef, the menu showed a little more variation here.

A smoked-salmon quesadilla, luscious with the fish and creamy cheese, was happily split for an appetizer. A flank-steak salad with strips of freshly grilled meat over crisp romaine, mushrooms, tomatoes, and cheese shreds was a pleasant variation on most Alaska menus.

It's hard for a kitchen to be all things to all diners, but this one tries and manages pretty well. It has a stunning setting on the waterfront, where you can watch the busy fishing fleet, but the windows needed a good washing on the day we visited.

Tina's Kitchen

907-772-2090
104 N. Nordic Dr., Petersburg, AK 99833
Open: Daily, spring–early fall

Price: Inexpensive
Credit Cards: No
Cuisine: Eclectic
Serving: L, D
Special Features: Take-out stand, heated dining tent, no alcohol.

Tina's Kitchen normally would be listed in the Food Purveyors section. You order at a window, and then get your food to go or take it to a heated tent on the premises. It's modest, low-key. But whenever we asked a local resident to name his or her favorite restaurant, Tina's Kitchen topped the list.

The menu is truly international, with Korean beef, burritos, halibut tacos, hot-and-spicy pork, and the Alaska soul food, halibut and chips. And it's all utterly fresh. Go by in the morning, and you hear Tina chop-chopping vegetables, and her assistant will be firing up the grill under an open-air shelter. Everything that comes off the grill, mixed with Tina's vegetables, and served in tortillas or buns, or with fries, comes to you moments after it's prepared.

Servings are extremely large. The halibut cheek tacos will take you through a whole day of fishing, or a trip to LeConte Glacier.

Sitka

Sitka offers larger restaurants, and a little more choice than some towns. They open as early as 4:30 AM for breakfast, perhaps for early-morning fishing.

The Channel Club

907-747-7440
sitkachannelclub.com
2906 Halibut Point Rd., Sitka, AK 99835
Open: Daily, except Jan.
Price: Moderate to Expensive
Credit Cards: Yes
Cuisine: Steakhouse re-invented
Serving: L, D
Special Features: Overlooking channel outside of town; reservations recommended; courtesy van service.

A large parking lot surrounds the Channel Club, giving it the look of a suburban steakhouse. It's outside of town and steak is the specialty, but the suburban comparison ends there.

In true steakhouse fashion, a large salad bar starts a meal here. The diner has many choices and could easily make a meal of the salad bar alone. The grill is beside the salad bar, and flames lick up over the meat, which gets perfect grid marks from the grill. Prime rib is another popular choice here, and it always comes out rosy red.

This being Alaska, fish and seafood certainly make an appearance on the menu. Buttery prawns and golden halibut are some of the choices. Elaborate desserts, including a killer chocolate cake and tarts, will satisfy the sweet tooth. It's one of Sitka's oldest, and newest, restaurants—in business since 1956, but it has new owners who rebuilt the structure.

Level II

907-747-3900
407 Lincoln St. in Bayview Building Sitka, AK 99835
Open: Daily, year-round
Price: Inexpensive to Moderate
Credit Cards: Yes
Cuisine: Eclectic
Serving: B, L, daily; D, Mon.–Sat.
Special Features: Sensational harbor view; very early breakfast; nonsmoking.

Level II, the former Bayview Restaurant, opens for breakfast at 4:30 AM, perhaps to catch the fishing crowd, and keeps serving all day long. The only meal they miss is Sunday dinner. The breakfast menu covers the gamut, with three-egg omelets, pancakes, and waffles. But the Dungeness crab eggs Benedict wins the breakfast popularity poll. At lunch, multiple variations of hamburgers, clam chowder, and halibut and chips get lots of takers. Many orders of the crab-albacore melt, perhaps the menu's most unique item, and Caesar salad with seafood seemed to whiz by in the bustling dining room. The dinner menu gets more creative, with shrimp stuffed halibut, seafood pasta, crab cakes, and beef tenderloin.

The restaurant's location, overlooking Crescent Harbor and busy Lincoln Street, attracts many people. And yet, because it's upstairs, it seems a bit removed from the shore-excursion hubbub.

Ludvig's Bistro

907-966-3663
ludvigsbistro.com
256 Katlian St., Sitka, AK 99835
Open Mon.–Sat. summer; Tues.–Sat. winter
Price: Moderate to Expensive
Credit Cards: Yes
Cuisine: Mediterranean interpreted with Alaskan seafood

Serving: D
Special Features: Small, stylish; Mediterranean fare; tapas, and oyster bar; reservations highly recommended.

This tiny restaurant attracts foodies from everywhere: People on cruise ships make reservations before they leave the Lower 48; Alaskans come to Sitka just to dine here. The stylish restaurant's reputation exceeds its size. It's tiny, with only about 10 tables and a counter seating eight. But its wild Alaskan paella and Julius Caesar (bacon-wrapped scallops over romaine with Caesar dressing) make it a dining destination.

The menu isn't long, but it gives many options. A steaming bowl of the spicy clam chowder with a house salad, and perhaps a plate of raw oysters, would be a lovely

Sophisticated diners come from near and far to enjoy Lidvig's Bistro in Sitka.

supper. More elaborate entrées include the Katlian special (catch of the day) with a local fish prepared in an innovative ways, perhaps with a red pepper sauce, cushioned against basil risotto.

A dessert, imaginatively named Picasso, consists of espresso flan studded with whole coffee beans and awash in caramel syrup. It's delicious, and though it delivers a caffeine jolt, is worth the risk of a sleepless night.

The vibrant décor matches the food. The mustard-yellow and electric-blue building stands out against its beige neighbors on Katlian Street. Inside, the same blue—the saturated color of Santorini roofs—covers the walls. Spanish tiles add accents, and tabletops glow with a copper top. It takes daring to choose such a décor in this tiny space. Owner-chef Colette Nelson does the same with the food.

And who is Ludvig? It's Nelson's late husky dog.

The restaurant generally closes for a few weeks after the summer season, and in the spring.

Nugget Restaurant
907-966-2480
600 Airport Dr., Sitka, AK 99835 in the airport terminal
Open: Daily
Price: Inexpensive
Credit Cards: Yes
Cuisine: American
Serving: B, L, D; Check hours
Special Features: Famous for pies.

When you have to eat at the airport or pick up something for a flight, of course you'll drop into the Nugget. But even if you don't need a thing, stop by the Nugget for some pie. Apple, cherry, blueberry—all the classic flavors. That's what's in all those boxes people are carrying away. Some people merely landing in Sitka jump off the airplane and dash in for a piece of pie, then re-board.

If you need something besides dessert, you'll find a full menu of breakfast items, sandwiches, soups, salads, and burgers. But the baked goods are what make this more than just a refueling stop.

Pizza Express
907-966-2428
1321 Sawmill Rd., Sitka, AK 99835
Open: Daily
Price: Inexpensive
Credit Cards: Yes
Cuisine: Mexican and pizza
Serving: L, D
Special Features: Strip-mall modest.

This is a good place for a quick, inexpensive meal, if you're visiting the Raptor Center. It's on the same road, a bit away from the main tourist attractions on Lincoln Street and the harbor. Although Pizza Express is the name, the restaurant is known for its Mexican dishes. The Mexican family who owns it brings their expertise to the enchiladas and tacos, and to the chips and salsa that appear the moment you sit down. And they also serve a credible pizza, and will deliver it to your hotel.

Raven Dining Room
907-747-6241
330 Seward St., Sitka, AK 99835
Open: Daily, year-round
Price: Moderate to Expensive
Credit Cards: Yes
Cuisine: Alaska American
Serving: B, L, D
Special Features: Hotel restaurant; handsome dining room.

Finding a restaurant open on a Sunday night in Sitka can be difficult. The top choices were closed, or booked. I found the Raven Dining Room in the Westmark Hotel. It stays open each day of the week and serves three meals during the summer season.

Huge posts, suggesting an Alaska lodge, support the bi-level dining room. Windows on one side overlook Lincoln Street. During the day, this is a busy center of action when the cruise ship crowds are here, and beyond, is the harbor. Adding to the color are the kites and windsocks from Fly Away Fly Shop that flutter in the wind. In the evening, the street seems empty, even in summer.

The menu covers the Alaska basics, with halibut and salmon, prepared on a cedar plank. It also ranges over continental dishes, including steak Oscar and trout almandine. The clam chowder, which is served on a sidewalk café outside the hotel at midday, was the thick variety with lots of vegetables. Bits of feta cheese and cranberries added tart zing to a poached-pear salad, dressed with a vanilla vinaigrette. King crab legs are a specialty here, and they arrive in leg clusters, ends pointed up on the plate like some exotic, carapaced flower. It looks intimidating, but the shell is soft, and the meat inside sweet.

WRANGELL

Dining is pretty basic in Wrangell. One of the more unusual venues, and a place to rub elbows with local folks, is the **Elks Club** (907-874-3716; 9126 Front St.). It welcomes the public most nights; on Saturday, it's likely to be serving a steak special. But don't count on its being open and whether or not you can get in; this may depend on the person at the door.

Stikine Inn Restaurant

907-874-3388
stikineinn.com/dining.html
109 Stikine Ave., Wrangell, AK 99929
Open: Daily
Price: Inexpensive to Moderate
Credit Cards: Yes
Cuisine: American
Serving: B, L, D

Special Features: Wonderful view over Zimovia Strait.

The Stikine Inn restaurant is appealing for its lack of pretension. Fresh flowers brighten Formica tables, and the rest of the room is in neutral gray or blond wood. The action is really at the windows that overlook Zimovia Strait, where gillnetters come in the morning to drop their fish in packing-shed boats, recreation boaters get picked up at the dock, and even golfers come by boat to play on the Muskeg Meadows Golf Course. It's quite entertaining, though what's on the plate is the real reason you're here.

The restaurant serves breakfast, lunch, and dinner for its guests and others. Local people come here for business meetings at breakfast, on a work break at lunch, and with their families at dinner.

In the morning, the country Benedict may mean you won't have to eat again for the day. It's a platter of split biscuits, ham, three fried eggs, and Yukon hash browns. At lunch, burgers, sandwiches, soups, and salads dominate. Cubes of potato and salmon give character to the creamy seafood chowder. It's served nicely side-by-side with a salad on a platter. Generously sized burgers come with all the trimmings.

At dinner, the menu is nicely written, with a wide, but not overwhelming, selection. In addition to some of the lunch offerings, dinner has steaks and chops, a pasta section, and a few unusual things. Halibut cakes were an interesting variation on crab cakes, or many versions of fried halibut. Served with a salad they made a fine, light entrée.

Three can share dessert, running to generous servings of cheesecake and ice cream. The waitstaff is altogether helpful, but sometimes haphazard. After extensive renovation, the hotel lounge reopened as a wine bar in 2008, and plans were underway to open a deck outside of the restaurant.

Zak's Cafe

907-874-3355
316 Front St., P.O. Box 1929. Wrangell, AK
99929
Open: Mon.–Sat., year-round
Price: Inexpensive to Moderate
Credit Cards: Yes
Cuisine: Alaska American
Serving: L, D
Special Features: Modest on the outside,
pretty inside; no alcohol.

Sometimes things come in unexpected
places. Zak's Café produced one of the best
pieces of halibut I have had in Alaska.
White, fluffy, pristine, it stood simply on
the plate with parsley flecks over the top. A
big scoop of rice and two small wedges of
watermelon completed the plate. The
utterly fresh fish, perfectly cooked, didn't
need anything more.

Modest is almost too effusive a word for
Zak's. It stands back slightly from the
street, in a faded turquoise building with a
scuffed sign. But inside, it's quite pleasing,
looking as if a feminine hand planned the
décor. A decorative band with a fruit still-
life spans the walls at near ceiling height.
Lavender valances top the windows, and
straw mats mark each place.

But still, it's simple. People help themselves to ketchup from a refrigerator, and
the salad dressing is served in a little cup
on the side. One person serves the room,
and is sometimes out of sorts.

In addition to beer-battered fish and
seafood, the menu has steaks, pasta, stir-
fries, and entrée salads. Head lettuce may
be the basis for the salad, but it's crisp and
fresh, and the grape tomatoes had reason-
able flavor. Wraps and a blackened-chicken
salad are popular at lunch; steak and stir-
fries top choices in the evening.

SOUTHERN PANHANDLE

KETCHIKAN

Waterfront restaurants in Ketchikan not
only serve salmon and halibut, but they
have nautical themes, appropriate for the
town known as the "salmon capital of the
world." A few of the older cafés in town
have also survived, and they offer an interesting change from the newer places. You're
also more likely to meet locals there. Unless
otherwise stated, restaurants are nonsmoking and are open year-round.

Alaska Fish House

907-225-4055 or 1-877-732-9453
alaskafishhouse.com
3 Salmon Landing, P.O. Box 8523,
Ketchikan, AK 99901
At the waterfront on Thomas Basin at the
end of Main St.
Open: Daily May–Sept.
Price: Inexpensive
Credit Cards: Yes
Cuisine: Alaska American
Serving: B, L, D
Special Features: Recreation of old fish
house; private dining for groups.

Looks may fool you. The big façade of the
restaurant looks like an old-fashioned fish
house. But the impressive structure just
houses the counter where you'll order, and
some food gift items. Tables are open-air,
out front. Should it be raining, you can have
food delivered to Fat Stan's, just across the
way. A small, private dining room is
upstairs, but it's available only by reservation to local residents.

The appealing menu makes you want to
try everything. Salmon, wild and troll-
caught, appears in several dishes. It may be
hot-smoked, alderwood-grilled, oven-
roasted, and served with a choices of glazes.
The two-salmon chowder combines oven-
roasted and smoked with corn, leeks, and
potatoes. It sounds utterly delicious, but by
a late lunch hour it was viscous. Everything
else fared much better: cornbread that
crumbled at the touch; spinach-fig-smoked
salmon salad that blended sweet and

Alaska Fish House presents a classic façade at Ketchikan's Salmon Landing.

savory; blueberry-and-rhubarb bread pudding to dream about, after you get home. Espresso drinks are made with Green Bean Coffee Company beans.

Construction began on an extension out back, in summer 2008.

Annabelle's Keg and Chowder House

907-225-6009
gilmorehotel.com/annabelles.htm
326 Front St., Ketchikan, AK 99901
In the historic Gilmore Hotel
Open: Daily
Price: Moderate to Expensive
Credit Cards: Yes
Cuisine: Alaska American
Serving: L, D
Special Features: Hugely popular; smoking in bar; reservations recommended for dinner.

With tufted-leather booths, dark paneling, and low lighting, Annabelle's looks as if mining barons and successful fishermen might bring their families here to dinner. The adjacent barroom, which may be as large as the restaurant, might attract ordinary miners or fisherfolk, with its long wood bar with brass rails and the murals of Creek Street at night in the old days. Annabelle's is in the 1927 Gilmore Hotel, listed on the National Register of Historic Places.

The lengthy menu offers many choices, from small plates and appetizers, to sandwiches and wraps, salads, and chowders, charcoal-broiled dishes, and pasta. Some of the recipes date to the hotel's early days—supposedly the hamburger is the same as it was in 1927. Clam chowder comes from a 1920s-era recipe. There's also an absolutely delicious smoked-salmon chowder that makes a stop to the restaurant worthwhile, and an Alaska seafood chowder that's a feast in a bowl. The pies are flaky, and taste homemade.

Bar Harbor Restaurant

907-225-2813

2813 Tongass Ave., Ketchikan, AK 99901

Open: Mon.–Sat.

Price: Moderate to Expensive

Credit Cards: Yes

Cuisine: Eclectic

Serving: L, D

Special Features: Tiny building; back deck; free wireless Internet; dinner reservations necessary.

Ketchikan residents always recommend this restaurant, located in a little house near the ferry dock. Its narrow end faces the street, and it's easy to miss. Dining areas are still divided into small rooms. Shelves hold knickknacks, and Christmas garlands may be hanging in May, which adds to its eccentric charm.

A large deck overlooks Tongass Narrows and about doubles the dining area. Heat lamps add to the comfort level, but Ketchikan's frequent rain may drive you inside. When the weather cooperates, sitting out there during the long sunsets is a memorable occasion.

The kitchen does original takes on the Alaska staples. Salmon and halibut appear, but chicken *satay* joins homey pot roast and *cioppino*. Sun-dried tomato sauce dresses up the crab cakes, which came with cheese on top that didn't add much. An expertly sautéed snapper filet got an added zing from capers. Steak salad with blue cheese is a real winner.

The attitude here simply makes Bar Harbor more endearing. A note on the door profusely apologized for a temporary lunch closure. When we weren't attended to immediately, the server, who wore a Hawaiian shirt, seem chagrinned.

Héen Kahidi Restaurant and Lounge

907-225-8001

capefoxlodge.com

800 Venetia Way, Ketchikan, AK 99901

In the Cape Fox Lodge

Open: Daily

The deck at Bar Harbor, overlooking Ketchikan's waterfront, rates high with dinner patrons.

Price: Moderate
Credit Cards: Yes
Cuisine: Alaska American
Serving: B, L, D
Special Features: Gorgeous view of Tongass Narrows through window wall; reservations recommended for dinner.

Halibut Olympia has appeared on the menu since this restaurant opened in 1990. Try it, and you'll understand why. A perfect piece of snowy halibut sits atop a bed of thinly sliced, gently cooked onions, crowned with a lovely browned sauce. The delicate fish benefits from this treatment. A trio of vegetables—baby carrots, broccoli, and cabbage, seasoned with caraway seeds—completed the plate one night.

Other choices run to salmon dishes, king crab, or one of the nightly specials, like a Portobello mushroom dish. Entrée salads offer a lighter alternative, which you may pair with a soup. Desserts are huge, and get shared at most tables.

A lengthy list of appetizers offers crab dip, quesadilla, and chicken wings. The restaurant sometimes fills with tour groups, so reservations are recommended. The dining room and bar are on two levels of a room that overlooks Tongass Narrows, a view of which can be enjoyed in the long summer twilight.

Good Fortune Restaurant
907-225-1818
4 Creek St., Ketchikan, AK 99901
Open: Daily, summer; Tues.—Sun. winter
Price: Inexpensive
Credit Cards: Yes
Cuisine: Cantonese and Szechuan Chinese
Serving: L, D
Special Features: Building set up on pilings, over rushing Ketchikan Creek.

Located at the top of Ketchikan's popular Creek Street, this is a good place for lunch between browsing in Ray Troll's Soho Coho, and learning about the ladies of the night at Dolly's Museum. It tends to be crowded at lunch and quieter at dinner. A lengthy Chinese menu has sections for Szechuan, Cantonese, and Mandarin cuisine, as well as noodle and rice dishes. You won't find surprises, but stir-fried dishes taste fresh and sauces are added with a light touch.

Good Fortune sits at the very end of Creek Street. It's easy to think the street has ended before you discover the modest-looking restaurant.

Diaz Café
907-225-2257
335 Stedman St., Ketchikan, AK 99901
Open: Tues.—Sun.
Price: Inexpensive
Credit Cards: No
Cuisine: Asian and American
Serving: L, D
Special Features: Longtime favorite Ketchikan restaurant with an Asian-American menu.

One day at lunch, the *pansit* delivered to one diner looked so appealing that it started a run on the Filipino dish. Several diners in a row just pointed and said, "I want that."

Since the 1950s, Ketchikan residents have been going here for the chicken adobo, *lumpia*, or the cheeseburgers, which have the reputation of being the best in town. The menu has sections for Chinese, Filipino, and American dishes. Chinese stir-fries join french fries with hamburgers, and potsticker soup keeps company with a list of sandwiches. Even the Chinese dishes come out somewhat Americanized: the Chinese chicken salad was offered with a choice of blue cheese, Ranch, French, or Italian dressing. But the big mound of greens arrived with stir-fried chicken, sesame seeds, and chow-mein noodles.

The restaurant has vibrant red and yellow walls, Formica tables, and a long counter. Most of the diners are local and conversations sometimes take place between tables. The restaurant shares a part of Ketchikan history; Asian families have owned restaurants on this street since the early 1900s.

Ocean View Restaurante

907-225-7566
oceanviewmex.com
1831 Tongass Ave., Ketchikan, AK 99901
Open: Daily
Price: Inexpensive to Moderate
Credit Cards: Yes
Cuisine: Italian and Mexican
Serving: L, D
Special Features: Pizza delivery; loud in color, and in decibels.

The menu has one foot in Mexico, the other in Italy. So you can order pastas or pizza, or chiles rellenos or fajitas. Even a few Greek dishes pop up on the Italian side.

It's a large, crowded room, with Latin-American music videos, and surreal murals, including one of Neptune. In spite of its name, the restaurant lacks a view, except for a few tables. But plenty of television sets give diners something to look at.

The guacamole and house-made salsa are excellent. It's hard not to keep dipping, even at the risk of spoiling the rest of dinner. The full bar provides margaritas.

The eclectic menu of two cuisines challenges any restaurant, but this one tries the balancing act. The pasta with red sauce is credible, and the fajitas, including a kind of "everything" version, are a feast. The pizza rates high in some diner's estimation. The restaurant will deliver to your hotel.

Pioneer Café

907-225-3337
619 Mission St., Ketchikan, AK 99801
Open: Daily
Price: Inexpensive
Credit Cards: Yes
Cuisine: Alaska American diner

Serving: B, L, D
Special Features: Reindeer sausage; open 24 hours; smoking allowed.

If you know anyone who lives in Ketchikan, and if you sit here long enough, they will come by. Locals love this restaurant, and come for breakfast, lunch, or dinner, or a cup of coffee anytime. It's open around the clock, so there's plenty of opportunity.

Servings are for Alaska lumberjacks: A taco omelet is made with four eggs. There are several variations of eggs Benedict, pancakes, french toast, and biscuits and gravy. The Alaska breakfast has two blueberry pancakes, two eggs, and two reindeer sausages. Happily, there are some alternatives. You can get two pancakes instead of a stack. They cover the plate, and come with blueberries or strawberries, as well as plain. Syrup will be maple or fruit flavored. Other unusual offerings keep the menu interesting, such as creamed-chipped beef on toast with hash browns. Later in the day, look for Alaska burgers with all the trimmings, Northwest clam chowder, chili, sandwiches, and fried halibut. No one leaves hungry.

A ROUTE 66 signs hangs on the wall, and Pioneer Café can certainly join the ranks of fabled diners, with its black-and-white linoleum floor, red booths and counter, and black table tops. The most negative thing is the smell of smoke that pervades the room.

Salmon Falls Resort

907-225-2752
salmonfallsresort.com
P.O. Box 5700, Ketchikan, AK 99901
About 20 miles north of Ketchikan
Open: Daily, May-Sept.
Price: Moderate to Expensive
Credit Cards: Yes
Cuisine: Alaska American
Serving: L, D
Special Features: Spectacular beamed dining room, wrap-around view.

Even if you don't spend the night at Salmon Falls, a spectacularly sited fishing lodge, it's worth an excursion out here (cruise ships offer them) or a drive to the end of the road to eat in this gorgeous dining room.

Enormous log beams support the octagonal room, which soars upward at its center to a section of the pipe from the Alaska Pipeline, repurposed to form part of the structure. Window tables line the periphery of the room spanning a 270-degree view over Clover Pass and several islands. The dining room is at two levels, to maximize the view. You'll watch eagles swoop onto the rock beach below, cascading waterfalls, and sea lions, whales, or porpoises swimming past.

The food seems almost an afterthought, but it's quite good. A lengthy appetizer list includes oysters, beef skewers, and a spinach and artichoke dip. Salmon and halibut may be ordered grilled or blackened, or in more elaborate preparations. A specialty, halibut crusted with crab, was fluffy and delicate beneath its seafood coat. Rib-eye and double-cut pork chop, roasted chicken, and New York strip steak will please meat lovers.

Steamers

907-225-1600
76 Front St., Ketchikan, AK 99901
Open: Daily, May–Sept.
Price: Moderate to Expensive
Credit Cards: Yes
Cuisine: Alaska American
Serving: L, D
Special Features: Second floor, view; smoking in lounge; dinner reservations recommended.

Sunny, or not, light floods into this high-ceilinged dining room from a wall of windows overlooking Front Street and the cruise ships. When ships are in town, passengers jam the restaurant and the mood seems more touristy than Ketchikan's smaller cafes.

Steamers is tucked into the second floor of this building on the Ketchikan docks.

Crab, halibut, and salmon star on the lengthy menu. Some of the small plates make an interesting lunch. Sandwiches and wraps, pastas and salads offer many other choices. Hearty appetites will find seafood and steak entrées. The smoked-salmon chowder here is among the best I've tasted in Alaska. Creamy and luscious, with smoky fish flavor, it's subtle and silky. A plate of halibut tacos also offered colorful, crunchy, chopped vegetables, salsa, and a creamy sauce, along with the soft tortillas and fish.

The bar offers several draft choices, and a unique way to serve them. A "column," a glass cylinder with a spigot, is filled with beer and placed on the center of the table, allowing imbibers to serve themselves.

PRINCE OF WALES

Dining choices are limited on the island. Most people eat at the fishing lodges, which often are not accessible by road.

Fireweed Lodge

907-755-2930
fireweedlodge.com
P.O. Box 116, Klawock, AK 99925
Prince of Wales Island
Open: Daily, Apr.–Sept.
Price: Moderate
Credit Cards: Yes
Cuisine: International
Serving: D
Special Features: Homey fishing-lodge dining room; no alcohol; reservations essential.

It's always possible for meals to be interrupted here. There might be a bear on the beach across the way, or a river otter on the dock. The homey dining room, an extension of the lobby that also looks like someone's living room, has an expansive view over lawns, to a river estuary and the dock.

I arrived tired, way past the dinner hour,

after driving across POW. But the young chef almost apologetically offered a pork chop with walnuts and gorgonzola sauce, and zucchini with sun-dried tomatoes. It was gourmet fare, and the fishermen who come here are well-fed indeed. The entrée changes nightly, or a halibut burger is offered. Even the halibut burger is something special, with pineapple, lettuce, and sauce, on a seeded bun. Pie or cake is set on a buffet, for those with a sweet tooth.

Ruth Ann's Restaurant

907-826-3377
300 Front St., Craig, AK 99921
Open: Daily year-round; closed Jan.
Price: Inexpensive
Credit Cards: Yes
Cuisine: American
Serving: L, D
Special Features: POW gathering spot; small rooms and alcoves.

The cheerful-looking building with the flower boxes at the waterfront is Ruth Ann's, a local gathering spot since the 1970s. Of course, local seafood is on the menu, along with steaks and burgers. Some sport anglers think Ruth Ann's dishes up the best steak sandwich in Alaska.

It's a good place to get Dungeness crab, either baked on a bun or on a salad plate. Wraps run to several varieties, including a BLT with warm, thick bacon that heated up the sandwich.

Colorful wallpaper, bright salmon-colored walls, and lace valances bring cheer to the inside. An enclosed porch at the back overlooks a pier, where families might be fishing or boats come and go. The menu has little tidbits about Craig's history, which gives you something to read while you wait for lunch. It's a good thing, because the wait may be long.

Most visitors to Prince of Wales Island make their way to distinctive Ruth Ann's in Craig.

FOOD PURVEYORS

You may not want to take time for a table-service restaurant when you have a whale-watching boat to catch, or want to spend an extra hour shopping. The following places work for a quick meal. Most of them do not offer table service, and they tend to close in the late afternoon or early evening.

Bakeries and cafés will usually provide sack lunches, and open very early. They are also good places to chat up locals, or the person behind the counter.

Each Panhandle town seems to have a coffee roastery with owners who choose beans with care and blend them with finesse. They also buy with a social conscience, since many sell only fair-trade coffees. Alaska coffees have imaginative names—Raven's Brew, Midnight Sun, and Jumping Goat.

Inside Passage towns have street stands during the cruise season. Even Alaska's frequent summer rain doesn't deter these sellers.

Bakeries, Cafés, and Delis

Bakers, cafés, and delis appear here together, because most of them serve light meals to the traveler in a hurry. Street stands (see below) are also popular near cruise ship docks in Juneau and Ketchikan.

NORTHERN PANHANDLE

|UNEAU

Capital Café: (907-586-2660; 127 N. Franklin St., in the Westmark Baranof Hotel.) The conversation at the next table may run to a gas-tax law or the proposed highway from Juneau to Skagway. This is where the state legislators hang out when they're in town. The kitchen has a way with skillets, scrambles, and omelets, which come in several variations. The sourdough pancakes are so sour they will curl your hair.

Breads come from Silverbow Bakery. At lunch, sandwiches, soups, and salads lead the way. Busy and bustling, and open for breakfast and lunch year-round.

Caribou Café: (907-586-5008; outside Caribou Crossings store, 497 S. Franklin Street.) This street stand even has a few tables and chairs where you can sip your cappuccino or latte along with a creamy gelato.

Costa's Diner or the Soup Queen: (Merchant's Wharf, 2 Marine Way.) In a state with superlative idiosyncrasies, this may top the diner list. You pick your selection from a board, write it down, and serve yourself coffee and even set your own place at the counter or a few tables. When it's time to pay, throw your money in a pail along with a tip; it's all on the honor system. At breakfast, this is Costa's Diner (named for owner Collette Costa); at lunchtime, it becomes the Soup Queen. Food is not bad—but it's not the reason to come.

Heritage Café Downtown: (907-586-1087; 174 S. Franklin Street.) When you see the clever sign in Northwest Coast-style carving, featuring a smiling bear, don't assume it's just another adaptation of Alaska Native design. The bear is clutching a steaming cup of coffee between its claws. The sign seems to be everywhere, since there are six Heritage Cafés in Juneau, and the coffeemaker in your hotel room will probably have packaged Heritage-brand coffee. The roastery has been toasting beans since 1974, and consistently wins awards as Juneau's best espresso.

The South Franklin café location is especially busy. Sit near the big windows. If you know even one other person in Juneau—a resident, or another traveler—chances are, they will pass by. The baristas will make any elaborate espresso drink that you can think up. In the morning, there are wonderful sweet, sticky things and huge muffins. Later in the day, packaged wraps and salads make a light meal. A gelato case tempts ice-cream lovers, with chocolate, vanilla, and more exotic flavors. Before you leave, be sure to check out the historic photographs at the back of this building.

Heritage Glacier Café: (907-789-0692; 9112 Mendenhall Road, in the Mendenhall Center.) This Heritage Café (with the familiar logo) seems to have more elaborate food than its sister cafés downtown. Perhaps I was just hungrier on my visit, but the breakfast pastries seemed especially plentiful and varied. It makes a good stop after a morning or afternoon at Mendenhall Glacier. It also can be a good place to pick up something to go, before a flight.

Silverbow Bakery and Back Room Restaurant: (907-586-4146; silverbowinn.com; 120 Second Street.) This is something of a Juneau institution. It's the Red Dog Saloon of the cool crowd. Bagels are the menu item of choice. Each day, more than 16 varieties are available. If you count all the options to spread on top, the condiments, cheese, and veggies, the choices reach into the scores. Two breads are also baked fresh daily, and are the basis for sandwiches at lunch and dinner. With sandwiches, you may make a healthy choice of carrot sticks, or opt for the salt and fat, with a dill pickle and chips. The kitchen makes lox from cold-smoked, wild Alaskan sockeye salmon. Being a bakery, there are cakes and cookies, including a decadent chocolate cheesecake or peanut-butter mousse cake. The dipwich—an ice-cream sandwich between two chocolate chunk cookies, dipped in chocolate—is enough for two.

Silverbow has at least two claims to historic fame. A bakery opened at this site in 1889, making this Alaska's oldest continually operating bakery. And the current owners started making traditional bagels in 1997—the first bagel in Alaska shop to do so.

To order, line up at the counter and fill out a slip, checking off what you like. You can then eat it up front, on a heated deck, or in the Back Room Restaurant, a room with walls painted the color of tomato soup and hung with artworks. Hope to be at Silverbow on Monday, Tuesday, or Wednesday nights, when free movies are shown in the Back Room Restaurant.

Tracy's King Crab Shack: Technically this is a street stand, so it's description appears below. But it's one of Juneau's most popular lunch stops for cruise ship passengers.

Valentine's Coffee House & Pizzeria: (907-463-5144; valentinescoffeehouse.com; 111 Seward Street.) Even if you don't want a latte or lunch, do go to Valentine's to see the "dress" displayed on the wall. It looks like a flounced thing ready for a flamenco perform- ance. But look again: the ruffles are coffee filters, and the squares on the bodice are coffee labels; every part of it is some disposable coffee necessity. It was actually worn once, to a Juneau event, and the employees, who call themselves "Valentine's Crew," made it.

The café offers a full coffee menu, sandwiches, including a delicious smoked salmon on focaccia, homemade soup, salads, and pizza and calzones: Quite an array for a simple cof- fee house, which is housed in the historic Valentine's Building. Much of the wood inside is from the original building and is more than a century old.

GUSTAVUS

Bear Track Deli: (907-697-2352; Quarter Mile Dock Road inside Bear Track Mercantile.) One morning, the hunger-producing aroma of frying onions wafted through the aisles of canned soup and souvenirs at Bear Track Mercantile. The deli cook was preparing for lunch, when sautéed onions are just one of the things you can get on your sandwiches. Quite a variety is available from this small space. Whole or half, toasted or not, sandwiches may be ordered with several bread choices and toppings.

This is a good place to stop before a fishing trip, hiking, or perhaps a dog-sled ride at the Husky Ranch just down the road.

HAINES

Box of Daylight Bakery: (Fort Seward Drive.) This bakery in the entrance hall to one of the large officer's houses in Fort Seward gets rave mention from everyone for its pastries. There's nowhere to eat on the premises, unless you sit on the porch steps. And it can be difficult to find it open. It's supposed to be closed on Thursday, but I've found it closed other days of the week. Keep trying.

Mountain Market and Café: (907-766-3340; 151 Third Avenue.) Don't be put off by peo- ple with shopping carts. This is a grocery store, with lots of organics, including the coffee roasted on the premises; it's sort of the "Whole Foods" of Haines. But you can also get a terrific breakfast or lunch to eat on the premises. Breakfast choices run the gamut, from

Haines's Mountain Market, seen in the background, is almost as iconic as the Haines horizontal totem pole.

fabulous sticky buns and huge blueberry muffins, to elaborate breakfast wraps and bagel sandwiches with eggs. At lunch, there are soups, sandwiches, wraps, and "naked wraps," which, in Alaskan argot, means a salad. A smoked-salmon naked wrap appears, with the luscious, cubed fish smoked Alaska-style, baby spinach, grape tomatoes, olives, avocado, and red onion. You'll order at the counter and pick up your breakfast or lunch after it's prepared. Meanwhile you can browse among the Alaska berry jams, birch syrup, and more smoked salmon. The coffee is fair-trade, and NPR is on the radio.

Open for breakfast and lunch, daily, year-round.

SKAGWAY

The Black Bean: (907-983-3225; Seventh Avenue, just off Broadway.) There are two kinds of beans here—the kind that fill a burrito and the kind used for coffee. Drawings of both appear inside this tiny, false-front building. This is a coffee stand with light fare, and a good stop for breakfast or lunch, though the choices are pretty much limited to burritos, bagels, or a few other baked goods. Open morning through late afternoon, seasonally.

Glacial Smoothies & Espresso: (907-983-3223; 336B Third Avenue.) A glacial smoothie is not what you may have in mind on a rainy, cool day in Skagway, which, even in July, is often the case. But this little café also has soups, sandwiches, and wraps. During the winter, locals come for breakfast bagels or a McMabel Muffin, along with an espresso drink made with Raven's Brew coffee. And, there are smoothies with exotic fruits and berries, if you're in the mood. A few Internet stations allow you to check e-mail. Open all year.

Haven Café & Catering: (907-983-3553; Ninth and State streets.) Espresso coffee drinks or an Italian soda are the reasons to drop by, but a toasted panini, Greek salad, smoked-salmon bagel, or crab chowder make Haven Café a fine lunch destination. At breakfast, an egg sandwich from the panini press, house-made granola, and yogurt shakes give the day a healthy start, and at teatime, a decadent dessert might just hit the spot. Order at the counter, and take your treats to a table.

This simple, but sophisticated café, is somewhat off the beaten tourist path. Coffee comes from Midnight Sun Coffee Roasters in Whitehorse. On warm days, seating extends to a brick patio. When you run out of conversation, a bookshelf offers things to read. Open year round.

Lemon Rose Bakery: (907-983-3558; 330 Third Avenue.) It's easy to overlook this small bakery situated on a cross street between Broadway and State Street. Inside it's barebones, but it doesn't really need any distractions from the cookies, pastries, and breads. Open Tuesday through Saturday, late morning through the afternoon, year-round.

Sweet Tooth Café: (907-983-2405; 315 Broadway.) Homemade breads, chowders, and soups lure travelers and locals into this downtown restaurant. The 6 AM opening will please

Sweet Tooth Café is sandwiched between Dedman's and Heart of Broadway in Skagway.

those who get hungry early, with breakfast ?platters overflowing with omelets, scrambled eggs, pancakes, and waffles. Doughnuts are homemade and a great favorite with locals.

At lunch, soup, sandwiches, burgers—beef and halibut—and salads appear on the menu. Sundaes and floats satisfy the "sweet tooth" promise. This family-owned restaurant has been open for more than 30 years. Printed wallpaper, wainscoting, and a pressed-tin ceiling hark back to the building's Gold-Rush origins. The window tables are prime for watching the steady stream of people passing on Broadway. It tends to be very crowded on cruise ship days, but it's also very popular with locals. It's the place they're likely to recommend for lunch.

YUKON

HAINES JUNCTION
Village Bakery and Deli: (867-634-2867; corner Kluane and Logan, across road from Kluane National Park Visitor Centre.) This is a perfect lunch stop if you're on the Golden Circle drive. Various baked savory items, including quiche, *spanakopita*, and a Mexican pie, tempt the hungry traveler. And if it's a cold day, lentil-veggie or other homemade soups hit the spot. They're served with the bakery's delicious bread, which a steady stream of locals come in to buy. It's down a gravel road, about 1½ blocks from the Alaska Highway. Ask anyone in town.

WHITEHORSE
Baked Café + Bakery: (867-633-6291; 108—100 Main Street.) The crowd lines up early, and keeps arriving in a steady stream for the delicious scones, muffins, coffeecake, croissants, and bagels. The variety is unbelievable. Scones and muffins may be made with different kinds of flour and filled with different berries or nuts. The lunch choices are just as diverse. Soups are served in generous bowls and often have exotic seasonings from the Middle East or Africa. Whitehorse has a fair number of mild, sunny days in summer, when you can nab a sidewalk table.

Chocolate Claim: (867-667-2202; 305 Strickland Street.) If you're one of those who could eat chocolate for breakfast, lunch, and dinner, and for appetizer, entrée, and dessert, well, heads up. The Chocolate Claim lives up to its name with terrific chocolate cookies, cakes, brownies and perhaps the best mocha in the territory. But other things will tempt palates, including ginger-carrot soup and pizza. Coffee is brewed from Bean North coffee beans.

Java Connection: (867-668-2196; 3125 Third Avenue.) This downtown coffee bar offers sandwiches and pastries along with brew. It's near the Westmark Hotel.

Midnight Sun Coffee Roastery: (867-633-4563; Fourth and Black streets.) The bright yellow and orange building, and glowing petal umbrellas make the Midnight Sun hard to miss. Inside you find an espresso bar with pastries from local bakeries, as well as freshly made sandwiches for breakfast and lunch. On warm days, a Mojo Shakin' shake will revive you. Owner-coffee roaster Zola Doré presides over all, as well as a downtown café (867-668-5780; 305 Main Street).

CENTRAL PANHANDLE

PETERSBURG
Coastal Cold Storage: (907-772-4177; coastalcoldstoragealaska.com; 306 Nordic Drive.)

The clam and oyster tanks gurgle just a few feet away from the table in this simple retail store that offers a limited selection of prepared food, and a vast selection of local fish in the refrigerators. Everyone in town recommends you go for the salmon-and-halibut salad sandwiches, shrimp burger, and Norwegian shrimp salad. The shrimp spread gets lots of takers who get a box of crackers to go with it. Seating is limited to a few tables. Should you be fishing yourself, Coastal Cold Storage will clean and flash-freeze or smoke your fish, and pack it for the flight home.

Common Grounds: (907-772-2299; 904 S. Nordic near the ferry dock.) This is for coffee on the run. Common Grounds has a drive-through space and walk-up window. Espresso drinks and bagels, muffins, and biscotti.

Helse Restaurant: (907-772-3444; 13 Sing Lee Alley.) This popular breakfast and lunch spot is known for its homemade bread and soups. Daily specials might be something based on black beans and rice or seafood chowder. Espresso drinks, ice cream, and cookies and other sweets add to the mix, and, to keep you healthy, Helse also has packaged vitamins.

Java Hüs: (907-772-2626; next to Scandia House Hotel, 110 N. Nordic Drive.) Only the hardest rain or snow seems to drive people away from the tables in front of the Java Hüs. The Norwegian habit of afternoon coffee and cake—and the American craving for caffeine, anytime—keep this popular and tiny coffee shop busy from early morning to early evening. If you want to see someone in town, just sit here long enough and they'll drop by. Open daily year-round.

La Fonda Mexican: (907-772-4918; Sing Lee Alley inside Kito's Kave.) Your tacos and enchiladas may be handed through the window or you can get them inside the bar, at Kito's Kave. Service starts at breakfast with Mexican dishes, and runs through the evening.

SITKA

Backdoor Café: (907-747-8856; 104 Barracks Street, in the back of Old Harbor Books.) If you want to meet locals, this is the place to do it, and have a latte along with a cranberry-walnut scone or a bagel sandwich. Salads, sandwiches, and soups join the offerings at lunch. Freshly squeezed juices are available for non-coffee drinkers. Not quite a full-scale restaurant, this is more elaborate than many other cafés. Closed Sunday. No credit cards, no reservations.

Café Mellow Days: (907-747-6000; 315 Lincoln Street.) Perhaps it's the quinoa pilaf, homemade bread, or the quiche abundantly filled with vegetables, but the food at this café right in the center of town seems so healthy. Zesty seasonings, perhaps curry or tahini, keep items interesting to the last bite. Geoduck clams go into the chowder and a salad comes with paninis. Breakfast starts at 6:30 AM and last service is at 6:30 PM. Closed Sunday.

Harry's Soda Shop: (907-747-8006; 106 Lincoln Street.) When was the last time you had a real malt, poured out of a cold metal container? You'll find malts, shakes, and sundaes at this old-fashioned fountain in a pharmacy.

Highliner Coffee: (907-747-4924; highlinercoffee.com; 327 Seward Street.) This is Sitka's coffee roastery, and you'll be able to get the full line of espresso drinks, plus bagels, breakfast croissants, muffins, butter cookies, and cakes. Wireless Internet is available, and vintage photos are on the wall. It's open late, for revelers who might want a caffeine fix at 2 AM.

Victoria's: (907-747-9301; 118 Lincoln Street in the Sitka Hotel.) Although it serves dinner, this place is best known for its breakfast and lunch. There's free wireless Internet so you can catch up on your e-mail in the otherwise frilly room.

WRANGELL

Diamond C Café: (907-874-3677; 223 Front Street.) Early in the morning, fishermen fill Diamond C, complaining about the latest limits on halibut or the government policy toward wolves. They fit right into the scene, with its nautical décor, lanterns, compasses, and a few signs with tart messages.

The café serves breakfast and lunch and covers the basics quite handily. Oatmeal doesn't just come with raisins and brown sugar, but with a warm berry compote. Fluffy biscuits may be had with gravy. Seniors get a reduction on eggs, hotcakes, or a french toast breakfast.

The lunch menu covers soups, sandwiches, salads, burgers, and grilled halibut. The shrimp and halibut are likely to be local, and fresh. Diamond C is in a complex with a modest inn and a Laundromat.

Jitterbugs Espresso to Go: (907-874-3350; 309 Front Street.) This may be the most aptly named coffee bar in Alaska. The espresso machine fills the entire counter space, often hiding the barista behind it. You will find a few plastic-wrapped breakfast bars to go with your coffee, but not much else. The shrimp truck parked outside emblazoned with the sign, MEMORIES, is indeed a memory. It no longer sells seafood.

Don't leave Ketchikan without drinking some Raven's Brew Coffee, or taking some home in a Ray Troll-decorated package.

Ketchikan Coffee Co. has a bar worthy of a saloon, but it dispenses espresso drinks.

SOUTHERN PANHANDLE

KETCHIKAN

Ketchikan does its share to keep up with the Alaska tradition of good coffee from locally roasted beans. It's home to Raven's Brew Coffee, served throughout the Panhandle, and two other coffee roasters, as well. Most cafés also serve muffins, scones, or coffeecake, though pastries may not be made on the premises. They may arrive by air from Seattle, and taste surprisingly fresh. Other places bake their own pastries. You'll have to ask, and habits change quickly.

Some Ketchikan restaurants allow smoking, so if you're sensitive, be sure to check before you enter.

Burger Queen: (907-225-6060; 518 Water Street.) Don't let the name fool you. This little colorful place just beyond the tunnel offers an Oriental chicken salad (somewhat popular in Ketchikan), halibut tartare, and low-carb dishes, in addition to burgers and chicken sandwiches. Rates high with locals.

Crab Cracker Seafood: (907-247-2866; inside Salmon Landing.) Just a counter with a few seats, some netting, ice, and bins of enormous king crab legs and Dungeness crab. You order by weight, wield the cracker, and enjoy the succulent, sweet crab. Generally open while ships are at the dock.

Ketchikan Coffee Company: (907-225-0246; 207 Stedman Street, beside the New York Hotel). Formerly the New York Café, this hip place has a bar worthy of a grand saloon, but mochas, lattes, cappuccinos, and several variations of the classic coffee drink are served up by baristas. Locally roasted Raven's Brew coffee is poured. Window tables look across the road to Thomas Basin, where huge cruise ships tower over smaller craft. Lots of people from those ships come over for muffins or scones in the morning, and delicious vegetable soup or a sandwich at midday. The café closes in late afternoon, except for Friday when small plates are offered at dinner; some weeks, live music adds to the festivities.

The Pour House: (907-225-7717; 324 Dock Street.) Raven's Brew coffee is the specialty at this aptly named coffee house. The premises are simpler than some, and the emphasis is on the coffee, or cold lemonade or iced tea. Biscotti and a few pastries are offered. Closes in late afternoon.

Refiner's Roast: (907-247-6278; 2050 Sea Level Drive in Plaza Mall.) The coffee aroma is rich here because the coffee is roasted right behind the order counter. All of the muffins, scones, cookies, and breads are made on the premises as well, which is unusual for a Ketchikan coffee house. "We do everything here except for chips and chocolate," said our order taker. A leather couch and comfortable chairs cozy up to a fireplace where a chess set is ready for players, or singles can simply enjoy a good book with coffee or tea in the comfortable seats. Several high tables accommodate those with more complicated orders, perhaps a pulled-pork sandwich or a bowl of soup. Closes at 6 PM; earlier on weekends.

PRINCE OF WALES ISLAND

Annie Betty's Bakery-Café: (907-826-2299; anniebettys@aptalaska.net; 302 Thompson Road, Craig.) The scent of Annie Betty's cinnamon rolls greets early risers. They're famous on POW, and beyond. Tully's Coffee is the basis for the espresso drinks and delicious frappéed coffee or mocha. Come lunch, there's panini, sandwiches, soup, and ice cream. If you don't have time to stop, you can get lunch at a drive-through window, but it's much more relaxing to take a seat at one of the comfortable black leather chairs. Open daily. No smoking.

Dockside Café: (907-826-5544; Craig, across from city docks.) The café boasts 100-year-old-sourdough pancakes—it's the yeasty starter that makes the claim to such age, not what's served on the plate. Opening hour is 5:30 AM, and a sack lunch will be prepared, a boon to the sport angler. The simple café has a three-seat counter and a few tables. Open daily. Smoking allowed.

The Voyageur: (907-826-2333; 801 Water Street, Craig.) This book and gift shop-café looks a little like Berkeley or Boulder, with a comfortably tattered look and high-quality offerings. The coffee bar dispenses French-roast coffee and espresso drinks. People line up at the counter for the freshly baked scones and muffins, and sit on comfortable chairs reading or chatting.

Breweries and Brewpubs

Handcrafted beer seems to be a flourishing art in Alaska. Maybe it's the long, cold winters; maybe it's the masculine culture of fishing and hunting, but several artisan breweries exist in the state. Most of them distribute beers locally with only a few outlets, or sometimes only at the brewery. The exception is Alaskan Brewing Company in Juneau. Their red-and-green neon sign with the boat promoting amber ale hangs in nearly every bar in the Alaska Panhandle.

Alaskan Brewing Company: (907-780-5866; akaskanbeer.com; 5429 Shaune Drive, Juneau.) When you drive out Glacier Highway toward the airport and notice the steam

The Alaskan Brewing Company brewing room must have 100 bottles of beer on the wall.

cloud rising in the Lemon Creek area, you've spotted Alaskan Brewing Company. This is from the barley water cooking away to becoming an ale, porter, or stout. Alaskan Brewing Company is too large to be a microbrewery, though it's beers are handcrafted. They are distributed throughout Alaska and 10 Western states.

Tours start in the tasting room, where you can sample specialty beers on draft. Sometimes beers not yet released are offered here, perhaps their Jalapeño IPA, said to be good with nachos. Next, you're taken into the brewery in a room beside the steam tanks, for a briefing about the process, and then it's possible to do more tasting and browse the gift shop. No food is served, so this is not a brewpub.

In its mining heyday, Juneau had 10 breweries, producing largely European-style beers. All of them had disappeared by 1986, when Geoff and Marcy Larson decided to start crafting beer based on a recipe from the old Douglas City Brewing Company.

Haines Brewing Company: (907-766-3823; 108 White Fang Way. Southeast Alaska Fairgrounds, Haines.) The bonus of visiting here as that you'll get to walk down the "Dawson City" street from the original *White Fang* movie. Haines Brewing Company creates its handcrafted beers in one of the storefronts. Beer connoisseurs rate the ales and stouts from this small brewery with approval. No food here, just the chance to taste some of the seven beers, including spruce tip, IPA, or amber ale. They are available by the growler (half-gallon jug).

Skagway Brewing Company: (907-983-2739; skagwaybrewing.com ; Seventh Avenue and Broadway, Skagway.) Although it has roots to 1897 when Skagway was born, this is also a relatively "new" brewpub. It re-opened in 2007 after being closed for several years. Seven handcrafted ales are created on site. The brewpub also offers other artisan beers along with some of its ales. The most famous may be their Spruce Tip Ale. The cheeseburger is the most popular thing on the menu, though you can get other sandwiches, salads, and soup. Open daily in summer, weekends in winter.

Cooking Schools

Chez Alaska Cooking School: (907-957-0327; chezalaska.com; 2092 Jordan Avenue, Suite 585, Juneau.) You'll take home more than just memories of delicious seafood and berry desserts from your Alaska vacation. A session at Chez Alaska Cooking School will teach you how to make delicious smoked-salmon pasta and barbecued halibut. In one-hour demonstration classes, a professional chef imparts favorite recipes for Alaska foods. Classes are expertly run, and end with samples of the food and a glass of wine. The sessions are offered through cruise ships or independently, and run throughout the year.

Alaska Garden Gourmet: (907-983-2289; skagwayinn.com; Seventh Avenue and Broadway, in the Skagway Inn, Skagway.) The cooking demonstration starts in the garden, where lettuces and herbs grow magically fast in raised beds on the long, summer days. The chef and guests pick the fresh ingredients and then proceed to the kitchen to prepare the meal. The main course may focus on Alaska fresh fish. Summer only.

Plans are underway to reopen Olivia's, the restaurant on the premises, for the 2009 season.

Fast Food

Fast-food chains have not taken hold in Alaska as they have elsewhere. Quick takeout, which might be a halibut taco or some stir-fried dish, usually comes from a mom-and-pop operation, not a chain franchise.

Sharon Barton demonstrates for students, many of them from cruise ships, at Chez Alaska cooking school in Juneau.

Southeast Alaskans have a certain attitude toward fast food. The first McDonald's in the Panhandle opened in 1982 in Juneau. Skagway residents wanted to be part of the action, so they chartered a Medivac airplane and placed an $800 order of hamburgers and french fries for the Golden Arches run, 95 miles to the south. (There is no road connecting the communities.) When the plane touched down, laden with its fatty high-carb load, the high-school band played "Old MacDonald Had a Farm" and a good bit of the town met it. It was well below zero.

To this day, Skagway doesn't have a McDonald's. If you're having a Big Mac attack or a yen for a Subway Sandwich, here is where you'll find them.

JUNEAU

McDonald's and **Subway Sandwiches** each have two locations in the state capital. The golden arches are downtown at 130 Front Street (907-586-6745) and in Mendenhall Valley at 2285 Trout Street (907-789-4653). The downtown Subway is 201 Seward Street (907-586-3331) and the Mendenhall location at 8777 Glacier Highway (907-789-2774).

SITKA

Look for **McDonald's** on the way out of town at 913 Halibut Point Road (907-747-8709) and **Subway Sandwiches and Salads** at 327 Seward Street (907-747-7827).

KETCHIKAN

The **McDonald's** is at 2417 Tongass Avenue, Suite 108 and **Subway Sandwiches** is right in the center of the old town at 417 Dock Street (907-225-3444) and in the Wal-Mart (4230 Don King Road, 907-247-6717.)

Fish Smoking and Processing

A thriving industry of processing and smoking fish exists side-by-side with Alaska's recreational and commercial fishing. Most fish processors will meet your boat on the dock at the end of the day. They will clean, fillet, vacuum-pack, and flash-freeze the fish, and pack it in airline containers or ship it home for you. It may also be smoked. Some fish processors have retail shops. A small package of alder-smoked salmon or halibut, perhaps seasoned with lemon-pepper or Cajun flavorings, is a coveted gift. Look for white king salmon, or for belly strips, which have a higher fat content and are considered a delicacy. Many fish-processing facilities are closed during the winter, but you may find the smoked fish in other retail stores.

NORTHERN PANHANDLE

JUNEAU

Taku Wild Alaska Seafood: (1-800-582-5122; takustore.com; 550 S. Franklin Street.) An array of hot- and cold-smoked salmon, in pyramids of jars or in the refrigerator case, tempts shoppers. Windows open to the smokery, allowing visitors to see the whole process, from fresh fish filet to smoked and packaged salmon or halibut.

GUSTAVUS

Pep's Packing: (907-697-2295; gustavus.com/peps/; Dolly Varden Road, ¼ mile from Gustavus Road.) Pep's will process your fish or has their own custom alder-smoked fish and wild king salmon for sale. A small retail shop at the processing facility has gifts including wine-bottle holders and unusual jewelry, including earrings made from halibut ear bones.

HAINES

Bell's Seafood: (907-766-2950 or 1-800-446-2950; 18 Second Avenue, Haines.) On cool days, it's fun to pop into this fish store and chat with Clyde Bell. His business, in the former Haines jail, has been here 50 years. Bell's father was a fisherman and so he knows his way with wild salmon, scallops, shrimp, and halibut, which is frozen quickly and shipped anywhere you might want it. He also has canned sockeye salmon. "It's only wild, and it's all Alaska," he says proudly. The stove, which he feeds with logs from out front, is from "Dawson," he says, just like an old sourdough.

Dejon Delights: (907-766-2505 or 1-800-539-3608; dejondelights.com; Portage Street in Fort Seward.) The store here is a little plainer than some of the fish smokeries, but the variety is astonishing. Tastes of almost everything are available, as well as cute gifts, such as a fish-shaped oven mitt. Birch Boy syrups, jams, and kelp pickles are other Alaska specialties to take home.

CENTRAL PANHANDLE

PETERSBURG

Petersburg is one of the most active fishing communities in the Alaska Panhandle. Several processing facilities in town will freeze or smoke and package the catch.

Coastal Cold Storage: See Bakeries, Cafés, and Delis section.

Northern Lights Smokeries: (907-772-4608; nlsmokeries.com; 501 Noseeum Street.) Smoked black cod, hot-smoked salmon, lox and many other varieties are available. The company will custom-process your fish.

Tonka Seafoods: (907-772-3662; tonkaseafoods.com; 22 S. Sing Lee Alley.) Handsome gifts as well as a full array of smoked fish are available in the store across from the Sons of Norway Hall.

SITKA

Absolute Fresh Seafoods, Inc.: (907-747-7566 or 1-877-747-7566; absolutefresh seafoods.com; 475 Katlian Street, Suite D.) The company will process your catch, or, in its retail store, will sell troll-caught wild salmon, smoked salmon, halibut, red snapper, lingcod, weathervane scallop, spot prawns, and king crab.

SOUTHERN PANHANDLE

PRINCE OF WALES ISLAND

Jody's Seafood Specialties: (907-755-8870; judyseafood.com; turnoff at Fireweed Lodge, Klawock). Jody Anderson will process your catch and if you don't fish you can purchase seafood or smoked fish directly from the counter. Open June 1–Sept. 25.

Fudge

Alaskans must spend long, winter nights thinking up the many inventive names for fudge. Every town has at least one store that sells homemade fudge, often cut freshly from big blocks. But names like "white chocolate, maple nut, or chocolate walnut" won't do. Instead look for "Glacier Chip," "Klondike Pecan," and "Alaskan Chewy" at the **Alaskan Fudge Company** in Juneau (907-586-1478; 195 S. Franklin Street). In Haines, at **Chilkoot**

Gardens (907-776-2703; 204 Main Street) it's "Northern Lights," "Sea Otter," "Bear Tracks," "Moose Drool," and "Dalton Trail."

Skagway has its own version of **Alaskan Fudge Company** (907-983-2052; Seventh Avenue and Broadway), and the same fanciful names as Juneau, though the fudge is locally made. **Kone Kompany** (907-983-3439; 485 Broadway) practices restraint with classic names: chocolate pecan, maple nut, and chocolate walnut.

Ketchikan's **KetchiCandies** (907-225-0900; 315 Mission Street) also is pretty straight forward. The fanciest they get is penuche.

Grocery Stores and Supermarkets

Grocery stores are essential to the traveler heading for a Forest Service cabin or a vacation rental, or RV trippers. They can also be useful for a quick bite to eat. In some remote places, such as Metlakatla or Yakutat, the hot bar in the grocery store is the place to eat in town.

Most of the stores listed below are large supermarkets with pharmacy items and other essentials. You'll see the initials "A & P" on stores throughout the Panhandle. It stands for Alaskan and Proud, not Atlantic and Pacific of yore. IGA stores are also common in the smaller Panhandle towns. AC (Alaska and Commercial) stores are Alaska's largest retailer in small communities.

NORTHERN PANHANDLE

JUNEAU

Alaskan & Proud: (907-586-3101; 615 Willoughby Avenue.) Known as the "A & P," This is a basic supermarket.

Breeze-In Grocery: (907-789-7878; 2200 Trout Street, Juneau; 907-586-1065, Douglas Island.) Going fishing? On a picnic? Head to Breeze-In for sandwiches.

Rainbow Foods: (907-586-6476; rainbow-foods.org; 224 Fourth Street.) Organic produce, whole-grain breads, and a hot bar with tables make this a good lunch spot. Set in a former church, it's near the State Capitol and Governor's Mansion.

Safeway: (907-523-2000; 3033 Vintage Boulevard.) The big California grocery chain has a mammoth Juneau store.

HAINES

Haines Quick Shop: (907-766-2330; 1 Haines Highway.) A large convenience store.

Howers IGA Supermarket: (907-766-2040; 3335 Main Street.) The town mainstay.

Mountain Market: See Bakeries, Cafés, and Delis section.

SKAGWAY

Fairway: (907-983-2220; Fourth Avenue and State Street.) Though it's not the New York market by the same name, this store covers the basics handily.

You Say Tomato Natural Foods: (907-983-2784; 21st Avenue and State Street.) This is the place to find organic produce, freshly baked breads, and ethnic foods, as well as vitamins and herbs.

YAKUTAT

AC Value Center: (907-784-3386; 716 Ocean Cape Road.) This store sells potatoes, and all-terrain vehicles (for $7,449), and everything in between. The store has a hot bar, which makes a convenient stop for lunch or dinner. The deli will pack sandwiches or wraps.

Mallott's General Store: (907-784-3355; 509 Max Italio Street.) The town community board is posted at the entrance to the store. Espresso drinks, and pretty complete groceries.

Monti Bay Foods: (907-784-3395; 552 Mallott Avenue.) Not huge, but slightly upscale. Tuxedo raspberry cheesecake, and fancy tea kits, beside oranges and onions.

CENTRAL PANHANDLE

PETERSBURG

Hammer and Wikan: (907-772-4811; 218 North Nordic Drive and 1300 Howdan.) The convenient Nordic Drive location is a True Value Hardware store with grocery items, and the more complete store is near the airport.

WRANGELL

Bob's IGA: (907-874-2341; 223 Brueger Street.) Located just off Front Street, this is a complete market with an excellent deli.

SITKA

Market Center: (907-747-6686; 210 Baranof Street.) The larger supermarkets are on Halibut Point Road, but this one is more convenient.

SOUTHERN PANHANDLE

KETCHIKAN

Alaskan & Proud: (907-225-1279; 3816 Tongass Avenue.) Just across the road from the ferry dock.

Safeway Food & Drug: (907-228-1900; 2417 Tongass Avenue.) Offers the widest selection of groceries and sundries, as well as a salad bar in the Plaza center.

Tatsuda's IGA: (907-225-4125; 633 Stedman Street.) Has a deli and bakery in addition to a full line of groceries. This family has had a grocery store for decades on Stedman Street.

METLAKATLA

Leask's Market: (907-886-4881; First and Milton streets.) A complete store with a good produce section. Nearby on Upper Milton Street, Leask's Mini Mart has a hot bar, and espresso drinks and Italian sodas.

PRINCE OF WALES ISLAND

Alaska and Commercial (A&C): (Craig, Hydaburg, Klawock Mall). The Klawock store is probably the largest, but all of them are essential.

Pizza

Many Panhandle restaurants include a pizza section on the menu. The following eateries focus pretty much on the pies.

JUNEAU

Juneau residents name **The Island Pub** (907-364-1595, theislandpub.com; 1102 Second Street, Douglas) as their favorite pizza place. It specializes in customs pies, and has salads and interesting appetizers. **Pizzeria Roma** (907-463-5020; 2 Marine Way) rates high with visitors who sit at the colorful tables sharing pies on tall stands. Some interesting veggie variations in the mix.

PETERSBURG

Everything is made from scratch at **Papa Bear's Pizza** (907-772-3727; 1105 S. Nordic Drive), with hand-thrown crust and a long list of toppings. Sandwiches, wraps, and baskets, are offered, as well as another kind of pie, in apple or cherry.

KETCHIKAN

Pizza Mill (907-225-6646; 808 Water Street) hand-tosses the crust and bakes the pies to a turn. Multiple variations run to inventive names, such as Dead Head and Fish Hippie, and may be delivered.

Street Stands

Street stands are popular with the traveler in a hurry. They shutter up the moment the last ship pulls away, and their season runs from mid-May to about mid-September.

NORTHERN PANHANDLE

JUNEAU

Bernadette's BBQ: (Seward and Front streets.) The delicious aromas wafting up from this street stand hint at the tasty Filipino fare served from the hot grill. Meat served in strips is a specialty.

Kettle Korn: (South Franklin Street.) You'll smell it a block away, and find the stand across from the Mount Robert's Tramway.

Tracy's King Crab Shack: (907-723-1811; kingcrabshack.com; outdoor stand on the dock at 356 S. Franklin Street.) It takes guts to grab enormous crab legs out of the boiling pot, but that's what it takes to work at Tracy's King Crab Shack. Tracy's crab legs are Alaska's most famous street food, and people from the cruise ships, towering above the stand on the dock, line up to get one of them. You'll have to manipulate the sweet meat out with a plastic fork, and eat at an outdoor table rain or shine, but it doesn't deter the fans. If you bring some friends, you can order them by the bucketful.

   In enthusiasm for the giant legs, people might overlook the delicate, mini-crab cakes or the crab bisque, made with king

Tracy of the eponymous King Crab Shack on the Juneau docks holds two specimens.

Sitka's Reindeer Redhots food stand attracts a line at midday.

and snow crab. It's so delicious, I'd make a trip back to Juneau to have this treat of cream and crab. You can also get a crab hoagie with coleslaw on top. Garlic rolls come with most things on the menu. After you're back home, you can order the king crab legs, Dungeness crab, and Alaska fresh salmon or halibut by mail. Open May through September during the cruise ship season.

HAINES

Top Frog: (Second Avenue across from the Visitor Center.) This green stand set up in the parking lot dispenses espresso drinks, smoothies, and soft ice cream through a window. It's set up in a vacant lot near the visitor center. You can't miss it for the lime-green color.

SKAGWAY

Popcorn Wagon: (565 Broadway.) Reindeer sausage, hot dogs, and drinks in addition to popcorn are available at the stand at Skagway Bazaar building.

CENTRAL PANHANDLE

SITKA

Ludvig's at Lincoln Place Soup Cart: (Tent behind Brenner's store at the foot of Lincoln Street.)This may be the longest name for the tiniest eating place in Sitka. The famous restaurant serves soup and sometimes crabs at this outdoor stand. Open summer only, Monday through Friday for lunch.

Cruise ship passengers love outdoor food stands, like these in Ketchikan, for lunch.

Reindeer Redhots: (Lake and Lincoln streets.) Dispensed out of a cart, the reindeer sausage and beef hot dogs make a quick tasty lunch. Beware of adding too much sauerkraut, chili, or mustard. Eating the delicious, juicy stuff in a bun without dripping challenges the tidiest of eaters.

Wrangell

Java Junkie: (Foot of Front Street at the dock.) Cars come and go all day long at this little stand that also books Stikine River and fishing trips. You'll usually have to wait in a short line for a latte or an espresso. Open during the summer.

SOUTHERN PANHANDLE

Ketchikan

Alaskan Surf: (On the dock at Berth 2.) As the name implies, you'll be able to get a fish sandwich, halibut taco, or chowder at this tiny, colorful stand in the shadow of cruise ships near Berth 2. Bar Harbor, one of Ketchikan's most popular restaurants, prepares the food in its kitchen and shuttles it to the open-air eatery.

Ketchikan Coffee Company: (On the dock at Berth 2.) Espresso drinks from Raven's Brew Coffee are offered from the same folks who have the café in the New York Hotel (See *Bakeries, Cafés, and Delis* section.)

Orca Kettle Corn: (907-225-1566; 602 Dock Street.) Free samples of the slightly sweet, crunchy, popped corn are dispensed. It's hard to stop with just a handful, so chances are you'll walk away with a bag.

RECREATION

Close Encounters with Wild Alaska

Spectacular scenery and wildlife lure people to the Alaska Panhandle. This chapter tells you how to experience and enjoy the mountains, forests, and sea. You can appreciate them at many levels: As a spectator on whale-watching and glacier excursions; being more active with fishing and hiking; and challenging yourself with glacier treks and ziplines.

Prices listed for each activity are average starting figures. Prices change, and the cost may be less at the beginning or at the end of the summer. In many cases, if a cruise line offers an activity as a shore excursion, it must be booked with the line if you are a passenger. Otherwise it can be arranged individually. Independent travelers can book these activities, though preference may be given to cruise passengers.

Almost everything listed here takes place June through September, only, unless otherwise indicated.

Skiffs and cabin cruisers will take people closer to Alaska's scenic wonders for glacier excursions and fishing.

BIKING

Southeast Alaska's unpaved roads and trails are bike-friendly. What's challenging is the mountainous terrain, though almost all communities have flat roads extending a few miles outside of town. Some cruise passengers find biking the ideal way to explore a port of call. Bed-and-breakfast inns often have bikes for guests. U.S. Forest Service offices have excellent trail maps. Rentals start at $14.

NORTHERN PANHANDLE

JUNEAU

Cycle Alaska: (907-780-2253; cycleak.com; 3172 Pioneer Avenue.) Rental bikes include tandems and children's bikes; also trail information and guided trips.

HAINES AND SKAGWAY

Sockeye Cycle Co.: (907-766-2869, Haines; 907-983-2851, Skagway; cyclealaska.com.) In addition to rental bikes, guided tours are offered out of Haines and Skagway. Multiday trips take in the Golden Circle route, or combine canoeing and biking.

CENTRAL PANHANDLE

PETERSBURG

Paved bike trails. Several B&Bs offer bikes.

SITKA

Sitka Bike and Hike: (907-747-7871.) Bike rentals, guided trips to Kruzoff Island, and multisport trips offered.

Travelers in this pickup on the Haines Highway come equipped to enjoy Alaska's wilderness.

Yellow Jersey: (907-747-6317; yellowjerseycycles.com; 329 Harbor Drive.) A complete shop, offers mountain-bike rentals suitable for Sitka's terrain.

WRANGELL

Klondike Bike: (907-874-2453 (BIKE); klondikebike.com; 502 Wrangell Avenue.) Rentals and trail information from full-service shop.

SOUTHERN PANHANDLE

KETCHIKAN

Southeast Exposure: (907-225-8829; southeastexposure.com.) A guided tour to the Clover Pass area north of Ketchikan is available as a cruise ship excursion.

BIRD-WATCHING

Birders come to Alaska to add to their life lists. In addition to Arctic species, many North American birds spend the mating-nesting-nurturing season here. Even nonbirders are thrilled with bald eagles, sitting regally on treetops along watercourses.

Birding will be part of any Alaska trip you take on water, especially while whale watching or glacier viewing. Huge colonies of **black-legged kittiwakes** live near the edge of glaciers. From a distance, they look like white confetti flying against the black cliffs. Occasionally **Arctic terns** gracefully loop near glaciers.

Boat trips into Glacier Bay pause at South Marble Island, where **tufted puffins** nest on the cliff and may fly close enough to show their orange beaks. **Pigeon guillemots** and **common murres** bob on the water. **Glaucous-winged gulls** are also common here and **black oystercatchers** may be spotted.

Northern shovelers, harlequin ducks, and **common mergansers** hover around harbors and coves. In late spring, rafts of thousands of **surf scoters** settle into the water, and dive and surface in wavelike motion. Migratory visitors are **Sandhill cranes** and **white-fronted geese**.

Trumpeter swans spend winter, though a few may linger in the summer and can be spotted from the swan observatory near Petersburg. **American robins** are your constant companions in town gardens. **Kinglets,** both ruby and golden-crowned, and **black-capped chickadees** may be heard twittering in the conifer forest. **Red-breasted sapsuckers** are heard and seen.

And, of course, the **American bald eagle**, a trophy sighting, is almost as common along some Panhandle waterways as pigeons back home. Simply look for the white head, like a golf ball, sitting on a shaggy body at the top of a Sitka spruce. Thousands of bald eagles congregate in Haines late October through February.

The **Alaska Department of Fish and Game Wildlife Viewing Guides** (wildlifeviewing.alaska.gov) have helpful information for birders and other wildlife watchers. They are published regionally, and are in information racks everywhere.

Birding Sites
Juneau: Mendenhall wetlands

Gustavus: Dude Creek Critical Habitat Area

Haines: Chilkat River Valley

Alaska's trophy bird is an American bald eagle

Sitka: Starrigavan Recreation Area and St. Lazaria Island

Petersburg: Swan Observatory, Blind River Rapids Trail

Wrangell: Zimovia Strait paved walking trail

Ketchikan: Deer Mountain Trail, for grouse and ptarmigan

DOGSLEDDING

Summer dogsledding takes place on glaciers, or on wheeled sleds over dirt roads, in the Northern Panhandle. Glacier sledding with flightseeing is the most elaborate and expensive option, starting at $450. Other trips start at $15.

JUNEAU

Alaska Icefields Expeditions: (907-983-2299; akdogtour.com.) Whisk by helicopter to Mendenhall Glacier and then whiz over the snow with an expert musher from the oldest dogsled company in Southeast Alaska.

GUSTAVUS

Great Alaska Husky Ranch: (alaskahuskyranch.com.) The Siberian or Mackenzie River huskies come yapping to greet you at the ranch. After a demonstration, you can either be the musher, or ride as a passenger. Summer mushing is on a track, winter mushing on snow.

SKAGWAY

Alaska Icefields Expeditions: (907-983-2900; akdogtour.com.) A 30-minute flight takes you to the dog camp on Denver Glacier. You'll have a 30-minute ride with a musher.

American Bald Eagle Festival
907-766-3094
baldeagle.org
Early Nov.
Cost: About $35 per day

Not only do thousands of bald eagles gather in the trees above the flowing, salmon-rich Chilkat River in late fall, but bird enthusiasts and photographers also converge for the American Bald Eagle Festival.

The Alaska Chilkat Bald Eagle Preserve has several turnouts with ample parking and good viewing from Haines Highway, MM 18–24. Birds nab the fish from the stream and devour them on the sandbars. Most of the time they sit in bare trees and wait for fish to turn up. The American Bald Eagle Foundation offers daily van tours to the site.

At foundation headquarters in Haines, workshops with wildlife photographers, lectures, and hands-on activities for children take place. An auction features handmade items, including gloves with open fingertips, so helpful for photographing in the cold Haines weather.

An artist of the year, usually a well-known wildlife artist, such as Randall Compton, attends the festival and shows paintings at foundation headquarters. The artist is usually on hand to talk with festival participants.

Although food is not available at the preserve, buses from Chilkat Cruises & Tours stay on hand, and serve as a warming refuge. Drivers also set up urns of hot cider in the parking lot.

A highlight of the festival is the release of rehabilitated birds. People bid for the privilege of releasing the birds, which come from the Anchorage Bird TLC and Juneau Raptor Center. Winning bidders either open the cage door, or literally hold the birds, and then open their arms and allow the birds to fly to freedom. Seeing the birds soar over the river is surprisingly moving.

Photographers focus on a bird at the American Bald Eagle Festival in Haines.

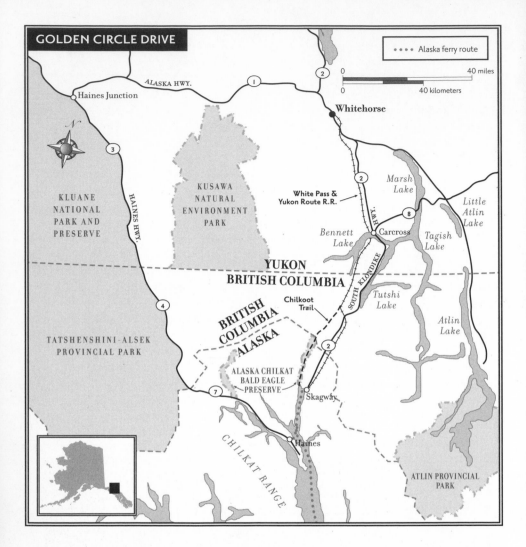

GOLDEN CIRCLE DRIVE

•••• Alaska ferry route

0   40 miles
0   40 kilometers

ALASKA HWY.

Haines Junction

1

2

Whitehorse

3

KLUANE
NATIONAL
PARK AND
PRESERVE

KUSAWA
NATURAL
ENVIRONMENT
PARK

White Pass &
Yukon Route R.R.

2

HAINES HWY.

Marsh
Lake

Little
Atlin
Lake

8

Bennett
Lake

Carcross

Tagish
Lake

YUKON
BRITISH COLUMBIA

SOUTH KLONDIKE HWY.

Tutshi
Lake

Atlin
Lake

4

TATSHENSHINI-ALSEK
PROVINCIAL PARK

BRITISH
COLUMBIA

Chilkoot
Trail

ALASKA

2

ALASKA CHILKAT
BALD EAGLE
PRESERVE

7

Skagway

Haines

CHILKAT RANGE

ATLIN PROVINCIAL
PARK

Excursions on Land

Drive the Golden Circle

Skagway is 14 miles from Haines, by ferry. By road, it's 364 miles—but getting there is more fun and you'll see more. The Golden Circle route traces three legendary highways, two countries, two provinces, and one state. The South Klondike Highway connects Skagway to Whitehorse, Yukon; the Alaska Highway goes from there to Haines Junction; from there, the Haines Highway connects to Haines in Alaska, through a sliver of British Columbia. Routes stay open all winter, though snowstorms may close them.

Mountains surround Skagway with almost claustrophobic nearness, and, indeed, when you leave town you'll immediately start the steep climb to White Pass. The highway traces the trail to the

Klondike, and closely parallels the White Pass & Yukon Route (WP&YR) train that replaced the trail. The White Pass Trail was less steep than the famed Chilkoot Trail nearby, but it was longer, and never became as popular.

Several turnouts allow you to stop, admire the mountains and deep gorge, and read historical information signs. Trees become more stunted, and finally disappear altogether, in a rocky and snow-streaked moonscape. At the 3,202-foot White Pass summit, the road cuts between two rock walls, so the pass can be easily closed in foul weather. The Canada–United States border was disputed into the early 20th century.

You'll reset your watch here. British Columbia, which you pass through briefly, and Yukon Territory both observe Pacific Time, an hour ahead of Alaska Time. Be sure to bring your passport to present to Canadian customs.

Turnouts continue to give access to jaw-dropping views on either side of the highway. At Log Cabin, the Chilkoot Trail National Historic Site has signage, but not a trace of anything else. Next, the Tutshi River Canyon suspension bridge allows you to stand on the swaying structure, 57 feet over the eye-popping gorge. Soon, Bennett Lake, where all those miners spent the winter of 1898, lies below the highway. And then, the Yukon surprises you at Carcross Desert, which looks as if it's straight out of the Mojave. It's made from glacial silt.

At Carcross, short for Caribou Crossing, the vivid red WP&YR station brightens the tiny town. Construction crews from Whitehorse and Skagway met here and laid the golden spike in 1900. Matthew Watson General Store is a good place for an ice cream, or to pick up postcards or an animal skin. Carcross rates an hour or two, with an interpretive mining center, a Yukon craft shop, and picture-pretty St. Saviour's Anglican Church.

A few miles to the north, Emerald Lake looks like an enormous opal shimmering below the road.

The Haines Highway climbs above the treeline at 3,493-foot Chilkat Pass on the Golden Circle Drive.

This enormous snowblower cleaned the White Pass & Yukon Route tracks in winter.

One of the few Gold Rush sites with any remaining buildings is the Robinson Roadhouse, a flag station for WP&YR. Ground squirrel holes punctuate the ground, and the wind howls around the leaning board structures. The vistas begin to flatten and widen as you reach the Alaska Highway and Whitehorse, the capital of Yukon Territory.

Whitehorse museums, restaurants, and hotels are listed in Chapter 3, Lodging, Chapter 4, Culture, and Chapter 6, Restaurants and Food Purveyors.

RVs lumber along on the Alaska Highway between Whitehorse and Haines Junction, where Kluane National Park headquarters is worth a detour. Days could be spent in the park, hiking in this vast wilderness.

Haines Junction to Haines repeats the same experience of crossing an international border, climbing to a pass and dropping down, but the pass is a little higher, and the progression seems more gradual, statelier somehow. Strangely, gulls soar around the snow-streaked, bleak mountains at the summit. Just past the U.S. border, 33 Mile Roadhouse is known for its hamburgers, pie, and friendly atmosphere.

Dropping down, the road hugs the edge of the braided Chilkat River. Bald eagles take up residence here, between MM 24–18, from October through February. Several turnouts with picnic tables offer views of the river and cliffs, where the white specks you see may be mountain goats. Light filters through the trees, and the Chilkat Range, which separates this valley from Glacier Bay, runs majestically along the horizon. It's a stunning picnic spot. And just up the road is Haines, hugging the base of mountains, a long way from the wide spaces of Haines Junction.

TRAINS

White Pass & Yukon Route

1-800-343-7373
whitepassrailroad.com
231 Second Ave., Skagway, AK 99840
Corner Second and Spring, near cruise ship docks
Operates: Early May–Sept.
Admission: Starts $103 round trip
Gift Shop: The Train Shoppe

About 500,000 people ride this train between May and September, making it Alaska's most popular tourism activity. Part of the reason is the mountain scenery: The train climbs 3,000 feet in 20 miles, around hairpin turns, over trestles, and through tunnels. But much of the lure is following the Klondike Gold Rush Trail and learning the stories of the stampeders, and their hardship and heroism. In the old days, the railroad connected Skagway to Bennett Lake, headwaters of the Yukon River, where prospectors picked up steamers to take them more than 500 miles downriver to the gold fields. Before the railroad was completed, they built their own boats.

Several options are possible, the most popular being the round trip to the summit and back. Chilkoot Trail backpackers may pick up the train at Bennett Lake, and day trippers can connect to Carcross with a train-motorcoach combination. The town of Bennett is gone, but an old train station exists as a restaurant.

The WP&YR station at Carcross now serves as a tourist information center.

> **Excursions on Water**
>
> These companies offer trips aimed at general wildlife sightings or combine wildlife viewing and fishing or rafting, and generally are longer than specific wildlife, glacier, and fishing tours, which are listed separately.
>
> These excursions run May through September. Cost for full-day, larger boat trips starts at about $150. Boats that carry four to six people start at about $200 per person for a half day, $400 for a full day.

Offbeat Tours

These are entertaining ways to tour in unconventional vehicles.

Alaska Amphibious Tours (907-225-9899 or 1-866-341-3825 (DUCK); akduck.com) vehicles ride high on wheels to take in Ketchikan's historic sites and natural vistas, and then drive right into the harbor for a boat tour along the busy waterfront.

Takshanuk Mountain Trail (907-766-3179; takshanuk@yahoo.com). 7 Mile Lutak Road near Haines. Drive-yourself tours on graded mountain trails in Kawasaki Mule utility vehicles.

NORTHERN PANHANDLE

Haines and Skagway

Alaska Fjordlines: (907-766-3395 or 1-800-320-0146; alaskafjordlines.com.) Once a day, the catamaran makes the round trip from Skagway and Haines down the Lynn Canal to Auke Bay at Juneau. A wildlife narration alerts passengers to glaciers, bald eagles, orcas, and a Steller sea lion colony. At Juneau, there's time for shopping, visiting historic sites, and Mendenhall Glacier.

Chilkat River Adventures: (907-766-2050 or 800-478-9827; jetboatalaska.com.) A jet-boat tour in the Bald Eagle Preserve near Haines often rewards those aboard with view of moose, trumpeter swans, brown bears, black bears, and bald eagles. Proper jackets provided.

Chilkoot Lake Tours (Alaska Eagle Tours): (907-766-3779; alaskaeagletours.com.) View bald eagles, moose, brown and black bears, mountain goats, mink, birds, and spawning salmon aboard pontoon craft and airboats on Chilkoot Lake. Fishing also available.

Eagle Preserve Floats: (907-766-2491 or 888-292-7789; raftalaska.com.) Half-day float trips on the Chilkat River for eagles, brown and black bears, and occasionally wolves. Takeout is near the Tlingit village of Klukwan. The company also offers multiday trips on the Alsek and Tatshenshini rivers, starting in Haines and ending in Yakutat, and on the Kongakut River in the Arctic National Wildlife Refuge.

Glacier Valley Wilderness Adventures: (907-767-5522; glaciervalleyadventures.net.) The company combines glacier viewing from the air, airboating, river rafting, and gold panning at Nugget Creek in the Tsirku Valley near Glacier Bay National Park with departure from all Northern Panhandle towns.

Klondike Tours, Inc.: (907-983-2075 or 1-866-983-2075; klondiketours.com.) The company offers a variety of tours and activities including wildlife viewing on the Lynn

Canal and at the Chilkat Bald Eagle Preserve, as well as rafting on the Taiya River combined with hiking the Chilkoot Trail.

CENTRAL PANHANDLE

PETERSBURG

Petersburg and Wrangell offer two spectacular wilderness sites: LeConte Glacier, the southernmost tidewater glacier in North America; and the Stikine River, the fastest free-flowing, navigable river on the continent. Each spring, tons of silt run downriver with the melting snow and drop out in the estuary. Boat operators have to make a trial run up the Stikine with a GPS unit to plot the course of the new riverbed.

PETERSBURG

Admiralty Bear Guide: (907-772-4878; admiraltybearguide.com.) Five-day, four-night trips take in LeConte and Baird glaciers, whale watching in Frederick Sound, and the brown bears on Admiralty Island. Departs Monday and returns Friday.

Alaska Island Charters: (907-772-3696 or 1-877-772-3696; alaskaislandcharters.com.) Guests do day trips out of Petersburg and return to town each night for lodging. Four-night packages are offered, with focus primarily on sightseeing and photography, but fishing, whale watching, and other options are available.

Kaleidoscope Cruises: (907-772-3736 or 1-800-868-4373; petersburglodgingandtours .com.) Capt. Barry Bracken is a marine biologist and naturalist who brings his interpretive skills to whale watching in Frederick Sound. Orcas, porpoises, sea lions, and seabirds are

Eric Yancy takes people far up the Stikine River on wildlife and glacier viewing trips in the Stikine Dream.

often spotted. A hydrophone on board the 28-foot *Island Dream* amplifies whale sounds. LeConte Glacier and custom photography trips available.

Summer King Adventures: (907-321-0847; summerking.net.) Trips out of Juneau and Petersburg may focus on lighthouses or whale watching, or be drop-offs for cabins or kayaking trips. Clients may also arrange fishing charters. The Armstrong Marine Catamaran has a hinged bow door that allows beach landings.

Wrangell

Breakaway Adventures: (907-874-2488 or 1-888-385-2488; breakawayadventures.com.) The *Stikine Dream* jet boat takes passengers up the Stikine River to Shakes Glacier with stops at Sergif Island and Shakes Hot Springs. In July and August, trips to Anan Wildlife Observatory for black bears are offered. LeConte Glacier trips run through the summer. A Motivator landing craft is used for photography trips, as a water taxi, and transport to Forest Service cabins.

Stickeen Wilderness Adventures, Inc.: (1-800-874-2085; akgetaway.com.) Trips up the Stikine River and to Anan Wildlife Observatory are offered. The company also does water taxi service to U.S. Forest Service cabins and fly-fishing trips. Travel is aboard heated, enclosed jet boats.

Fishing Charters

Anyone excited by tension on a rod or the glint of a salmon or trout in the water dreams of an Alaska fishing vacation. Some people come to fish for several days, a week, or more,

Fishing boats tethered at Thomas Basin at Ketchikan rest in the shadow of the Golden Princess.

and stay at a fishing lodge (See Chapter 3, *Lodging*), where all arrangements are made. Cruise ship passengers and independent travelers who want to spend a day or two fishing sign up with one of the charter boats in every town from Ketchikan to Yakutat. This section lists charters available for single-fishing days.

The services usually provide tackle and gear, and they may have rain jackets and boots. Some of them also sell Alaska fishing licenses or permits; lunch may be provided. Experienced guides will know good fishing spots, communicate with other boats, and use sonar fish finders.

Salmon and halibut are caught in the ocean almost anytime, though king salmon have a migratory pattern. Spawning salmon may be caught in estuaries or rivers. Steelhead and trout are also caught in rivers. The Alaska Department of Fish and Game strongly encourages catch-and-release practices for steelhead and some trout varieties, which are considered threatened. The main fishing season runs May through September, but some boats go out earlier, and others push into November.

Charter boat crews will clean and pack fish, or deliver the catch to a fish processor. Most Panhandle lodgings have freezers for storing your fish until you go home.

Cruise ship passengers may book a charter through the cruise line, or they can make independent arrangements with operators not under contract to the cruise lines. Some people prefer to wait to see what the weather is like and what's biting. Docks are also good places to pick up very fresh fish, a boon to those staying in a cabin or condo, or driving in a recreational vehicle.

Brokers make the process of finding a charter boat much easier than finding one on your own. They may charge a fee, but it may be worth the time saved. **Alaska Charter Boats** (907-523-0897 or 1-888-530-2628; alaskacharterboat.com) offers charters statewide, with access to more than 70 motor yachts and sailboats suitable for day trips or extended sailings. A crew skippers the boat, prepares your catch, and sees to your comfort.

Cost for sport fishing ranges about $150–$200 for a half day; double that for a full day. Processing fish is additional. Stream fishing will cost less, unless you need to fly into the spot.

NORTHERN PANHANDLE

JUNEAU AND HOONAH

Juneau isn't known as a fishing town, perhaps because there are other distractions, but several charters leave from Auke Bay. Most will pick up clients from the cruise docks or hotels.

Alaska Galore Tours & Charters: (907-364-3455 or 1-888-364-3455; alaskagalore.com.) The company does customized tours of several days, or day trips in the Juneau area with Professional Mariners' Group, a charter fleet.

Alaskan Marine Adventures: (907-789-3474; charter-alaska.com.) Three generations of a Juneau family run this charter, which specializes in custom trips on the 35-foot *Can Can*. Fishing from two hours to multiday expeditions.

Alaskan Raven Charters: (907-723-3429; alaskanravencharters.com.) Halibut is the fish of choice on the *ChilKat 30*, a catamaran built for stability. Half- and full-day options available.

Auke Bay Sportfishing & Beartrack Charters: (907-723-2799; aukebay.com or experience
alaska.com) Captain Todd has been fishing for salmon and halibut for more than 20 years.
Half- or full-day trips on the 42-foot *Beartrack*, which has two cabins.

Juneau Sportfishing & Sightseeing: (907-586-1887; juneausportfishing.com.) "Cruise
ship-style" fishing on boats with bathrooms, kitchens, and cozy cabins is the mode of the
day; some are handicapped accessible. The company provides all tackle and gear and rain
clothing, and also has fishing licenses available for sale.

HAINES

Alaska Explore Charters: (907-314-3021; akexplore.com.) Fishing on a 24-foot
Hewescraft with a cabin and marine head for comfort, on the Upper Lynn Canal, for five
species of salmon and halibut, as well as fly fishing. Photography, wildlife viewing, and
water taxi are other available options.

Happy Salmon Charters: (907-314-3080; happysalmoncharters.com.) Fishing out of
Haines and Skagway for salmon and "barn door" halibut, as well as fly fishing with light
tackle on the Chilkat and Chilkoot rivers. Nature tours with certified naturalist offered.

GUSTAVUS

The Alaska Department of Fish and Game rates the Gustavus fishing grounds in Icy Strait
the state's prime halibut fishing area. Halibut, which are bottom feeders, may be caught in
shallower water here than elsewhere. Of course, salmon, lingcod, and rockfish are caught
as well. Another benefit is that you'll fish among whales, since humpbacks also favor the
area. At the end of a fishing day, the stories may be as much about the whales spouting as
about the halibut catch.

Gustavus is also a center for fly fishing for steelhead, Dolly Varden, cutthroat trout, and
sockeye and coho salmon. Catch-and-release practices are encouraged on freshwater
streams. Most people who fish at Gustavus spend one day on a Glacier Bay cruise.

Fairweather Adventures: (907-923-3065 or 907-697-2334; fishglacierbay.com.) An official concessionaire of Glacier Bay National Park, the service uses 26-foot C-Dory sportfishing boats. The experience combines wildlife viewing as well as fishing for salmon and
halibut.

Glacier Bay Sportfishing: (1-800-445-2112; glacierbaysportfishing.com.) A range of saltwater and freshwater fishing is available, giving variety to the catch.

Gustavus.com: The online service offers links to several charter and sportfishing services
in the Gustavus area.

YAKUTAT

Yakutat has both ocean and river fishing, since the estuary of the Situk River meanders
around the city. Anglers connect with lingcod and rockfish as well as salmon and halibut.
The Situk boasts huge steelhead runs in April, May, and November. Yakutat is a much
smaller community than some Panhandle fishing towns, so choices don't overwhelm
fisherfolk.

Yakutat Charter Operators: (907-784-3433 or 1-888-317-4987; yakutat.net/charters
.htm.) This Web site lists eight Yakutat charters for Yakutat and Disenchantment Bay.
Contact them by linking to their Web sites, or by telephone.

CENTRAL PANHANDLE

PETERSBURG

Fishing has always been Petersburg's lifeblood. It's why Peter Buschmann settled here, and today, more than 400 commercial and sportfishing boats are based here. The town still has three large canneries and fish processing facilities. Petersburg waters support huge schools of pink salmon, the mainstay of the canned salmon industry.

Petersburg also has boat rentals at **Doyles Alaska Boat Rentals** (907-772-4439 or 1-877-442-4010; doylesboatrentals.com). Most Petersburg fishing charters also do LeConte Glacier trips or whale watching. You may well see the whales on a fishing trip.

Magicman Sportfishing Charters: (907-772-9255; magicmansportfishing.com.) The company aims to make beginning fishermen comfortable on the trip to inlets, bays, and sounds near Petersburg. Trips may be booked for a half, whole, or multiple days on the 32-foot *Reel King*.

Petersburg Creek Charters: (907-772-2425; alaska.net/~psgcreek.com.) Half- and full-day charters for halibut, salmon, and steelhead. The captain has been guiding fishing and glacier trips for more than 30 years.

Secret Cove Charters: (907-772-3081; secretcovecharters.com.) The 28-foot boats are designed to get to fishing areas quickly.

SITKA

Numerous islands stud Sitka Sound, making this an attractive as well as rich fishing ground.

Sitka Charters: (907-747-0616 or 1-888-409-0616; sitkacharters.com.) The company arranges half-day charters for cruise ship passengers or fishing packages of several days. All captains are year-round Sitka residents, and know the waters and fishing grounds. The company matches your interests to the right charter.

Sitka Rose Sportfishing Charters: (907-747-9373; fishsitkarose.com.) Long-time Sitka resident Rey Gutierrez helped design the 28-foot aluminum boat that gets people to the fishing areas quickly.

Fishing for Money

Most Alaska communities have salmon derbies during the summer. Local businesses sponsor the events, and contribute cash or prizes. Entrants pay a fee, and the proceeds often benefit a local charity. Derbies may run over a weekend, or a month or more. Participants hope to catch the big ones and bring them to be weighed before a deadline. Boats often race to the dock just before the deadline. During 2008, most winning fish weighed between 45 and 50 pounds.

Most Panhandle salmon derbies take place during late spring and early summer, during the king salmon run. Some of the Panhandle's best known are: **Baranof Island (Sitka) Salmon Derby** (sitka coc.com); **Haines King Salmon Derby** (haines.ak.us); **Golden North (Juneau) Silver Salmon Derby** (goldennorthsalmonderby.org/); **Ketchikan King Salmon Derby** (ketchikancharr.com/Templates/mainderby.htm); **Petersburg** (Petersburg.org); and the **Wrangell King Salmon Derby** (wrangellchamber.org/derby.php).

Sitka's Secrets: (907-747-5089; sitkasecret.com.) The charter supplies all you need, it claims, except luck in catching fish. King salmon are sought in early summer, coho later, and halibut anytime. The 27-foot boat accommodates six comfortably.

WRANGELL

Commercial fishing is still very active here, as well as sport fishing.

Alaska Peak & Seas: (907-874-2454; wedoalaska.com.) Half-day to multiday adventures aboard the 53-foot *Bear Necessity* or the jet boat, *Stikine Spirit*. Fishing or hunting trips are usually several days. The company also offers wildlife trips, and whale-watching trips, which include a sonar device.

Fish Wrangell Alaska: (907-874-2590; fishwrangell.com.) Fly fishing on freshwater streams or saltwater angling for salmon and halibut are offered. Don't know how to fly-fish? Not to worry. Capt. Marlin Benedict will teach you how.

Timber Wolf Charters: (907-874-4157 or 1-888-993-2750; alaskaupclose.com.) Salmon and halibut fishing on salt water, or guided freshwater fly fishing from a fourth-generation Alaska family.

SOUTHERN PANHANDLE

KETCHIKAN

Ketchikan is called "Salmon Capital of the World." Lots of anglers think it lives up to the name. Scores of fishing charters are available. A good source of information is the booklet from the **Ketchikan Visitors Bureau** (907-225-6166; visit-ketchikan.com.), which is free on every rack in town.

Alaskan Fishing Adventures: (907-225-4043; alaskanfishingadventures.com.) Half-day and full-day trips, boat rental for unguided fishing, and packages of several days offer flexibility. Excellent salmon and halibut fishing not far from the dock.

Bering Sea Crab Fishermen's Tour: (1-888-239-3816; 56degreesnorth.com.) You'll be an observer aboard the F/V *Aleutian Ballad*, which has been filmed for the Discovery Channel's *Deadliest Catch*. You'll go out with the crabbers, seated in a comfortable observation area, and watch them pull up and empty crab pots. This is a rare opportunity to go out with a commercial fishing boat.

Experience One Charters: (907-225-2343; latitude56.com.) The company specializes in charters for cruise ship passengers. The M/V *Experience* can accommodate 16 passengers and wheelchairs.

Ketchikan Charter Boats, Inc.: (907-225-7291 or 1-800-272-7291; ketchikancharter boats.com.) Their fleet of boats ranges in size from 24 to 40 feet, providing fishing for up to 60 people. The service accepts walk-up passengers, but highly recommends reservations.

Northern Lights Charters: (907-247-8488 or 1-888-550-8488; ketchikanfishing.net.) Several options are offered by three charter services, including standard half- and full-day trips. In addition, Northern Lights offers evening fishing in the long twilight, and Island Wings has fly-out fishing trips.

Salmon Quintuplets

A salmon isn't just a salmon. Five varieties of salmon live in Alaska waters. Fishermen prize areas with all five species. Salmon tend to spawn at different seasons, so visitors time fishing trips to the avail-ability of the variety they want. During spawning season, the salmon can be caught near beaches or along the spawning streams, though some people do not like to eat the flesh of spawning salmon. A good time to spot black and brown bears is during the salmon spawning season, along streams.

Though the flesh is pink like salmon, steelhead are actually sea-run rainbow trout. Salmon and steelhead are anadromous fish, which means they are born in fresh water, migrate to salt water where they mature, and return to spawn in their birth streams. Sometimes the flesh of king salmon is white, which some people con-sider a delicacy. (This information comes from the Alaska Department of Fish and Game.)

King or Chinook: The largest and most prized variety for sport fishermen, it is also the most rare. It passes through Southeast Alaska waters April through June, to spawn in streams farther south. The exception is the Stikine River near Wrangell, though it's closed to king salmon fishing.

Sockeye or red: Some people prefer sockeye for its vibrant color, taste, and ability to fight. Few of these are caught in salt water. Most anglers fish with flies and spinners in July.

Coho or silver: These are abundant in the Petersburg-Wrangell area and average 8 to 10 pounds. They reach a peak in salt water in mid-August, and in bays and estuaries late August through October, when they spawn.

Chum or dog salmon: Sport fishermen rate this variety at the bottom of the list and generally catch it incidentally when trolling or fly fishing for something else.

Pink or humpies: The salmon most often canned is abundant in Southeast Alaska waters, travel-ing in schools numbering in the thousands. Anglers catch them in salt water throughout the summer. People often fish for pinks from the shoreline, mid-July through August. They develop distinctive humps on their backs as they spawn, earning their nickname.

An angler smiles broadly with her impressive salmon. Kristen Kemmerling/Alaska Tourism Marketing Council

Ketchikan Kayak Fishing: (907-225-1272; yakfishalaska.com.) Paddle to uninhabited islands not far from the Ketchikan shore in a comfortable, stable kayak with top seating. Fishing is normally for salmon; inexperienced anglers are welcome.

Fishing Multiday Trips

Live-aboard fishing trips often are a leisurely, luxurious way to fish the Panhandle bays and channels. Think of them as floating fishing lodges.

JUNEAU

Alaska Yacht Adventures: (907-789-1978 or 1-800-725-3913; alaskayachtcharters.com.) Week-long trips out of Juneau, Sitka and, in the early season, out of Ketchikan, are the itinerary for the 73-foot *Sea Mist.* She was designed as a stable, yacht fishing vessel.

Wild Alaska Sportfishing and Cruises: (907-723-1596 or 1-866-945-3252; wildalaska cruises.com.) The 85-foot *Perseverance* takes guests to remote salmon and halibut fishing grounds and combines fishing with ecotourism and wildlife viewing. Cruises depart from Juneau or Petersburg.

HAINES

First Out, Last In: (907-766-2854 or 1-877-881-2854; firstoutlastin.com.) Private, live-aboard cruises in Glacier Bay, Icy Strait, Elfin Cove, and Pelican on a 45-foot Bayliner with three staterooms and galley. Fishing, wildlife viewing, photography, dinghy shore excursions.

PETERSBURG

Alaska Sea Adventures: (907-772-4700 or 1-888-772-8588; yachtalaska.com.) Emphasizes wildlife viewing and photography in addition to fishing. Seven- to ten-day trips aboard the four-cabin M/V *Alaska Adventurer.*

A fishing guide fillets a halibut for fishermen after a day of fishing at Yakutat.

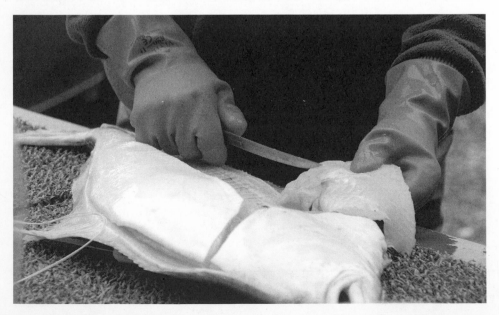

Visitors peer into tanks where young salmon and steelhead are raised at Deer Mountain Tribal Hatchery & Eagle Center in Ketchikan.

KETCHIKAN

Classic Alaska Charters: (907-225-0608; classicalaskacharters.com.) Five-day, four-night trips are planned with guests that may include visits to Misty Fjords, photography, or ecotourism. The 40-foot *Saltery C* has a covered fishing deck.

Fish Hatcheries

Almost every community has a fish hatchery, which generally is open to the public. You'll learn a great deal about the life cycle of anadromous salmon at these facilities, which are aimed at replenishing salmon streams.

One of the best is **Deer Mountain Tribal Hatchery & Eagle Center** (907-228-5530; kictribe.org; 1158 Salmon Road) in Ketchikan. You start with a visit to the bald eagle facility, where injured birds are kept. Then a tour guide walks you through the hatchery, explaining the remarkable process of harvesting only 30 to 35 adult spawning salmon, which yield thousands of eggs that hatch in "incubators." Sac fry still have a bit of the yolk attached. They grow to fingerling and finally smolt stage, when they can survive in salt water and are released. The hatchery raises king and coho salmon, and steelhead. At **Macaulay Salmon Hatchery** in Juneau, (907-463-4810; dipac.net/Macaulay_hatchery .html; 2697 Channel Drive) visitors get a briefing on the life cycle of the salmon from an elevated viewing area of the operation. They move on to interpretive exhibits and saltwater aquarium displays with more than 100 species of marine life.

FLIGHTSEEING

Ask anyone how they enjoyed their Alaska vacation, and, chances are, the first thing they will talk about is a flightseeing tour. Companies in every community provide this excitement.

With the exception of Ketchikan, where you'll usually visit Misty Fjords, most flightseeing focuses on glaciers of the great icefields. Petersburg and Wrangell flights take in LeConte Glacier; Juneau, its icefield and series of glaciers; Gustavus, Glacier Bay; and Haines-Skagway, Davidson and Rainbow glaciers, and sometimes Glacier Bay.

Flightseeing may be in helicopters or small airplanes; starts at about $150; with landings, about $200 or more.

NORTHERN PANHANDLE

JUNEAU

Era Helicopters: (907-586-2030; flightseeingtours.com.) Glacier-walking boots are provided for a four-glacier air tour with a landing; a company signature tour.

TEMSCO Helicopters: (907-789-9501; temscoair.com.) Glacier sightseeing and landings with dog-sledding on the Juneau Icefield are the specialty. The company pioneered glacier helicopter touring in Alaska. Departures are also from Skagway and Petersburg. The company celebrated its 50th anniversary in 2008.

Wings Airways: (907-586-6275; wingsairways.com.) Operates out of a downtown dock with float planes on two itineraries: Juneau Icefield glaciers and Taku Glacier Lodge.

HAINES AND SKAGWAY

Alaska Mountain Flying Service: (907-766-3007 or 1-800-954-8747; flyglacierbay.com.) The service offers itineraries over Glacier Bay, with the option to land on a glacier or the beach. The service also ferries skiers and mountaineers with drop-offs and pickups on ski planes.

Earthcenter Adventures/Fly Drake: (907-314-0675 or 907-766-3679; flydrake.com.) Passengers wear stereo headsets for easy conversation on sightseeing flights over an arm of Glacier Bay. Drake Olson will customize flights with beach or glacier landings. He also ferries rafters and gear for Tatshenshini and Alsek River trips, and offers support for skiers and hikers.

GUSTAVUS

Air Excursions: (907-697-2375; airexcursions.com.) The air taxi service does touring over Glacier Bay, Admiralty Island brown bear viewing and landing, and the Juneau Icefield.

Fjord Flying Service: (907-697-2377; gustavus.com.) High-wing Cessna 206 aircraft provide good viewing over Glacier Bay or the Juneau Icefield.

YAKUTAT

Alsek Air Service, Inc.: (907-784-3231; alsekair.com.) Trips over Russell Fjord take in Hubbard Glacier, the largest tidewater glacier in North America, views of the St. Elias Range, and the large tidal area of the Situk River. Glacier landing in a ski plane an option.

A helicopter flies over Mendenhall Glacier near Juneau. Robin Hood/Alaska Tourism Marketing Council

CENTRAL PANHANDLE

PETERSBURG

Nordic Air: (907-772-3535.) An amphibious airplane, with wheels attached to its floats, is used for flightseeing.

Pacific Wing: (907-772-4258; pacificwing.com.) The Stikine Icefield and River are the primary areas taken in by float plane and amphibious aircraft.

WRANGELL

Sunrise Aviation: (907-874-2319 or 1-800-874-2311; sunriseflights.com.) The Stikine River, LeConte, and Shakes glaciers are some of the territory covered.

SITKA

Harris Aircraft Services: (907-966-3050; harrisaircraft.com.) A deHavilland Beaver and Cessna 185 provide scenic flights over Sitka Sound and islands and Baranof Island.

SOUTHERN PANHANDLE

KETCHIKAN

Pacific Airways: (907-225-3500 or 1-877-360-3500; flypacificairways.com.) Float plane tours to Misty Fjords land in the water; also tours of Revillagigedo Island.

Promech Air: (907-225-3845 or 1-800-360-3845; promechair.com.) The Misty Fjord trip combines float plane transportation with a catamaran ride in the national monument. Also Neets Bay for black bear viewing, and glacier trips.

Taquan Air: (907-225-8800 or 1-800-770-8800; taquanair.com.) The company operates the largest fleet of deHavilland Beaver float planes in Alaska. Misty Fjords, glaciers, black bear habitats, and a "seaplane safari."

GLACIERS

Glaciers rate alongside bears and whales as something visitors want to see in Alaska. The Panhandle offers several chances to visit glaciers. The northernmost is Hubbard Glacier, with a 6-mile front wall, the largest in North America. The glaciers spilling into Glacier Bay from the Brady Icefield and Fairweather and Chilkat ranges come next. Juneau Icefield is the source of several glaciers, including popular Mendenhall and several on Taku Inlet. South of Juneau, Tracy Arm leads to North and South Sawyer glaciers. The southernmost tidewater glacier is LeConte and its tributaries near Petersburg.

John Muir experienced a state of ecstasy when he visited glaciers, which he chronicles in *Travels in Alaska*. He describes light as keen as diamonds radiating from ice crystals: "It was perfectly glorious to think of this divine light burning over all this vast crystal sea in such ineffably fine effulgence, and over how many other of icy Alaska's glaciers where nobody sees it."

Whether viewing a glacier head on, flying over its endless river of ice, or trekking on it, remember Muir's rapture.

Even in the rain, people come to view Mendenhall Glacier.

NORTHERN PANHANDLE

JUNEAU

Mendenhall Glacier (Tongass National Forest)

907-789-0097

fs.fed.us/r10/tongass/districts/mendenhall

8465 Old Dairy Rd., Juneau, AK 99801

Accessible: By car and city bus Route 3 and 4 in the Mendenhall Valley area of Juneau

Open: Year-round

Admission: $3 May–Sept.; free, Oct.–Apr.

Gift Shop: Fine books on glaciers, wildlife, DVDs, caps, T-shirts, handwarmers

Mendenhall is sometimes dubbed the "drive-in glacier" or "bus stop glacier." Both are true. It is one of the most visited glaciers in the world.

It stretches 12 miles from the Juneau Icefields to Mendenhall Lake at its toe. Like most glaciers, Mendenhall is shrinking. Its terminal moraine is about 1½ miles from the visitor center, which stands where the glacier ended in the 1930s. Start your visit there for the excellent exhibits explaining glaciers, their origin, and their effect on the landscape.

Several trails surround the visitor center. Photo Point Trail drops down to the lake, for good photo-op spots. The visitor center and Photo Point loop trail are wheelchair accessible.

Be forewarned: It's not always clear here. One winter day when I visited, the glacier never once emerged from the fog. But on another visit at dusk in mid-summer, the light was rosy on the glacier and fireweed framed the foreground.

Steep Creek Trail follows a spawning salmon stream, and others show glacial action on the landscape. Interpretive signs point out striation in the rocks, caused by glacial movement over them. Bear sightings are frequent along these paths, so be alert.

Note: The city bus stop is about 1½ miles from the glacier.

Sawyer Glacier

Located about halfway between Juneau and Petersburg, South and North Sawyer glaciers are visited by cruise ships and some day trips out of Juneau. Tracy Arm, a narrow channel with waterfalls, gives access to both. The channel twists a bit so you don't see the glaciers until you are quite close.

They are active glaciers so it's sometimes not possible to get close to them. Occasionally they will calve underwater, and icebergs will suddenly burst through the surface.

Adventure Bound Alaska (907-463-2509 or 1-800-228-3875; adventureboundalaska .com.) does Tracy Arm day trips out of Juneau.

Gustavus
Glacier Bay National Park and Preserve
907-697-2230
nps.gov/glba
P.O. Box 140, Gustavus, AK 99826
Accessible only by boat or plane.
Open: Year-round, though services limited in winter. Visitor Center at Glacier Bay Lodge, open May–early Sept. Boat tours operate during same period.
Admission: None. Fees and permits for camping, boating, kayaking from Visitor Information Center at Bartlett Cove at head of dock. Open May–Sept.
Gift Shop: Books, DVDs.

When Captain George Vancouver visited Glacier Bay in 1794, he found only a slight indentation where Bartlett Cove is today. But the glaciers were already in retreat. When John Muir came by in 1879, the glaciers had shrunk about 48 miles up the bay to Tlingit Point. Today the retreat stands at about 65 miles, creating a great, Y-shaped fjord. Muir Glacier, the one he described so rhapsodically in *Travels in Alaska*, is not even visible from the bay.

Muir is generally credited with the "discovery" of Glacier Bay, though Tlingits were well aware of it. They had lived along the bay, but the "Little Ice Age" of the 1700s drove them away. To this day, some Tlingit groups consider Glacier Bay their ancestral home.

People visit Glacier Bay on cruises or by spending the night at Gustavus or Glacier Bay Lodge. Alaska Airlines serves Gustavus in summer; air taxis are available the rest of the year. A park service concessionaire runs a tour boat out of Bartlett Cove with a park ranger naturalist on board.

I once had a magical experience on a small boat between islands near the Glacier Bay mouth. A mother black bear with two cubs started to cross the channel ahead of the boat. The captain cut the motor and we floated silently. One of the cubs swam right beside her, but the other one whimpered in the water, far behind. The mother turned around, picked up the reluctant cub, put it on her back and swam to the far shore. The baby whimpered all the way, and the mother's breath came in gulps. When she reached the beach, she and the cubs shook off water; we all let our breath out.

Most boats pause at South Marble Island for the Steller sea lion colony, and the puffins and kittiwakes. Brown bears are usually spotted on the beach a bit north of here. Then boats make their way up Tarr Inlet to famed Margerie Glacier, a wall of ice about a mile long. People crowd the decks and gawk at the corrugated white, blue, and gray face of the glacier. Sometimes they're rewarded with calving ice. The first indication is usually a bit of movement, as small ice pieces chip off, and then a portion of the face simply hits the water with a thunderous clap.

Most ships make a wide turn at Grand Pacific Glacier, which looks like a vast, dirty, river of ice. Lamplugh and Reid glaciers usually merit a stop on the way out. Nearby Johns Hopkins Glacier is so active that boats rarely get closer than 2 miles.

A limited number of cruise ships visit Glacier Bay. The park service runs a daily tour in a high-speed catamaran (visitglacierbay.com) during summer. For other boat tours, flight-seeing, rafting, mountaineering, see the national park Web site.

YAKUTAT

Hubbard and Malaspina glaciers are near Yakutat. Hubbard puts up the most spectacular façade and is the most frequently visited.

Hubbard Glacier
Wrangell–St. Elias National Park and National Preserve
907-784-3295
nps.gov/wrst or Yakutatalaska.com

Hubbard Glacier's front wall stretches for 6 miles in Yakutat Bay.

Yakutat Visitor Center, Mallott Highway near Ace Hardware

Hubbard Glacier is the exception to the shrinking-glacier rule. It's getting thicker and it's advancing. Visiting this glacier in a small boat, low in the water at its 6-mile front wall, bedazzles the most jaded tourist.

First you'll cross wide Yakutat Bay, and enter narrower Disenchantment Bay. Turner and Valerie glaciers introduce Hubbard. Icebergs dot the water, and then cluster thicker and thicker. A skilled boat operator, like Mark Sappington of the Yakutat Charter Boat Co., guides the boat to the right shore, and zigzags a path through the bergs, which nudge the boat like bullies. Finally, closer to the face, the ice seems to open a bit. We move past the endless wall of towers, pinnacles, and ice caves, in colors from gray-white to deepest blue, like the façades of castles set end to end. He stops the boat, so we can "hear" the glacier. And indeed, it hisses, pops, and sometimes thunders from calving. Often, we see just the icy, mist aftermath. The glacier ends at Russell Fjord, and we have to backtrack, hoping the iceberg path hasn't closed.

In 1986, Hubbard shed so many icebergs that they dammed up the fjord, and threatened to flood Yakutat when they released.

Yakutat is the gateway to Hubbard, the largest tidewater glacier in North America. You'll need to charter a boat or arrange for flightseeing over the glacier. A visitors center for Wrangell–St. Elias National Park in town serves as a good source of information. The rangers are helpful, though be aware that in summer 2008, hours were limited to Monday, Wednesday, and Friday mornings.

Wrangell–St. Elias is the largest U.S. national park. Its Kennecott Visitor Center is almost 200 miles from Yakutat.

For boat charters, visit **Yakutat Charter Operators** (yakutat.net/charters.htm) or flightseeing **Alsek Air** (907-784-3231; alsekair.com) or **Yakutat Coastal Airlines** (907-784-3831; flyyca.com).

CENTRAL PANHANDLE

PETERSBURG

LeConte Glacier

fs.fed.us/r10/tongass/forest_facts/resources/geology/stikineicefields.htm

Petersburg is the jumping-off point for LeConte Glacier, the southernmost tidewater glacier in North America. The glacier is born in the Stikine Icefield and makes its way into LeConte Bay, a narrow, deep outlet.

The boat trip into LeConte Bay is particularly pleasing, with the water changing from deep marine to turquoise. Icebergs appear long before the glacier is visible. At times, access is limited because harbor seals are berthing on the icebergs in front of the glacier.

LeConte throws off icebergs like a popcorn machine. Some of them calve underwater, and are known to pop to the surface as much as 1,000 feet away. Boats approach cautiously, and often get nudged from side to side as some of the bergs hit the boat. LeConte is one of Alaska's most active glaciers, and most of its motion is backward. It has retreated 2½ miles since it was first charted in 1887.

Every year since 1983, students at Petersburg High School have measured the position of the glacier. While it has retreated overall, some years it extended farther into the bay than previous years.

Day cruises out of Petersburg take in the glacier. **Viking Travel** (907-773-4818; 101

North Nordic Drive) will book cruises or flightseeing. **Breakaway Adventures** (907-874-2488) and **Kaleidoscope Tours** (907-772-3736) are popular.

Glacier Trekking

NorthStar Trekking: (907-790-4530 or 1-866-590-4530; northstartrekking.com.) Three levels of trekking on the Juneau Icefields offer opportunities for everyone from novices to experienced ice climbers. The treks range from one-hour walks on fairly level terrain to three-hour trips in rugged terrain of remote parts of the glacier. Transportation to the glacier site is by A-Star helicopters.

Icy Origins

All North American glaciers originate in the vast ice fields of Alaska and Northern Canada that once covered huge areas extending from the polar regions of Earth. They still cover a lot. Worldwide, glaciers and polar ice store more water than lakes and rivers, groundwater, and the atmosphere combined. Glaciers cover as much land as farms.

Glaciers form when snowfall in the mountains exceeds snowmelt in the spring and summer. The snow gets warm, melts a bit and forms ice. Then the next year, more snow falls, and the process repeats itself, adding a bit more ice.

But glaciers don't just grow deeper and deeper. They move downhill with gravity and eventually reach the sea, where they calve, or reach a valley.

When snowfall does not exceed snowmelt, the glaciers begin to retreat, as they are now. Almost all glaciers worldwide are retreating, though not all of them. Taku Glacier, formed out of the Juneau Ice Fields, has been growing, and over the past several years, achieved stability. As glaciers advance, they carve deep valleys and, once they retreat, leave behind moraines.

Glaciers that reach the sea are tidewater glaciers, like those in Glacier Bay, or Sawyer and LeConte in the Panhandle. A hanging glacier, such as Rainbow Glacier near Haines, ends high in a mountain valley. They usually are at right angles to the main U-shaped valley. Glaciers that end in freshwater lakes, like Mendenhall, are lacustrine glaciers. Many have a small lake at their foot where melting water accumulates.

As the glaciers move, they carve valleys and when they melt, they leave behind debris that they've pushed. John Muir observed U-shaped valleys at Yosemite in California, and came up with the idea that glaciers had made these valleys. When he came to Alaska, he confirmed his ideas when he saw glaciers in the act of carving the valleys.

Glaciers also act like sandpaper. The rocks and boulders they pick up scrape against rock farther along. Rock faces in the path of retreating glaciers have striations. The piles of debris they leave behind are called moraines.

As the great ice masses retreat, the earth "rebounds" and rises, much like a cushion re-inflates after someone gets up. The shore at Gustavus is 5 feet higher than it was 40 years ago.

Another phenomenon is the reappearance of plants on the rock left barren by the glacier. Scientists study this scrubbed rock to watch as plants begin to take hold. They're interested in the species and the time it takes to restore a forest. They call it glacial succession, which gets as much attention as the retreat.

GOLF

Golfing anywhere in Alaska is unique. It shuts down completely during the winter, but during the summer you can play from about 3 AM to 10 PM without difficulty. So over the course of a year, the golf hours may be about the same as Florida. And golf costs less. Expect to pay $15–$20 for nine holes.

GUSTAVUS

Mt. Fairweather Golf Course

907-697-2214

Dock Rd., about ¾ mile from Gustavus Rd.

The rough is truly rough muskeg at this nine-hole, par 36 golf course, but the fairways and greens are clipped and tidy. You can warm up on a driving range. It may have the most informal arrangement of any golf course in the country. Scorecards, tees, and even rental golf clubs and handcarts sit in an open shed with shelves. Select what you need, and drop your money in a jar. It's not unusual to see moose, black bears, or foxes, and almost certainly bald eagles from the holes near Icy Strait.

HAINES AND SKAGWAY

Valley of the Eagles Golf Links

907-766-2401 or 907-314-0760

hainesgolf.com

Haines Hwy., Mile 1.5

The Mt. Fairweather Golf Course at Gustavus operates on the honor system, including rental clubs.

This may be the most unique golf course in the world. Located on tidelands, the nine-hole course is occasionally awash in water since it is subject to high tides. The setting makes it a true links course. The original "links" were sited on estuaries in Scotland.

The fairways often have a slightly burned look. This may be from frost, or because no pesticides or herbicides are used. Although you won't usually encounter wild animals, expect to see moose and bear tracks. Artificial turf covers the tees and greens to provide even playing surface and to extend the playing season. The setting, beside the Lynn Canal and surrounded by coastal mountains, is gorgeous. A driving range is beside the course.

SITKA
Sea Mountain Golf Course
907-747-5663
seamountaingolf.com
301 Granite Creek Rd. off Halibut Point Rd.

Builders carved the course out of the natural terrain at this nine-hole par 36 golf course, which opened in July 2008. Fairways overlook Sitka Sound and Mount Edgecumbe in the distance. It's considered a challenging course with somewhat hilly terrain and narrow fairways. A driving range, restaurant, and lounge are amenities. Rental clubs are available. The restaurant is open for lunch Friday through Sunday, and for dinner Tuesday through Sunday. Van service is available.

WRANGELL
Muskeg Meadows
907-874-4653
wrangellalaskagolf.com
Ishiyama Drive, near the airport

Rental clubs and handcarts are available at this private course, which is open to the public. Volunteers created the nine-hole, 36 par course with materials donated by the Alaska Pulp Corporation. In spite of its name, trees, rather than muskeg, line most fairways. Ocean and mountain views are spotted between the fairways. Covered boxes keep driving range players dry. An eight-station putting green is also available.

The course has a special "Raven Rule." Should one of the ever-present black birds snatch your ball, you may replace it with no penalty, provided there is a witness.

GOLD MINE TOURS

Gold brought many people to the Panhandle in the late 19th and early 20th centuries, though the big prizes were in Canada's Klondike or Cassiar gold fields. But Alaska yielded some nuggets as well. You'll be able to visit mines at Juneau and near Haines.

JUNEAU
AJ Mine/Gastineau Mill Enterprises: (907-463-5017.) The excellent tour explains the process of milling ore at two outdoor sites with clear canopies and heaters. The only hard rock gold mine tour in Southeast Alaska includes a drilling demonstration given by a miner. You'll wear earplugs to mute the din. The museum has fascinating exhibits, including a scale so sensitive that it can register the weight of a pencil line drawn across paper.

The gift shop has gold nugget jewelry costing four figures, and inexpensive rhodinite bracelets. Pickup by a bus or van is from the Mt. Roberts Tramway.

Last Chance Mining Museum: (907-586-5338; 1001 Basin Road.) You'll hike a short distance up the hill to get to the museum located in the old compressor building, listed on the National Register of Historic Places. This is where Joe Juneau and Richard Harris originally found gold.

HAINES
Big Nugget Gold Mine: The Porcupine Mine, the largest placer mine on Porcupine Creek, is open to tourists. You get to keep the gold you pan.

HELI-SKIING

The Chilkat Range surrounds Haines, making this a base for heli-skiing. Many peaks offer the chance to accumulate 25,000-foot vertical descents in a day. Skiing terrain starts at the saltwater shore, and extends several miles inland with five different microclimates in the area. The season runs February through April, when days are longer. Helicopters do not have to travel far to drop skiers. Cost starts at about $600 per day for heli-skiing, $200 for Sno-Cat.

Alaska Heli-skiing: (907-767-5745; alaskaheliskiing.com.) Groups of five taken up to ski or snowboard about six or more runs per day. Depending on terrain, skiers may take as many as 10 runs per day. Ski-plane and Sno-Cat skiing, as well as intermediate skiing for families. Certified guides accompany all trips.

Southeast Alaska Backcountry Adventures: (1-877-617-3418; skiseaba.com.) Helicopter and Snow-cat skiing with a high percentage of first descents and vertical feet. Six-day packages offered.

HIKING

Hiking in the Panhandle is a win-win situation. You're either looking at jaw-dropping scenes of icefield-crowned mountains or shimmering bays studded with islands. Or you're in the temperate rainforest, where the light itself seems green from the sheer density of growing things. The ground springs back underfoot from the constantly dropping needles, compacted by the frequent rain.

Maybe the rain isn't part of the win equation. Just wear a rainproof jacket with a hood. It rarely rains hard, and the hood will keep you warm if it gets windy.

Trails, some of them famous, lace the Panhandle's mountains, which rise abruptly from the sea. Those listed below are easily accessible from towns.

Guided Hikes
When time is short or you don't know an area well, a guided hike may be the answer. Cost starts at about $65.

JUNEAU
Gastineau Guiding: (907-586-8231; stepintoalaska.com.)
Rainforest nature hikes, glacier overlook walks, photography safaris, wildlife viewing, and

Two hikers are prepared to do some serious backpacking in the Alaska Panhandle.

a tram-trail combination are among the choices from this well-known company. The company will also plan a custom itinerary and activities for those with specific ideas in mind, such as day hikes to remote destinations or private whale watching.

The truly adventurous may opt for one of the helicopter-glacier walking or dogsledding tours, or icefield adventures. The company works with various helicopter companies for remote itineraries.

Chosen Juneau's top tour company by Princess Cruises, Gastineau limits hiking groups and tours to 14 people. Guides offer frequent interpretive comment. The company runs the Mount Roberts Nature Center at the top of the tram, where interpreters give frequent deck talks and a self-guided Alpine audio tour, "Tracks and Trails."

WRANGELL
Rainwalker Expeditions: (907-874-2549; rainwalkerexpeditions.com.) Trips range from history and cultural walks in town to more extensive outings in the rainforest to Rainbow Falls, Mill Creek, and Virginia Lake and overnight trips to Telegraph Creek in British Columbia. The company also rents kayaks and bikes.

SITKA
Island Fever: (907-738-1535; islandfeverdiving.com.) Hikes in several Sitka areas range from a gentle rainforest walk to a climb of Mount Edgecumbe, only for the reasonably fit.

The company has Tongass National Forest permits for access to some trails.

KETCHIKAN
Misty Fjords National Monument
Island Wings Air Service: (907-225-2444; islandwings.com.) The company offers both guided and unguided hiking in Misty Fjords. Transport is by float plane with sightseeing along the way. The guided hike has several options, including one trail beside a waterfall. The unguided hike begins at an Alpine lake and follows a trail through old-growth forest along a river.

Trails
The U.S. Forest Service sells trail maps to Tongass National Forest, which takes in most of the Panhandle. All the major Panhandle towns have Forest Service Visitor Centers, though they are often closed because of federal government cutbacks. You'll also find maps at the Southeast Alaska Discovery Center in Ketchikan or Mendenhall Glacier Visitor Center. Local visitor guides available in all the towns also have information and maps for trails closest to town.

In spring, be aware of avalanche areas. In the rainforest, be bear savvy. Always make noise as you walk. Should you meet a bear, don't challenge it, but don't run away. Be calm, and slowly back off. Never carry food. I've been given pepper spray to carry when hiking around Yakutat, and I've seen 12-year-olds carry shotguns to protect themselves against bears.

Slap, Squish, Repel
Mosquitoes. They're called Alaska helicopters or the state bird. A Tlingit legend tells about a blood-sucking monster that turns into a swarm of mosquitoes. These buzzing giants have plagued people as long as the two have coexisted in Alaska. Jokes about two mosquitoes carrying off a victim to devour are rampant. Anything you do outdoors in Alaska from spring to fall will be in the company of mosquitoes.

So, what's the best remedy? Start by covering as much of your skin as possible with long sleeves, long pants, and a hat. Some people swear by the Avon product, Skin So Soft, generally used in the bath or rubbed on the skin after a shower. Lately herbal mosquito-repelling products have become popular. Others insist the product must have DEET, which can be up to 95 percent. Heed all the warnings on the labels and use exactly as directed. Avoid getting it on your camera or binoculars.

NORTHERN PANHANDLE

JUNEAU

Downtown Juneau huddles against Mount Roberts and Mount Juneau, affording easy access to trails. Just walk up Sixth Street to Basin Road, then walk to its end and you're on **Perseverance Trail**, a 3-mile popular trail. Or continue straight on Sixth, and you'll be on the **Mount Roberts Trail.** An even easier way is to take the Mount Roberts Tramway up to the 1,800-foot level, where you'll meet the trail. This gives access to the Mount Roberts loop, a strenuous climb, and even in June was still snow covered.

These trails are along cascading streams with waterfalls, and follow old mine roads. The hill is honeycombed with tunnels. During the winter, there's an avalanche threat, so hiking is not recommended.

The Mendenhall Valley and Auke Bay areas also have splendid and numerous hiking opportunities. From many vantage points here, the glacier looms in the distance. The 2.1-mile **Mendenhall River Trail** offers views of the glacier across a meadow, and follows the river to Montana Creek. The trail is paved and handicapped accessible.

Two challenging hikes are on either side of Mendenhall Glacier. The **East Glacier Trail** is the easier of the two and takes you to a Nugget Falls overlook and is a loop trail. The **West Glacier Trail** gains 1,400 feet in elevation and leads to the edge of the glacier with its ice pinnacles, caves, and gorges. Do not venture onto the glacier unless you are with an experienced trekker.

HAINES AND SKAGWAY

Haines has mountain and shoreline trails. The 7-mile **Seduction Point Trail** follows the western shore of Chilkat Peninsula, offering spectacular views over the inlet, Rainbow and Davidson glaciers, as well as pretty coves and the rainforest. No need to travel the entire length to be rewarded with glacier views and wildlife. Much of the trail is through the dense rainforest where the trail is discernible only with a change of texture on the loamy, needle-covered soil. Boardwalks traverse boggy places.

For eagle's-eye views, pick the 7-mile **Mount Riley Trail** on the Chilkat Peninsula or the challenging climb to 3,650-foot **Mount Ripinsky** where you'll encounter snow until midsummer.

Skagway gives access to world-famous, world-class **Chilkoot Trail**, the 33-mile path blazed by Klondike miners. It also happens to be international. Backpackers cross into Canada at Chilkoot Pass and need passports or certified proof of birth and photo ID. It takes four to five days one way, depending on your fitness level.

Almost anyone will recognize the famed photo with gold seekers struggling in the snow over the almost vertical pass, or Golden Stairs, as it's sometimes known. A map, "A Hiker's Guide to the Chilkoot Trail," is available from the **Alaska Natural History Association** (907-274-8440). It's also a good idea to view the video at the Klondike Gold Rush National Historical Park Visitors Center, at Second and Broadway in Skagway. Permits are required June 1 through September 5, and cost $50 for the U.S. and Canadian segments, $15.70 for the U.S. portion only. Reservations may be made in advance for an additional fee. You may hike the trail before or after those days without paying the fee, but you must still register for a permit at the park visitor center.

Other Skagway hikes: **Dewey Lakes Trail**, either a short jaunt to Lower Dewey Lake 500 feet above Skagway, or a 3,097-foot climb to Upper Dewey Lake; 5-mile **Laughten Glacier**

Trail up the Skagway River to the jagged glacier; 7-mile **Sturgill's Landing Trail** to a woodcutter's camp on Taiya Inlet.

CENTRAL PANHANDLE

PETERSBURG

You're almost sure to spot whales walking out North Nordic Drive to **Hungry Point**, where Wrangell Narrows meets Frederick Sound. About ½ mile farther is the whale observatory. A shipwright in town built the shelter and patterned it after Norwegian stave churches. Continue on to **Sandy Beach**. If the tide is low, walk across the mudflats to the point at the left of the beach. Petroglyphs that seem to outline the human face are etched on the rock. Sometimes rangers on the beach will point out pegs from prehistoric fish traps, visible at very low tides.

For a fine muskeg hike, take Mitkof Highway about 14 miles south of town to **Blind River Rapids**. A boardwalk leads over the muskeg from a parking area and runs along the river with its gentle rapids for a short distance. It's a popular fishing spot.

SITKA

Mountains surround Sitka and provide excellent hiking with vantage points over the town, harbors, and surrounding islands. These are easily accessible from the center of town.

Take Baranof Street to its end for the **Gavin Hill Trail**, which climbs to 2,650 feet. Steps are built into the trail to ease the climb, and the view at the end is magnificent. **Indian River Trail**, off Indian River Road, traces a stream through old-growth and 100-year-old, second-growth forest and leads to a waterfall.

WRANGELL

Mount Dewey is the hill to climb to get a good view of Wrangell. The steep but short climb is accessed from Third Street. John Muir built an enormous fire on Mount Dewey during a rainstorm. Reflections from its flames danced on the clouds, and terrified some town residents. **Petroglyph Beach State Historic Site** is just a short walk from downtown. South of Wrangell, 4½ miles on Zimovia Highway, **Rainbow Falls** overlook and trail south of town is an easy trail popular with hikers.

SOUTHERN PANHANDLE

KETCHIKAN

The **Deer Mountain Trail** climbs 3,000 feet just behind Ketchikan for an awesome view over the town and Tongass Narrows. Plan a whole day for the strenuous climb, and you may have to wait until the snow melts to do it. Even in July you may encounter snow patches near the summit. Access the trail from Deer Mountain and Fair streets.

Don't Touch or Brush

Learn to recognize the plant called devil's club. Its leaves and stems bear barbed stickers that will adhere to your skin and cause a sting as nasty as a bee's. It has large, maple-like leaves and, in late summer, red berries. It grows everywhere.

Ward Lake near Ketchikan makes a good hiking destination.

Ward Lake Nature Trail, 8 miles from downtown, is a pleasant walk around the lake with interpretive signs along the way.

HUNTING

Hunting, though not attracting quite as many people as fishing, has its seasons and followers. Bears, wolves, mountain goats, Dall sheep, deer, elk, and moose are all hunted on the Alaska Panhandle. Bears are generally hunted in the spring or fall, mountain goats in the late summer and fall. Nonresidents must hunt with a licensed guide, who will generally manage licensing, permits, and tags. Guided hunts, which run from about three days to a week or more, range about $3,000–$10,000.

NORTHERN PANHANDLE

JUNEAU
Southeast Alaska Guiding: (907-586-1168; seaguiding.com.) A 50-foot yacht is home base for hunting brown bears on Admiralty Island and the Coastal Range for brown bears, black bears, and mountain goats.

HAINES AND SKAGWAY
The Chilkat and Chilkoot rivers and surrounding mountain ranges provide prime territory for prized brown and black bears, and mountain goats. Black bears in the Chilkat Valley sometimes have reddish coats, similar to brown bears, and are called "cinnamon bears."

Mountain goat terrain may be some of the most challenging in the world. These white, woolly creatures cling to tiny shelves and outcroppings hundreds of feet above the valleys and above the timberline. Hunters must be in good condition to stalk this prey.

Alaska Fair Chase Guiding: (907-767-5775; geocities.com/alaskafairchase.) Owner-guide Larry Benda makes it a policy to take out only experienced hunters for brown and black bears, and mountain goats.

John Katzeek Guiding Service: (907-766-2168; johnguiding.com.) This native Tlingit guides hunters in the Chilkat Valley and uplands for black and brown bears, wolves, and mountain goats.

YAKUTAT

John and Fran Latham: (907-784-3287; johnlatham.com.) One of Alaska's most well-known hunting and fishing guides, John Latham runs big game hunts in Alaska's interior at permanent camps. The spring bear hunts originate in Yakutat. Latham is a fishing guide during the summer.

CENTRAL PANHANDLE

SITKA

Annahootz Alaskan Adventure: (907-747-2608; annahootz.com.) Longtime guide Jim Phillips leads boat-based hunts on Baranof and Prince of Wales islands for black bears, brown bears, and mountain goats.

SOUTHERN PANHANDLE

KETCHIKAN AND PRINCE OF WALES ISLAND

Alaska Glacier Adventures: (907-738-5000; alaskaglacieradventures.com.) The service arranges hunting out of a boat to remote parts of POW. Seasons determine the hunt: spring for wolves and black bears; fall for mountain goats; winter for ducks and Sitka black-tailed deer.

Muskeg Excursions: (907-225-9513; muskegexcursions.com.) Prince of Wales Island and the Misty Fjords area are the two main hunting regions. Some camps are cabins, others in more remote locations with tents or backpacking.

Hunting Rules

Alaska Department of Fish and Game has many regulations for hunting and trapping large and small game. So baroque are the rules that they fill a 23-page booklet. The state is divided into hunting units, which may have different regulations. Units 1–5 cover the Alaska Panhandle.

Nonresident hunters for brown or black bears must be accompanied in the field by a guide/outfitter or a relative who is an Alaska resident. A list of licensed guides and transporters, and other guiding information is at commerce.state.ak.us/occ/apps/ODQuery/cfm.

You will need a license, appropriate locking tag, and a harvest ticket for all large game. If hunting demand exceeds the sustainable game population, a limited number of permits are issued.

Hunting regulations change frequently, especially as demand has increased against harvestable surplus, so check **Alaska Department of Fish and Game** hunting regulations (wildlifealaska.gov).

KAYAKING

One memorable Alaska adventure is to be taken out to a remote bay, perhaps along Glacier Bay, and be dropped off with kayaks and camping gear in waterproof canisters. People usually stay out five days to a week, and then get picked up. Glacier Bay tour boats routinely check pickup points.

More than any other activity, kayaking places you within the awesome scale of Alaska. There you are, in a little polyethylene shell, sitting at water level. The water is often clear enough to see the glint of a salmon or a pink sea anemone. Sometimes it reflects the sky, as if you're floating on cloud-studded blue. Porpoises might skim over the bow; an iceberg, reaching stories above you, might sit massively in the water; and, suddenly, a humpback whale might breach. You'll look up at its flukes.

Costs for a day trip usually range $85–$200, and for multiday trips $650–$2,000 or more, depending on length and level of support.

In addition to challenging sea kayaking wilderness trips, every Panhandle town has some opportunity for renting kayaks. Paddle at the edge of a boat harbor in Petersburg, or on Ward Lake at Ketchikan. (Even five-year-olds can manage the latter.)

Most people who rent a U.S. Forest Service cabin will want to take a kayak for small trips once they get to the cabin.

NORTHERN PANHANDLE

JUNEAU

Kayak activity in Juneau is out of Auke Bay. Longer trips often explore the glaciers south of Juneau off Tracy or Endicott arms. You'll be transported on either a large boat or float plane.

Alaska Boat and Kayak Center: (907-789-6886; juneaukayak.com.) Rental kayak and canoes are available, as well as classes to hone your skills. A half-day trip near Juneau takes paddlers to a quiet cove where you may see a humpback whale, sea lions, porpoises, and seabirds. Longer trips may take in Taku Glacier or Admiralty Island.

GLACIER BAY

In Glacier Bay, kayakers not only see and hear the glaciers calving, they ride the waves generated in the water, and may be sprayed. It's possible to rent a sea kayak from an outfitter to explore on your own, or join a guided trip. If you aren't sure of your skills, it's better to join a guided trip. No one who has never paddled before should attempt sea kayaking in Glacier Bay. Day kayak trips run about $100–$150. Multiday trips may be proportionately more expensive since meals and overnight arrangements are included.

Alaska Discovery: (1-888-687-6235; mtsobek.com/alaska_Discovery/.) Paddlers explore the west arm of Glacier Bay, with a chance to see wildlife as well as the glaciers. There's hiking as well as kayaking, and three nights camping.

Alaska Mountain Guides and Climbing School: (See *Mountaineering* section below.) Multiday trips on Glacier Bay, as well as trips at Haines and to Pack Creek Bear Station on Admiralty Island.

Glacier Bay Sea Kayaks: (907-697-2257; glacierbayseakayaks.com.) Guided half- and full-day kayak tours out of Bartlett Cove park headquarters. The company also has rental kayaks and outfitting for multiday independent excursions, along with instruction.

GUSTAVUS

Spirit Walker Expeditions: (907-697-2266 or 1-800-529-2537; seakayakalaska.com.) This large company has numerous trips designed for novices to experienced paddlers. It takes small groups to seldom-visited Fords Terror Wilderness to experience the turbulent fjord, and up Endicott Arm to explore the waters near Dawes Glacier.

CENTRAL PANHANDLE

PETERSBURG

The glacier-fed bays and inlets near Petersburg provide more kayak opportunities.

Tongass Kayak Adventures: (907-772-4600; tongasskayak.com.) Day trips are in Petersburg Creek, or teamed with a powerboat to LeConte Glacier. Multiday trips are in LeConte Glacier Bay or along Frederick Sound.

WRANGELL

Rainwalker Expeditions: (907-874-2549; rainwalkerexpeditions.com.) Rental tandem and single kayaks available.

SOUTHERN PANHANDLE

KETCHIKAN

Misty Fjords National Monument is the long-distance paddle trip of choice out of Ketchikan. Near town, Revillagigedo and Gravina islands provide lots of nooks and crannies.

Southeast Exposure: (907-225-8829; southeastexposure.com.) Day trips take in the Tatoosh or Eagle islands in Clover Pass. Misty Fjords is the destination for six-day camping-and-kayaking trips. Single or tandem kayaks available; some trips only for experienced paddlers.

Southeast Sea Kayaks: (907-225-1258 or 1-800-287-1607; kayakketchikan.com.) Paddlers are transported by launch to remote Orcas or Pennock coves for a half- or full-day paddling with naturalist-guides and see humpback whales, orcas, bald eagle nests, Sitka black-tailed deer, and other wildlife. Misty Fjords trips range from a single-day to five-day trips.

MOUNTAINEERING

Alaska Mountain Guides & Climbing School: (907-766-3366 or 1-800-766-3396; alaskamountainguides.com.) Almost everything with a vertical component—rock and ice climbing, mountaineering courses, backcountry skiing and glacier hiking—are the company's specialties. Departures are April through September and vary with the activity. The company also has sea-kayaking programs in Glacier Bay and hiking the Chilkoot Trail. Costs vary with activity.

NATURE AND WILDLIFE CENTERS AND GARDENS

An interpretive center might well be your first stop in Alaska. It will introduce you to the wonders you'll meet outdoors.

NORTHERN PANHANDLE

JUNEAU

Mount Roberts Tramway Nature Center

907-463-3412
goldbelttours.com
490 South Franklin St., Juneau, AK 99801
Open: Daily, May–Sept.
Admission: $24.95 (for tram ride)
Gift Shop: Nature-themed books

The Mountain House atop the Mount Roberts Tramway houses the Juneau Raptor Center with a live bald eagle exhibit and interpreters on hand to explain the bird rehabilitation program. The nature center has both exhibits and sale items. Touch and feel displays, animal information, minerals, and books focusing on wildlife, plants, trails, and geology are available. Occasionally a Gastineau Guiding naturalist gives talks on the deck. Access to the Mount Roberts Trail is from the center.

Glacier Gardens Rainforest Adventure

907-790-3377
glaciergardens.com
7600 Glacier Hwy., Juneau, AK 99801
Open: Daily, May–Sept.
Admission: $21.95
Gift Shop: Garden gifts and Wild Berry Café

Petunias spill over the sides of hanging pots at Glacier Gardens visitor center .

This is an extreme example of making lemonade when handed lemons. Steve and Cindy Bowhay purchased the property that became Glacier Gardens after a devastating landslide wiped out a stream and a slice of forest on Thunder Mountain. They decided to reclaim the stream. Steve worked with a bulldozer to move rocks and trees. One tree trunk seemed particularly stubborn, so he slammed it into the earth upside down. It stuck. Bowhay, who ran a nursery, decided to plant some flowers in the dirt-encrusted roots. The plants thrived, so Bowhay "planted" another and another upside-down tree, giving the entrance to the facility a fanciful look, like a child's storybook illustration.

Inside the tented visitors center, which houses a garden shop and a café, brilliant begonias and petunias spill over hanging pots. It's like walking through a forest of flowers.

But this is only the beginning. You'll ride up a rainforest trail on Thunder Mountain in golf carts with guides who point out the false azalea and devil's club, and take a boardwalk to a deck overlooking Gastineau Channel and the airport below. The stream tumbles down once again; the rainforest is recovering.

HAINES
American Bald Eagle Foundation
907-766-3094
baldeagles.org
113 Haines Hwy., P.O. Box 49, Haines, AK 99827
Open: Daily during summer, by appointment during the winter
Admission: $3
Gift shop: Eagle-themed gifts

An enormous diorama filling an auditorium-size room represents the entire 48,000 acres of the Chilkat Bald Eagle Preserve. Almost 200 animals, including mountain goats, black bears, moose, lynx, and wolves are presented in natural settings, along, of course, with American bald eagles.

In another room, a mural high on the wall depicts Tlingit life from prehistory through the Yukon Gold Rush with a backdrop of nearby Klukwan.

The gift shop has books, eagle-themed jewelry and gifts, and photographs and posters with artworks by American Bald Eagle Festival artists. The foundation sponsors the Bald Eagle Festival in November.

The center results from the inspiration and dedication of founder David Olerud, who quite literally built its headquarters and museum, and who paid the price with a devastating injury that keeps him in a wheelchair. It hasn't killed his spirit. Hope he is there to tell you about the eagles and how they fit into the area's ecology and Tlingit myth.

Kroschel Films Wildlife Center
907-767-5464
kroschelfilms.com
kroschelfilms@aptalaska.net
Haines
Open: By appointment
Admission: $20

You may have never heard of Steve Kroschel, but you've probably seen his work. The animals that he has nurtured in wild conditions appear in wildlife films for National Geographic, the Discovery Channel, Walt Disney, and many more. Since childhood he has had a gift for interacting with wild animals. He now has Alaska wildlife, including wolves, wolverines, foxes, lynx, deer, and others, which are used in the films. Visitors get to see interaction with the animals and learn about his non-zoo techniques. Cruise ship shore excursions take in visits here, and the center is open on certain weekdays.

SKAGWAY
Jewell Gardens
907-983-2111
jewellgardens.com
P.O. Box 536, Skagway, AK 99840
South Klondike Hwy. at Skagway River Bridge
Open: Daily, early May–late Sept.
Admission: $12, or $18 with transportation from downtown

This hybrid attraction is a garden, glass-blowing studio, café, and G-scale model railroad at the edge of Skagway. It's located on the former Clark farm, where vegetables thrived. It's now an organic garden of both flowers and vegetables, and continues to raise the monster rhubarb that made the farm famous.

The glass studio offers a hands-on option of allowing visitors to blow their own glass ornaments. Garden tours are offered, and the café offers a fixed menu with items from the garden. On Thursday through Sunday evenings, it becomes Poppies and serves a full dinner menu.

YUKON
Yukon Beringia Interpretive Centre
867-667-8855
beringia.com
Mile 914 Alaska Hwy., Whitehorse, Yukon, Canada Y1A 2C6
Open: Daily, mid-May–late Sept.; Sun. afternoons rest of year
Admission: $6 Canadian
Gift Shop: Books

We all learned as children that Asian people migrated over a land bridge into what is now North America, 10,000 years ago or more. The Beringia Interpretive Centre gives real substance to the notion, with films, exhibits, signage, and artworks. Maps show the land bridge, perhaps 1,000 miles wide, that formed when the sea level dropped during the Ice Ages. Glaciers never formed here because the area was too dry. Instead, vast grassland supported woolly mammoths, Jefferson ground sloths, scimitar cats, and people, who became Alaska Natives and First Nation people in Canada. Examples of all of these animals are here. A diorama shows a winter camp with a skin tent amidst the snow and wolves.

Fossils offer evidence of Beringia in the Yukon and on some of the Bering Sea Islands. Docents at the center are eager to help interpret the exhibits.

CENTRAL PANHANDLE
SITKA
Alaska Raptor Center
907-747-8662 or 1-800-643-9425
alaskaraptor.org

100 Raptor Way, Sitka, AK 99835
Open: Sun.–Fri., May–Sept.
Admission: $12 adults, $6 children 12 and under
Gift Shop: Native Alaska gifts and eagle-themed notecards, posters

This may be the closest you will be to a bald eagle. Although the goal of the Raptor Center is to release birds into the wild, some are too badly injured to survive, and so they are kept at the center in expansive outdoor aviaries. Visitors can see their fierce eyes, yellow bills, and beautiful feather patterns.

The Alaska Raptor Center treats 100–200 injured birds annually, including golden and bald eagles, hawks, falcons, and owls. It's located on 17 acres that have numerous outdoor display areas. It's beside the Indian River and near the Sitka National Historical Park.

Fortress of the Bear

907-747-3032
fortressofthebear.org
4639 Sawmill Creek Road, about 5½ miles from downtown, Sitka, AK 99835
Open: Daily, May–Sept.; Wed.–Sun., Oct.–Apr.
Admission: $11

This facility provides a shelter for orphaned brown bears unable to survive in the wilderness. A covered shelter provides viewing of the bears in the ¾-acre site. There were two young bears in 2008, and the facility has room for more. **Sitka Wildlife Tours** (907-747-8443) takes in the site on two-hour tours of the area.

SOUTHERN PANHANDLE

KETCHIKAN

Southeast Alaska Discovery Center

907-228-6220
fs.fed.us/r10/tongass
50 Main St., Ketchikan, AK 99901
Near the cruise ship docks
Open: Daily, May–Sept.; Tues.–Sat., Oct.–Apr.
Admission: $5 May–Sept.; free, Oct.–Apr.
Bookstore: Gorgeous books focusing on Alaska's natural history

This excellent Forest Service center will introduce Alaska's natural areas and people with appealing exhibits. The lobby has three totem poles, carved by contemporary master carvers and representing the three native groups: A flamboyant house-post style Tlingit pole; a massive Haida pole with eagle, bear, and killer whale; a Tsimshian pole with the four clan crests.

Visitors follow curved paths to exhibits, with something new around each turn. Motion activated narrations start as soon as you walk into an area. Themes are Alaska Native people, represented with a fish camp; the rainforest; fishing, mining, and timber industries, and eco-systems. A film *Mystical Southeast Alaska* is screened periodically.

The bookstore, run by the Alaska Natural History Association, has comfortable seating areas, and, cleverly, has a DVD running on a monitor within a fireplace.

At Ketchikan's Southeast Alaska Discovery Center evocative displays such as this one with a salmon-smoking rack and canoe, bring to life Alaska Native life and the state's natural gifts.

PARKS AND PRESERVES

National Parks

NORTHERN PANHANDLE
Glacier Bay National Park and Preserve
See Glacier section.

Klondike Gold Rush National Historical Park
See Chapter 4, Culture.

HAINES JUNCTION, YUKON
Kluane National Park
867-634-7250
pc.gc.ca/kluane
Visitor Center: Haines Junction
Open: Daily, mid-May–late Sept.

This Canadian national park shares borders with Wrangell-St. Elias and Glacier National parks in the U.S., and British Columbia's Tatshenshini-Alsek Park. The combination of parks makes up a World Heritage Site. Its terrain covers glaciers, mountains, foothills, valleys, rivers, lakes, and First Nation villages. Most of it is inaccessible except by float plane or backpacking.

The visitors center has excellent interpretive exhibits about this diverse terrain, and a spectacular view through soaring windows.

The visitor center at Kluane National Park in Haines Junction, Yukon, looks out to a sweeping view of the St. Elias Mountains.

CENTRAL PANHANDLE
Sitka National Historical Park and Southeast Alaska Indian Cultural Center
See Chapter 4, Culture.

KETCHIKAN

SOUTHERN PANHANDLE
Misty Fjords National Monument
fs.fed.us/r10/tongass/forest_facts/resources/wilderness/kawld.html
Misty Fjords is as far south in Alaska as you can go and still be in the United States. It hugs the British Columbia border about 22 miles south of Ketchikan. It's accessible only by float plane or boat, most often as a day trip out of Ketchikan (see *Flightseeing* section).

Granite cliffs soar 2,000–3,000 straight up from the water. Their bases may be forested, but the tops are bare rock and often swathed in mist. Waterfalls cascade off the sides. It's a wild place of deep mystery. Some petroglyphs exist in places that seem impossible to reach. Kayakers love it. A good way to see it is with a trip that combines flightseeing in one direction, with a boat trip in the other.

Tongass National Forest
907-225-3101
fs.fed.us/r10/tongass/
649 Mission St., Ketchikan, AK 99901

Tongass National Forest encompasses the entire Alaska Panhandle. The only regions not included in it are Glacier Bay National Park and Preserve, and Admiralty and Misty Fjords National monuments. It stretches over nearly 17 million acres, making it the largest U.S. National Forest.

Much of the forest is wilderness, but opportunities for boating, fishing, hiking, and picnicking exist in many places.

The Forest Service has about 150 rustic cabins (see Chapter 3, *Lodging*) as well as hundreds of shelters along hiking trails.

CAMPGROUNDS AND RECREATION AREAS

Forest Service campgrounds have a 14-day limit and are open from May 1 to Sept. 30. Fees vary, from free to $30. Reservations: 1-877-444-6777 or visit recreation.gov. These areas are also open to day visitors for hiking, birding, fishing, and boating. Most of them have covered picnic shelters or grills.

Juneau: Mendenhall Lake, 69 sites and Auke Village, 12 sites.

Sitka: Starrigavan, 35 sites and Sawmill Creek, 11 sites. The Old Sitka State Historic Site, with interpretive panels, boat launch, and barrier-free muskeg trail is near the campground.

Petersburg: Ohmer Creek, 10 sites.

Wrangell: Nemo Campsite, eight sites, and Lower Salamander Recreation Site, three sites.

Ketchikan: Ward Lake Recreation Area, 44 sites.

Prince of Wales Island: Eagles Nest, 11 sites, and Harris River, 14 sites.

State Parks, Preserves, and Recreation Sites

The state park system has recreation sites, sometimes near the Forest Service campgrounds. Some state parks have cabins. These are good places for day hikes or for camping or RV sites for those staying longer. **Alaska State Parks,** 907-465-4563 or dnr.state.ak.us.

NORTHERN PANHANDLE

JUNEAU

Point Bridget: Located 38 miles north of Juneau on Glacier Highway. The park is known for its meadows, Cowee Creek, hiking trails, Chilkat Range views, and beach along Lynn Canal. Cross-country skiing in winter.

HAINES

Alaska Chilkat Bald Eagle Preserve
907-766-2292
dnr.state.ak.us/parks/units/eagleprv.htm
Haines Highway MM18–24
Open: Year-round
Admission: Free

The Bald Eagle Preserve is one of the reasons people visit Haines, and this stretch north of town is known as Valley of the Eagles. About 2,500–3,000 bald eagles make their home on this 6-mile stretch along the Chilkat River from about October to February, one of the largest gatherings of eagles in the world. About 200–400 make this their home year-round. They come because of a late salmon spawn, and because warmer water from an underground source keeps the Chilkat running longer than other rivers in Southeast Alaska. About 48,000 acres has been set aside in the preserve for the protection of the eagles.

At any given time during the peak season, a dozen or more may be seen perching on the limbs, occasionally tearing at some salmon held down with their claws. They also hover on the sandbars of the braided river. Black and brown bears are often spotted along the river when salmon are present. Mountain goats appear like white specks on the mountain on the opposite side of the road. Be sure to bring binoculars. The park has no facilities, except for restrooms, but there are frequent turnouts along the river for eagle and other wildlife viewing. Good signage appears at around MM 21. The road is narrow and rarely has a shoulder, so park only in the designated turnouts. A developed path along the river connects the pullouts in the area of highest eagle concentrations.

Chilkat State Park

dnr.state.ak.us/parks/units/haines.htm
Mud Bay Road, 7 miles south of Haines
Open: May–mid-Sept.
Admission: Free
Camping: 15 sites; 32 RV pull-through sites

The park is beautifully situated on a narrow strip of land in Lynn Canal, with spectacular views of Rainbow and Davidson glaciers. Spotting scopes at the visitors center enable visitors to see seals, porpoises, and whales in the inlet, and even mountain goats and bears across the way.

The park has three hiking trails: Seduction Point and Battery Point trails run along the beach and alternate between woods and beach; the Mount Riley Trail (see hiking section) is more challenging, and rewards hikers with spectacular views of the area. A boardwalk on Battery Point helps hikers get over the boggy sections of the forest, which is part conifer and part deciduous.

A boat launch ramp gives access to the inlet, which has excellent fishing, especially during the king salmon run in June.

Chilkoot Lake State Recreation Site

dnr.state.ak.us/parks/units/haines.htm
10 miles northeast of Haines by Lutak and Chilkoot River roads
Open: May–Sept.
Admission: Free
Camping: 80 sites, $10 per site per night. 32 RV spaces

Located at the south end of Chilkoot Lake, the site is heavily wooded with Sitka spruce and hemlock. Hiking trails spread out from the parking area at the park. Thick moss encrusts many of the trees and logs in this temperate rainforest. At certain times of the year carnivorous plants and slime mold—called "the blob" by locals—are present in the forest.

The lake has fine salmon fishing, with four runs between mid-May and mid-October. Because of the plentiful salmon, this is also a favored bear haunt. It's essential to be familiar with bear safety precautions for campers and hikers. A boat launching ramp provides access for boating, which is popular on the lake. Look for rafts of surf scoters, mergansers, and, near the park, harlequin ducks.

Sitka spruce trees shelter the 80-site campground, which has a seven-night limit. There is also a picnic shelter.

CENTRAL PANHANDLE

SITKA

Halibut Point State Recreation Site: About 4 miles north of town on Halibut Point Road, the waterfront site has covered picnic areas and a ½-mile trail through the spruce-hemlock forest. It's a good bird-watching area.

WRANGELL

Petroglyph Beach State Historic Park (See Chapter 4, *Culture*.)

SOUTHERN PANHANDLE

KETCHIKAN

Totem Bight State Historical Park: (See Chapter 5, *Alaska Native People*.)

SKIING

Cross-country skiing is as accessible as anyone's backyard and, along with snowshoeing, is a popular winter activity. In spite of the mountain terrain, downhill skiing is more rare. The City of Juneau runs **Eaglecrest** (907-586-5284; juneau.org/ecrestftp/index.php) the Panhandle's only downhill ski area. It has 31 Alpine runs and three Nordic trail loops. Heli-skiing is popular at Haines, and of course, lots of people improvise by schussing down slopes without a lift.

SNORKELING AND SCUBA DIVING

Brrrrr! The idea of snorkeling in Alaska's chilly waters makes most people shiver. But enthusiasts insist you're never chilly more than a few seconds. Those who wear a dry-suit claim they're warm before they hit the water.

Panhandle waters shelter beautiful creatures. Sea anemones grow as large as dinner plates and come in a spectrum of pinks, greens, and mauves. Sea urchins look like extravagant pincushions. Starfish seem larger and brighter than their tropical cousins. A wide variety of fish live in the kelp beds and other exotic creatures on the floor.

Cold water is clearer than warm, so you can see farther. Michelle Gundaker of Island Fever in Sitka prefers winter to summer for scuba diving because of increased clarity.

Although you could snorkel and scuba dive on your own, strong currents and large tidal surges exist on the Inside Passage, so guided trips are safer.

Snorkeling cost starts at about $90 and scuba diving, $160.

CENTRAL PANHANDLE

SITKA

Island Fever: (907-747-7871; islandfeverdiving.com.) The company offers dry-suit snorkeling from a boat. The suit is worn over regular clothing, keeping the swimmer more buoyant, which benefits those new to the sport. Snorkelers swim over kelp and eel grass beds, and the rocky bottom of Magic Island at Halibut Point Recreation Site. The company also offers diving to several sites. For four-hour charters, divers must be cold-water certified. Deep water is 38 degrees winter and summer. For longer trips, divers can become certified.

SOUTHERN PANHANDLE

KETCHIKAN

Snorkel Alaska: (907-247-7783; snorkelalaska.com.) Snorkeling is off Mountain Point south of Ketchikan in calm, clear water. Shallow tide pools make snorkeling comfortable even for beginners. Bring a swimming suit or shorts to wear under the wet suit, which is ¼-inch thick and has a hood. Surface water temperature averages 55 degrees in summer. Clothing is changed in heated quarters and prescription masks are available. The company offers scuba dives along a wall at Mountain Point that starts at the surface and drops to 100 feet. Cold-water diving is strenuous because of the heavier wet suit and currents. The dive is open only to those with advanced certification and cold-water experience.

SUBMERSIBLE BOAT TRIPS

Two Panhandle companies offer a chance to be eyeball-to-tentacle with the undersea life without getting your face wet or donning a wet suit. Cost starts at $49.

SITKA

Sea Life Discovery Tours: (907-966-2301 or 877-966-2301; sealifediscoverytours.com.) The 49-passenger semi-submersible vessel has an underwater viewing chamber 3 feet below the surface. A live video feed also provides images on flat-screen monitors. A diver appears during the excursion to help passengers identify creatures.

KETCHIKAN

Alaska Undersea Tours: (907-247-8889 or 1-877-461-8687; alaskaunderseatours.com.) The 60-foot *Nautilus V* semi-submersible prowls the Tongass Narrows with the chance to see moon jellyfish, sea urchins, sunflower starfish, sea cucumbers, pile perch, and perhaps a wolf eel. Viewing is through windows and on flat-screen monitors. An enclosed deck allows above-water viewing.

SURFING

Alaska even has a surfing beach at Yakutat. The long rollers steam in across the Pacific to the flat beach. They're long, glassy, and attract surfers from around the world, who brave the 55-degree water in thick wet suits. **Icy Waves Surf Shop** (907-784-3226; icywaves.com) in town tells you where to find the waves and what to wear in the water. Other surfers look for action on Lynn Canal in Haines. **Lost Coast Surf Shop** (907-314-0335; lostcoastsurf.com) at the corner of Main and Second has information and all the gear you'll need.

WHALE WATCHING

Alaska waters, especially during summer, are happy hunting grounds for whales. Ten whale species make their home in Alaska; three varieties—humpbacks, orcas, and minkes—live in Panhandle waters. You'll most likely see humpback whales May through September—they're summer visitors, like the tourists. They gorge in nutrient-rich cold water and build up blubber for their long trip back to Hawaiian waters, where they winter off Maui and don't feed at all.

Boat charters offer whale-watching trips out of Juneau, Hoonah, Gustavus, Petersburg, and Sitka. Whale watching is often part of fishing or glacier-viewing trips. Porpoises, Steller sea lions, sea otters, and harbor seals may also be spotted. You may see whales in Southern Panhandle waters, but they don't congregate here as they do in Frederick Sound, Icy Strait, or Glacier Bay.

Humpback whales, named for their prominent dorsal fins and arched backs, are aquatic acrobats. They break the surface and slap their tail flukes hard when they dive. Sometimes they leap far out of the water, almost dancing on its surface.

Hope that you might see bubble feeding. You'll first notice that large bubbles break the surface, spaced in a rough circle. This may go on for awhile; you may see the silvery glints of small fish within the bubble. Suddenly the surface explodes with several humpbacks thrusting their mouths out of the water and taking in great gulps of seawater filled with the fish. The water spurts out of their mouths through the fringed baleen, which catches the small fish and krill like a sieve.

Whale-watching trips range from $100 to $400 for a day trip. Additional companies are listed in the Wildlife Viewing section below.

NORTHERN PANHANDLE

JUNEAU

Juneau whale-watching boats depart from Auke Bay, about a 20-minute drive from downtown. Most companies will pick you up and return you to the cruise ship docks or hotel.

Alaska Whale Watching: (1-888-432-6722; akwhalewatching.) Six people or fewer are taken out in 30-foot Ciera Command bridge cabin cruisers for customized whale watching.

Dolphin Jet Boat Tours: (907-463-3422 or 1-800-719-3422; dolphintours.com.) The operator guarantees $100 back if you don't see whales. Pickup is downtown for the three-hour tour in the bright red boats. Binoculars provided.

Harv and Marv's: (907-209-7288; harvandmarvs.com.) Never more than six passengers are taken out in the boats on customized trips on three- or four-hour tours.

Orca Enterprises: (907-789-6801; orcaenterprises.com.) The company's fast jet boats designed for whale watching whisk passengers from Auke Bay to the feeding grounds.

GUSTAVUS

Gustavus sits at the edge of Icy Strait and near the entrance to Glacier Bay, prime whale habitat during the summer. One of the highest concentrations is at Point Adolphus across the strait.

Spirit Walker Expeditions: (1-800-529-2537; seakayakalaska.com.) The kayaking trips are offered to two locations, Point Adolphus or Pleasant Island Wilderness Area, and aim for novice or advanced paddlers. Gear and boots provided.

Woodwind Adventures: (907-697-2282; sailglacierbay.homestead.com.) The 40-foot sailing catamaran, the *Great Sea*, was built in Gustavus. The company offers whale watching in Icy Strait and Glacier Bay, combined with kayaking at Point Adolphus. A national park concessionaire, Woodwind Adventures also has Glacier Bay trips.

Kayaking Glacier Bay offers a transcendent experience for Alaska travelers. Robin Hood/Alaska Tourism Marketing Council

HOONAH

Humpback whales congregate in great numbers at Point Adolphus on Chichagof Island near Hoonah. The mist from a whale blowhole is almost never out of sight. Sometimes the huge creatures are close enough to hear them and sniff the rank sea smell of their exhaled breath.

Occasionally a humpback whale bursts out of the water so you will see the barnacles on its cheeks, and water cascading off the flukes before it dives.

Icy Strait Point: (icystraitpoint.com.) Naturalists on board explain the behavior of whales and help spot other wildlife on the cruise to Point Adolphus aboard the catamaran *Baranov Wind*. A large open upper deck allows maximum viewing.

CENTRAL PANHANDLE

PETERSBURG

Petersburg is near the junction of Stephens Passage and Frederick Sound. Where the currents meet, the water teems with krill, fish, and other nutrients, and whales come to feed. **Admiralty Bear Guide, Kaleidoscope Cruises,** and **Summer King Adventures** (see *Excursions on Water* section) offer whale watching. Additionally, **Whale Song Cruises** (907-772-9393; whalesongcruises.com.) tours Frederick Sound aboard the 28-foot *Glacier Titan*.

SITKA

Whale watchers in Sitka usually spot sea otters as well. The reason the Russians settled here was because of the abundance of sea otters, which they hunted to near extinction.

Sitka Wildlife Quest: (907-747-8100; allenmarinetours.com) Morning and evening whale-watching trips are aboard comfortable catamarans with open upper-deck viewing and a marine naturalist on board. Departure is from Crescent Harbor Dock, and reservations are not necessary. The company also offers whale watching in Juneau on wheelchair-accessible boats, and wildlife trips out of Ketchikan.

ONE-STOP BOOKING

A few tour services can arrange your fishing, wildlife viewing, and town itineraries for a day or a trip of several days.

Juneau Alaska Adventures and Tours: (juneau-guide.com.) This online site, run by Pearson's Pond Luxury Inn, offers a wide spectrum of packages and activities.

Viking Travel: (907-772-3818 or 800-327-2571; AlaskaFerry.com; 101 North Nordic Drive, Petersburg, AK 99833.) The company can make reservations for any activity or plan the trip.

WILDLIFE VIEWING

Most Alaska visitors hope to see two "trophy" animals—bears and whales. Many companies offer wildlife-viewing tours, though you may see wild creatures anywhere, anytime. Misty whale spouts appear in open bays or channels, and black bears have been known to meander down to the cruise ship docks in Juneau.

Water drips form a humpback whale's flukes while another swims nearby at Point Adolphus near Hoonah.

Grizzly bears are more people wary, but you may well see them on the beach from a cruise ship or the Alaska ferry, especially where the vessels travel narrow channels.

These companies offer excursions aimed specifically for bears, though whales and other wildlife will be seen. They frequently also run fishing charters and glacier viewing.

Bears

Brown and black bears congregate along streams or falls when salmon spawn in mid- to late summer. This is the best time to see them at Anan Wildlife Observatory near Wrangell, or at Admiralty Island near Juneau. These areas area accessible only by boat or float plane.

NORTHERN PANHANDLE

PACK CREEK

The Tlingit people call Admiralty Island "Kootznoowoo," which means "Fortress of the Bear, " and indeed, the island has the largest concentration of brown bears—about 1,500—in the world. Visitors see them at Pack Creek Bear Viewing Area, where a permit is required.

Researchers believe that about 25 bears inhabit the area around the creek. The brown bears come to the estuary and tidal flats when the salmon spawn, mid-July through late August, and wander about the beach and through sedge grasses.

Reached by a 1-mile trail, a viewing platform has been set up on Upper Pack Creek. The viewing platform is about 60 yards from the creek, so binoculars and a telescopic camera lenses are recommended.

Access is by boat or float plane. If you go on your own, you will need to get your own permit; on guided trips, companies will get it for you. **Contact Alaska Fish and Game** (907-465-4327) or the **U.S. Forest Service** (907-225-3101).

Pack Creek lies at Windfall Inlet on Admiralty Island, about 20 air miles from Juneau. The following companies offer Pack Creek day trips, or three- or four-day trips out of Juneau. Cost starts at about $400 per person for a day trip.

Alaska Fly 'N' Fish Charters: (907-790-2120; alaskabyair.com.) Binoculars, boots, and rainwear provided. The wildlife guide pilot may choose to visit another site on Admiralty Island if the bear viewing is considered better. Departure from Juneau International Airport.

Alaska Mountain Guides: (1-800-766-3396; alaskamountainguides.com.) You'll hike to two different sites to watch for the brown bears on the day trips. Three-day trips offer the option to camp and kayak to the mouth of the creek.

Alaska Seaplanes Service: (907-789-3331; flyalaskaseaplanes.com.) The plane will drop you at the beach in the morning, and pick you up in the afternoon. You will have to get your own permit and bring your own boots and rain gear.

CENTRAL PANHANDLE

ANAN WILDLIFE OBSERVATORY

Black bears are the main attraction here, though brown bears, mink, river otters, and harbor seals are present. The area is 35 miles south of Wrangell on the mainland's Cleveland Peninsula. The season runs July through August, when 64 daily permits are issued to

Paddling to Pack Creek

The adventurous and strong of spirit might canoe or kayak to Pack Creek from Juneau. The U.S. Forest service calls it an "unrivaled opportunity for solitude." It involves a shortcut of a canoe/kayak portage by a rail-mounted hand pushcart of I mile. If you wanted to avoid this portion, you'd have to kayak an extra 80 miles around Glass Peninsula.

An easier way is to do it on an organized day trip. Fly to Windfall Island, where you'll pick up sea kayaks and paddle the short distance to the creek mouth. Contact **Juneau Alaska Adventures and Tours** (juneau-guide.com.)

Mountain Travel-Sobek's Alaska Discovery (1-800-586-1911; mtsobek.com) offers three days with roughly the same itinerary, but more kayaking possibilities.

groups and individuals. Viewing requires a half-mile boardwalk hike to a covered viewing platform. Most companies also offer Stikine River and LeConte Glacier trips.

Alaska Peak and Seas: (907-874-2454; wedoalaska.com.) The 16-passenger jet boat *Stikine Spirit* takes people to Anan Wildlife Observatory.

Alaska Waters: (907-874-2378 or 1-800-347-4462; alaskawaters.com.) The guide from the Tlingit-owned company guide offers local and native history and information on flora and fauna on the six-hour trip. Three hours is planned at the observatory and photo blind.

Breakaway Adventures and Stickeen Wilderness Adventures also offer Anan trips. See Excursions on Water section.

SOUTHERN PANHANDLE

TRAITOR'S COVE

This bear-viewing area is about a 20-minute float plane ride from Ketchikan. Black bears converge here mid-August through September to feed on the salmon in Margarite Creek. Visitors board vans for a 1-mile drive from the shore, followed by a short boardwalk hike to the bear-watching observatory.

Island Wings: (907-225-2444; islandwings.com.) The company offers flights to Anan Creek July through August, and to Traitor's Cove mid-August through September.

Seawind Aviation: (907-225-1206; seawindaviation.com.) The trips are offered during August and September.

Wildlife Photography Tours

These companies offer a variety of wildlife and outdoor activity trips, often incorporating photography, though specific trips may focus on a single wildlife variety. They may be day trips or longer. Costs start at about $50.

Alaska Nature Tours: (907-766-2868; alaskanaturetours.net.) Guided hiking, birding, wildlife photography, and cross-country skiing in and around the Chilkat Bald Eagle Preserve. Fall-winter trips focus on the Bald Eagle Preserve, and spring-summer trips on

> **Brown Bears by Any Other Name**
>
> You'll hear Alaska brown bears (*Ursus arctos*) called various names: grizzly bear, Kodiak bear, or brown bear. They're all correct, and they all refer to an animal of the same species, though there are some variations, often related to its locality.
>
> The Alaska Department of Fish and Game uses "brown bear" for all of them. They recognize different terminology. "Grizzly bear" generally means inland bears, which are smaller (if 800 pounds can be small) because their diet consists of berries and roots. Brown bears dwelling on the coast eat a salmon-rich diet, and generally grow much larger. Kodiak bears live on Kodiak Island, and they are the biggest of the breed, with males weighing up to 1,500 pounds.
>
> Usually a beautiful cinnamon brown, the color may vary from pale blond to almost black.
>
> Black bears (*Ursus americanus*) are smaller, and a distinct species.

mountain and rainforest hikes. The company is associated with Alaska Backcountry Outfitters, which offers a full line of outdoor clothing and gear.

Rainbow Glacier Adventures: (907-766-3576; joeordonez.com.) Bear-viewing tours, coastal rainforest hikes, kayaking and biking-kayak combos, photography, flightseeing over Rainbow and Davidson glaciers, and customized itineraries out of Skagway or Haines. Wildlife trips take in Chilkoot and Chilkat Bald Eagle Preserve. Tours are small and customized.

ZIPLINES

Ziplines are the latest travel fad. Those who love heights and speed line up for the adrenaline-boosting plunge; those who fear heights line up, too. And afterwards they love to brag about conquering their fears. Zipline course tours start at $138.

JUNEAU

Alaska Canopy Adventures: (907-523-2920 or 1-877-947-7557; alaskacanopy.com.) The course covers rainforest terrain above the Treadwell Mine site on Douglas Island. There are 10 ziplines, two suspension bridges, and rappelling from the last platform to base camp. Transport across Gastineau Channel provided.

Alaska Zipline Adventures: (907-321-0947; alaskazip.com.) This course through old-growth forest at the Eaglecrest ski area crosses streams and traverses a natural clearing to minimize impact on the forest, on seven ziplines and a suspension bridge. April through October.

HOONAH

Icy Strait Point ZipRider: (icystraitpoint.com.) This is a single swoop down a mountain, 5,330-feet long and 1,300 down, the longest zipline in the world. Three riders in seat harnesses go at the same time on parallel cables, reaching speeds up to 60 miles per hour. The ride sometimes starts in the clouds, drops into the forest canopy, and then opens to views over Icy Strait buildings, and the channel. Cost: about $90.

KETCHIKAN

Alaska Canopy Adventure: (907-225-5503 or 1-877-947-7557; alaskacanopy.com.) Designed as a rainforest experience, two courses are available in a wildlife habitat at Herring Cove. The Bear Creek zipline is suitable for beginners, has four dual cables, a sky bridge over a waterfall, rainforest swing, and mountain slide. The Eagle Creek course has three suspension bridges and eight dual cables. Both rides end with hot chocolate and a snack.

Shopping

Totems to Trolls

An Alaska travel industry survey found that people listed wildlife viewing as the number one reason to visit the state. But they actually spent more time shopping.

Shopping opportunities abound in Panhandle towns, especially in the three big cruise ports: Juneau. Ketchikan, and Skagway. Handcrafted items, either by Alaska Native artists or other Alaskan artisans, offer appealing choices. The powerful and harmonious interlocking designs of Northwest Coast people (Tlingit, Haida, and Tsimshian in Alaska) appear on silver jewelry, totem poles, masks, drums, and bentwood boxes. The haunting and sometimes whimsical images of Inupiat and Yup'ik Eskimo people appear in whalebone carvings and ivory jewelry, and Aleut baskets, with their tiny flowers, charm many others.

Of course, numerous spin-offs, some of them gaudy and schlocky, cram many shops. The spectrum of T-shirts and coffee mugs embellished with totem designs staggers the imagination. Many visitors covet T-shirts, especially those sporting humorous Alaska-teasing cartoons from Ray Troll (see *Culture* chapter). Some visitors come to Alaska with requests to bring them back to friends.

Mukluks (boots), *ulu* (curved knives), and *qiviut* (musk ox) yarn from the Eskimo cultures, and scrimshaw expand the possibilities. And almost everyone takes home bear claws, the wooden hand-shaped paddles for pasta or salads.

The Panhandle's Russian heritage reappears with nesting *matryoshka* dolls, lacquer boxes, blue-and-white porcelain, and amber jewelry, especially in Sitka.

Food is an increasingly popular item both for gifts and to serve your friends when you get home. Native Alaskans have smoked salmon for centuries. It's often packaged in attractive cedar boxes with Northwest Coast designs. Syrups and jams from berries or birch tree sap or spruce tips are other popular items. There's even a delicious Alaska-made chocolate, Theobroma from Sitka.

Locally made soaps, including those infused with glacier silt, pop up fairly frequently.

Silversmiths create beautiful jewelry inspired by Northwest Coast designs. Especially popular are the cuff bracelets with the designs incised and carved into the silver. Alaska Natives originally pounded out silver dollars to make the bracelets. Often jewel-like, but much less expensive, are enameled pins and zipper pulls in similar designs. Look for those by William Spear and Greg Horner.

High-quality outdoor wear, which you will need for ship decks, hiking, and even just cool days in port, is plentiful. Many people underestimate how cool an Alaska summer can be, and need to buy a fleece or water-repellent jacket.

Many shops, especially those selling gems and jewelry, cater to cruise ship passengers. Companies that have long set up in the Caribbean, such as Diamonds International or Tanzanite International, and Little Switzerland open for the summer cruise season in Ketchikan, Juneau, and Skagway. Local residents often resent these shops, which have appeared on the scene only since about the mid-1990s. They open only during the cruise season.

The listings in this chapter focus on places that offer distinctly Alaskan goods, so there will be no mistaking that what you take home will be from this part of the world. Most of them are locally owned. Some shop owners put a sign in the window indicating the shop is locally owned.

Galleries dedicated to art, especially those having changing exhibits, are listed in Chapter 4, Culture. Many of their prints, small carvings, and jewelry cost no more than gift shop items. Museum shops, which often have an excellent selection of Alaska-made gifts and books, are listed with museums in that chapter.

NORTHERN PANHANDLE

JUNEAU

Sometimes it seems the sidewalks on South Franklin Street should have grooves worn from shoppers trekking from the cruise ships to the many stores. Shopping can be a contact sport along here. As in most places in Alaska, Northwest Coast designs dominate many objects. The designs appear on mass-produced platters, T-shirts, coffee mugs, and scarves, as well as one-of-a-kind Alaska Native objects. Be aware of quality, and try to stick with the authentic thing. Unless otherwise noted, shops are open year-round.

This Juneau shopping jaunt will take you from the waterfront near the cruise ship dock up Franklin Street, with a few jogs on other streets in downtown. Starting near the waterfront and across from the tram station, **Caribou Crossings** (907-586-5008; caribou crossing.com; 497 S. Franklin Street) offers work by 60 Alaska artists and artisans. It has many carvings in stone and whalebone made by people in the Arctic regions. Open May through September, and at Thanksgiving and Christmas. "Or bang on the door," said the owner.

A Gift from Each Town

If you were to buy one inexpensive item to remember each place, here are some suggestions.

Juneau: Rie Muñoz small print

Gustavus: Pep's Packing halibut ear bone earrings

Haines: Greg Horner zipper pull

Skagway: Buckwheat Donahue Robert Service CD

Petersburg: Hardanger embroidery Christmas ornament

Sitka: Devil's Club lip balm

Wrangell: Petroglyph silver pendant

Ketchikan: Salmon Etc. smoked salmon

Metlakatla: Tiny cedar basket

The largest Christmas ornaments I've ever seen were at **Nor'Westerly** (907-586-6055, 439 S. Franklin Street). They're spectacular, but a challenge to carry home.

Many Alaska visitors find they need just one more sweater for the cool summer days, and make steps to **Invisible World** (907-586-3339; invisibleworld.com; 369 S. Franklin Street). Handsome silk, alpaca, wool, and cashmere sweaters in intriguing patterns and gossamer shawls fill the store. The owners import the yarns largely from Peru, Ecuador, and Bolivia, as well as China. Rustic and brightly patterned sweaters come from Otavalo, the Ecuador market town. More elegant versions with refined patterns would be perfect for dinner on a cruise ship or at a cocktail party. Open April through September, and December.

The Jade Shop (907-463-5551; alaskajadeshop.com; 321 S. Franklin Street) had what may be the coolest object in a Franklin Street window—a jade teapot standing on a jade placemat. Surely this is lavish use of this beautiful green stone found all over the Pacific coastal areas of Alaska and British Columbia. It also had the stone stacked in an *inukshuk*, one of the human-shaped cairns used by native people as markers on the tundra. (The *inukshuk* is the symbol for the 2010 Winter Olympics in Vancouver.) Nephrite jade is the Alaska gemstone. Open May through September only.

Ad Lib (907-463-3031; 231 S. Franklin Street) has high-quality artworks and gifts, including elegant Northwest Pewter platters and bowls with traditional designs made by Alaska Native former prisoners in a halfway house in Lemon Creek. Embroidered black T-shirts with embroidered Northwest Coast designs, wooden toys, and bright pillows, throws, and cards all beckon to be taken home. Owned by a Juneau mother and daughter,

This jade teapot in a South Franklin Street window may be one of the more unusual things to buy in Juneau.

the shop also features Sitka beadwork, artisan jewelry, and limited-edition prints. Most items are from Juneau artisans.

Across the street, the scent from the **Alaska Soap and Candle Company** (907-586-4404; alaskasoapcompany.com; 230 S. Franklin Street) wafted out to the street, even on a winter day when the door was closed. Inside, a rainbow of candles and soaps tempts shoppers. The soaps are infused with glacial silt, which serves as a sort of skin scrubber. Jars of lotions and body balms stood open to be slathered on hands.

Once in a Blue Moose (907-463-4311; 219 S. Franklin Street) has high-quality, Alaska-made items and some inexpensive items, including T-shirts and canvas tote bags. The **Senate Mall** building (175 S. Franklin Street) offers one-stop shopping with several shops. **Alaska Fly Fishing Goods** (907-586-1550; www.alaskaflyfishinggoods.com) offers an array of flies, and the feathers, sparklers, and hooks to make your own flies that quite dazzle the eye. The hot pink fly, the owner told me, actually irritates the fish so they strike at it. Of course, everything else you need for fly fishing is here, as well as advice on the best spots to try. **Skeins** (907-463-5678) has rare *qiviut* musk ox yarn in two different weights, and a few items such as small caps made from strands as soft as baby's hair. It also has anything else the knitter or embroiderer may want. Skeins also has a Mendenhall Valley location at 9121 Glacier Highway near Juneau International Airport.

Pin collectors make tracks to **Wm. Spear Design** (907-586-2209; wmspear.com; 174 S. Franklin Street #201) above Heritage Coffee. The bright jewel-like enamel pins and zipper pulls come in scores of images, including fanciful wildlife, Alaska Native designs, Juneau downtown, and fishing lures. Inexpensive and small, they are beautifully crafted. A selection of them is in the coffee shop window downstairs. **Mt. Juneau Trading Post** (907-586-3426; 151 S. Franklin Street) is well named. Every inch of floor, shelf, and wall space shows

Southeast Alaska artists and crafts people created almost everything at Ad Lib, including the Northwest Pewter platters.

A unique casserole tempts the shopper at Annie Kaill's.

Northwest Coast carvings, whalebone figures, ulu with cutting boards, bracelets, ivory, Russian nesting dolls, mukluks, pasta claws, and totem poles, some of them massive. The store aims to sell artworks and gifts made by Alaska Natives. "Then we look for Alaska, then the Lower 48, and finally China," the store owner said. The store has been in business 50 years.

At the clock, turn left at Front Street for **Annie Kaill's** (907-586-2880; annieandco juneau.com; 244 Front Street), which could also take its place among the gallery listings. Watercolors and prints by Alaska artists cover the walls. But casseroles, scarves, glassware, jewelry, notecards, and even sauces and dips fill up shelves, display cases, and tabletops. It's an attractive jumble and hard to leave the store without a filled Annie Kaill shopping bag.

Cruise ports-of-call always attract jewelry and gem shops. **The Jewel Box** (907-586-2604; 248 S. Front Street), a Juneau fixture for 50 years, specializes in Alaskan gold jewelry.

Several gem companies from the Caribbean and Bahamas open their doors during the May through September cruise season: **Diamonds International** (907-586-6363; 207 S. Franklin Street) and **Tanzanite International** (907-586-3550; 455 S. Franklin Street).

One of the best shops in Juneau isn't on South Franklin Street. It's the **Friends of the Alaska State Museum Store**, and it has two locations. One is inside the museum (907-465-4840; foasm.org/store.html; 395 Whittier Street) and the other is in the historic downtown (907-523-8431; 124 Seward Street). Inupiat soapstone and whalebone sculpture, colorful Tlingit masks and massive boxes, Athabascan birch-bark baskets, and Yup'ik dolls are arranged tastefully on shelves. Finely woven baleen baskets, made from the fibers in a whale's mouth, and the exquisitely carved silver bracelets are coveted Alaska gifts.

Nesting dolls and carved birch boxes, almost baroque in elaboration, represent Alaska's Russian period.

The books and DVDs cover Alaska history and its people, including intriguing stories devoted to Benny Benson, the little boy who won the competition to design the Alaska flag. The state's beauty is celebrated in coffee-table books with photographs of glaciers, forests, mountains, and seacoasts. There are also high-quality inexpensive items, like embossed notecards and small notebooks with narwhals, caribou, and other Alaska creatures, perfect for making notes on your trip.

The downtown site may actually be the larger of the two because it seems to have more objects than the museum store.

MENDENHALL VALLEY SHOPS

Some interesting possibilities for Alaska gifts exist in the Mendenhall Valley outside of downtown Juneau. **Hummingbird Hollow** (907-789-4672; hummingbirdhollow.net; Juneau International Airport, 1873 Shell Simmons Drive) makes a long wait for a flight worthwhile. The shop has much better quality and selection of Alaska handmade pieces than one might expect of an airport shop. You'll find carved silver jewelry, stone and whalebone figures, dolls, baskets, and ivory. Particularly charming soapstone figures have baskets filled with beads—blue for blueberries, red for salmonberries.

Ulu and carving boards, bear paw salad and pasta servers, and field drinking glasses make practical gifts. Military souvenirs and *matryoshka* dolls paid homage to Alaska's Russian heritage.

Nugget Mall (907-789-4439; 8745 Glacier Highway) in the Mendenhall Loop area is Southeast Alaska's largest retail mall. Juneau residents shop here for clothing, books, wrapping paper, cell phones, and pots and pans under an enclosed roof. It's also home to **Nugget Alaska Outfitters** (907-789-0956 or 800-478-6848), just the place for terrific rain jackets, fleece pullovers, and hand-embroidered Icelandic sweaters. The name for the mall comes from the Outfitters, which had a store in this area before the mall was built. When people came here, they called it Nugget Mall for the nearby shop. The name stuck. The mixture of stores is pretty much like any strip mall in the Lower 48, but you know you're in Alaska when you see the big stuffed bear in the center of the hall.

You may be curious about the **Pull-Tab** shop outlet. You see them all over the Panhandle. Pull-Tab is a state-regulated game of chance run for nonprofit organizations. Pull the tabs open and try to match with winning money tabs.

Also out on Glacier Highway, the local box store is a **Fred Meyer** (907-789-6500; fred

---

Rainbow-Bright Ammolite

Shoppers may notice a stone colored as vibrantly as the rainbow set into pendants and earrings in Alaska jewelry stores. It looks almost synthetic, but it's not. The opalized gemstone is formed on the fossilized shells of ammolites, found on the eastern slopes of the Rocky Mountains. Most of the jewelry is made from the ammolite found in Canada, where it's the Alberta gemstone. Its vibrancy wins over some, but not all people.

Look for the Logos

When you're hunting for something Alaska made, look for two logos. Objects made by Alaska Natives bear a black oval logo with a silver hand and the words: "Authentic Native Handicraft from Alaska." The backside has space for the artisan's name and Native group. For objects made by an Alaska residents who are non-Natives, look for a similar logo with a white mother bear and tiny black cub with the words, "Made in Alaska."

Shops are often proud of their Alaska-made products and gifts, and advertise this symbol boldly in the window, especially in Ketchikan, Juneau, and Skagway.

MADE ɪɴ ALASKA

Shop owners are often proud of the "Made in Alaska" logos attached to their gifts and artworks.

meyer.com; 8181 Old Glacier Highway), an Alaska staple in Anchorage and Fairbanks as well as Juneau. They will even deliver to the bush if need be.

GUSTAVUS

This tiny hamlet may have Alaska's most unique shop: **Gustavus Dray** (907-697-2481; Four Corners, Gustavus and State Dock roads) is a service station with pre-World War II pumps, a petroleum museum, and a gift shop. At one time, it was the fuel and electric company for Gustavus. Give yourself plenty of time to browse the handsome patchwork quilted bags, a booklet describing the 1957 Gustavus plane crash, Northwest Pewter, Glacier Ice soap, and locally made Kim Ney pottery. You can also get Theobroma chocolate bars for less than they cost in Sitka, where the chocolate is made.

Bear Track Mercantile (907-697-2358; State Dock Road) doubles up as a grocery store and drugstore, deli, video and DVD rental, and gift shop. Locally made pottery and Alaska T-shirts are tucked among the other merchandise. **Pep's Packing** (907-697-2295; gustavus .com/peps/ Dolly Varden Road, ¼ mile from Gustavus Road) may have Alaska's most unique gift: earrings made from halibut ear bones. In addition, the shop at the fish-packing facility has other handmade jewelry, wine bottle holders, and Christmas gifts. It also sells its alder-smoked salmon.

HAINES

Haines is less touristy than many other Panhandle towns, so it seems easier to separate the dross from the real things at its shops. It's home to Alaska Indian Arts, where the tradition of Tlingit carving is kept alive, and the town also has artists who have moved here from the Lower 48. You'll find their work at local galleries and in shops.

Fort Seward has several galleries, which are covered in Chapter 4, Culture, but also one distinctive shop, **The Wild Iris** (907-766-2300; 22 Tower Road). A sign in its attractive garden beckons, "This way to shop." Follow the path, climb the stairs to the enclosed

Antique gas pumps stand at Gustavus Dray, part museum, part gift shop.

porch, and you'll meet the very friendly owner, Fred Shields, the former Haines mayor. He will introduce himself, and then immediately pinpoint where you are from and what your occupation is. He's uncanny.

But don't let this distract you from the attractive hand-screened T-shirts, sweatshirts, and canvas bags made by his wife Madeleine, who is also a plant expert and master gardener, and responsible for the lovely garden. There is also bright trade bead jewelry, gold jewelry from nuggets pulled at Haines, made by both Fred and Madeleine, and prints and hand-screened cards. Carved Eskimo ivory pieces are from St. Lawrence Island. Almost everyone who comes to Haines eventually makes her (or his) way to this shop. They aren't sorry and usually end up buying something.

Dejon Delights (907-766-2505 or 1-800-539-3608; dejondelights.com; 37 Portage Street), not far from The Wild Iris, is the place to shop for smoked salmon and halibut. Both the smokery and a retail outlet are here, so you'll get a sense of the operation. Smoked wild salmon and halibut are the specialties, with several variations in seasonings and other dishes based on the wild smoked fish. You can take it with you, or they will ship anywhere in the world. There's also a retail outlet in Skagway.

Besides smoked fish, you can get salmon caviar, jams, jellies, exotic mustards, kitchen gear, and even Japanese glass fishing floats. Birch and Sitka spruce tip syrups are available here, as well as cranberry, rhubarb, and wild blueberry syrups.

Shopping in the main part of Haines covers a few galleries (see Chapter 4, *Culture*), gift shops, and outfitters. Sports enthusiasts who come to Haines for heli- or cross-country skiing, fishing, hiking, or climbing will have no trouble getting outfitted. Even if you don't need a thing, stop in at **Outfitter Sporting Goods** (907-766-3221; Mile Zero Haines Highway) for the display of taxidermy specimens. A greater kudu, an African antelope is displayed alongside mountain goat, Dall sheep, caribou heads, and various deer antlers. You can get any type of gun, ammunition, fishing rod, tackle, camouflage pants, waders, fleece jackets, half mittens, and cap or hat that you might need to hunt these animals. The wildlife mounts on the walls are trophies bagged by the owner and store manager with a bow and arrow.

Alaska Backcountry Outfitter Store (907-766-2876; alaskanaturetours.net; 111 Second Avenue) covers a similar range of everything you need to participate in any outdoor adventure. As well as selling gear, the owners offer kayak, ski, and snowboard rentals, and also lead hikes and wildlife and bald eagle-viewing trips in Haines and the Chilkat Valley.

Chilkat Valley Arts & Treasures (907-766-3230; www.chilkatvalleyarts.com; 209 Willard Street) is part antiques shop, part art gallery, and part bead shop, with items ranging from vintage china, costume jewelry, and postcards, to prints, fine jewelry, and carvings. Every color of the rainbow and shape of bead sits in bins and boxes, or is strung on thread in the bead shop. The gallery features work by Haines artists, including Debi Knight Kennedy. The store now has a small annex in Fort Seward, beside the garden entrance to The Wild Iris. Look for **Tom Lang's** small books profiling Alaska denizens, such as salmon, bears, eagles, and moose. The Haines resident combines the familiar with modern pop psych ideas, such as anger management (bear) and fear of commitment (bald eagle). They're about the size of a first-grade reader and will bring a chuckle. The annex is closed in winter.

Chilkoot Gardens (907-766-2703; www.chilkootgardens.com; 204 Main Street) combines a Hallmark shop with collectibles, a florist and nursery, clothing, books, maps, and terrific fudge. It was the fudge the kept us browsing, if nothing else for its names: northern lights, sea otter, bear tracks, moose drool, Dalton Trail. This place has fairly inexpensive and good-quality souvenirs.

Bell's Alaska Gifts and Clothing sits next to Bell's Seafood (see Chapter 6, *Restaurants and Food Purveyors*). When I visited, a sign on the gift store read, . . . GO NEXT DOOR AND ASK FOR CLYDE OR DORIS. Next door, another sign on the locked door read, WE'RE AT THE AIRPORT.

Gold nuggets can still be pulled here, and some of the precious metal makes its way to **Gold Spot** (907-766-2772; 8 Second Avenue) and **Helen's Shop** (907-766-2266; 221 Main Street). Another place for gold, as well as Native Alaskan-made gifts is the **Trading Post** (907-767-3195; 128 Second Avenue). The carved wooden bear and moose antlers on the log building go a long way toward looking the part.

The **Lost Coast Surf Shop** (907-314-0335; lostcoastsurf.com; corner Second Avenue and Main Street) has lots more than surfboards and wet suits—it has a full line of Patagonia and other outdoor wear. New to town is **Gill Netter Gear** (Main and Front streets) for nautical-themed clothing, art, and gifts. It's in the Alaska Fjordlines ticket office.

Outside of town, **Birch Boy Products** (907-769-5660; birchboy.com; 18 Mile Haines Highway), is home to the syrups you'll find at Mountain Market, Dejon Delights, and many other places in the Alaska Panhandle. They will ship any one of a dozen flavors of syrup made from Alaska products. Imagine Russian-American cherry, rhubarb, highbush cranberry, red currant, wild blueberry, salmonberry, Sitka spruce tip, and, of course, birch syrups.

SKAGWAY

Tromping along Skagway's board sidewalks like a Klondike stampeder makes shopping fun. Most shops line Broadway, the wide street that serves as Skagway's spine. Lots of interesting storefronts are also on the numbered cross streets. The shopping area stretches for about six short blocks, but multiply that by about three or four cross streets, and it adds to a heavy shopping day.

Most Skagway shops are open mid-May through mid-September only, unless otherwise noted. Shops in this section are listed roughly as you would come to them along Broadway and a few of its side streets, starting nearest the waterfront.

Skagway has the typical mix of gifts, art galleries (see Chapter 4, *Culture*), and out-of-town jewelry stores, though gift shops seem to predominate. Both the **Train Shoppe** (907-983-2022; wpyr.com; 213 Second Avenue) and the **Klondike Gold Rush National Park Visitor Center** (907-983-2921; nps.gov/klgo/; Second and Broadway), which sit side by side, offer numerous books, memorabilia, caps, and other gifts geared to Skagway's historic past or train lore. The Alaska Natural History Association maintains the excellent shop in the national park visitors center and has an excellent selection of books.

Starting up Broadway from the national park visitors center, **Taiya River Jewelry** (907-983-2637; taiyariverjewelry.com; Second Avenue and Broadway) has gold jewelry that owner Casey McBride creates from nuggets found in Alaska, Yukon, and British Columbia. The store also has work by other jewelry designers, and McBride will custom-design a piece if you wish.

Alaska artists and artisans created the unusual and exquisite beadwork, silver, ivory, and gold nugget jewelry, and even Father Christmas figures at **Heart of Broadway** (907-983-3773; 305 Broadway). There are a few exceptions, including Romanian lace china, displayed seductively in the window. Even this has an Alaska connection: One of the patterns has the state flower, forget-me-knots, on the translucent white surface.

Nearby **Dedman's** (907-983-2353; 331 Broadway) in the little blue building is a good place for camera batteries, memory cards, or film, as well as some artworks. The owner is descended from a Gold Rush pioneer. This is Skagway's oldest family-owned business, and it's open year-round.

Rushin' Tailor's Quilt Alaska (907-983-2397; quiltalaska.com; 370 Third Avenue) where Alaska-made quilts are available, as well as the patterns and fabrics to make them, year-round; and **Changing Threads** (907-983-3700, changingthreads.com; 326 Third Avenue), where you can get *qiviut* musk ox yarn as well as Alaska-themed quilt kits. Both stores feature Northwest Coast and Barbara Lavallee designs. Both shops are open year-round with limited winter hours. Bins of nails in the hardware store don't have much appeal for vacationing shoppers. However, almost everyone makes the pilgrimage to **Skagway Hardware** (907-983-2233; skagwayhardware.com; 400 Broadway) to see a true old-fashioned hardware store where it is still possible to buy one nail, a pipe joint, or, this being Alaska, a battery blanket. The store does have a large selection of souvenirs and children's toys as well.

Klothes Rush (907-983-2370 or 1-800-664-2370; klothesrush.com; 499 Broadway) has souvenir belt buckles, T-shirts, caps, and sweatshirts, but also high-quality outdoor gear, including items by The North Face; open year-round.

High on the bluff above downtown, a gigantic pocket watch with the name Kirmse's Curios is painted on the rock, a cross between graffiti and an old-fashioned billboard. Kirmse's is long gone, though the building is at Broadway and Fifth Avenue, and totem poles line its side as they might have in the old days.

Side-by-side **Tundra Ted's** and **North to Alaska** (907-983-3070 or 1-888-595-4556;

Tundra Ted's in Skagway has a little bit of everything.

northtoalaskagifts.com; 634 Broadway) manage to pack in almost every kind of gift or souvenir you will find anywhere in Alaska. Eskimo dolls, ulu knives and bowls, and Alaska-themed caps, shirts, coffee mugs, and cocktail napkins are here. So are Siberian birch bark boxes, *matryoshka* dolls, and lacquer brooches from Russian America. It has a large selection of Alaska-related cooking utensils—bear claws for pasta or salad, cedar and alder baking planks, and cookbooks.

"At Your Service"

Hope that you might be in Skagway when Buckwheat Donahue does readings from Robert Service at the auditorium in Klondike National Historical Park Visitor Center. He also does them on small cruise ships. A way to take home a bit of the Klondike is on his CD, *Buckwheat at Your Service: The Readings of Robert Service,* which includes famed examples, "The Cremation of Sam McGrew," "The Shooting of Dan McGrew" and "The Spell of the Yukon" among its selections.

Buckwheat has also narrated Jack London's novel, *The Call of the Wild,* and three other short stories, on a five-disk CD set. The CDs are available at Skaguay News Depot and Hearts of Broadway, or by visiting buckwheat.info.

Buckwheat, a tall man with a salt-and-pepper beard, loves the lore of the Klondike Gold Rush and is well versed in its adventures.

Glacier Silt for the Skin

Glacial silt does more than wash down streams. It's used for facials, rubs, and scrubs in beauty products such as **Alaska Glacial Mud**. Rub it on your face, let it dry, and rinse it off. Good as a salon facial, the company claims. Its grit is filled with minerals, deemed to make the skin glow.

Glacier Smoothie isn't something to drink; it's glacial silt soap. It both exfoliates and smoothes the skin. It's sold in attractive drawstring bags with brass number tags, the kind used by gold miners at Juneau's famous mines. Find it at a little stand on the docks off South Franklin Street.

Yukon

WHITEHORSE

Since the 1940s, travelers have beaten a path to **Murdoch's** (867-667-7403; murdochs.ca; 207 Main Street), mostly a jewelry store but part museum, part Whitehorse institution. In addition to jewelry from gold nuggets, Canadian diamonds, and ivory, you'll find Klondike Kate's silver belt and a large wooden statue of a panning gold miner. Store designers create the gold nugget jewelry in house. **North End Gallery** (867-393-3590; northendgallery.ca; 118,117 First Avenue) has elegant Inuit carvings, gold nugget and ivory jewelry, art glass, and oil paintings, as well as unique northern artworks. These include images made by biting flattened and folded birch bark, creating floral and other decorative patterns. Other flower pictures are made by tufting the hair of moose and caribou. Elegant rolling pins, chip-dip sets, and pretty pottery wildflower plates offer less-expensive choices. Yukon artisans make most of the items.
S'igèdí Gifts & Things (867-456-4157; sigedi.com; 101-100 Main Street), just across the street from the train station, has souvenir T-shirts, caps, and fleece, as well as First Nation carvings, dolls, and slippers.

CENTRAL PANHANDLE

Shopping opportunities in the Central Panhandle relate to the number of cruise ships that stop. Sitka, the largest community, has by far the most shops, including some of the chain jewelry shops. Shopping is more limited in Petersburg and Wrangell, but each of these places has some interesting things with specific local ties.

PETERSBURG

Bright rosemaling festoons every Petersburg storefront, making shopping here a happy event. Many shop items, too, relate to the town's Norwegian heritage, including gorgeous

Northwest Pewter Co.

Any Panhandle gift shop selling high-quality gift items with have lustrous silvery platters and bowls with Northwest Coast designs done in relief. Alaska Native transitional prisoners at a halfway house for the Lemon Creek Correctional Center make the patterns for these lead-free pewter serving pieces. Several platters, including one shaped like a salmon, and a large serving bowl are among the items. These handsome pieces will be perfect for serving the smoked salmon you bring home from Alaska, and for years remind you of the trip.

Nordic sweaters and rosemaling kits. Petersburg shops may not have street numbers posted. They are listed here when available. This section starts with Nordic Drive shops at the north end of downtown and moves south. Shops are arranged more or less as they appear when you are walking along the street.

Wild Celery (907-772-2471; 400 N. Nordic Drive) sits behind the lovely wildflower mural on this corner building. Inside the array runs to eclectic items including folk art painted furniture, contemporary lamps, candles, whimsical teapots, wearable art, rosemaling, Alaska Native designs, and paintings and prints. **Hammer & Wikan** (907-772-4811; 218 N. Nordic Drive) is a hardware store, but it also has souvenirs and gifts. Across the street, **Seaport Gallery** (907-772-3015; 219 N. Nordic Drive) has high-quality Alaska Native carvings, jewelry, and baleen baskets, and prints by well-known artists Rie Muñoz and Barbara Lavallee. The antler zipper pulls, at $5, fill the bill for inexpensive gifts.

Lee's Clothing (907-772-4229; 212 Nordic Drive) beckons with bright Norwegian, Swedish, and American flags suspended over the sidewalk. Inside the colors are just as bright, with racks and racks of gorgeous hand-knit Norwegian and Icelandic sweaters. If you pop into the Sons of Norway Hall you'll see large, group photographs of people wearing these sweaters. Lee's Clothing has everything else to outfit you for the rainy summer or cold winter. Heidi Lee and her sister Cynthia Lee Mathisen own the store, which has been a family business since the early 1970s. Their grandfather was a Petersburg pioneer.

The carved moose antler in the window at **Diamonté** (907-772-4858; 210 Nordic Drive) stops shoppers in their steps. Inside you'll find everything from gold nugget jewelry to carved ivory, Petersburg blankets, and stuffed moose toys.

At Scandia House hotel, Sing Lee Alley breaks off Nordic Drive. It's filled with unusual boutiques. Note that the buildings have historical markers. Today's shops are often quite removed from the buildings' origins.

Quilts with salmon, halibut, and killer whales brightly announce **WildCat Quilts** (907-772-4848; 14 Sing Lee Alley). Inside Grazyna Froelich may be at the longarm sewing machine at work on these bright patches that hang on the wall or on a rack outside, ready for you to take a bit of Alaska home. **Kinder Komfort** (907-772-4100; 15 Sing Lee Alley) jogs local shoppers' memory in the cleverest way: A list of birthdays of the month for Petersburg children is posted outside the shop. Inside, everything those children might want may be found among the toys and gifts.

Moving along the street, the **Cubby Hole** (907-772-2717; 14 Sing Lee Alley) has more children's books and toys, as well

Maya Lee Holmes wears a Norwegian sweater from Lee's Clothing, owned by her mother.

Cool Book Shops

NORTHERN PANHANDLE

Juneau

The long, dark winter may be conducive to settling down with a book. Juneau seems to have an unusual number of independently owned bookshops, and they stay open through the winter. Every Juneau visitor should stop for at least a few minutes at **The Observatory** (907-586-9676; observatorybooks.com; 299 N. Franklin Street) to browse its extraordinary selection of books focused on Alaska, Russian America, and polar regions, but also to chat with Dee Longenbaugh. The engaging owner seems to know the contents of every book in the jammed shop, especially anything to do with Russian Alaska. She knows equally as much about the intellectual and social life of contemporary Juneau. An afternoon evaporates in her company, and in the wonderful collection of antique and antiquarian books.

Be sure to ask her how the shop got its name. There is no observatory on the roof. The inspiration behind the name shows the reach of her interests and lively mind.

Hearthside Books has two locations: One is downtown (907-586-1726; hearthsidebooks.com; 254 Front Street at the clock) and the other, the largest in Nugget Mall (907-789-2750). Both have an excellent selection of books devoted to the state's social and natural history, literature, and Alaska Natives. If you want a coffee table book of the gorgeous glaciers, mountains, and the Inside Passage fjords, this is the place to find it. People working in the shop will guide you to the one that matches your interests. The store also covers bestsellers, literary works, and children's books. Upstairs, a little nook with children's books is a perfect place to retreat on a rainy day. Local authors often make appearances on First Friday evenings. If you need something to read, a mystery set in Alaska might add to the pleasure of the trip.

The store also serves as something of a community center. Tickets are sold to Juneau theaters and other events, and people in the store know what's going on in town. It's hard not to walk out with a stack of books.

The aptly named **Rainy Day Books** (907-463-2665; juneaubooks.com; 113 N. Seward Street) places new books beside used books on its crammed shelves. "We don't see any reason to separate them," said shop manager Royce Metz. It's another place that tempts spending an afternoon and browsing the many Alaska titles and unusual books. To encourage

Dee Longenbaugh, owner of Observatory Books in Juneau, knows everything about Russian America and the modern Alaska capital.

lingering, you're invited to get coffee or tea next door at Valentine's and bring it into Rainy Day. Both the café and bookshop are in the historic Valentine Building.

Friends of the Library has a bookstore at the **Juneau Airport Shopping Center** (907-789-4913; 9121 Glacier Highway), the perfect place to be selling something to read. **St. Nicholas Orthodox Bookstore** (907-586-1023; 325 Fifth Street) has religious and history books.

Another place to spend an afternoon or a day absorbed in a book is at the **Juneau Memorial Library** (907-586-5324; 292 Marine Way). An award-winning architectural tour de force, the library is located on the top floor of a multistory parking garage near the waterfront. Comfortable chairs at the floor-to-ceiling windows look out over the Gastineau Channel.

Haines

You'll learn what's going on in town at **Babbling Book** (907-766-3356; 223 Main Street), both from the friendly people who work there and the notices posted on the wall. As much a gift as book shop, it also has cards, calendars, maps, and toys.

Skagway

The store name, **Skaguay News Depot and Books** (907-983-3354; 264 Broadway), is not mis-spelled. The town was originally spelled this way, after a Tlingit word, roughly Skagua in English. Early miners added a "y," to make it more "English." Eventually a few people, including the U.S. Postal Service, changed the "u" to "w," so the spelling stuck.

You'll learn this and other arcane northern facts in this small, friendly store. It's well stocked with Alaska and Yukon titles, including fiction and nonfiction about Skagway. Open year-round.

Yukon

Whitehorse

Part community center, part social club, and part intellectual institution, **Mac's Fireweed Books** (867-667-2434; 203 Main Street) is a large bookstore with an excellent selection of books that cover Canadian literature, First Nation books, and northern and polar history. It's an excellent center for maps and magazines—"the best magazine rack north of the 60th parallel," the store claims. Poetry readings are frequent, so try to time a visit to one of these events.

Central Panhandle

Petersburg

Books about the town's history, natural history, local character, and characters, are available at the **Clausen Museum** shop (see Chapter 4, *Culture, Museum* section). A lot has been said and written for a community the size of Petersburg.

Sing Lee Alley Books (907-772-4440; 11 Sing Lee Alley) sits back on a wide expanse of lawn in what was once comfortable a private house, and a fishermen's boarding house. It's still comfortable, especially for browsing the many rooms of books, well organized and divided by subject. The Alaska Reading Room looks especially inviting, with titles that will add interest to your trip, including *Where the Sea Breaks Its Back* by Corey Ford, the story of Georg Steller, the naturalist for whom sea lions and jays are named. Wildlife guides and maps are perfect for interpreting Alaska. Good-quality reading lights on sale will ensure bedtime or ferry reading even in poor light. A cheerful room at the back is reserved for youngsters.

Sitka

Old Harbor Books (907-747-8808; 201 Lincoln Street) has an excellent selection of Alaska subjects, including natural history, ecology, travel guides, marine history and fishing, children's books, and Native American and Alaska Native subjects. It also has Alaska fiction, including mysteries by Sitka native John Straley, the former Alaska State Writer Laureate. The usual selection of popular and topical nonfiction and fiction is here as well. The staff has read the books and makes intelligent suggestions.

People gather here and greet each other and browse, and then duck into the back entrance of Back Door Café (see the *Food Purveyors* section in Chapter 6). The store even has a vision statement: "The right book for the right person at the right time."

SOUTHERN PANHANDLE
Ketchikan

Hidden among the galleries and gifts on Creek Street is **Parnassus Books** (907-225-7690; 5 Creek Street). Just look for the sign and stairs near Ray Troll's Soho Coho gallery in the Star Building. Like other Creek Street buildings, this one had a racy past. "The Star," as it was known, was a dance hall with a few rooms upstairs. The upstairs is now the bookstore.

Parnassus Books carries many Alaska titles, including those on Alaska and Pacific Northwest Native art, natural history, literary titles, and cookbooks. Ketchikan authors and artists are represented, including neighbor Ray Troll. There also are offbeat titles that the staff might suggest, and children's books.

Prince of Wales Island

Voyageur Book Store (907-826-2333; 801 Water Street, Craig) is a town meeting place, toy shop, café, and very good book shop in a remote location. Worn couches make an appealing place to read a book with a cup of coffee.

as craft and hobby supplies, including rosemaling kits. Across the street, **Tonka Seafoods** (see Chapter 6, *Food Purveyors* section) has gift baskets of alder-smoked salmon, halibut, and other things.

Backtracking a bit on Nordic Drive, you'll find **Dawn Eagle Engraving** (907-772-4998; Nordic Drive and Lumber Street). Haida engraver Malcolm J. Miller makes silver bracelets that combine Native and Nordic imagery with Eagle, Raven, and Devils Thumb (a mountain near Petersburg) in the center, and a rosemaling design on the side. It's unique to Petersburg. J, as he is known, is Petersburg's only Native carver. His wife Mary makes Tlingit regalia. If the shop isn't open, simply knock at the door. This is their home.

SITKA

Russian nesting *matryoshka* dolls stand in rows on shop shelves throughout the Panhandle, but nowhere in the numbers and sheer variety of Sitka. The fat bowling pin-shaped figures, especially at home in the former capital of Russian America, may be painted in bright folk art garb, Eskimo parkas, Father Christmas costumes, and even Japanese kimonos. (*Matryoshka* dolls originated in Japan and migrated to Russia in the late 1800s.)

Sitka shops have other Russian gifts—lacquer boxes, samovars, Lomonosov porcelain, and Fabergé and amber jewelry.

Shopping choices also benefit from some well-known, local Tlingit carvers and jewelry makers whose work is available. The Sheldon Jackson Museum, Sitka National Historical Park, Alaska Raptor Center, and even St. Michael's Cathedral have shops with high-quality items (see Chapter 4, *Culture,* and Chapter 7, *Recreation*). Galleries tend to be on the north side of Lincoln Street, shops on the south. The street divides at St. Michael's Cathedral at the corner of Cathedral Way.

Sitka shops tend to stay open through the winter, though they often cut back on hours, which may vary from week to week.

Shops begin at the foot of Lincoln Street just steps past the dock for small cruise ships and run all the way to Jackson Sheldon College, making Sitka a good shopping town. Sitka was founded on fur trade, so it's no surprise to find two or three shops with pelts hanging from the doorway, and fur underwear in the window. **Sitka Fur Gallery** (907-747-5577; 108 Lincoln Street) is among the larger ones. Lots of choices among fur vests, jackets, and

Pelts or completed jackets, vests, and coats from Sitka Fur Gallery are designed to keep people warm.

parkas. Dark, rich, north woodsy color characterizes the clothing, table linens, and other high-quality items at **Brenner's Fine Clothing and Gifts** (907-747-3468; 124 Lincoln Street). **Random House** (907-747-3354, 134 Lincoln Street) may have the largest lacquer box ever. Most of these black boxes with fairytale scenes are small enough to sit on a dresser. This one stands on the floor, and is the size of a coffee table. Inside the store, all things Russian, including nesting *matryoshka* dolls and Fabergé eggs fill the shelves. But whalebone carvings from Arctic Alaska also join the mix.

A short detour across Totem Square brings you to **Rain Country** (907-747-6422; 201 Katlian Street) beside the Totem Square Inn. Really a small department store, it has useful items as well as gifts, including bright boots for the rain.

Across the street, **Baranov's** (907-747-8092; 205 Lincoln Street) has an especially handsome collection of Lomonosov blue-and-white porcelain.

Pick out some Raven's Brew Coffee, Alaska jams, and smoked salmon at **Alaska Basket** (907-747-7922; 202 Lincoln Street), the perfect gift for a foodie friend, and then pack it with some attractive napkins in a basket. A treat awaits at **Fairweather Gallery and Gifts** (907-747-8677; 209 Lincoln Street). They make an Alaskan Dream ice cream bar, dipped in Belgian light or dark chocolate and then almond toffee crunch. They also specialize in Alaska-made gifts and boutique clothing with hand-painted petroglyphs and folk art animals, and ivory and silver jewelry.

A few scraps of cloth, needle, and thread are transformed into sea otters, killer whales, and even glaciers on the quilt wall hangings at **Abby's Reflection Apparel and Quiltworks** (907-747-3510; 231 Lincoln Street). Apparel ranges from serious outdoor wear from The North Face to cute socks at **Mountain Miss Gear and Gifts** (907-747-5050; 322 Lincoln Street).

No one will miss the **Fly Away Fly Shop** (907-747-7301, 100 Lake Street in the Westmark Hotel) with the bright butterfly-shaped banners and windsocks fluttering in the wind out front. The door is almost hidden behind all the brightness. Inside, anglers will find everything they need for fly fishing, including an Alaska fishing license and rental gear. A wide array of caps, sweatshirts, undershorts with racy messages, and the vibrant flags and windsocks are available.

Charming children's T-shirts brighten the window at the **Shepherd's Heart** (907-747-5005; 334 Lincoln Street). The store also has devil's club ointments, lip balm, and oils made by Pauline Duncan.

During the day in summer, a van pulls up near the Coliseum Theatre on Lincoln Street, where Catharine Weaver displays her hand-blown and fused glass beads, pendants, and marbles. She may even demonstrate her skill with molten glass in this mobile **FiredDesires Studio.**

Sitka Rose (See the *Art Gallery* section of Chapter 4, *Culture*) and **WinterSong Soaps** (907-747-8949; 419 Lincoln Street) share the Hanlon-Osbakken historic house. The pleasing scent draws shoppers into WinterSong, with its enormous range of Alaska-scented soaps. Wild berry, fireweed, seaweed, and forget-me-knots all perfume the handsome bars made in Sitka. There are soaps to wash your dog and fishy-smelling hands, and devil's club salve to heal sunburns and cuts.

The large **Bay View Building** (407 Lincoln Street) houses the **Russian American Company** (907-747-6228; russianamericancompany.com) where hundreds of *matryoshka* dolls, lacquer boxes, amber, and samovars dazzle the eye on the second level. Even more dazzle is across the hall, at **Goldsmith Gallery** (907-747-5744; alaskajewelry.com), with some fine bracelets by Tlingit artists, gold nugget jewelry, and art glass. On cool Sitka days, unprepared tourists head downstairs to **Work and Rugged Gear Store** (907-747-6238) for fleece shirts, woolen caps, and windbreakers in muted colors.

Turn down Harbor Drive, at Sitka's only stop light, for a few more opportunities, including **Baranof Arts & Crafts Association** shop (330 Harbor Drive in Centennial Hall). The cooperative gallery features work by several local artists in wide-ranging media, including watercolor, prints, textiles, jewelry, and pottery. Frog Raven yarn in rainbow colors, and Sailor's Choice coffee roasted in Sitka are available. Open in summer only.

At **Simple Pleasures** (907-747-3880, 300A Harbor Drive), Renee Pierce gives you a warm welcome, as if you've arrived in her home. She offers hot tea, brewed in the samovar and sweetened, if you like, in the Russian manner with salmonberry jelly. The shelves are bright with jars of jelly, syrups, pickles, and vinaigrette from Alaska products, including all the wild berries, spruce tips, and kelp. The tea is imported from Russia, and may be purchased in tins.

A bit off the beaten shopping path, **Taranoff's Sitkakwan Gifts** (907-747-8667; 208 Katlian Street), features Alaska Native jewelry and carvings.

WRANGELL

Wrangell gets small cruise ships only a few times a week and so lacks the jewelry shops that line streets at other ports. Residents own the shops, and some of the items are locally made. The **Wrangell Museum Shop** in the Nolan Center (see Chapter 4, *Culture*) is a good place to start shopping, with a wide range of Alaska gift foods, petroglyph jewelry, cedar basket necklaces, and a wide range of books.

Wrangell has one shopping experience that shouldn't be missed. Local youngsters set

Matryoshka *dolls and more* matryoshka *dolls line shelves at Russian American Company in Sitka.*

Willis Osbakken carved this alder bowl, seen at Sitka Rose Gallery. An Alaska Native, he grew up in the Hanlon-Osbakken house, which now houses the gallery.

up stands near the ferry terminal or at the covered shelter at City Dock at the foot of Front Street and sell **garnets**. The gems come from an area that was mined in the late 20th century on the Stikine River mouth. In 1962, mine owner Fred Hanford deeded the property to the "children of Wrangell." Each spring families, go up with picks and shovels and harvest the magenta stones embedded in gray rock. It's hard work. Youngsters sell the loose garnets for about $5–$15. They're not gemstone quality, but still it's a bargain, and even more fun to meet these youngsters. Local artisans often join the children under the City Dock shelter. Everyone sets up when a cruise ship or the Alaska ferry docks.

Wrangell shops generally fall into the gift and souvenir category, rather than art galleries. Murals on buildings brighten many shops along Front Street. Shops geared primarily to tourists open May through September, and often only in the afternoon or when cruise ships are at City Dock. Stores that combine gifts with practical things, such as **Stikine Drugs,** are open year-round.

The order of stores generally starts at City Dock on Front Street and proceeds toward Chief Shakes Island. Note: A street number is added when possible, but Wrangell businesses and residents pick up their mail at the post office, and use their post office boxes for mailing addresses. Street addresses have been assigned to residences and businesses, but they are rarely used, and many stores do not put numbers on the building.

Front Street Shops
A few stores cluster just beyond City Dock beside the **Stikine Inn** (107 Stikine Avenue): **Alaska Waters** (see Chapter 7, *Recreation*), primarily a booking agency, also has logo wear and other items; **A Bliss Design** (907-874-3880), hand-screened custom-screened T-shirts and sweat shirts in Alaska-inspired designs; and **Simply Sterling** (907-874-

4144). The latter attracts notice with a handsome silver wine coaster/candle holder that gleams in the window. It's adorned with a single, simple spiral, a universal symbol found among the petroglyphs on the beach. The company specializes in silver jewelry fashioned after the shapes of Alaska petroglyphs, including those found on Wrangell's Petroglyph Beach. The jewelry is also available at the Wrangell Museum shop, Clausen Museum in Petersburg, and Exploration Gallery and Southeast Alaska Discovery Center in Ketchikan.

Angerman's Clothing & Sporting Goods (907-874-3640; 2 Front Street) and nearby **Angerman's Outlet** (907-874-3636; 10 Front Street) serve as general stores for both visitors and Wrangell residents. The list of medium and top-line sportswear runs to dozens of brands, including Grundens gear for fishing, Mustang survival gear, and Spalding. Campers, hunters, and anglers will find all they need. They also will help with fishing and hunting licenses and tags. And if you need just a small gift, they have that too, especially at the outlet store.

Plenty of things small enough to tuck in a suitcase tempt shoppers at **Alaskan Gift Shop** (907-874-3726; 22 Front Street), including pretty blue etched glass plates and jackets; and **Norris Gifts** (907-874-3810; 124 Front Street): paintings, picture frames, crystal figures, and small stuffed animals. Even **Ottesen's** (907-874-3377; 104 Front Street), a True Value Hardware store, has gifts among the tools, fishing tackle, and bikes.

Trevor, Calleigh, and Garrett Miller sell garnets at the Wrangell ferry dock.

Look for the prints of marine artist **Brenda Schwartz-Yeager** (907-874-3508; marine artist.com; 7 Front Street), who uses nautical charts as backdrops for her watercolors of the Alaska coastline, towns, and boats. She runs a charter boat and sketches at the sites, and then creates the paintings and prints. They are found in many Panhandle galleries, as well as gift shops on the Alaska Marine Highway ferries. The shop/studio is also her booking agency for glacier and bear trips.

SOUTHERN PANHANDLE

KETCHIKAN

Ketchikan is one of the Panhandle's "shop until you drop" towns, primarily because it's a large cruise ship port. For many passengers, it's the first port of call in Alaska, and the shopping urge runs strong. Shops are just steps from the cruise ships, which berth along the waterfront from Thomas Basin to the tunnel. Salmon Landing and Spruce Mill Mall, which stands on the site of the old mill, are two waterfront complexes. Shops line Front, Mission, Dock, and Main streets behind these complexes. Of course Creek Street, Ketchikan's iconic lane, has galleries and shops where brothels and dance halls once reigned.

Ketchikan art galleries (see Chapter 4, *Culture*), the Southeast Alaska Discovery Center (see Chapter 7, *Recreation*), and Saxman Totem Village (see Chapter 5, *Alaska Native People*) provide other shopping possibilities. Ketchikan may have more Tsimshian and Haida art than elsewhere in Southeast Alaska since the southern Panhandle is closest to their home villages.

Ketchikan is also home to Ray Troll's Soho Coho gallery (see the *Gallery* section of Chapter 4, *Culture*). A Ray Troll T-shirt is Ketchikan's most distinctive souvenir.

Ketchikan has its share of cruise port jewelry stores, many of which are in Salmon Landing and Spruce Mill complexes. This section focuses on stores with distinctive Alaska products. Streets get jammed with people and cars near the docks, but crossing guards ensure that pedestrians get their right-of-way.

Most visitors swarm to Creek Street like salmon in the adjacent creek during July. At the corner, the **Blue Heron** (907-225-1982; blueheronalaska.com; 123 Stedman Street) has handmade items from throughout the state: ulus, ivory jewelry, Christmas ornaments, and an especially charming teapot and cup with forget-me-knots, the state flower.

Several souvenir shops, **Carver at the Creek** (see the *Art Gallery* section in Chapter 4, *Culture*) and Dolly's Museum fill the bottom of Creek Street. Moving along with the salmon, you'll come to **Fish Creek Company** (907-617-0867; fishcreekcompany.net; 3 Creek Street). Salmon-skin leather wallets, enchanting spirit dancer carvings, and soap made from rainwater in every color imaginable are some of the eclectic choices. Photographer Hamilton Gelhar, who owns the shop with his wife Karla, has a once-in-a-lifetime photo—an image of a mother bear with two cubs. One bear is brown, another black, and the third white. They are all black bears, but color variations occur in the species.

Cross over the footbridge to get a good view of the creek, and jog on to other shopping possibilities on Mission Street. It has some fine galleries (see the *Art Gallery* section in Chapter 4, *Culture*). One of those only-in-Alaska combinations exists under a single roof: **Barnaby's Old Town Curios** (907-247-2002; 422 Mission Street), **Tall Tale Taxidermy**

(907-225-2025; talltaletaxidermy.com; 449 Mill Street), and a post office substation. They're separate with separate entrances, and yet you can walk from one to the other.

Luscious and exquisitely formed chocolate truffles, barks, and marzipan from **KetchiCandies** (907-225-0900; ketchicandies.com; 315 Mission Street) would make a welcome gift for someone back home. The most popular item: chocolate-covered Oreo cookies, which come in white, milk, and dark chocolate versions. One of these cookies, which swell to about twice their normal size from the chocolate coat, revives the weary shopper. Salmon is king at two other food shops: one with a roll-up facade, topped with a huge sign saying simply, **Salmon** (907-225-5249; 200 Main Street); and nearby **Salmon Etc.** (1-800-354-7256; 322 Mission Street). Both sell Ketchikan's most famous product in jars, cans, and flat packages.

Scanlon Gallery (907-247-4730; 310 Mission Street) takes time to browse; "Aloska" shirts by Jon Van Zyle, which are Alaska's answer to Hawaii's aloha shirt; pottery ranging from modern stoneware to whimsical pieces, and antler lamps. Founded in 1972, Scanlon Gallery also has some fine art carvings and sculpture, but most of its items are gifts.

At the waterfront, **Sockeye Sam's** (907-225-3260 or 1-888-230-7267; 425 Water Street) is proud that most items bear the Alaska-made logo. **Tongass Trading Co.** expanded for the first time in 1913, and has now grown to three stores in the center of Ketchikan. The main store (907-225-5101; tongasstrading.com; corner of Dock and Front streets) is as much department as gift store. At Tongass Dock Store, across the street, a life-size stuffed moose towers over the windbreakers and sweatshirts. The curio store, at the corner of Front and Mission streets, focuses on trinkets and gifts.

Moving back toward Creek Street, **5 Salmon Landing** offers several temptations: bright wall hangings at **Silver Thimble Quilt Shop** (907-225-5422; silverthimblealaska.com) and another combination gift-hobby shop at **Dockside Gallery/Bead and Yarn Shoppe** (907-225-2858).

Nearby, the **Jade Shop** (907-225-6625; 300 Spruce Mill Way), part of the same company as the Juneau store, has handsome carvings and jewelry made from the nephrite jade mined in British Columbia.

Ketchikan's big mall where local people shop is the **Plaza Mall** (907-225-7000; plazaketchikan.com; 2417 Tongass Avenue) and **Wal-Mart** (907-247-2156; 4230 Don King Road), which will send a van for you at the cruise ship dock or in downtown hotels.

Smoked Salmon Spread

It's fun to serve guests the smoked salmon you bring home from Alaska. It allows you to regale them with stories about the trip along with a tasty treat. Of course, you can just put the fish on a pretty plate with crackers. Or you can make a salmon spread, especially if it's the leftover pieces from a filet. Bring 8 ounces of cream cheese to room temperature. Flake I cup smoked salmon, and blend with soft cream cheese. Add 2 tablespoons each of lemon juice and minced green onion, and I tablespoon fresh chopped dill, or ½ teaspoon dried dill. Add salt and pepper to taste. Put in a small crock, or shape into a ball. Chill. Serve with crackers or toasted baguette slices. It can be blended in the food processor, but leave some small flecks of smoked salmon. You may use herbed cream cheese instead of adding dill, or add chopped capers.

PRINCE OF WALES ISLAND

If you're at one of POW's fly-in fishing lodges, shopping will pretty much be limited to the resort's logo wear. But if you have a rental car, there are some opportunities. **Westwind Plaza** in Craig has the **Clothes Co.** (907-826-3939) for hunting, fishing, and outdoor gear, as well as shoes, boots, and T-shirts. Possibilities at **Alaska Gifts** (907-826-2991) range from smoked salmon to gold nugget jewelry. **Bearly Threaded Quilting** (907-826-2234) is a place to find unique Alaska patterns and fabrics, and chat with quilters.

One thing you won't be able to carry home in your bag is a carving from **Stone Arts of Alaska** (907-826-3571; Craig-Klawock Highway). Abstract sculpture, garden art and furniture, and even raw stone for carvers are available here. This is the stone yard, not only a shop—so chances are the artist Gary McWilliams will be at work. Look for the sign on the highway across from the high school.

Quilts from the Silver Thimble bring a rainbow of color to 5 Salmon Landing in Ketchikan.

9

INFORMATION

Practical Matters, Enriching Matters

AMBULANCE, FIRE, AND POLICE

For fire, police, or medical emergencies, call 911. The following fire and police numbers are for information only. Alaska towns may have both a police department and Alaska State Troopers. Smaller communities may have only State Troopers, who are responsible for statewide law enforcement and safety.

NORTHERN PANHANDLE

JUNEAU
Fire Department: 907-586-5322
Police Department: 907-586-0600
State Troopers: 907-465-4000

GUSTAVUS
Police–Glacier Bay National Park: (907-697-2230) rangers cover Gustavus law enforcement.

HAINES
Klehini Valley Volunteer Fire Department: 907-767-5550
State Troopers: 907-766-2552

HOONAH
Police Department: 907-945-3655
State Troopers: 907-945-3620

SKAGWAY
Volunteer Fire Department: 907-983-2450
Police Department: 907-983-2232

YAKUTAT
State Troopers: 907-784-3220

CENTRAL PANHANDLE

PETERSBURG
Volunteer Fire Department: 907-772-3355
Petersburg Police: 907-772-3838
State Troopers: 907-772-3983

Sitka
Fire Department: 907-747-3233
Police: 907-747-3245
State Troopers: 907-747-3254

Wrangell
Fire Department: 907-874-3223
Police: 907-874-3304
State Troopers: 907-874-3215

SOUTHERN PANHANDLE

Ketchikan
Fire Department: 907-225-9616
Ketchikan Police: 907-225-6631
State Troopers: 907-225-5118

Metlakatla
Volunteer Fire Department: 907-886-7922
Police Department: 907-886-4011

Prince of Wales Island
State Troopers: 907-755-2918

Area Code, Local Government, Population, and Zip Codes

The telephone area code for Alaska is 907. Some Panhandle communities are city governments with a mayor-council structure; others are consolidated borough-cities, with the city and borough government being the same body. Population (pop.) figures are rounded to the nearest 100.

NORTHERN PANHANDLE
Juneau City and Borough: Pop. 31,000. 907-586-5240
Gustavus: Pop. 400. 907-697-2451
Haines Borough: Pop. 1600. 907-766-2711
Hoonah: Pop. 800. 907-945-3663
Skagway: Pop. 800. 907-983-2297
Yakutat City and Borough: Pop. 700. 907-784-3323

CENTRAL PANHANDLE
Petersburg: Pop. 3,000. 907-772-4687
Sitka City and Borough: Pop. 8,800. 907-747-3294
Wrangell: Pop. 2,300. 907-874-2381

SOUTHERN PANHANDLE
Ketchikan: Area pop. 14,000. 907-225-3111
Ketchikan Gateway Borough: 907-228-6625

Bill Ray painted this Juneau City Hall mural, which depicts the Tlingit myth of raven discovering humankind in a clam shell.

Metlakatla: Pop. 1,400. 907-886-7491
Prince of Wales Island: Pop. 3,900. 907-755-2261

Postal Zip Codes

NORTHERN PANHANDLE
Juneau: 99801, 99802, 99803, 99821, 99824, 99811
Gustavus: 99826
Haines: 99827
Hoonah: 99827
Skagway: 99840
Yakutat: 99689

CENTRAL PANHANDLE
Petersburg: 99833
Sitka: 99835, 99836, 99840
Wrangell: 99929

SOUTHERN PANHANDLE
Ketchikan: 99901
Metlakatla: 99926
Prince of Wales Island: 99925

BANKS

Almost every tiny community has a bank branch with an ATM facility. Large tourist stores also have ATMs. First Bank, First National Bank Alaska, and Wells Fargo branches serve the larger communities. The banks listed below are in the main tourist areas of towns; Juneau and Ketchikan have additional branches. Web sites are listed under the first references to the banks, which appear in Juneau.

NORTHERN PANHANDLE

JUNEAU

Alaska Pacific Bank: 907-586-1010; alaskapacificbank.com; 301 N. Franklin St.
First Bank: 907-586-8001; firstbankak.com; 1 Sealaska Plaza
First National Bank Alaska: 907-586-5400; fnbalaska.com; 238 Front St.
Wells Fargo Bank: 907-586-3324; wellsfargo.com; 123 Seward St.

HAINES

First National Bank Alaska: 907-766-6100; 123 Main St.

SKAGWAY

Wells Fargo Bank: 907-983-2264; 601 Broadway

CENTRAL PANHANDLE

PETERSBURG

First Bank: 907-772-4277; 103 N. Nordic Dr.
Wells Fargo Bank: 907-772-3833; 201 N. Nordic Dr.

SITKA

Alaska Pacific Bank: 907-747-8688; 315 Lincoln St.
First National Bank Alaska: 907-747-7000; 318 Lincoln St.
Wells Fargo Bank: 907- 747-3226; 300 Lincoln St.

WRANGELL

First Bank: 907-874-3363; 224 Brueger St.
Wells Fargo Bank: 907-874-3341; 115 Front St.

SOUTHERN PANHANDLE

KETCHIKAN

Alaska Pacific Bank: 907-228-4650; 410 Mission St.
First Bank: 907-225-7090; 331 Dock St.
Wells Fargo Bank: 907-225-2184; 306 Main St.

PRINCE OF WALES ISLAND

Wells Fargo Bank: 907-826-3040; 1330 Craig-Klawock Hwy.

CHAMBERS OF COMMERCE AND VISITORS BUREAUS

Visitors bureaus or associations provide excellent information for the traveler. Addresses are for public information centers or kiosks. Printed material is also available on racks in any tourist area. The **Alaska Official State Vacation Planner** is free, and has a large section on Southeast Alaska (travelalaska.com).

NORTHERN PANHANDLE

Juneau Chamber of Commerce: 907-463-3488; juneauchamber.com

Juneau Convention and Visitors Bureau: 907-586-2201 or 1-888-587-2201; travel juneau.com. Centennial Hall Visitor Information Center, 101 Egan Drive, and in the building next to the Mount Roberts Tramway on South Franklin Street.

Gustavus Visitors Association: 907-697-2105 or 907-697-2451; gustavusak.com

Haines Convention and Visitors Bureau: 907-766-2234; haines.ak.us. 122 Second Avenue.

Visit Hoonah: visithoonah.com

Skagway Convention & Visitors Bureau: 907-983-2854; skagway.com. Broadway between Second and Third.

Yakutat Chamber of Commerce: 907-784-3933; yakutatalaska.com

Yukon-Whitehorse: 867-667-6401;visitwhitehorse.com. 100 Hanson Street.

The Alaska Brotherhood Hall, where the Skagway Visitor's Bureau makes its home, has 8,933 pieces of driftwood decorating its surface.

CENTRAL PANHANDLE

Petersburg Chamber of Commerce: 907-772-3646; petersburg.org. First and Fram streets.

Greater Sitka Chamber of Commerce: 907-747-8604; sitkacoc.com.

Sitka Convention & Visitors Bureau: 907-747-5940; sitka.org. Harrigan Centennial Hall.

Wrangell Convention & Visitors Bureau: 1-800-367-9745; wrangell.org. Nolan Center, 296 Campbell Drive.

SOUTHERN PANHANDLE

Ketchikan Visitors Bureau: 907-225-6166 or 1-800-770-3300; visit-ketchikan.com. 131 Front Street at the docks; and another building on the docks closer to Berth 3.

Metlakatla Indian Community: 907-886-4441; metlakatla.com

Prince of Wales Chamber of Commerce: 907-755-2626; princeofwalescoc.org

CLIMATE AND WEATHER REPORTS

In spite of its northern latitudes, the Alaska Panhandle has a temperate rainforest climate, with fairly moderate winters and cool summers. Precipitation is high throughout the region. Fisherman and recreational boaters will be interested in marine forecasts.

National Marine Fisheries Service, Alaska Forecast: fakr.noaa.gov/weather.htm

National Weather Service, Juneau Forecast Office: http://pajk.arh.noaa.gov

DRESS

Layers always, with a cotton or other lightweight shirt, sweater or fleece, and outer waterproof jacket.

Plaid flannel shirts and jeans will make you blend in best with the locals. Even in the best restaurants, casual wear is de rigueur. Only politicians and lobbyists wear suits in Juneau.

HOSPITALS AND CLINICS

The Panhandle's largest medical facility is Juneau's **Bartlett Regional Hospital** (907-796-8900; bartletthospital.org; 3260 Hospital Drive). It provides comprehensive health care and wellness programs. **Ketchikan General Hospital** (907-225-5171; peacehealth.org/SoutheastAlaska/; 3100 Tongass Avenue) offers trauma, inpatient, outpatient, home health services, and a long-term care facility. Sitka has two facilities: **Mt. Edgecumbe Hospital** (907-966-2411; searhc.org; 222 Tongass Avenue), run by a tribal health consortium; and **Sitka Community Hospital** (907-747-3241; sitkahospital.org; 209 Moller Avenue), a city-owned acute care facility.

Petersburg Medical Center (907-772-4291; 103 Fram Street) is a small hospital and clinic; **Wrangell Medical Center** (907-874-7000; wrangellmedicalcenter.org; 310 Bennett Street) serves the area with acute, emergency, and preventive care. Other Panhandle communities have clinics, but not acute care hospitals.

MEDIA

Newspapers

NORTHERN PANHANDLE

Juneau Empire: 907-586-3740; juneauempire.com; 3100 Channel Drive. Daily, the Panhandle paper of record.

GUSTAVUS
The Fairweather Reporter: 907-697-2806; fairweatherreporter.com. Monthly.

HAINES
Chilkat Valley News: 907-766-2688; chilkatvalleynews.com; Main Street. Weekly.
The Skagway News: 907-983-2354; skagwaynews.com; 264 Broadway. Twice monthly.

CENTRAL PANHANDLE

Petersburg Pilot: 907-772-9393; petersburgpilot.com; 211 N. Nordic Drive. Weekly.
Sitka Sentinel: 907-747-3219; sitkasentinel.com, 228 Harbor Drive. Daily.
Wrangell Sentinel: 907-874-2301; thewrangellsentinel.com; 205 Front Street. Weekly, more than 100 years old.

SOUTHERN PANHANDLE

Ketchikan Daily News: 907-225-3157; ketchkiandailynews.com; 501 Dock Street. Daily.
SitNews.com: A Ketchikan-based news Web site.

RADIO

NORTHERN PANHANDLE

JUNEAU
Most Juneau stations serve Glacier Bay area, Haines, Hoonah, and Skagway.
KBJZ–FM 94.3: Variety radio
KTOO–FM 104.3: Public radio
KTKU–FM 105.1: Country music
KSUP–FM 106.3: Rock
KJNO–AM 630: News, talk
KINY–AM 800: kinyradio.com; 24-hour Web-based newscasts.

HAINES
KHNS–FM: 102.3 and 91.1 Public radio serving Haines, Skagway, and Klukwan.

CENTRAL PANHANDLE

PETERSBURG AND WRANGELL
KFSK–FM 100.9: Public radio
KRSA–AM 580: Religious radio

SITKA
KSBZ–FM 103.1: Country music
KCAW–FM 104.7: Public radio

KIFW–AM 1230: Oldies

SOUTHERN PANHANDLE

KETCHIKAN

KFMJ–FM 99.9: Rock oldies
KGTW–FM 106.7: Country
KRBD–FM 105.9: Public radio
KTKN–AM 930: Talk

TELEVISION
Major networks are available by cable and satellite in Alaska's larger communities.

JUNEAU
KATH–TV Channel 5: NBC, available throughout Southeast Alaska
KJUD Channel 8: ABC affiliate
KTOO–TV Channel 3: PBS

SITKA
KSCT–TV Channel 5: NBC affiliate
KTNL Channel 13/6: CBS, available throughout the Northern Panhandle

KETCHIKAN
KUBD Channel 4: CBS affiliate

ANNUAL EVENTS

Timing a visit to a local festival adds immeasurably to the trip. Salmon derbies (See Chapter 7, *Recreation*) also draw visitors May through September.

MARCH
Buckwheat Cross-Country Ski Classic: (907-983-2127; skagway.com/events.html; Skagway.) Skiers for 50k, 25k, and 10k converge, along with snowshoers for a 5k event in the annual race held along the historic Trail of '98. Late March.

APRIL
Alaska Folk Festival: (907-463-3316; akfolkfest.org; Juneau.) Rockabilly to Celtic rock, Renaissance dance to Revolutionary-era hymns, come together on a mid-May weekend.

MAY
Little Norway Festival: (907-772-3646; petersburg.org; Petersburg.) The entire town dresses in Norwegian costumes and Viking helmets to enjoy a weekend of parades, music, dance, special food, and children's activities. Celebrates Norway's Constitution Day, May 17, U.S. Armed Forces Day, and the start of the fishing season. Third weekend in May.

JUNE
Celebration: (907-463-4844; seaalaskaheritage.org; Juneau.) More than 2,000 Haida, Tlingit, and Tsimshian people converge to celebrate their culture with dance groups, workshops, and juried exhibits. Biennial in even years, early June.

Many people at Petersburg's Little Norway Festival dress in embroidered costumes, like this Leikarring dancer photographed at Sons of Norway Hall.

Petersburg sneakers are usually worn on the feet, but they make a good vase as well, as seen in Petersburg.

JULY

Southeast Alaska State Fair: (907-766-2476; seakfair.org; Haines.) Alaskans show off animals, crafts, baked goods, and flowers at this event. Horseshoe and fiddle contests, logging show and rodeo, plus kids activities, contribute to the fun. Late July, sometimes early August.

AUGUST

Blueberry Festival: (907-225-2211; ketchikanarts.org; Ketchikan.) Juried art show, a fun run, eating contest, and famed slug race attract locals and cruise ship passengers. First weekend in the month.

SEPTEMBER

Klondike International Road Relay: (867-668-4236; klondikeroadrelay.com; Skagway.) Relay teams run through the night on the Skagway-to-Whitehorse 100-Mile Relay race on Labor Day weekend.

OCTOBER

Alaska Day Festival: (907-747-6738, or 907-747-8604; cityofsitka.com/alaska day/; Sitka.) The transfer ceremony of Russia to the United States is re-enacted, along with a period ball. Dinners, contests, and a parade. Several days including October 18.

NOVEMBER

Alaska Bald Eagle Festival: (907-766-3094; baldeaglefestival.org; Haines.) Bird and photography enthusiasts converge along with bald eagles, on the Chilkat River. Wildlife and photo workshops. Early November.
Sitka WhaleFest: (907-747-7964; sitkawhalefest.org; Sitka.) Lectures from marine biologists along with whale-watching boat trips highlight the event. Early November.

BIBLIOGRAPHY

Borneman, Walter R. *Alaska: Saga of a Bold Land*. New York; Harper Perennial, 2004. 608 pp., $16.95.

Conner, Cathy and O'Haire, Daniel. *Roadside Geology of Alaska*. Missoula, MT; Mountain Press Publishing Company, 1988. 251 pp., $18.

Ford, Corey and Darling, Lois (illustrator). *Where the Sea Breaks Its Back: The Epic Story of Early Naturalist Georg Steller and the Russian Exploration of Alaska*. Portland, OR; Graphic Arts Center Publishing Company, 2003. 224 pp., $14.95.

Garfield, Viola E. and Forrest, Linn S. *The Wolf and the Raven: Totem Poles of Southeastern Alaska*. Seattle, WA; University of Washington Press, 1948/1961. 151 pp., $14.95.

Holm, Bill. *Northwest Coast Indian Art: An Analysis of Form*. Seattle, WA; University of Washington Press, 1965/1970. 133 pp., $18.95.

Krakauer, Jon. *Into the Wild*. New York; Anchor Books, 1997. 224 pp., $13.95.

Lende, Heather. *If You Lived Here, I'd Know Your Name*. Chapel Hill, NC; Algonquin Books, 2006. 281 pp., $12.95.

London, Jack. *The Call of the Wild: And Selected Stories*. New York; Signet Classics, 1998. 179 pp., $4.95.

London, Jack. *White Fang*. New York; Puffin Classics, 2008. 307 pp., $4.99.

Mallory, Enid. *Robert Service Under the Spell of the Yukon*. Victoria, BC; Heritage House Publishing, 2008. 288 pp., $18.95.

McPhee, John. *Coming into the Country*. New York; Farrar, Straus and Giroux, 1991. 272 pp., $17.

Michener, James. *Alaska*. New York; Random House, 1989. 1,073 pp., $8.99.

Muir, John. Introduction by Edward Hoagland. *Travels in Alaska*. New York; Modern Library, 1915/2002. 247 pp., $10.95.

Purdy, Anne Hobbs as told to Specht, Robert. *Tisha: The Story of a Young Teacher in the Alaska Wilderness*. New York; Bantam Books, 1984. 341 pp, $7.50.

Raban, Jonathan. *Passage to Juneau: A Sea and Its Meanings*. New York; Vintage, 1999. 435 pp., $15.

Schooler, Lynn. *The Blue Bear: A True Story of Friendship and Discovery in the Alaskan Wild*. Ecco, New York. 2003. 272 pp., $13.95.

Schorr, Alan Edward. *Alaska Place Names*. Juneau, AK; The Denali Press, 1991. 192 pp., $25.

Service, Robert William. *Collected Poems of Robert Service*. New York; Penguin Group, 1989. 752 pp., $25.95.

Service, Robert. *The Very Best of Robert Service*. Todd Communications, Anchorage, AK. 2002. 216 pp., $12.95.

Smelcer, John E., editor. *The Raven and the Totem: Traditional Alaska Native Myths and Tales*. 1992. A Salmon Run Book, Anchorage, AK. 149 pp., $14.95.

Straley, John. *Big Both Ways.* 2008. Portland, OR; Alaska Northwest Books. 350 pp., $16.95. Straley is the former Alaska Writer Laureate.

Straley, John. *The Woman Who Married a Bear: A Cecil Younger Investigation.* 1992/2005. New York; Soho Press. 225 pp., $12.

GLOSSARY

Many of the terms in this glossary appear in the *Viking Visitor Guide* published by the Petersburg Chamber of Commerce.

Banana Belt: The Panhandle area, warmed by Pacific Ocean currents that keep winter temperatures in the 27–43-degree range.

barn door: A halibut weighing in at more than 250 pounds.

bergie bits: Small ice pieces that break off glaciers.

Bottom fish: Refers to bottom-dwelling fish, such as halibut, black cod, and rockfish.

break-up: The end of winter; or marriages that don't last through those dark, winter nights.

cabin fever: Boredom, restlessness, or anxiety caused by a prolonged stay in a confined space, like an Alaska cabin in winter.

Cheechako: An Alaska newcomer; a greenhorn or tenderfoot.

Chinook: A warm wind or another name for Alaska king salmon.

devil's club: A prickly, broad-leaved plant that grows in damp habitats.

Dungie: Nickname for Dungeness crab weighing two to three pounds.

fish traps: Used by Alaska Natives and commercial fisherman to harvest salmon near spawning streams, now outlawed statewide.

Eskimo candy: Belly strip of smoked salmon, done on racks over alder or other Alaska wood. The heat caramelizes the edges, giving it a faint sweetness.

gunkholing: Cruising from cove to cove, lodge to lodge, or town to town on a multiday fishing trip.

highliners: The title given commercial fisherman harvesting the largest catch during a fishing season.

hooligan: A smelt-like, oily fish that runs up rivers, especially the Chilkat and Stikine, each spring. It's sometimes spelled eulachon or ooligan and it's also known as candle-fish.

humpy: Pink salmon or humpback salmon; named for the hump formed on spawning males.

in country: In Alaska.

Lower 48: What many Alaskans call the 48 contiguous American states.

Marine Highway: The Alaska Marine Highway System or ferry system.

mug up: Time for grub and coffee.

muskeg: Grassy, wet, boggy soil, incorporating decaying plant matter that covers much of the Panhandle.

outside: Outside of Alaska; the Lower 48.

This fanciful sign pole at the Wrangell dock guides visitors to local sites.

Panhandle: The nickname for Southeast Alaska, including the Alexander Archipelago and the narrow mainland strip running 400 miles from Ketchikan to Yakutat.

Permanent Fund: The fund made up of 25 percent of proceeds of all mineral lease revenue received by the state. Qualified state residents receive a permanent fund dividend (PFD) check each year from the $30 billion account. Sometimes called a reverse tax.

Petersburg sneakers: Called Wellingtons in England, the brown rubber books are worn year-round by locals, for fishing and camping trips, hikes, weddings, and funerals. Also known as Sitka slippers, Ketchikan sneakers, or by whatever place you happen to be.

potlatch: Ceremonial feasts celebrated by Alaska Natives, who gather for gift-giving, storytelling, dancing, and other festivities, to mark totem pole dedications, weddings, deaths, and other rites of passage.

slime line: Area of cannery where fish are gutted and cleaned prior to canning or packaging.

South: The Lower 48, especially the Seattle area. Sometimes "Down South."

sourdough: Yeast and flour mixture used to make hotcakes, bread, and other baked goods; an early settler or prospector in Alaska or anyone who has lived in Alaska for most of his or her life.

spotter: A pilot who spots schools of herring or salmon for commercial fishermen.

taiga: Arctic region supporting small spruce and sparse vegetation.

tundra: Treeless area covered with low-lying plants.

ulu: Traditional Eskimo rounded knife used for cutting and scraping.

termination dust: First snow on the mountains, signaling the end of summer.

williwaw: Violent, strong wind gusts that reach speeds of 100 miles per hour or more.

General Index

Lodging Index

Dining by Price

Inexpensive	Entrées $15 or less
Moderate	$15–$25
Expensive	Most entrées more than $25

Expensive
The Gold Room, 164–65
The Raven, 185

Northern Panhandle

Inexpensive
Chan's Thai Kitchen, 163
Donna's Restaurant, 163–64
Homeshore Café, 174–75
Lighthouse Restaurant and Harbor Bar, 179
Mi Casa Restaurant, 165–66
Mosey's Cantina, 179–80
Sweet Dream Teas, 166–67
33 Mile Roadhouse, 175

Inexpensive to Moderate
Bamboo Room and Pioneer Bar, 176–77
A Bear's Nest Café, 170–71
Bonanza Bar & Grill, 181
Chilkat Restaurant and Bakery, 177
Douglas Café, 164
Fireweed, 178
Hangar on the Wharf, 165
Klondike Rib and Salmon BBQ, 186–87
Port of Call, 181
Red Dog Saloon, 132
Red Onion Saloon, 132–33
Seong's Sushi Bar and Chinese Take-Out, 166
Skagway Fish Company, 181–82
Starfire, 182
T. K. McGuire, 167
Yakutat Lodge, 184

Moderate
Fort Seward Lodge, 178–79
Glacier Bear Lodge, 184
Grandma's Feather Bed, 165
Stowaway Café, 183
Twisted Fish Company, 167–68
Zephyr Restaurant, 169

Moderate to Expensive
Cellar Steakhouse and Wine Bar, 186
Commander's Room Restaurant and Officers' Club
  Lounge, 177–78
Giorgio's Cuccina, 186
Glacier Bay Lodge, 171
Gustavus Inn at Glacier Bay, 173–74
Wild Spice, 168
Zen Asian Fusion Restaurant, 168

Central Panhandle

Inexpensive
Nugget Restaurant, 192
Pizza Express, 192
Tina's Kitchen, 189–90

Inexpensive to Moderate
Joan Mei, 189
Level II, 190–91
Rooney's Northern Lights Restaurant, 189
Stikine Inn Restaurant, 193
Zak's Cafe, 194

Moderate
Beachcomber Inn, 188–89

Moderate to Expensive
The Channel Club, 190
Ludvig's Bistro, 191–92
Raven Dining Room, 192–93

Southern Panhandle

Inexpensive
Alaska Fish House, 194–95
Diaz Café, 197–98
Good Fortune Restaurant, 197
Pioneer Café, 198
Ruth Ann's Restaurant, 200

Inexpensive to Moderate
Ocean View Restaurante, 198

Moderate
Fireweed Lodge, 200
Héen Kahidi Restaurant and Lounge, 196–97

Moderate to Expensive
Annabelle's Keg and Chowder House, 195
Bar Harbor Restaurant, 196
Salmon Falls Resort, 198–99
Steamers, 199–200

Dining by Cuisine

Northern Panhandle

Alaska American
Bamboo Room and Pioneer Bar, 176–77
Bonanza Bar & Grill, 181
Fireweed, 178
Glacier Bay Lodge, 171
Glacier Bear Lodge, 184
Red Dog Saloon, 132
Red Onion Saloon, 132–33
Skagway Fish Company, 181–82
33 Mile Roadhouse, 175
T. K. McGuire, 167
Twisted Fish Company, 167–68
Yakutat Lodge, 184

American
Chilkat Restaurant and Bakery, 177
Donna's Restaurant, 163–64
The Gold Room, 164–65
Grandma's Feather Bed, 165
Hangar on the Wharf, 165

Asian
Sweet Dream Teas, 166–67
Wild Spice, 168
Zen Asian Fusion Restaurant, 168

Barbecue
Klondike Rib and Salmon BBQ, 186–87
Wild Spice, 168

Breakfast
Chilkat Restaurant and Bakery, 177
Donna's Restaurant, 163–64
Douglas Café, 164

Chinese
Seong's Sushi Bar and Chinese Take-Out, 166
Starfire, 182

Contemporary
Commander's Room Restaurant and Officers' Club,
  177–78
Fort Seward Lodge, 178–79

Continental/International
Cellar Steakhouse and Wine Bar, 186
The Raven, 185

Eclectic
Douglas Café, 164
Wild Spice, 168

Greek
Giorgio's Cuccina, 186

Homey/Home-Cooking
A Bear's Nest Café, 170–71
Chilkat Restaurant and Bakery, 177
Douglas Café, 164
Gustavus Inn at Glacier Bay, 173–74
Homeshore Café, 174–75
Lighthouse Restaurant and Harbor Bar, 179

Italian
Giorgio's Cuccina, 186
Port of Call, 181
Zephyr Restaurant, 169

Mediterranean
Giorgio's Cuccina, 186
Zephyr Restaurant, 169

Mexican
Grandma's Feather Bed, 165
Mi Casa Restaurant, 165–66
Mosey's Cantina, 179–80

Middle Eastern
Port of Call, 181

Mongolian Barbecue
Wild Spice, 168

Organic
A Bear's Nest Café, 170–71
Fireweed, 178

Sandwiches and Pizza
Douglas Café, 164
Homeshore Café, 174–75

Seafood
Commander's Room Restaurant and Officers' Club
  Lounge, 177–78
The Cookhouse, 180
The Crab Station, 180
The Gold Room, 164–65
Gustavus Inn at Glacier Bay, 173–74
Klondike Rib and Salmon BBQ, 186–87
The Landing Zone, 180
Stowaway Café, 183

Southwestern
Starfire, 182

Steakhouse
Cellar Steakhouse and Wine Bar, 186

Sushi
Seong's Sushi Bar and Chinese Take-Out, 166